VAN DIEMEN'S LAND

MURRAY JOHNSON has taught Australian History and Indigenous Studies at the University of Queensland, the Australian National University and the University of Tasmania. He has published widely in both fields, with his most recent book being *Australia's Ancient Aboriginal Past: A global perspective* (2014). Murray has also been heavily involved in the historical underpinnings of Native Title claims in Queensland.

IAN MCFARLANE has taught Aboriginal Studies at the University of Tasmania. He specialises in studies of Aboriginal people from Tasmania's north-west region, and has been a contributor to the 'History Wars' debates. He has published widely, with his best-known work *Beyond Awakening: The Aboriginal tribes of North West Tasmania, a history* released in 2008.

VAN DIEMEN'S LAND

An Aboriginal History

MURRAY JOHNSON AND IAN McFARLANE

UNSW PRESS

TABLE OF MEASURES

VOLUME

One imperial gallon = eight pints = 4.55 litres

CURRENCY

One penny (1d.) = one cent (1c.).
  Comparison: 1d. in the 1920s = 42 cents in 2000
One shilling (1s.) = twelve cents (12c.).
  Comparison: 1s. in the 1920s = $5 in 2000
One pound (£1) = two dollars ($2).
  Comparison: £1 in the 1920s = $100 in 2000

AREA

One acre = 0.404 hectares
One square mile = 2.58 square kilometres

WEIGHT

One ounce (1oz.) = 28.3 grams
One pound (1lb.) = 16 ounces = 0.45 kilograms
112 pounds (112 lbs.) = one hundredweight (1cwt.) = 50.8 kilograms

ABBREVIATIONS

AA	*Australian Archaeology*
ADB	*Australian Dictionary of Biography*
CT	*Colonial Times*
CSO	Colonial Secretary's Office
HRA	*Historical Records of Australia*
HRNSW	*Historical Records of New South Wales*
HTG	*Hobart Town Gazette and Van Diemen's Land Advertiser*
KM	*Koori Mail*
TAC	Tasmanian Aboriginal Centre
TAHO	Tasmanian Archive and Heritage Office
THRA	*Tasmanian Historical Research Association Papers and Proceedings*

CONTENTS

FOREWORD

by Henry Reynolds

Tasmanian settlers were keen to change the Island's name from Van Diemen's Land to Tasmania in the 1850s when the British government brought convict transportation to an end and the colony was accorded the right to establish its own parliament with wide powers of internal self-government. But a name change could not expunge the legacy of the turbulent and tragic events of the first half of the nineteenth century any more than Tasmanians born after 1850 could ignore the enduring presence of the imposing architecture of the convict era which was an everyday presence in town and country alike.

The past lived on in other ways as well. Tasmanians have continually reflected on and written about their history. At the same time, long periods of economic and demographic stagnation prevented them from embracing that common colonial habit of looking eagerly to a beckoning future. Tasmanians have consequently been avid collectors of memorabilia, raconteurs, antiquarians and family historians. Serious history has been produced in every generation since the 1830s. As a result nineteenth century Tasmania left behind a richer historiographical legacy than any other part of Australia. At the forefront of this body of work stands the great two-volume *History of Tasmania* by Congregational minister John West published in Launceston in 1852. Two themes attracted West's attention: the convict system and the tragic fate of the Tasmanian Aborigines. These subjects still elicit more interest from contemporary historians than any competing ones.

It is easy to see why the Aborigines have been an abiding subject of curiosity from the late eighteenth century when French and British expeditions found welcome shelter from the roaring forties in the bays and estuaries of south-eastern Tasmania. Every generation since has found aspects of the story worthy of investigation or conducive of compassionate concern. There were so many reasons for Europeans to speculate about the Tasmanians. They had lived in isolation for as many as 300 generations after the flooding of Bass Strait. The earliest occupation of what had been the Tasmanian Peninsula went back 30 000 years into the heart of the Ice Age. For the seafarers who visited Tasmania before the first British settlements were established in 1803 and 1804, the Aboriginal bands they encountered represented natural man untouched by civilisation and were variously viewed as noble or primitive savages. Later in the nineteenth century the Tasmanians were seen as the most primitive people on earth and of great sociological and scientific interest because their way of life represented the earliest infancy of the human race. Ascendant evolutionary theory fixed on the death of Truganini in 1876 as an event of global importance. Here was what appeared to be inconvertible, well documented proof of the rapid destruction of a unique race of people. It was compelling evidence of the operation of the laws of evolution which also presaged a like fate for native peoples all over the world. Generations of Tasmanians consequently grew up with the belief that there were no Aborigines on the Island. The truth of the matter was a further cause of interest in Island history. The emergence of an assertive, self-conscious Aboriginal community in the middle years of the twentieth century was a confounding experience for the wider community. But the implications of Aboriginal renaissance were once again of great historical significance. The survival of a distinct Aboriginal identity against almost impossible odds is a story of universal interest.

Given the richness of interpretation and the great wealth of documentation available in Tasmania, it was not surprising that the history wars of the first decade of the new millennium focused on the local story and in particular on the frontier conflict of the 1820s and the early 1830s. And one direct consequence of the intense debates of that period has been that a new generation of scholarship has appeared, often emerging from research at the University of Tasmania. With *Van Diemen's Land: An Aboriginal History* we have a new and valuable addition to the burgeoning literature. Its provenance differs from a number of the recent books which began their life as post-graduate theses. The authors Murray Johnson and Ian McFarlane both worked as teachers in Aboriginal studies at the University of Tasmania's regional campuses at Launceston and Burnie respectively. This gives the book some clear and advantageous characteristics. As experienced and successful teachers, the authors kept their lectures up to date with reference to the most recent literature in a range of related fields. Much of this material will not be readily available to the general reader. A book like this one which emerges from years of undergraduate teaching has a number of other advantages. It is, as it were, already road-tested. Johnson and McFarlane both know which topics and which interpretations most clearly engaged their students. They have had to spend considerable thought into the ways in which they could arouse and maintain under-graduate interest over a long period of time. And what worked with students will clearly also work for the putative general reader.

What we have here then is a book that provides us with a highly readable survey of the latest scholarship on the Tasmanian Aborigines and a study that will remain as an essential reference work relevant for years to come. The reach of the narrative is impressive. Two chapters outline what we currently know about traditional life drawing on a wide range of sources from many disciplines. Six chapters cover the great tragedy which befell the Aboriginal bands during the early nineteenth century up until their exile on Flinders Island and in a further one Johnson and McFarlane trace the sad story of the decline and death of the remnant population which returned from Flinders Island to mainland Tasmania in 1847. Two impressive chapters survey the little known story of the mixed descent community which grew up on the islands of eastern Bass Strait in the second half of the nineteenth century. The authors explain how what was essentially a new and distinctive people emerged as a result of the mixing of Aboriginal and European traditions in conditions of almost complete isolation from mainstream Tasmania. The account is brought to a fitting conclusion with a survey of the resurgence of Tasmanian Aboriginality over the last generation and once again it is a story that will be little understood beyond the island State.

In their conclusion Johnson and McFarlane observe that the Tasmanian Aborigines have 'been engaged in a journey of epic proportions, an odyssey which continues to wind its way towards the future'. This book provides us with a thorough well-written account of where the odyssey began, how it unfolded and where it might now be heading.

INTRODUCTION

Lying between latitudes 40°–44° South, the island of Van Diemen's Land (renamed Tasmania in 1855) is separated from the mainland of Australia by Bass Strait, a 240 kilometre-wide stretch of shallow turbulent water. Much of the island's 62,409 square kilometres was sculpted by glaciation, and it continues to be whipped by gales of the 'Roaring Forties' which swirl across unchallenged from South America. Van Diemen's Land/Tasmania is also the most mountainous state of modern Australia, and while much of its rugged landscape remains heavily forested, continual leaching has left its soils anything but rich. The island experiences clearly defined seasons, with cool to cold winters and relatively brief summers, though there are regional variations. The vegetation in the west largely comprises temperate rainforest, wet sclerophyll forest and button grass moorlands, a consequence of cooler conditions and greater precipitation ranging from 1200–3600 millimetres per annum. By way of contrast the eastern half of the island receives between 500–1200 millimetres of rain every year and although temperate rainforest occurs in the north-east the dominant vegetative pattern is dry sclerophyll forest. Central Tasmania forms a transitional zone between these two extremes.[1]

Briefly visited by Dutchman Abel Tasman in 1642, who named it in honour of Anthony van Diemen, then governor of the Dutch East Indies, the island was ignored by European mariners until the late eighteenth century, when first the French and then the British found it a useful location to reprovision in these southern climes. It was the French who made the initial contact with the Indigenous people, and it was the activities of the former which also prompted their British rivals to take possession of Van Diemen's Land in 1803. It was thus Britain's second colonial outpost in the antipodes, effectively extending their sphere of influence from the fledgling settlement of Sydney in New South Wales. With this one bold stroke the Aboriginal inhabitants were stripped of their customary rights to their homelands and became — theoretically at least — subjects of the British Crown. It was a dispossession which did not go unchallenged.

While it is known that the Aboriginal people penetrated into the far south-west of what was then the Tasmanian Peninsula by at least 35 000 years ago, occupation was neither permanent nor extensive. It may not have been until the Holocene epoch, perhaps within the last 10 000 years, that the east and south-east were permanently occupied. Over that immense span of time, however, the Aboriginal people were impacted upon by environmental and climatic conditions. Change was also a result of isolation caused by the flooding of the Bassian Plain some 10 000 years ago, when genetic inflow from mainland Australia completely ceased. Nor were they one people. Three, possibly four, separate groups of Aboriginal people settled in Van Diemen's Land. They spoke different languages and possessed distinctive cultural traits, though over time and right throughout the island technology was reduced to its most basic form. It was the supposedly 'simplistic' material culture, coupled with biological adaptation, which convinced many early observers and theorists that the Indigenous people of Van Diemen's Land were not Aborigines at all. Their variable pigmentation, often short stocky bodies and woolly hair were held to be of 'negrito' origin. Depending on the theorist, the original homeland of the Tasmanians was said to be New Caledonia, Papua New Guinea, Indonesia, Africa or, in one instance, South America.

Long before these strange and varied ideas were finally dispelled and the Tasmanians were recognised for what they are — Aboriginal people — their societies had been irrevocably shattered by British colonisation, warfare and exile. That process occurred so rapidly that knowledge of their pre-contact lives is full of lacunae. Mere snippets are known of their languages, religion and spiritual beliefs, political and social relationships. Other aspects of customary life, such as technology and food sources, are reasonably well understood, but even here they are far from complete. Whether the Tasmanians used boomerangs and spear-throwers in the ancient past remains unknown; they certainly did not have them during the contact period. Bone tools apparently disappeared around 3700 years ago, so it is possible that the Tasmanians once made warm cloaks. In the contact period they sufficed with a wallaby or kangaroo skin thrown over one shoulder. None of this is to suggest, as archaeologist Rhys Jones once did, that cultural development retrogressed. The invention of the distinctive bundled canoe in southern and north-west Tasmania within the last few thousand years is a reminder that the cultural universe of the Aboriginal people was continuing to expand. Archaeology has nevertheless played a key role in our understanding of pre-contact Aboriginal societies right throughout Australia, and Van Diemen's Land is no exception. The pioneering work by Rhys Jones and Sandra Bowdler in the 1960s revealed much and they are owed a great debt by the modern Tasmanian Aboriginal community. Importantly, their efforts were continued.

For all that, there is no denying that the impact of early European mariners, and especially British colonisation from 1803, had a devastating impact on the Aboriginal people. In the first two decades of the nineteenth century, though, conflict and collaboration often went hand-in-hand. Indeed, the first clash between the colonised and colonisers in February 1804 was instigated by the Aborigines, who drove off a survey party without any known injury to either side. The so-called 'Risdon Massacre' occurred the following May, an incident which has often been grossly exaggerated. On this occasion there was certainly loss of life, but to refer to it as a 'massacre' is naïve at best. The evidence does not support any large-scale killing, a myth which came into being decades after the event and still captures the public imagination.

It also needs to be borne in mind that the Aborigines were not simply passive victims when widespread conflict did erupt, particularly from the mid-1820s in eastern Van Diemen's Land. Their defensive and, at times, offensive measures were much more successful than is usually credited. Nor was the so-called 'Black War' an all-out war. Conflict was generally localised and, even at the height of violence, customary internecine war between Aboriginal groups continued unabated. A similar scenario was played out in the north-west, where customary animosity seriously weakened resistance against the incursions of the Van Diemen's Land Company, which was granted huge areas of land in that region and became virtually a law within itself. And it was here that the conflict lasted longest, continuing until at least February 1842, almost a decade after hostilities had concluded in the east.

The struggle in the south and east between 1826 and 1832 was nonetheless a major turning point in Van Diemen's Land. Towards the end of the horrendous conflict, surviving Aborigines were only too willing to accept the overtures of peace proffered by George Augustus Robinson, one of the most controversial figures in the island's history, whose 'Friendly Mission' ultimately led many into exile and slow death. It is not surprising then, that the spectacular demographic collapse of Aboriginal societies within three decades of British colonisation has raised the spectre of genocide. It has ensured that Van Diemen's Land has figured prominently in virtually all historiographical discussions of the colonial impact on the Aboriginal people of Australia. The first major salvo in this particular arena of the 'History Wars' was fired off in 2002 by social commentator Keith Windschuttle in his self-published tome, *The Fabrication of Aboriginal History Volume One: Van Diemen's Land 1803–1847*. In this work Windschuttle challenged the orthodox interpretation of the frontier conflict which erupted throughout the island, but it needs to be remembered that the 'History Wars' are not history per se. They are an argument over control of the past as a political resource. The term itself was first used in the United States during 1994, when an intellectual clash took place between academics who had long touted the positive and patriotic side of American history, as opposed to those who had begun to critique those glossy images by dwelling on the negative aspects of the past. In this first instance it concerned the morality of dropping atomic bombs on Japan in 1945.[2]

In Australia the battleground has encompassed broad areas of the past: gender and ethnic relations, 'big man' versus 'little', the Anzac myth, suburbia and the bush, the environment, the convict era and, of course, Aboriginal history. Former conservative Prime Minister John Howard was heavily involved in the preliminary rounds, accusing those who sought to highlight the tragedies of the past as being motivated by a partisan political cause.[3] The so-called 'black armband' historians did not necessarily deny that allegation. The problem is that history is not set in concrete; there are only pieces of evidence from which to reconstruct a picture of the past, and it is not all that unusual to have two conflicting interpretations from the same available evidence. On top of that is the inbuilt bias and life experiences which influence any interpretation. No matter how objective we wish to be, an element of subjectivity will always creep in. Above all, history is a form of knowledge which is constantly being supplemented and reworked as new evidence comes to light.

The media also plays a role because the blood from academic battles invariably seeps in to the public arena where it is eagerly lapped up by journalists in search of a juicy story. Generally speaking, though, the 'History Wars' themselves have a narrower cast of players whose personalities and foibles of character become indelibly entwined with the overarching story. Unfortunately, some of them have been vilified merely for the stance they have taken as the 'History Wars' rely heavily on allegation and ridicule — not to say outright abuse. A good example is the pillorying of Manning Clark, one of the nation's great historians, whose six-volume history of Australia is held to have a powerful left-wing bent and was later castigated by Clark's own publisher, Peter Ryan, as 'an imposition on Australian credulity'.[4] It went even further. Clark is said to have been a close confidante of Soviet intelligence agents, an association that only ended with his death in 1991.[5] On the other side of the ledger, however, stands Geoffrey Blainey, one of Clark's former students and another of Australia's great historians. His outspoken criticism of the high level of Asian immigration in 1984 under the Hawke Labor government led to vitriolic abuse and ultimately Blainey's resignation four years later as Professor of History at Melbourne University.[6] One from the left, one from the right, with both men undeservedly having their reputations tarnished.

The 'History Wars' have also been generated and propelled by pressure groups, 'think tanks' and a political coterie. As Stuart

Macintyre has pointed out, they 'operate on the martial principle of conquest, of us against them, right and wrong, of a single supposedly correct view' of the past.[7] In the midst of all this stands the Aboriginal history of Van Diemen's Land. There is evidence which suggests to some that British policies in the island colony were genocidal in their intent; others have contended that there were only local and unofficial genocidal incidents, while a small number of commentators have been at considerable pains to play down the level of violence in the frontier conflict between the Aborigines and colonists.

Among the latter group is Keith Windschuttle, who has argued that Van Diemen's Land 'probably saw the least indigenous blood ... deliberately shed' on the Australian frontier. The Aboriginal casualty figures he provided for the period from 1803–1834 amounted to just 118, the majority — 72 — occurring from the first ripples of open conflict in 1824 until 1831. At the same time, wrote Windschuttle, 187 colonists were slain by the Aborigines. Given these figures it is thus 'bizarre and offensive' to compare them with the killing fields of Cambodia during the Pol Pot regime, or Stalinist Russia or the Holocaust of Nazi Germany. While admitting that 'full-blooded' Aborigines did disappear in Van Diemen's Land during the nineteenth century, Windschuttle attributed their demise to two factors. One was disease; the second was their alleged practice of trading and prostituting women 'to such an extent that they lost their ability to reproduce themselves'.[8] Although disease was certainly a factor in the very early contact period, with the exception of the far south-west there is little evidence of widespread disease after British colonisation, and even then it was invariably a consequence of incarceration. Similarly, while others have agreed that the trade and prostitution of Aboriginal women was extensive (specifically in north-eastern Van Diemen's Land), we will see that this, too, is based on the flimsiest evidence.

Windschuttle's explanation has much in common with the archaic reasoning of Count Paul de Strzelecki in 1843.[9] Importantly, though, Windschuttle argued that disease and the prostitution of women were simply nails in the coffin as the Indigenous population of Van Diemen's Land was already in serious decline prior to the arrival of Europeans. With the wave of a seemingly magic wand, he dismissed all reasoned estimates of the pre-contact Aboriginal population to come up with a figure of less than 2000,[10] assuring readers that Aboriginal societies were 'primitive and internally dysfunctional' and already on the verge of collapse. The mere presence of the colonists was enough to push the Aboriginal people over the edge of an abyss already yawning in front of them. Thus, the survival of the Van Diemen's Land Aborigines until the first decade of the nineteenth century was due more 'to good fortune than good management'.[11] It is not a convincing argument. As John Hirst has rightly stated, however, Windschuttle's forensic examination of the works of certain historians did uncover the 'wilful and careless misuse of sources'.[12] Indeed, it went further in one instance by revealing particularly sloppy scholarship. It was a good wakeup call for historians dealing with the Aboriginal history of Van Diemen's Land, one which was not universally appreciated or acknowledged. To ignore Windschuttle's warning merely serves to perpetuate falsehoods and myths, which have no place in legitimate historical research.

Yet rather than a historian it was a journalist who made the most extraordinary attempt to explain the rapid destruction of Van Diemen's Land Aboriginal societies in the early contact period. Before ceasing publication in 2008, the *Bulletin* was generally considered to be a highly-reputable journal with an intelligent and mature readership. In February 1982, an article by Patricia Cobern slipped through the editorial safety net and unfortunately entered public discourse. Entitled 'Who really killed Tasmania's aborigines?', the article began with the bold and unsupported statement that 'the descendants of the early settlers of Tasmania have been branded as the children of murderers'. The defensive direction the article would take was immediately apparent, and it comes as no surprise to find that Cobern was a descendant of two prominent colonial families who made their fortunes in Van Diemen's Land. In one huge generalisation she described all the early free settlers as 'peace-loving folk' who were only given their passage to the colony on account of their 'high moral character'. Few, argued Cobern, had ever 'used a gun or weapon of any kind and they knew nothing about hunting and fighting'. Such an assertion flies in the face of all the evidence and this, of course, leads to an appraisal of their Indigenous foes. Unlike the newcomers, the Aborigines were 'war-like hunters' who were 'fickle and unstable' in temperament, descending upon isolated farms to 'flick the spears from between their toes and plunge them into the hapless frontiersman and his wife and children'. More British colonists, argued Cobern, were killed in the 'Black War' than Aborigines: 'The most Aborigines killed in any one melee was 41 of a force of several hundred who *attacked* the Royal Marines' [emphasis added].[13]

If the Aborigines were so 'war-like' and aggressive we might rightly ask what became of them. For a start, Cobern was swayed by a maximum figure of 700 for the entire population, 'and they were, even then, fast dying out' as a result of six crucial factors. First on the list were their eating habits, which alone was sufficient 'to wipe them out'. Cobern's second factor was childbirth, with pregnant women abandoned when they could no longer keep pace with their compatriots. If the mother and her new-born infant survived they then faced the risk of 'strange tribes' who 'would kill and probably eat them'.[14] There is not one recorded case of anthropophagy in Van Diemen's Land. Yet, according to the Cobern thesis, it appears that very few women who gave birth managed to re-join their kin.

The third factor cited by Cobern was a distinct lack of hygiene. Then there was supposed marriage practices. Without any understanding of the term 'Elders' or Tasmanian marriage rites, Cobern insisted that only old men were permitted to take wives. Many younger men met their death attempting to 'steal wives from another tribe' and 'naturally, the old men were not so fertile as the young bloods and few children were born to their women'.[15] The fifth factor relating to the disappearance of the Aboriginal people was their 'dangerous "magic" surgery' which was fortunately left unexplained.[16] Finally, there was exposure to the harsh climate, something the Aborigines had been successfully contending with for at least 35 000 years, including the extremely bitter conditions of the Last Glacial Maximum. Not so, argued Cobern, 'exposure to the weather was a common cause of death before the coming of the white man'. Nor did the angelic 'peace-loving' British colonists introduce venereal disease, which 'was already making inroads on the natives of Tasmania when Europeans first arrived'. One can only ponder where it may have come from. Cobern concluded:

> My research [surely a misnomer] has shown that the only massacres carried out were those on the white people by the natives. The killer that stalked the Tasmanian Aborigine tribes was the traditions and customs of the race, its face was not white.[17]

In the Van Diemen's Land context there has certainly been too much emphasis placed on 'massacres'. With a few notable exceptions violent clashes were mostly small-scale affairs, but there can be no denying that copious amounts of Aboriginal blood was splashed on the island's wattle. Nor was it any surprise that Cobern's naïve account attracted a storm of protest. The distinguished archaeologist, Dr Sandra Bowdler, was among the many who responded:

> I have been engaged in research in the field of Tasmanian Aboriginal studies since 1973, and in that time I have read some pretty awful stuff, but never anything so spectacularly dreadful as the article by Patricia Cobern. It is unbelievably inaccurate, ill-informed and racist. If it were not for its racist implications, it would be hysterically funny.[18]

Contrary to the Cobern thesis the Aboriginal people of Van Diemen's Land did not die out, and Truganini was definitely not the 'Last of the Tasmanians' as has often been stated.[19] The progeny of Aboriginal women and European sealers in Bass Strait were destined to form an entirely new society which held strongly to its Aboriginal origins, though with a few notable exceptions a very different scenario was certainly played out on the mainland of Van Diemen's Land. As hostilities drew to a close many Aborigines laid down their arms on the understanding that their grievances would be addressed. Others, particularly those on the west coast, were rounded up by the government's so-called 'conciliator', George Augustus Robinson, occasionally at the point of a gun. No attempt was made to conclude satisfactory arrangements for the Aborigines to remain in their customary homelands. Instead, they were exiled to Bass Strait, first to Gun Carriage (Vansittart) Island, then to Flinders Island. A small group of 15 accompanied George Augustus Robinson to Port Phillip (Victoria) in 1839 following his appointment as Protector of Aborigines on the southern Australian mainland. Most were later returned to Flinders Island, but a few died from natural causes during their sojourn, two were executed for resurrecting the frontier conflict across Bass Strait, and at least three were allowed to remain. There were to be further Aboriginal links between Tasmania and Victoria as the nineteenth century advanced.

Apart from Robinson's party, only one other Aborigine escaped the confines of the Wybalenna Aboriginal Establishment on Flinders

Island before it was finally closed down. That fortunate individual was Woretemoeteryenner, who was granted permission to live with her daughter, Dolly Dalrymple, at Perth in northern Van Diemen's Land. She died a free woman in 1847, the very same year the 46 surviving exiles on Flinders Island were repatriated to Oyster Cove, just to the south of Hobart. Their new abode was a former penal station which had been condemned as unfit for convicts. Not surprisingly, death continued to stalk the new residents. As their numbers declined, however, the free population on the islands of Bass Strait steadily climbed. The islanders forged a unique lifestyle which blended customary Aboriginal and European practices, at the core of which was the annual harvest of the short-tailed shearwater or mutton-bird (*Puffinus tenuirostris*). It worked, but only just, as a heavy reliance on seasonal resources also meant a constant struggle for sheer survival. The situation was exacerbated by governmental neglect. In 1881, 6000 acres (2430 hectares) of land was finally set aside on the western end of Cape Barren Island as a reserve for descendants of European sealers and Aboriginal women, but this was more an attempt at social control than genuine assistance. Further legislation in 1912 was similarly unsuccessful. Yet, despite grinding poverty, the islander community persevered through two world wars and an economic depression, concomitantly developing a new sense of identity largely based on their Tasmanian Aboriginal origins. Customary dissension nevertheless remained a powerful force. While many islanders openly embraced their Aboriginality others did not, and Aboriginality was consistently denied by the Tasmanian government.

The situation began to alter considerably from the 1960s when the resurgence of Aboriginal identity on mainland Australia flowed across Bass Strait, providing a springboard for larger numbers of islanders to assert their own distinctiveness — and to make political gains — a process which continues to the present day. It has not been without controversy. Notwithstanding a measure of continuity from the past, much has been lost. Attempts have been (and are continuing) to be made to recreate language and customary practices, not always successfully, with their authenticity at times highly questionable. The problem is that the Aborigines of Van Diemen's Land never were, and are still not, a single entity, customary separateness making a mockery of the post-colonial construct of 'Palawah'. While the creation of the Tasmanian Aboriginal Centre (TAC) in 1977 as the representative body for all Tasmanian Aborigines has certainly been fruitful, even today it cannot and does not speak for all Tasmanian Aboriginal people.

Tasmanian Aboriginal intellectual property is yet another divisive issue. This was highlighted in late 2013 with the publication of the Cotton Papers as *Land of the Sleeping Gods*, reputedly a collection of Aboriginal mythology, religion, rituals, language, customs and oral history. Initially compiled by the Quaker, Joseph Cotton and his family, along with Joseph's life-long friend, Dr George Fordyce Story, the material is said to have been collected from a previously unknown and unrecorded secret-sacred group of Aborigines from the late 1820s. It is claimed that the original documents were accidentally destroyed in a fire in 1959 and reconstructed from memory by William Jackson Cotton, who published his work two decades later as *Touch the Morning*. They were again rewritten and published by William Cotton's daughter, Jane Cooper.[20] These assertions have been refuted by the research of Dr Nicholas Brodie, who suggests that the stories 'read like early twentieth century historicist and fantasist literature, demanding a willing suspension of disbelief'.[21] They are clearly not of Aboriginal origin. Theresa Sainty, an Aboriginal linguistic consultant with the TAC, was another who questioned the authenticity of the work, yet lamented that publication had occurred without consultation with the Aboriginal people. Conversely, and once again emphasising the difference which has characterised Tasmanian Aboriginal societies from the remote past, other members of the community fully endorsed Cooper's decision to place the material in the public domain.[22] Unfortunately, as time goes on, these stories may well be uncritically accepted as authentic Aboriginal mythology — which they most assuredly are not.

This again is a consequence of the rapid decimation of Van Diemen's Land Aboriginal societies in the first half of the nineteenth century. But all is not lost. The discovery of the Schayer Papers in a Berlin archive, the unearthing of Robert Lawrence's journal by Eleanor Cave and the ongoing research of Nicholas Clements into the 'Black War' have all provided new and insightful information on the Aboriginal history of Van Diemen's Land. They serve as building blocks for future reconstruction, which is something the Aboriginal people of the past — and present — rightly deserve. Their history has been a lengthy one, and their struggle against almost insurmountable odds is one which is worthy of respect and admiration. This book has been written to provide a comprehensive and critical account of that epic journey, and it does so by emphasising the regionalism and separateness which has been a consistent feature of Aboriginal life since time immemorial on the island now known as Tasmania.

1

ORIGINS ... IN FACT AND FICTION

Owing to physical and cultural differences between the Tasmanian Aborigines and their mainland Australian counterparts, an array of theories were put forward during the nineteenth and early twentieth centuries in an attempt to explain their presumed origins. It was quite clear to most contemporary European observers that the turbulent waters of Bass Strait had acted as a natural barrier and prevented any interaction between the two Indigenous groups. Very few Europeans could therefore accept the Tasmanians as Aboriginal people, a perception reinforced by their pigmentation and their often woolly hair. Coupled with a unique lifestyle and limited material culture, the Tasmanians were often ranked at the lowest levels of humanity.[1]

Thomas Huxley, assistant surgeon and naturalist on HMS *Rattlesnake*, which voyaged around the world between 1846 and 1850, claimed that the Tasmanians were an Asiatic Negrito people closely related to the indigenous inhabitants of New Caledonia.[2] Although Captain Owen Stanley twice defied Admiralty orders by briefly visiting Hobart and Launceston respectively, it is not known whether Huxley even saw any of the island's Indigenous inhabitants.[3] It certainly did not deter him from theorising that the Tasmanians had migrated south from New Caledonia along a chain of islands east of the existing Australian coast until they reached their final destination in Tasmania. Those islands, insisted Huxley, were later submerged by rising seas, effectively marooning the migrants in Tasmania where they subsequently lost their maritime skills.[4] Huxley apparently based his theory on the existence of Norfolk and Lord Howe Islands. In 1935 the distinguished Professor of Anatomy at Melbourne University, Frederic Wood-Jones, put a slightly different spin on Huxley's theory by insisting that the New Caledonians made a direct voyage to Tasmania.[5]

During this time even more bizarre theories abounded. Commenting on Francis Allen's argument that the Tasmanians came from Africa, Hyde Clarke drew attention to a language remarkably similar to the Tasmanians which was spoken by the 'Nyam-Nyam' people of the 'African Lake regions'.[6] Allen himself disagreed with another contemporary, Professor Harry Govier Seeley, who believed the Tasmanians had migrated from Africa across a long-submerged land bridge extending from Madagascar through the Seychelles to Borneo, at which point they turned south. Allen could see no reason why the eastward migration could not have been undertaken around the existing coastline and down through the islands of South-East Asia. Upon reaching the Australian landmass they had simply continued to its southernmost extremity.[7] Indeed, that was almost certainly the route taken by the original Aboriginal colonisers of Australia, with the then Tasmanian peninsula as far south as they could go. Of course, neither Allen nor Seeley recognised the Tasmanians as Aborigines: to them they were a distinctly separate African Negrito people.

Even more extraordinary was a theory briefly held in some quarters that the homeland of the Tasmanians lay in Patagonia, the southernmost region of South America. According to this wild claim the people had migrated westwards, skirting the Antarctic ice sheet before turning north to settle permanently in Tasmania.[8] What could have sparked this mass migration — even if the technology had been available — remained undisclosed, and through want of any evidence the proposition was quickly dismissed. Nor was there any evidence to suggest that the Tasmanians were autochthonous or,[9] as historian James Bonwick argued in 1870, a Negrito people whose origins lay on a long-lost continent.[10]

Then there were the tri-hybrid theories. In 1899 the Reverend John Mathew held that the Tasmanians were of Papuan stock and colonised the Australian landmass before their displacement by later arrivals. Mathew reasoned that the original colonisers crossed into Tasmania via a land bridge which was later inundated by rising waters prior to the arrival of more technologically advanced and aggressive Dravidian people.[11] Far-fetched though it may have sounded, Mathew was at least correct about an ancient land bridge. It was just that he had no way of proving its ancient existence. In this respect Mathew was well ahead of most, because well into the 1930s anthropologists and like-minded individuals were still grappling to explain how the Tasmanians could have crossed the formidable sea barrier of Bass Strait. In 1936 a self-proclaimed authority on Tasmania's Indigenous people, Archibald Meston, suggested that they might have used canoes to cross from Wilson's Promontory in Victoria to north-eastern Tasmania using the Kent and Furneaux Islands as staging posts.[12]

One thing these theories all had in common was a mistaken belief that the Tasmanians were a Negrito people both physically and culturally distinct from the Australian Aborigines. It was a denial that continued into the 1960s when archaeologist Rhys Jones raised the spectre of an Indonesian origin. Entering north-western Australia and finding the continent already occupied by Aborigines, this migratory group continued south and then east before stumbling on the uninhabited Tasmanian peninsula which, of course, was later separated from the mainland.[13]

Supposed Negrito people, which included the rainforest dwellers of north-east Queensland as well as the Tasmanians, figured prominently in the tri-hybrid theory of anthropologist Norman Tindale and his American associate Joseph Birdsell. They called the original colonisers of Australia the Barrineans, after Lake Barrine in the Atherton Tableland of north-east Queensland. These were short and slightly built people with woolly hair who were later displaced by a fairer-skinned group ostensibly related to the Ainu of northern Japan who Birdsell and Tindale labelled the Murrayians. Their theory held that the Barrineans only survived in isolated pockets of rainforest in north-east Queensland and Tasmania, where flooding of the Bassian Plain occurred before the Murrayians had spread so far south. The Murrayians were later displaced across northern Australia by the Carpentarians, a Dravidian people who were tall and thin, rather like northern Aboriginal people today.[14] There is, in fact, some evidence that people of Dravidian stock entered northern Australia during the mid-Holocene epoch, but there is no evidence for either the Barrineans or the Murrayians.[15] That, of course, is not to say that Birdsell (in particular) was necessarily wrong: evidence of earlier migrations into Australia may yet emerge. All we can be certain of is that both the Tasmanians and the rainforest people of north-east Queensland were — and are — Aborigines who exhibit a range of physical variation in common with any other group of modern humans.

In June 2002, however, Keith Windschuttle and Tom Gillin resurrected the Barrineans in a discussion specifically focusing on the rainforest people of north-east Queensland. They did so to argue that pre-contact Australian history has been politicised, with evidence of earlier inhabitants deliberately suppressed to avoid undermining the Aboriginal claim to be Australia's first people.[16] While the language of the rainforest dwellers certainly does possess a number of unusual linguistic features, it belongs firmly within the Pama-Nyungan language group which extends across much of the Australian landmass.[17] It also encompasses the Aboriginal languages of Tasmania.[18]

Although only fragments of Tasmanian languages have survived, it was sufficient for the late John Taylor to postulate on the origin of their speakers. Taylor believed there were three, possibly four waves of migration across the Bassian Plain which connected Tasmania to mainland Australia prior to its inundation by rising seas around 10 000 years ago. Until 40 000 years ago entry into the then Tasmanian peninsula was not possible owing to extreme aridity, bitterly cold conditions and sparse food resources. Approximately 40 000 years ago increased precipitation provided the first real opportunity for Aboriginal people to extend their range further south. They seized the initiative and by the time the last great Ice Age began Tasmania had resident populations.[19] Interestingly enough, the giant Australian megafauna, which suddenly began to disappear from the landscape around 46 000–47 000 years ago, apparently survived in Tasmania until c.41 000 years ago, closely coinciding with Taylor's estimate of the earliest human presence.[20]

Taylor believed the original human colonisers of Tasmania came from the Murray River Basin and crossed the western side of the Bassian Plain, which included a section of higher ground that is today's King Island. Having reached Tasmania proper they spread down the west coast and penetrated inland along the river valleys.[21] Archaeological evidence has confirmed the presence of Aborigines in south-west Tasmania at least 35 000 years ago.[22] They were in fact further south than any humans on earth, an achievement not equalled for at least 25 000 years when hunter-gatherers began to make their presence felt on Tierra del Fuego at the extreme tip of South America. Even then, permanent settlement of Tierra del Fuego may not have been accomplished until as recently as 5000 years ago.[23] The initial colonisers of Tasmania also spread into the north-east, though expansion down the east coast was blocked by the prevailing cold, windswept and arid conditions. Those same climatic factors ensured that eastern and south-eastern Tasmania was largely devoid of adequate food resources, thus acting as a brake on human colonisation.[24]

Towards the end of the Last Glacial Maximum, possibly as early as 15 000 years ago when climatic and environmental conditions slowly began to improve, the eastern section of the Bassian Plain was crossed by successive waves of Aboriginal people from today's south-eastern Victoria. They ultimately merged with, or displaced, the resident population in north-east Tasmania before expanding in two directions. One spread into the north-west, reaching their southernmost limit around Macquarie Harbour, thereby confining their predecessors to the south-west. A second group penetrated the centre of Tasmania as far as the southern Midlands.[25]

Taylor argued that a third group of people from the south-western Victoria and south-eastern South Australia region arrived in Tasmania towards the end of the Pleistocene epoch, not long before the Bassian Plain was submerged by rising seas. These people were eventually to settle the eastern and south-eastern regions of Tasmania, though it was not until around 6000 years ago that conditions were conducive for permanent occupation of the Derwent estuary and surrounds.[26] While all Taylor's claims remain highly conjectural, they nevertheless exhibit a considerable degree of plausibility, and linguistic evidence has proved extremely useful in establishing early human settlement patterns in other parts of the world. If his evidence is accepted, it means that it was not until the Holocene epoch of the last 10 700 years that these three (possibly four) socio-cultural groups reorganised themselves into the nine relatively distinct but loosely knit political entities based on geographical territories that are believed to have existed at the time of European contact.[27] That there were a number of Tasmanian languages is undeniable, notwithstanding that at least some of them appear to have been dialects of a mutually shared language.[28]

In early 2010, however, sensational reports appeared in the press that an archaeological discovery on the Jordan River in southern Tasmania had confirmed an Aboriginal presence beyond 40 000 years.[29] The announcements were greeted rapturously by the modern Tasmanian Aboriginal community, members of whom subsequently made vigorous efforts to prevent major roadworks being carried out in the area. Their endeavours proved unsuccessful, but perhaps that was only to be expected.[30] The interim archaeological report, along with peer reviews, quickly made it clear that it was the sediments, not the Aboriginal artefacts, which had been dated.[31] Nor had conjoint analysis, whereby two pieces of a broken artefact from different levels are matched to determine their true position in the stratigraphy, been undertaken. Further work disclosed that burrows of earthworms and rabbits had led to both Aboriginal and post-colonial artefacts filtering downwards to the lower sediment levels. How old the site actually is remains contentious, with a number of archaeologists favouring a Pleistocene occupation beyond 11 000 years.[32] Yet, apart from John Taylor's linguistic interpretations, it is known that prior to the Holocene this entire region was virtually uninhabitable, with conditions alternating from glacial to extreme aridity. The chill factor was exacerbated by constant winds, and combined with minimal precipitation this was an extremely sterile environment.[33] The previous archaeological excavation of a Jordan River midden and a number of sites in the Derwent estuary as well as pollen analysis at Lake Tiberias all point to the occupation of this region as having occurred no earlier than 6000 years ago.[34]

The river valleys of south-west Tasmania were a very different matter. This region was definitely inhabited by Aboriginal people around 35 000 years ago, though it needs to be stressed that all archaeological sites located thus far all point to limited seasonal occupation. Rather than the south, though, it was in the north-west that archaeologist Rhys Jones gained the first real insight into ancient Tasmanian Aboriginal societies. In 1965 Jones began excavating two seaside caves at Rocky Cape, where he was able to trace occupation back to 8000 years. One cave contained five small hearths which revealed that the occupants had feasted upon abalones and other molluscs, scale-fish, birds, small mammals and seals. There was also evidence of vegetable foods such as bracken fern, a lily tuber and grass tree pith.[35] Yet the diet had been anything but constant, with a major transition in the economy occurring around 3700 years ago. The earliest deposits contained the shells of intertidal molluscs as well as scale-fish, but from 3700 years ago the Aboriginal harvesters directed their attention towards sub-littoral resources, particularly abalone and crayfish.[36] At the same time fish bones disappeared from the camp refuse, a phenomenon that was subsequently recorded at a number of widespread locations around the Tasmanian coast. Artefacts at Rocky Cape included stone scrapers, flakes and choppers and a stone mortar used for grinding vegetable foods. There were also bone points made from wallaby fibulae (lower leg bones), but these implements disappeared from the deposits at roughly the same time as fish bones, cessations that will be discussed in the following chapter. When the cave finally became choked with refuse some 5500 years ago it was abandoned in favour of another 300 metres away, which continued to be used until 500 years ago.[37]

Early the following decade Sandra Bowdler excavated the first Pleistocene site at Cave Bay Cave on Hunter Island off the north-western tip of Tasmania. When it was first occupied just over 22 000 years ago the cave was situated well inland on a broad peninsula jutting into the waters of Bass Strait. The site was intensively occupied for around 1000 years, after which it slowly fell from favour. It contains a number of stone hearths and artefacts, with prey species largely consisting of small- to medium-sized mammals, the largest of which was the red-necked wallaby (*Macropus rufogriseus*). Birds were also part of the diet. From 20 000 years to 18 000 years ago (at the height of the Last Glacial Maximum) occupation was less intensive, and apart from one stone hearth which has been dated to 15 500 years ago this large siltstone cave was effectively abandoned.[38] Indeed, it was not reoccupied until 6600 years ago and then abandoned once again when rising waters severed the peninsula from the Tasmanian mainland. Occupation only resumed when Hunter Island was recolonised by the Aboriginal people some 2500 years ago.[39]

By the mid-1970s the Aboriginal occupation of Tasmania had thus been extended beyond 22 000 years. In 1977 a geomorphologist named Kevin Kiernan stumbled on a cave in south-west Tasmania which revealed that Aboriginal people had also penetrated this far south by 20 000 years ago. Excavations at Fraser Cave, or Kutikina, commenced in 1981, with the archaeological results playing a significant role in the campaign against the proposed Gordon-below-Franklin Dam. The successful outcome of that unprecedented environmental protest ensured that a substantial section of south-west Tasmania was ultimately protected by World Heritage legislation. This was particularly fortunate, for if dam construction had gone ahead Kutikina and even older Aboriginal sites would have been lost for all time.[40]

Kutikina was a temporary base camp which was occupied for a few weeks every year by a group of 20–30 people, who returned here from foraging to butcher and cook their game. Fragments of bone littered the floor of the cave in immense quantities, and as at Cave Bay Cave in the north-west, the major prey species was the red-necked wallaby,[41] a species which remains common today with a distribution extending from southern Tasmania to central Queensland.[42] Along with animal bones were thousands of stone implements made from chert, quartz, quartzite and Darwin glass, a natural glass formed from a meteorite strike at Mount Darwin, just south of Queenstown, 800 000 years ago. Darwin glass varies in colour from black to white or light and dark green, and is found across an area of 410 square kilometres north, south and east of the impact crater. Although rare in the crater itself,[43] small fragments are picked up from the ground or gathered among the roots of upturned trees. When fractured, Darwin glass has extremely sharp edges.[44] Yet despite its obvious importance, implements made from Darwin glass only appeared in the deposits from the end of the Last Glacial Maximum, around 14 000 years ago.[45]

Previously, 70 per cent of all stone artefacts had been made from quartzite.[46] The remainder were manufactured from chert, hornfels and quartz, some of which came from distant quarries. Like Darwin glass, however, quartz only became prominent from the end of the Last Glacial Maximum.[47] Tool types excavated at Kutikina include a number of scrapers, particularly thumbnail scrapers which, as their name suggests, are roughly the size of a human thumbnail. Despite their small size they were clearly an important component in the toolkit as the edges of many had been retouched to maintain their cutting qualities.[48]

Analysis of the cutting edges of Darwin glass implements revealed traces of collagen and haemoglobin, the latter from red-necked wallabies. It appears almost certain that they were used for butchering these animals.[49] Bone points made from wallaby fibulae were also uncovered from the deposits, leading to speculation that at least some of them may have been used as awls to make fur cloaks,[50] garments that were unknown among Tasmanian Aborigines at the time of European contact. Importantly, though, the discovery of Kutikina Cave provided the impetus to conduct a more rigorous archaeological survey of the south-west Tasmanian river valleys, greatly assisted by the Southern Forests Archaeological Project initiated by Melbourne's La Trobe University in 1988.[51]

Kutikina is a large cave. The roof reaches five metres in height, with a main chamber 20 metres long and 12 metres wide.[52] The floor covers approximately 100 square metres, but it is only one of more than 20 caves in south-west Tasmania which have now been identified as Pleistocene occupation sites. Warreen Cave, with occupation dating beyond 34 000 years, is the oldest discovered thus far.[53] Then, around 11 000 years ago all but one of these caves was abandoned following the onset of warmer and wetter conditions which led to dense and unproductive rainforest encroaching on the tundra-like grasslands with their patches of alpine shrubs. Gone were the glaciers which existed on the Central Plateau and in a number of river systems, including the upper Mersey.[54] Despite the intense cold, the south-west had been the most productive environment in Tasmania, with the mixed grasslands the preferred habitat of red-necked wallabies.[55]

These macropods stand around 90 centimetres in height and weigh between 13–18 kilograms. Their remains comprise approximately 90 per cent of all animal debris in the Pleistocene occupation sites of Tasmania's south-west.[56] Many of the bones from the hind limbs and feet had been split along their longitudinal axis to extract marrow,[57] the carbohydrates essential for metabolism in a high-protein diet which may have included only limited quantities of vegetable foods. Unlike their larger cousins, red-necked wallabies tend to be solitary and fairly sedentary animals. Their home ranges average between 15–20 hectares in extent and their grazing and browsing feeding activity only expands approximately 30 metres every two or three years. In other words, these animals are virtually tethered to relatively small patches of ground, yet another reason why they were targeted as prey during the Pleistocene.[58] Given that larger animals were available, it appears that this species was specifically hunted for its marrow, with meat merely a by-product.[59]

Exploitation was certainly not a random affair. Red-necked wallabies live to more than six years of age, and an examination of their archaeological remains has revealed that animals above two years of age were the preferred quarry. It seems clear that consideration was taken regarding both age and quality. Remains of very young wallabies are entirely absent from the human refuse in all south-west Tasmanian Pleistocene sites, and the evidence further suggests that hunting occurred in autumn, when these macropods were in prime condition, and late winter, a particularly lean time for the Aboriginal people. Exploitation of the red-necked wallaby in late winter thus represented a low-cost high-energy return for expended effort.[60]

Other prey species included the common wombat (*Vombatus ursinus*), whose bones comprise around 12 per cent of the animal debris. Fragments of wombat crania suggest that this species may have been primarily targeted for their brains, once again an important source of essential carbohydrates. The long bones of wombats were also split to extract marrow. Brush and ringtail possums, pademelon and eastern grey kangaroo provided additional mammalian food sources. Although the remains of both the Tasmanian devil (*Sarcophilus harrisii*) and the eastern quoll (*Dasyurus viverrinus*) have also been recovered from the deposits their provenance is less clear. Conversely, birds such as the Tasmanian native hen (*Gallinula mortierii*) and the extinct Tasmanian emu (*Dromaius novaehollandiae diemenensis*), do appear to have been part of the diet,[61] but it is only at Nunamira Cave further south in the Florentine River valley that the eggs of the Tasmanian emu appear in Pleistocene domestic refuse. Amino-acid analysis of the eggshells has also made it possible to estimate the mean temperature at the time they were gathered, a cool 4°C. ± 1°C.[62] These were tough people living in a very harsh environment, though they were not entirely immune to extreme conditions. The available evidence suggests that these ancient hunters moved seasonally along the river valleys, but there was also a degree of altitudinal mobility, with the highest caves only utilised during the warmer months.[63]

The caves of the south-west have also provided the first evidence of Pleistocene art in Tasmania. Although hand stencils have long been known from three rock-shelters in south-east Tasmania, it was generally believed they were executed by New South Wales Aborigines brought to Tasmania in the late 1820s and early 1830s to assist in tracking down and forcibly removing Indigenous survivors of the 'Black War'. They appeared to be relatively fresh and all three sites were located close to early European settlements.[64] Then, in January 1986, hand stencils were discovered in the remote Maxwell River valley. They have since been recorded from three caves — Ballawinne, Weld and Wargata Mina — with radiocarbon dating of human blood which was mixed with ochre to produce the paint returning a date of approximately 10 700 years ago.[65] This roughly coincides with the very time the caves of the south-west were abandoned. On the other hand, the legacy of the Pleistocene hunters still lives on to the present day. Many, if not most, of the button-grass plains existing in the south-west are the result of ancient burning regimes, a human artefact that makes a mockery of any claims that south-west Tasmania represents a vestigial stand of untouched wilderness.[66]

Slightly to the north, Parmerpar Meethaner in the Forth River Valley is the only cave in the general south-west region of Tasmania where continuous occupation extended into the Holocene. The earliest deposits date from 34 000 years ago, while the youngest are from 780 years. Even at the height of the Last Glacial Maximum the Forth River Valley remained free of ice,[67] partly explaining why this particular site continued in use. But there are a number of features which distinguish Parmerpar Meethaner from the caves further south. Stone artefacts, for example, were manufactured from a range of materials, all of which were sourced locally. Prior to 18 000 years ago quartzite flakes dominated the assemblage, but as at Kutikina quartz provided the bulk of the raw material between 15 000 and 18 000 years. Quartz was superseded by hornfels, a hard metamorphic rock, around 10 000 years ago and it remained the preferred material for stone tools until 3500 years ago. Although thumbnail scrapers made from Darwin glass are extremely prolific at Mackintosh Cave only 35 kilometres west, they are entirely absent from Parmerpar Meethaner. Mackintosh Cave, in fact, marks the northernmost limit of Darwin glass artefacts, which extended southwards to the Florentine River valley.[68]

Their absence from the Forth River valley is nevertheless difficult to explain, and nor did the ancient inhabitants of this area hunt red-necked wallabies. The remains of wombats are also very sparse in the deposits. The economy of Parmerpar Meethaner revolved around the exploitation of small- to medium-sized animals, including ringtail possums, pademelon, potoroo, blue-tongue skinks and fish.[69] It could well be that Parmerpar Meethaner marked the southern limits of a more northerly people with their own distinctive culture, and it was possibly elements of this group who occupied Warragarra rockshelter in the upper Mersey River valley around 10 000 years ago. The main prey species at this location were once again small- to medium-sized animals, particularly macropods and possums. Warragarra was abandoned in the mid-Holocene and then reoccupied some 3400 years ago.[70] Whatever the explanation behind the differences which existed at Warragarra and Parmerpar Meethaner, they serve as powerful reminders that the Tasmanian Aborigines should not be regarded as a single cultural entity. While there were certainly many similarities, there were also considerable differences between the various groups.

Physical variation, on the other hand, may not have been pronounced. Skeletal remains excavated at Nanwoon Cave in the Florentine River Valley in 1987 and dated to 16 000 years belonged to a gracile individual. Another gracile individual dating from 14 000 years was unearthed on King Island, both remarkably similar to the slightly built people who lived around Lake Mungo in south-western New South Wales 44 000 years ago.[71] They were quite different from the later robust inhabitants of Lake Mungo and the Murray River valley.[72] It was once believed that King Island retained a relict population after flooding of the Bassian Plain. The general consensus today is that the island was abandoned shortly before it was separated from mainland Tasmania,[73] though there is intriguing evidence of an Aboriginal presence on King Island during the late Holocene. Of the 22 identified Aboriginal occupation sites, all but two have been dated to the Pleistocene. One at Cataraqui Point, however, has been dated to 1980 years BP, while another at Quarantine Bay is even more recent — 1100 years BP. Both sites were occupied only briefly, with no suggestion of extended use. Molluscs formed at least part of the diet, and at both sites artefacts made from spongelite (a form of chert) have been found. Although it is possible that a local deposit of spongelite has long since been submerged by the sea, the only known source of this material is an old Aboriginal quarry at Rebecca Creek in north-west Tasmania. The artefacts could have been carried on watercraft that were driven north by winds and currents, perhaps from Hunter Island, which had been recolonised during the late Holocene.[74] If such was the case the marooning was likely to have been permanent, as those same winds and currents would have prevented any return to the Tasmanian mainland.

A very different scenario was played out on Flinders Island at the opposite end of Bass Strait. Extensive shell middens provide ample testimony to the existence of an island population long after the flooding of the Bassian Plain. They survived on Flinders Island until 4500 years ago, when any further trace of these people disappears from the archaeological record. Their fate is one of the many mysteries of pre-contact Aboriginal history. While there may have been sufficient food sources to sustain a small population indefinitely, the availability of fresh water was another matter again. Flinders Island was (and still is) subject to extreme drought during the summer months, with Pats River the only reliable source of fresh water. The disappearance of the Flinders Islanders coincided with a particularly arid climatic phase, and it is well within the realm of possibility that fresh water supplies completely dried up.[75]

On the other hand, the long-term survival of any isolated human population requires at least 500 individuals, preferably with an equal gender ratio. That is the minimum figure: any less and the population becomes highly susceptible to extinction through in-breeding, age disparity and contagious illness.[76] Nor is it likely that the Flinders Islanders reached the Tasmanian mainland. Watercraft only appeared in Tasmania within the last 3000–4000 years, and their distribution was confined to the southern and north-west coasts.[77] There would have been no escape for the population on Flinders Island.

Notwithstanding the false hype regarding the Jordan River levee site in 2010, no Pleistocene sites have yet been identified in the south-east or east of Tasmania. In the late 1960s Harry Lourandos conducted some important archaeological work at Little Swanport where extensive Aboriginal middens had been known to exist since 1891. Some of them are 2 metres thick, mostly comprising mollusc shells and the exoskeletons of crayfish. They are also relatively recent, the oldest deposits dating from 4750 years ago. For all that, it was the warmer and wetter conditions of the Holocene which resulted in a major demographic shift in Tasmania from west to east. There can be little doubt that when Europeans first arrived in Tasmanian waters from the seventeenth century the largest Aboriginal populations were located in the south-east, east and north-east as well as the Midlands. While it remains entirely debatable, the largest concentration may have been in the north-east where a more temperate climate and a wide range of ecosystems were to be found. The landscape included savannah grasslands and open forests interspersed with numerous moorlands and lakes, while the coastline was indented with bays and estuaries rich in marine resources:[78] a complete reversal of conditions during the Pleistocene. Unfortunately, it was the Aboriginal people of north-east Tasmania who were the first to have extensive contact with Europeans, resulting in a dramatic demographic collapse within a remarkably short span of time.[79] This, of course, raises the question of how many Aboriginal people existed in Tasmania at the time of European contact.

During the mid- to late-nineteenth century European estimates of the pre-contact population ranged from 700 to as many as 20 000.[80] On one hand there appears to have been a deliberate attempt to play down the numbers, perhaps to exonerate colonists from any charges of genocide in relation to the frontier conflict. Conversely, Henry Melville's claim of 20 000 people may have been intended to chastise his fellow Europeans for their brutality during the so-called 'Black War'.[81] The best estimate, however, falls on the work of George Augustus Robinson, whose 'Friendly Mission' brought in most of the surviving Aborigines from the frontier. Robinson and many others used (and continue to use) the word 'tribe' to identify different groups associated with specific geographical areas. In the Australian context the word itself is something of a misnomer as it implies that the Indigenous people were organised into federated bodies. This was very rarely the case.

Robinson was certainly aware of the importance of territory, using such terms 'Port Davey tribe' or 'Cape Portland tribe' to identify each of these groups. Having traversed much of Tasmania during the course of his work with the 'Friendly Mission', Robinson recorded 46 of these so-called 'tribes'.[82] He was also aware that numerous others had become extinct long before he began his peregrinations, possibly as a result of disease inadvertently introduced in the late eighteenth century by European mariners. Taking all this into account, Rhys Jones proposed that there could have been as many as 70 'tribes' in the pre-contact period, and from Robinson's figures each of them consisted of from 30 to 80 individuals. By accepting there were between 46 and 70 territorial entities the total population would have been somewhere between 3000 and 5000.[83]

On a regional basis 'tribes' shared a common language and culture, but there is no direct evidence of their total size. On the Australian mainland linguistic groups vary from 100 up to 1500 individuals, with the average around 500.[84] The available evidence suggests there were nine socio-linguistic groups in Tasmania,[85] and if the mainland figure bears any comparison it results in an Indigenous population of approximately 4500. Although Tasmania has an area of 62 409 square kilometres, perhaps as much as 25 per cent of it was never permanently occupied by the Aborigines. The point here is that if the pre-contact population was in the order of 4500–5000 it was a density comparable to the richest coastal districts of the southern Australian mainland.[86] That figure is probably very close to the mark. At the time of contact with Europeans the physical universe of the Tasmanians was also expanding. The appearance of watercraft within the last four millennia enabled the exploitation, and in some instances the resettlement, of islands in the south and north-west. Although material culture was in other ways maintained at a minimal level it was more than sufficient to fulfil every possible need. We now need to examine the cultural aspects of Tasmanian Aboriginal societies before they were impacted upon by outsiders.

2

LIFE-WAYS AND MATERIAL CULTURE OF PRE-CONTACT VAN DIEMEN'S LAND

Despite the misconception of many early Europeans, the Tasmanians actually differed little from their mainland counterparts in physical appearance except through biological adaptation and isolation in the cooler and moister climate of their island home. Adaptation and genetic drift produced woolly hair and generally short, stocky bodies, an important means of conserving body heat. But there were clear exceptions to this. Not all the Tasmanians had woolly hair, and many of the men in the immediate post-contact period were described as extremely tall — above 1.8 metres in height — notably those on the colder west coast.[1]

Pigmentation was also variable, ranging from black to reddish-brown,[2] though there were clear gender divisions in non-biological appearance. Men, for example, wore their hair long and in ringlets, coated with fat and ochre which superficially resembled modern dreadlocks.[3] They also smeared their upper body, head and neck with powdered charcoal. Women tended to use powdered charcoal as facial decoration, and unlike the men their hair was shaven or close-cropped. In coastal areas women smeared their bodies with seal fat, partly as decoration, but more importantly for insulation as it was the women who dived into the often frigid waters for abalone and crayfish.[4] Both men and women further decorated themselves with shell necklaces, ornamentation which is still made by a number of modern Tasmanian Aboriginal women.[5]

While the Tasmanians may have used warm fur cloaks during the Pleistocene (which at least appears likely) their adaptation to the environment over millennia left them in minimal need of wearing apparel. Their only covering was a shoulder cape made from wallaby or kangaroo skin, usually though not exclusively worn by women.[6] There are also reports of women wearing aprons to conceal their genitals. The Tasmanians normally went barefooted, but if their feet were injured they made a type of moccasin from wallaby or kangaroo hide which was laced around the foot.[7] Both men and women were scarified with cicatrices, the design partially intended to signify the band to which they belonged. The outer skin of the neck, torso and upper limbs was cut with a sharp instrument such as a mollusc shell and ochre, fat or wood ash rubbed into the wound to leave permanently raised scars forming a pattern that was replicated on the opposite side of the body.[8] Interestingly, it appears to have been women who scarified the young men when the latter reached puberty.[9]

Although Brian Plomley was led to believe that scarification was solely intended as 'tribal identification',[10] its full meaning lies much deeper than this. George Augustus Robinson mentioned motifs representing celestial bodies among the cicatrices of Aboriginal females 'on each side of the backbone and about the hips'. As he was aware that the sun and the lunar satellite were regarded as major sources of power and healing, Robinson concluded that such cicatrices were 'intended to remove inflammation and having the power of those luminaries [Aboriginal women] imagine it will have the same influence on the part affected'.[11] While Robinson's understanding of Aboriginal spirituality is at times questionable, there is no reason to doubt this connection between psychological power and Aboriginal well-being. On a more practical level there is no evidence that the Tasmanians practised tooth avulsion, circumcision or subincision, as was often the case on the Australian mainland.[12]

Their toolkit was certainly refined, though in regard to stone tools that was at least partly attributable to the use of superior materials, including chert, breccia and, in the north-west, spongelite.[13] It is not known whether the Tasmanians used boomerangs or spear-throwers in the distant past as wooden implements rarely survive in the archaeological record. They certainly did not use them in more recent times, and it was owing to their less sophisticated toolkit, the perception that they lacked adequate apparel, a misguided belief that they were incapable of producing fire, and their long-term isolation that led Rhys Jones to question whether the Tasmanians were already on the path to extinction: were they 'doomed to a slow strangulation of the mind?' he asked rhetorically.[14] In view of the limited knowledge then available as well as indications in the archaeological record, this was not an entirely unreasonable speculation. Only later did it become clear that the cultural universe of the Tasmanians had begun to expand within the last four millennia, and was still expanding at the time of European contact.

A degree of rigidity nevertheless applied to social organisation, and it is here that the term 'tribe' looms large, especially owing to its interchangeable use with the word 'band' in the Tasmanian context. This has led to considerable confusion. Rhys Jones, for example, applied the word 'tribe' to the nine large socio-linguistic entities, and 'band' for smaller social units simply as a matter of convenience. George Augustus Robinson, on the other hand, used the word 'tribe' when he was actually referring to bands who occupied specific tracts of territory within the larger socio-linguistic groupings.[15] Bands enjoyed political and economic autonomy, and all had names which identified them to others. As noted in the previous chapter the bands varied in size from around 30 to 80 individuals. When Robinson first made contact with the Port Davey or Ninene people of the south-west in 1830 he recorded 20 adults. To be a viable social unit, however, there would have been an almost equal number of children, making the Ninene band around 40 strong.[16] In 1802 the Baudin expedition counted 60 Aborigines on Bruny Island in the south-east, though as Brian Plomley pointed out, the absence of the aged and very young probably meant that the band was slightly larger.[17] When James Kelly's expedition circumnavigated Tasmania in a whaleboat in 1815–16 he estimated there were 50 Aboriginal men on Hunter Island off the north-west coast, with the 'women out of sight'.[18]

As in southern Victoria but in very few other regions in Australia, Tasmanian bands were led by a respected male warrior and hunter, whom Europeans referred to as a chief. There were no councils of Elders. The bands themselves comprised families or hearth groups, usually a nuclear family and perhaps a few close relatives, numbering anywhere from two to more than a dozen individuals.[19] Hearth groups camped and cooked around their own fires. The ex-convict explorer and police constable, Jorgen Jorgenson, described the living arrangements which he observed during the seasonal movements of a Tasmanian band. Each hearth group constructed their own bark shelter at some distance from the others for privacy, with every shelter having its own fire for cooking and warmth.[20] Families, then, travelled either individually or collectively when hunting and gathering, coming together as a band to exploit seasonal resources or for cultural reasons. There is some evidence that a number of bands occasionally came together, with large congregations of 'several hundred' people observed by early European settlers.[21]

This was particularly necessary to fulfil cultural obligations, including marriage. It can be accepted that there would have been a clear understanding from at least childhood that future marriage partners would have to be found outside the band owing to their limited size.[22] Jorgenson cited one instance where a Ninene woman from Port Davey in the south-west accompanied Robinson's 'Friendly Mission' for the sole purpose of seeking a marriageable partner. Her quest was successful, with the woman marrying into a band 110 kilometres from her home territory.[23] But it was not only women who left their homeland for marriage. Wymurick from Robbins Island off the north-west coast married into a band whose territory lay further down the west coast of the mainland. After taking up residence with his wife's people, Wymurick was later chosen by other members of her band as their leader.[24] In common with the Australian mainland, there was no formal wedding ceremony: cohabitation, acceptance by the families of both partners and an exchange of gifts was sufficient to consummate the marriage. This usually occurred when both partners were in their late teens.[25] Notwithstanding that Tasmanian Aboriginal societies were strictly patriarchal and that cuts were inflicted by husbands on wives with stone knives to mark their marital status,[26] Robinson observed that husbands were often very fond of their spouse, with both sharing great affection for their children.[27] With extremely rare exceptions marriage in Tasmania was monogamous.

The nine large socio-linguistic groups were devoid of formal structure, collective land ownership, integrated authority and leadership. They did not even possess a name.[28] And despite language, customs and kinship ties through marriage, the relationship between the smaller composite bands was occasionally strained. Bands could only enter the territory of neighbours under mutually agreed conditions, with any trespass or breach of protocol potentially resulting in violence. When George Augustus Robinson was in north-west Tasmania in February 1834 he was informed by members of the Tarkiner band from Sandy Cape that they had recently been involved in a deadly skirmish with the Tommeginer band of Table Cape. The Tommeginers had visited Tarkiner territory, bringing with them highly-prized ochre to presumably exchange for access rights. Unfortunately, a request by the Tarkiner for the ochre had been refused, sparking a fatal clash with casualties on both sides.[29] From this incident it can be understood that the supply of ochre and access to seasonal resources of others was carefully regulated and reciprocation expected. In the majority of cases these regulations probably worked quite satisfactorily, bringing benefits to both parties.

In common with Aboriginal groups throughout Australia there was a gendered division of labour, though in Tasmania women played a particularly significant role. It was women who gathered bird eggs, women who hunted seals and dived for abalone and crayfish, women who scaled trees to catch possums, and women who mined ochre, using a stone hammer and wooden chisel, grinding it into a powder with ballywinne stones. As on the Australian mainland, ochre (more correctly haematite) was a major cultural resource of the Tasmanians, but on the island it was women who were responsible for its preparation. In 1793 the French naturalist, Jacques Labillardière, also noted that Tasmanian women could remain submerged for twice as long as the best French divers.[30] Women wove a number of different types of baskets from grass or kelp to gather food, and they also made water containers from the fronds of bull kelp. The sides were drawn up with a string of vegetable fibre and thin sticks inserted through the edges to form a box-like shape. These were usually fitted with a handle and to further reduce spillage grass was sprinkled on top of the contents.[31]

Women certainly bore the brunt of labour, and although men are known to have been involved in gathering plant foods,[32] the principal male activity was to hunt the larger game and defend the hearth group or band. Their main accessories were the spear and waddy or club.

Although lacking the spear-thrower, or woomera, men were able to hurl their spears with remarkable accuracy over considerable distances. At George Town in September 1831, Robinson arranged a contest between two Tasmanian men and their opposite number from New South Wales who used spear-throwers: the Tasmanians won easily.[33] A similar demonstration was organised by Jorgen Jorgenson at Hobart, with Lieutenant-Governor George Arthur among the spectators. A door frame was erected and from a distance of 60–70 metres the men were able to hurl their spears through the opening. One man then placed a crayfish on top of a spear and threw three missiles from a distance of 60 metres. Two of them lodged in the target.[34]

Tasmanian spears were made from either tea-tree (*Melaleuca sp.*) or dogwood (*Pomaderris apetala*), and were generally around 3 metres in length. The point was first sharpened and then the bark removed from the shaft, which was then straightened by alternately heating a small section over a fire and bending it straight with the teeth. Spears were neither barbed nor fitted with a stone or bone point as was often the case on the Australian mainland.[35] The waddy, on the other hand, was a wooden club with a rounded head between 60–70 centimetres long. Hand-held in fighting, the waddy was thrown with a rotary motion when hunting, a particularly useful means of bringing down possums or birds on the wing. Tasmanian men were equally adept at throwing stones when hunting or fighting, their precision readily acknowledged by Europeans.[36]

Animals were also trapped or snared using a variety of ingenious techniques. One method was to dig burnt stakes into the ground, with their sharpened points projecting roughly 60 centimetres above the surface. Burning and burying the stakes stalled decay, and apart from wounding wallabies and kangaroos, this type of trap also served a military function by incapacitating bare-footed enemies.[37] Another trap consisted of a small grass hut, just large enough to conceal the hunter. A fish weighted by a stone was placed on a flat rock beside the wall and when crows alighted in anticipation of a feast the hunter simply reached through the grass to seize his prey. A similar technique was used to catch ducks, with worms providing the bait.[38] While travelling on the west coast, Robinson recorded an even more sophisticated trap consisting of a small dome-shaped basket with a small hole in the top, presumably baited inside. This, too, was apparently used to procure birds.[39]

Unlike many Aboriginal groups on mainland Australia, the Tasmanians did not cook their food in ground ovens: it was simply roasted over an open fire. Mammals were thrown into the ashes until the fur was singed off and then scraped and cleaned of entrails before being returned to the ashes for a final roasting. On Flinders Island in the post-contact period Quaker missionary James Backhouse recorded the Aborigines roasting mutton-birds (*Puffinus sp.*) on spits after their feathers had been singed off in the flames.[40]

Meat staples included all forms of macropods — eastern grey kangaroo, wallabies, pademelons and potoroos.[41] Holocene Tasmanians differed from their Pleistocene ancestors in being general rather than specialised hunters and gatherers. That said, there is some evidence that restrictions were placed on the taking of eastern grey kangaroo, though whether this applied to the age or sex of the animals or hunting at particular times of the year remains unclear.[42] It does appear to have been some form of conservation measure, and it could be relevant that the eastern grey kangaroo was rapidly exterminated across wide areas of Tasmania following the arrival of Europeans. This species is today largely restricted to the north-east, where European settlement came late and large areas still remain unoccupied.[43] Similar prohibitions applied to wallabies, though in this case it is definitely known to have been based on the gender of the animal.[44] It was probably women who hunted small mammals such as bandicoots and native rodents,[45] and they certainly took pride in their ability to climb the tallest trees with fibre ropes in pursuit of possums.[46] On the Australian mainland this was invariably a male activity.[47] Although platypus, echidnas, wombats and quolls also featured regularly in the Tasmanian diet,[48] there is no direct evidence that the largest marsupial predators — thylacines and Tasmanian devils — were prey animals. Whilst Robinson was told by his Aboriginal guides on the 'Friendly Mission' that 'they had speared plenty' of thylacines, this does not confirm consumption.[49]

On the coast beached whales provided bountiful feasts for all, but the hunting of seals devolved solely on women. They usually swam out to the seal colonies in groups, closely imitating the movements of their quarry (to the extent of scratching themselves and rolling from side to side) until the animals had become accustomed to their presence. At a given signal the women suddenly rose, with each clubbing a selected target to death.[50] A wide range of avian fauna and their eggs also featured regularly in the Tasmanian diet, with black swans and the Tasmanian emu considered particular delicacies.[51] Emus were once widespread throughout Tasmania, their rapid extinction resulting from European hunting:[52] the last emu, a captive specimen, was reputedly drowned in 1873.[53] Penguins and seagulls were among other birds hunted on the coast, though the role played by shearwaters or mutton-birds in the customary Aboriginal diet has almost certainly been overstated. An authority on mutton-birding, the late Irynej Skira, noted that the appearance of shearwater rookeries on mainland Tasmania and a number of close offshore islands is a very recent natural phenomenon — certainly within the post-contact period. The factors relating to this expansion of the breeding range of shearwaters are still not fully understood,[54] but it does mean that apart from isolated instances (and perhaps the north-west was a major exception) these birds were largely inaccessible to the Aboriginal people.[55] In a similar vein, the commercial harvesting of mutton-bird chicks for their oil and feathers is a cultural legacy of early European sealers.[56]

Along with crayfish, molluscs — especially abalone — were important items in the coastal diet. Again, it was women who harvested both abalones and other sub-littoral molluscs prised from submerged rocks with wooden spatulas and collected in woven baskets suspended around their necks.[57] It is with scale-fish that problems arise. Archaeology has clearly shown that the Tasmanians consumed at least 31 different species of fish prior to c.3700 years ago, when fish bones disappear from coastal middens.[58] The correlation (if any) with bone tools which were apparently discarded at almost precisely the same time adds a second element to this intriguing enigma. One argument that has been used to counter the claim that fish disappeared from the Tasmanian diet is the presence of fish-traps in the north-west. Their construction, perhaps best exemplified by a trap at Freestone Cove, required a considerable amount of time and labour. They also signify the development of a sustainable and reliable resource as well as a strong attachment to place. Having said that, however, there is an ongoing debate as to whether some of these traps, notably those at Rocky Cape and Boat Harbour, were built by Aboriginal people or early European settlers.[59] But first we need to take a step back.

When the absence of fish bones from coastal middens around 3700 years ago was initially recognised by Rhys Jones, the debate focused on the reasons why this important food resource had suddenly been abandoned. To Jones it was a major plank in his over-arching theory that the Tasmanians experienced cultural regression, particularly as he considered fish to have been a significant food item in the past.[60] Yet even by Jones's reckoning seals and molluscs comprised the bulk of the coastal diet prior to 3700 years ago. From 3700 years ago seal consumption only increased from 67–70 per cent of the total diet, while the consumption of wallaby on the coast increased from 7–18 per cent.[61] Clearly, the absence of fish did not result in a radical dietary change.

Both David Horton and Sandra Bowdler argued that Jones had placed far too much emphasis on scale-fish in the pre-3700 year diet,[62] an argument that has been resurrected in more recent times by Peter Hiscock, who contended that they only represented 5–10 per cent of the Aboriginal meat intake on the coast.[63] A different slant was provided by Harry Allen, who believed that abandoning fish from the diet was a sensible decision, given that cooler climatic conditions prevailed around 3700 years ago.[64] Josephine Flood later expanded on Allen's argument by suggesting that coastal economies were probably transformed to place greater emphasis on high-energy foods such as seals and seabirds at the expense of scale-fish, which have less nutritional value and require more energy to harvest.[65]

In 1994 Tim Flannery entered the debate by suggesting that scale-fish may have been dropped from the Aboriginal diet as a response to mass poisoning occasioned by the dinoflagellate, or algal bloom, known as 'red tide'. As specialist artisans could have been among the victims, this theory also attempted to explain the concomitant disappearance of bone tools.[66] But it is difficult to see how such a reaction could have been triggered right around the coast at virtually the same time. And there still remains the possibility that scale-fish never did feature significantly in the diet of the Aboriginal people. In 2004 Everett Bassett raised the possibility that fish bones at ancient coastal archaeological sites could merely be discarded remains from the stomachs of butchered seals.[67]

Rhys Jones examined the ethnological accounts of early European mariners, finding that virtually all of them confirmed an abhorrence of fish in any form. In 1777, for example, William Anderson, surgeon on James Cook's third and final Pacific expedition, noted that Bruny Islanders recoiled in horror when offered a gift of elephant fish. Cook himself mentioned that the Aborigines at Adventure Bay in southern Tasmania refused all scale-fish that was offered, though it needs to be added that they also rejected gifts of bread, iron and fish-hooks.[68] In February 1792 William Bligh, previously one of Cook's officers, returned for a third time to Adventure Bay with his own command and closely examined Aboriginal middens. All of them comprised mollusc shells and the remains of crayfish: fish bones were entirely absent.[69] The following year Bruny d'Entrecasteaux's expedition found 'no debris of fishes' in any Aboriginal middens,[70] while in 1802 Nicolas Baudin recorded how the Tasmanian Aborigines made unmistakeable signs that they did not eat fish.[71]

There is nevertheless evidence to the contrary. In 1772 Lieutenant Le Dez, an officer on Marion Dufresne's expedition, commented that 'one notices easily the place where they [the Aborigines] had slept around a mound of ash and one sees, nearby, fishbones and many burnt shells'.[72] An experienced mariner such as Le Dez is unlikely to have confused fish bones with the remains of other animals. In contrast to the remarks of his commander, Jacques Labillardière, naturalist on Bruny d'Entrecasteaux's expedition observed that the Nuenone people on Bruny Island 'acquainted us that they lived upon fish'.[73] It is, of course, quite possible that either Labillardière or the Aborigines actually meant 'shellfish' rather than scale-fish, but it could equally be true that in some areas of southern Tasmania the Aborigines continued to include scale-fish in their coastal diet — a timely reminder that considerable diversity existed among the island's Indigenous population.

Emmanuel Hamelin, commander of the Baudin expedition's second ship, *Naturaliste*, found that the Aborigines readily accepted a proffered stingray. The following day the Frenchmen found the stingray on the beach minus its liver, which Hamelin recalled was a delicacy among the Aboriginal people on the west coast of the Australian mainland. Baudin also mentioned that one night members of his crew observed Aborigines along the shoreline with torches, evidently involved in some form of fishing activity.[74] Fishing with torches and spears is a popular means of catching flounder in Tasmania today,[75] though once again this particular group could just as easily have been fishing for squid or some other marine invertebrate attracted to light.

In the post-contact period European commentators were similarly mixed in their assessments as to whether the Tasmanian Aborigines consumed scale-fish. This was no less so in the observations of George Augustus Robinson, who had the most extensive contact with the Indigenous people. At his initial Aboriginal establishment on Bruny Island in April 1829 Robinson recorded that after cooking some perch and rock cod it was only 'with great difficulty' that he managed to persuade the Aborigines to 'partake of some'.[76] As explained shortly, there may have been a valid reason for this reluctance. Two years later Robinson responded to Chief Justice John Pedder's argument that exiling the Aborigines to an offshore island would only result in them pining 'away in consequence of the restraint' by countering that they 'would be enabled to fish, dance, sing, and throw spears and amuse themselves in their usual way'.[77] Whether he meant fishing for food is not altogether clear. The following year Robinson narrowly escaped death at the hands of the Tarkiner people on Tasmania's north-west coast. From across the Arthur River the Tarkiner shouted at Robinson's guides that 'when I got these people to the island I should feed them on fish, and mimicked the pulling up of the fish with a line'.[78] These obviously disparaging remarks could have been condemnation of the guides falling under European influence — or, alternatively, the Tarkiner may have been voicing their superiority over people who included fish in their diet. Finally, in 1833 when Robinson was again on the west coast near the Wanderer River, he recorded in his diary that while his female guides readily enjoyed catching native trout (galaxiids) with hook and line the entire catch was presented to himself and his sons.[79]

Although much can be read into the 'conciliator's' remarks his nephew, James Young, later recalled that Aborigines confined at Wybalenna on Flinders Island regularly caught parrot fish (wrasse) and bluefish with hook and line, which they subsequently consumed.[80] Substantial quantities of fishing tackle for the Aborigines were regularly forwarded to Wybalenna from the government ordinance stores at Hobart.[81] John West also recorded that Tasmanian Aborigines warned Europeans that toadfish were poisonous,[82] knowledge that at least implies some experience of the edible qualities of certain species. In recent years Rebe Taylor combed through the private papers of Ernest Westlake, an English collector of Aboriginal artefacts who visited Tasmania in 1908–09. Westlake jotted down the reminiscences of many old colonists and their descendants who were adamant that scale-fish featured regularly in the diet of Tasmanian Aborigines. The telling point was perhaps their insistence that while the Aboriginal people had no hesitation eating fish caught by themselves they refrained from accepting any fish offered by Europeans in the belief that it may have been poisoned.[83] Fear such as this can explain why the Aborigines recoiled in horror when early European mariners had offered fish, but the real meaning behind it remains elusive. Why they thought the fish might have been poisoned still awaits a satisfactory explanation. There may, of course, have been specific cultural reasons or even a taboo against the consumption of certain species.[84] The descendants of Aboriginal people who formed communities in the

Furneaux Islands later in the nineteenth century readily consumed scale-fish — as they still do. Whether this can be seen as evidence of cultural continuity, or alternatively another component of the cultural baggage of European forefathers, is another matter again.[85]

All of this brings us back to the stone fish traps of north-west Tasmania, which were first systematically analysed by archaeologist Jim Stockton. The mean tidal range along this section of the coast exceeds 2 metres, ideal conditions for the construction of stone fish traps.[86] It is known that at least some of those in the Burnie area were built by Europeans as recently as the 1950s. Others may well be Aboriginal; Stockton was unable to establish whether the traps at Rocky Cape, Sisters Beach and Boat Harbour were of European origin, and it could be relevant that all of them lie within the former territory of the Tommeginer people.[87] As previously mentioned, the stone fish trap adjacent to Table Cape near Freestone Cove is almost certainly of Aboriginal construction. It is located a considerable distance from the nearest early European settlement of Alexandria, although today it lies across the Inglis River from Wynyard. With the exception of those near Burnie, all the traps in the north-west are close to old Aboriginal campsites, which allowed them to be closely monitored. As the tide ebbs, any fish caught in the shallows fall easy prey to scavenging seabirds which can make short work of an entire catch. The case for the stone fish trap at Sisters Beach is further strengthened by the claims of the original settlers' descendants, who insist the trap was already present when their forebears arrived.[88]

Rhys Jones examined the stone fish trap at Rocky Cape in 1963, initially convinced that it was of Aboriginal origin. After discovering that fish had apparently been dropped from the diet around 3700 years ago — and that the trap appeared to be more recent — he altered his thinking. The trap is now known to be of considerable antiquity. Jones was led astray by Europeans living in the area who had rebuilt the walls to ensure themselves of a regular supply of fresh fish. In the absence of any evidence to the contrary, all these traps in the north-west are deemed to be Aboriginal and are currently protected by legislation. The absence of fish bones from coastal middens can also be explained in a number of ways. They may, for example, have been directly disposed of in fires rather than being cast aside. Alternatively, they could have been scavenged by Tasmanian devils or seabirds,[89] though none of this is to deny that there was an obvious systemic transition of the coastal economy around 3700 years ago. Clearly, the Aboriginal people around Tasmania changed their focus from the exploitation of the inter-tidal to the sub-littoral zone. At the same time, however, it does not necessarily mean that scale-fish was entirely eliminated from the diet right around the Tasmanian coast.

With the possible exception of the blotched blue-tongue skink (*Tiliqua nigrolutea*) there is also a question mark over the Aboriginal exploitation of reptiles and amphibians in Tasmania.[90] Nor do we know a great deal about insect foods or even the vegetable diet. Notwithstanding that the intake of fatty foods was probably higher in Tasmania than most other parts of Australia, plant foods remained essential for a well-balanced diet and general well-being. The Tasmanians are known to have consumed the roots of bracken fern and the fronds of other fern species may have been harvested. Fruits included pigface, native plum, native currants and the kangaroo apple. Pods of acacias (wattles) were certainly eaten, along with a wide variety of berries. Leaf bases of the grass tree (*Xanthorrhoea sp.*) and a number of fungi, including the large subterranean species colloquially known as 'native bread', were important dietary articles. Edible seaweeds were gathered on the coast, while elsewhere there were reeds, sedges and storage roots, notably the native carrot and the roots of certain orchids. Herbs such as samphire and native celery were probably chewed, while wattle gum and eucalyptus flowers served as sweeteners.[91]

A number of Tasmanian Aboriginal groups had the rare opportunity in the Australian context of accessing an alcoholic beverage prior to the arrival of Europeans. This was the sap of the cider gum (*Eucalyptus gunnii*), which flourishes on the Central Plateau. George Augustus Robinson described how the trunk of the tree was pierced with sharp stones a short distance above the ground and a depression made at the base. Into this cavity the sap first flowed and then fermented, with up to a litre of liquid gathered at any one time. Robinson noted that 'The natives are very fond of the juice and I am told it frequently makes them drunk.'[92] It was not surprising that this Aboriginal practice was later followed by European pastoral workers.[93]

Despite a relative paucity of edible plant foods in Tasmania, with many species restricted in distribution and others seasonal, there was more than sufficient to cater for the needs of the Aboriginal people. Importantly, the plant foods that are known to have been available 'were as well stocked with carbohydrate as the vegetable foods available in the western diet'.[94] They were either eaten raw or roasted on hot coals,[95] and it is clear that a well-balanced diet combined with hard physical exercise ensured that by contemporary standards the Tasmanian Aborigines were a generally healthy people prior to contact with outsiders. There is no evidence of any serious endemic diseases, and the iodine deficiency of Tasmania's soils and waters was almost certainly overcome by seasonal visits to the coast and the consumption of seafood.[96] Early European mariners did record a number of medical disorders, including ulcerated legs, possibly the bacterial infection known as yaws. The interesting thing about yaws is that it offers some protection from syphilis, and apart from gonorrhoea — which is known to have been responsible for a high rate of infertility among Tasmanian women in the post-contact period — the incidence of other sexually-transmitted disease was substantially lower in Tasmania than on the Australian mainland.[97]

In March 1772 a young Aboriginal man was killed during an altercation with a French landing party in southern Tasmania. Lieutenant Le Dez recorded that his mouth 'was full of worms which came out of his stomach', almost certainly nematodes, an intestinal parasite.[98] Apart from traumatic injuries, other medical disorders at first contact included a cancerous sore on an elderly woman, a young girl who suffered from spasms, an adolescent girl with an undeveloped left breast, and another who was lame from a congenital condition of the hip. In 1777 members of Cook's third expedition to the Pacific were entertained at Adventure Bay by a red-haired hunchback who had probably been born with a defective vertebral column. Noted for his wit and humour, he was still living comfortably 11 years later when William Bligh returned to Adventure Bay. Red hair is an extremely rare mutation among Tasmanian Aborigines — so rare, in fact, that only one other case is known.[99] The average life expectancy of the pre-contact Tasmanians cannot be ascertained, but early European mariners did note a number of people who appeared to be up to 50 years of age.[100] At that time their longevity probably equalled if it did not exceed that of their uninvited guests.

Although perhaps as much as 25 per cent of the Tasmanian land mass saw very little Aboriginal activity, the remainder was a carefully managed landscape dependent on Aboriginal burning regimes. Fire served a range of purposes well beyond the provision of warmth and cooking. By using fire to encourage the growth of new shoots the Aboriginal people created pasture lands, each separated by copses of brush and trees to provide sanctuary for grazing and browsing prey animals during the day. They operated in much the same way as modern fences, with hunters knowing exactly where their quarry could be located when required.[101] As on mainland Australia, fire was also used to herd animals when hunting, and to clear pathways through dense bush. It was an important means of destroying vermin and venomous snakes around campsites, and it was used by hearth groups and bands to signal their whereabouts to others.[102] Over countless generations the topography of Tasmania was transformed by Aboriginal burning regimes or 'firestick farming' as it is often known. Bill Gammage, who has examined this practice in great depth, believes that burning regimes in Tasmania were conducted in 1–3-year cycles for grasslands and 3–5-year cycles for open forest. Wet forest was rarely burnt.[103] As a result of this deliberate policy the vegetation was radically adjusted, the legacy of which can still be seen today with stands of eucalypts tucked away in rainforest and ancient logs lying in the most unlikely places.[104]

Despite this, as well as the observations of eighteenth-century mariners, who observed large areas of the land mass ablaze as they sailed along the coast, it was once believed that the Tasmanian Aborigines had been incapable of generating fire by artificial means. It is an erroneous belief that has persisted in some quarters to this very day, which is even more remarkable when it is considered that the Aboriginal presence in Tasmania extends back tens of millennia when climatic conditions were extremely harsh. Claiming the absence of such knowledge also served to place the Tasmanians further down the steps of the evolutionary ladder as one of the most 'primitive' people on earth.[105] Nothing could have been further from the truth. It was nevertheless a myth that easily arose because no-one actually witnessed the Aborigines making fire. Early British settlers noted that the Tasmanians carried their firesticks — sections of rotting wood or twists of bark which had been carefully selected to smoulder very slowly — at all times.[106] Even the experienced George Augustus Robinson once commented:

> As the chief always carries a lighted torch I asked them what they did when their fire went out. They said if their fire went out by reason of the rain they was compelled to eat the kangaroo raw and to walk about and look for another mob and get fire of [*sic*] them. They must give fire and sometimes they would fight afterwards.[107]

Much has been made of Robinson's statements, which have been taken out of context. They were almost certainly directed at the immediate circumstances rather than fire-making more generally, as Robinson was well aware that the Aborigines could produce fire. When preparing for the first 'Friendly Mission' at Bruny Island in February 1830 he noted the Aborigines possessed a stone resembling flint which they used to sharpen their waddies 'and by means of which they strike fire'.[108] Sharing fire also appears to have been a universal policy, even with mortal enemies. The use of fire-sticks was simply a more convenient and certainly a more reliable means of having fire readily available in the cooler moister climate of Tasmania. A number of commentators in the nineteenth century were well aware that the Tasmanians were capable of making fire, but most accepted that they used a wooden fire-drill as was common on mainland Australia.[109] But there is a substantial body of ethnographic information pointing to the production of fire through percussion.

In 1773 Tobias Furneaux examined an Aboriginal hut at Adventure Bay and found small woven baskets containing flints and bark tinder, which he presumed were used to strike fire. William Bligh found similar baskets containing flints and soft bark when he revisited the same location in 1792. Like Furneaux, Bligh was of the opinion they were used for making fire. So, too, was Jacques Labillardière, naturalist on d'Entrecasteaux's expedition, who discovered pieces of 'silica' wrapped in soft bark at Recherche Bay the same year.[110] More telling were the comments of Louis Ventenat, another member of the expedition. Ventenat followed an Aboriginal pathway between Southport Lagoon and Southeast Cape and noticed large open areas which had been burnt. Notwithstanding that he did not actually see the Aboriginal people strike fire, Ventenat suspected that it was produced to drive kangaroos and other game animals towards waiting spearmen. This is one of the earliest references anywhere in Australia of Aboriginal burning regimes effecting ecological change.[111]

At the height of frontier conflict in 1830 four muskets were recovered from an Aboriginal camp which were found to be loaded and in perfect condition. The Aborigines had fitted two of these weapons with 'native flints' to produce a spark through percussion. The supposed use of flint has nevertheless been challenged on the grounds that true flint does not exist in Tasmania. Flint-like chert does, a material widely used by Tasmanians for millennia, and sparks can also be produced from either quartz or quartzite.[112] Yet this is not to deny that fire could also have been produced by friction using a wooden fire-drill. Like percussion, there is a substantial body of second-hand reports mentioning this very possibility. Whether one or the other method was geographically restricted in Tasmania — or perhaps preferred — is difficult to say.[113] What can no longer be disputed is that the Tasmanians were quite capable of producing fire by artificial means.

When it comes to Tasmanian Aboriginal spiritual beliefs, however, there is a distinct paucity of information. One of the main problems when investigating Aboriginal cosmology is that many of the Europeans who had first-hand knowledge of their beliefs were more intent on supplanting Aboriginal religion with their own Christian faith.[114] While George Augustus Robinson is without doubt the most important source of information regarding Tasmanian Aborigines in the first half of the nineteenth century, he was also one of the most fervent catechists.[115] Other contemporary Europeans such as Henry

Melville simply assumed the Aborigines had no spiritual beliefs as they did not appear to have any rites or ceremonies.[116] Melville, though, was writing at the very time Aboriginal societies were in a state of collapse. Nor is it possible to compare Tasmanian religion with that of mainland Aboriginal societies. From what little we know there appears to have been a number of significant differences.

There is only one known myth which demonstrates a clear connection between ancestral beings, people and land similar to those on mainland Australia. This particular example comes from Bruny Island even though it relates to Cox's Bight in the south-west. It concerns a large stone, said to be an ancestral being or Star God known as Moihernee. It was Moihernee who created Parlevar, the first man, who lacked joints in his legs and was endowed with a tail, imperfections rectified by another ancestral being named Droemendeneer. These two ancestral beings later fought one another, the defeated Moihernee falling from the heavens to spend the remainder of his days at Cox's Bight. His wife followed him down to dwell in the sea close by, and when Moihernee died he turned into the large stone which still stands. It is known that the victor of the celestial battle, Droemendeneer, was closely associated with the star Canopus, but there is no mention of Moihernee's stony remains ever being regarded as a sacred site or as a source of supernatural power.[117] There are also a number of other creation myths which relate to the heavens. At Cape Portland, in north-east Tasmania, certain stars in the Milky Way were held to have created the rivers; others are associated with fire, and still others with people and animals.[118]

Creation was one thing, death was another. Although there are unsubstantiated reports that the Tasmanians interred their dead or lodged their bodies in trees, the usual practice was cremation. While bones and ashes of the deceased were often kept by grieving relatives to ward off evil spirits and for healing purposes,[119] it appears that in the southern Midlands (if not elsewhere) cremated remains were subsequently interred.[120] With death there is another important link with the spiritual world. In some areas of Tasmania the spirits of the deceased were believed to return to the stars, while in the north the spirits were understood to dwell on an island in Bass Strait.[121]

As initiation rites are unknown in Tasmania, ceremonies appear to have served a very different function from those on mainland Australia. It is known that the most important ceremonies were held during the phase of the full moon, clearly a time of great reverence for the Tasmanian Aborigines. GT Lloyd, an early British settler, witnessed one such event and described the participants with their upturned eyes and outstretched arms as if supplicating to a lunar spirit. Lloyd was convinced that their actions were designed to invoke mercy and protection.[122] Major ceremonies were carefully orchestrated, preceded in all instances by song and dance. Very few Europeans were privy to the final sequence, a void which led Brian Plomley to conclude that Tasmanian ceremonies were merely leisure activities, with song and dance performed around a fire to celebrate natural phenomena.[123] The kangaroo and emu dances have been well documented, as have the horse and dog dances, natural wonders introduced by Europeans — and in the case of canines, rapidly incorporated into Aboriginal cultural life.[124] But these were simply the preliminaries, not the main event. Adolphus Schayer, a German authority on sheep who was employed by the Van Diemen's Land Company in north-west Tasmania between 1831 and 1842, witnessed a remarkable spectacle at Cape Grim on 14 April 1834. Schayer described the preliminary performances of the kangaroo and emu dances, but later that same night:

> The warrior, because it is with this in mind that they seem to choose their roles, stands in the middle of a circle formed around a fire, now singing and now reciting, and makes a short speech,

> which doesn't seem to evoke much of an impression on his companions, whilst he himself gets so worked up that, after a few minutes he can hardly speak, and can only utter inarticulate sounds and perform actions accompanied by movements expressing anger and the love of fighting, and in that way he comes to a state of mind which is close to madness. This moment seems to be the specific aim of the whole performance, because it's then that the men rush towards him, and giving vent to their frightful screams, begin a dance as ordered by the chief. They rush around the fire in such a way as to make the spectators dizzy, and from time to time slap the ground with the palms of their hands, then jump back, with both legs in the air. When this frenzy has to all appearances reached its highest point, the women rush forward in their turn; they hurl themselves into the narrow circle formed by the men, perform dances which are even more savage, if that's possible, raising their arms and uttering frightful cries. They usually conclude by rushing upon the fire, and overturn the burning wood with their feet, and by their leaping and jumping put out what's left of the fire. We have never been able to understand the real significance of this strange enactment ...[125]

Although Schayer did not understand it, his description does contain elements of shamanism, a dimension of Tasmanian religious life which has largely gone unnoticed. Perhaps that is not surprising given that George Augustus Robinson, the recognised authority on Tasmanian Aborigines in the first half of the nineteenth century, attended this very same ceremony and left no record of the proceedings. He did, however, document a women's dance which paid homage to fire spirits;[126] the supernatural world of the Tasmanian Aborigines was populated by a number of spirits, both the good and the malevolent, notably Wraeggowraper, the most dreaded of all.[127]

In common with Aboriginal groups on the Australian mainland, the supernatural beliefs of the Tasmanians were not frozen in time. In 1792 a gunner from the *Espérance*, one of Bruny d'Entrecasteaux's two vessels, carved a realistic image of a human head into a tree at Recherche Bay. When Robinson visited the area in 1831 — 39 years later — he was informed by Woorrady, one of his Bruny Island guides, that the tree had been the haunt of the huge and hideous Wraeggowraper, the harbinger of death. So terrified had the people become that the men finally summoned the courage to destroy the tree.[128] Woorrady was aware that the carving had been made by the first Europeans to land at the location, but it is interesting that not only was this first contact mythologised, it was also closely associated with death. Some of d'Entrecasteaux's crewmen who had personal contact with the Aborigines are known to have been suffering from tuberculosis. Cases of smallpox had also been identified on his vessels,[129] providing strong circumstantial evidence that it was this expedition which unwittingly unleashed a devastating epidemic in southern Tasmania 11 years before the permanent arrival of the British in 1803. During the 'Friendly Mission' Robinson traversed extensive areas of empty country in the south which, he was assured by his guides, were the territories of people who had long since disappeared.[130] It is quite probable that they had fallen victim to deadly microbes, with the dreaded Wraeggowraper evoked as a means of explaining the unseen and therefore the unknown.

Petroglyphs, or stone engravings, from north-west Tasmania near the Arthur River and Mount Cameron West — among other locations — may have been linked with religion. Many of the motifs are circles,[131] and in other parts of the world carved stone circles are explicitly linked with religious beliefs. As Brian Plomley noted, Robinson made a number of trips between Cape Grim and Mount Cameron without seeing these outstanding examples of petroglyphs. Robinson had observed them elsewhere, but on no occasion were they ever pointed out by the Aborigines. Although the Mount Cameron site was likely to have been obscured by sand and vegetation, the obvious reluctance of the Aboriginal people to disclose the whereabouts of any petroglyphs suggests that they may indeed have been sacred sites.[132] Yet, it does seem odd that this particular art form was restricted to just one geographical region. While petroglyphs are certainly known from north-east, east and southern Tasmania, all of them comprise branched lines; there are no concentric designs.[133]

Stone arrangements, on the other hand, have been found in many parts of Tasmania: the Bay of Fires in the north-east, near Ross in the Midlands, Maria Island in the south, as well as the west and north-west.[134] They, too, were possibly associated with religious ceremonies, though what the actual connection was can no longer be determined. Some consist of cairns, while others, including the fine example at the Bay of Fires, are long lines of flat stones resembling a pathway. This particular arrangement is approximately 56 metres in length, and there is another arrangement close by on a similar north-south alignment. Excavations at both sites have revealed that this location was a regular campsite,[135] and that raises the subject of housing.

Given their adaptation to the climate, it is not surprising that in the more mild areas of east and north-east Tasmania Aboriginal shelters were at best rudimentary, often merely bark windbreaks. In the colder, wetter and windier regions, especially along the west coast, quite elaborate structures were built. Some of them were up to five metres in diameter and two metres in height, capable of housing up to a dozen individuals in relative comfort. They were shaped something like a beehive, the framework of wooden hoops first thatched with rushes and overlain with grass packing. Sheets of peppermint bark provided the outer covering. These huts featured a narrow entrance around one metre high which faced away from the prevailing winds and could be closed off with a bark door.[136] The interiors were often decorated with bark paintings of people, animals and heavenly bodies, artistic skills which impressed early European observers.[137] In some areas of Tasmania the Aboriginal people occasionally camped beneath rocky overhangs, but they refrained from entering deeper caves which were feared as the haunt of evil spirits.[138]

Notwithstanding a considerable degree of conservatism, the intellectual and physical world of the Tasmanians was expanding long before the arrival of Europeans. Right across Australia there is abundant evidence of a dramatic demographic upsurge between 3000 and 4000 years ago. On mainland Australia it was a time when improved technologies, new foods and intellectual ideas appeared, some of them possibly introduced from overseas.[139] But internal stimulus triggered by climate change cannot be entirely discounted, as evidenced by developments in Tasmania. The climate became cooler and drier and, as already mentioned, this was the very time that coastal economies underwent a major transition from exploitation of the intertidal zone to the sub-littoral. The bones of scale-fish disappeared from middens and bone tools were discarded. Around 2500 years ago the Aboriginal people began to visit Hunter Island off the north-west tip of Tasmania, the resources of which had remained untouched by humans for thousands of years.[140] In the south, Bruny Island was abandoned 5000 years ago and then recolonised 2000 years later.[141] And in the south-west the Aborigines began exploiting the resources of Maatsuyker Island, 22 kilometres south of the Tasmanian landmass. This was the farthest south they ever ventured, a feat of epic proportions.[142] All of this territorial expansion was made possible by the invention of a unique form of watercraft.

There is no evidence of any watercraft in Tasmania before 3000 years ago, and the distribution of the bundled canoe was restricted to the southern and north-western coasts. In the east it was found no further north than Maria Island and Great Oyster Bay,[143] while along much of the west coast where there were no offshore islands, makeshift rafts made from driftwood or convenient timber were sufficient to cross rivers.[144] These craft were unique in Australia, a purely local innovation which consisted of three bundles of either stringybark (*Eucalyptus obliqua*) or paperbark (*Melaleuca sp.*) bound tightly together with vegetable fibre. The central bundle was positioned lower to provide most of the buoyancy, with the outer bundles acting as stabilisers. The bow and stern were sightly upturned,[145] with the largest of them capable of accommodating up to six or seven people. They were propelled by either a long pole or swimmers alongside,[146] though they did have one major drawback. After a few hours they usually became waterlogged and had to be dried ashore before re-use.[147] Notwithstanding this problem, bundled canoes were still capable of reaching the remote Maatsuyker Island, and while it has been suggested that such voyages would have required a stopover on De Witt Island, no Aboriginal hearths or middens have yet been identified to support this.[148]

The fact that the bundled canoe was a relatively recent invention should put paid to any speculation of cultural regression. On the contrary, Tasmanian Aboriginal societies were undergoing a demographic and intellectual resurgence. By the later eighteenth century Tasmania's Indigenous population had reached its optimal peak, and one can only wonder what the future of their isolation may have been. Unfortunately, the fleeting visits of outsiders were precursors for the permanent settlement of Tasmania by the British in 1803, with the end of isolation ushering in catastrophic change.

3

FIRST ENCOUNTERS AND BRITISH COLONISATION

Europeans first touched on Tasmanian shores in 1642, after Abel Tasman was commissioned by the Governor-General of the Dutch East Indies, Anthony van Diemen, to search for unknown parts of the great Southland and the south-east coast of New Guinea and to determine whether the two land masses were connected. Tasman was further instructed to search for any riches or sources of trade that might be found in either location. When he left Batavia in August of that year Tasman first sailed west to Mauritius to refit his two ships and stock adequate provisions for a lengthy voyage that was largely into the unknown.[1] The *Heemskerck* (*Home Church*) and the *Zeehaen* (*Sea Cock*) departed Mauritius in October and after battling heavy seas, fog and snow they sighted the coast of Tasmania near Macquarie Harbour on 24 November. Sailing south they found refuge in what is now Tasman Harbour and briefly went ashore. Continuing around the coast the ships came to anchor in Frederick Henry Bay (now North Bay) on 1 December. The following morning pilot-major (chief navigator) Franchoys Jacobszoon Visscher ventured ashore with four musketeers and six crewmen, accompanied by a boat from the *Zeehaen*. They found a number of edible herbs and noted what looked like fine stands of timber, but they failed to make any contact with Indigenous inhabitants.[2]

One suspects that Visscher and his companions were content to avoid any contact. They heard a noise which sounded like a gong or trumpet, and in their reconnaissance the Dutch observed notches cut into the trunk of a tree that were fully 1.5 metres apart, surmising they had been made by humans to rob bird nests in the treetop. From the distance between the notches they also suspected that these people were either extremely tall or they used an artificial device to assist them in the ascent. Holes burnt into the bases of a few trees appeared to be fireplaces, and they examined some 'tiger' tracks in the sand — almost certainly those of a thylacine. All in all, this appeared to be a forbidding place indeed. Tasman's ships remained in North Bay for three days and during that time clouds of smoke could be seen further inland.[3] Although under no illusions that the landscape was uninhabited, in accordance with his instructions Tasman ordered a carpenter to swim ashore and erect a pole on the south-east shore of the bay where the flag of the Stadtholder of the Netherlands was raised. By this action Tasman formally took possession of Van Diemen's Land, 'undiscovered' territory named in honour of his sponsor.[4]

What the Aborigines thought of these strange happenings before the Dutch disappeared over the horizon as quickly as they had come can only be guessed. Tasman went on to 'discover' New Zealand, Tonga and a number of Fijian islands before returning to Batavia, today's Jakarta. From the perspective of the Dutch East India Company, however, his voyage had been a failure, yielding very little in the way of riches.[5] Although the Dutch were to become familiar with the west coast of the Australian landmass, they never again ventured this far south and the Tasmanian Aborigines were to be left undisturbed for another 130 years before outsiders again arrived on their shores. Rather than the Dutch it was the French who were to make the next landfall, and on this occasion it was to have fatal consequences.

Like Tasman, Marc-Joseph Marion Dufresne set out from Mauritius, but in his case the objective was to return a Tahitian named Aotourou to his home island while carrying out a little exploration along the way for commercial and strategic purposes. Aotourou had been taken to France by Louis Bougainville in 1768. The two vessels under Marion Dufresne's command departed Mauritius on 18 October 1771, and after sailing south-east his crew sighted the coast of Van Diemen's Land on 3 March the following year, anchoring in the sheltered waters of Marion and North Bays, close to where Tasman had moored his vessels. The commander subsequently led a party ashore, and unlike the experience of his predecessor he immediately made contact with the Indigenous inhabitants.[6] The meeting was not to have a happy outcome.

As Marion Dufresne's two boat crews made for the shore they espied a number of Aborigines running along the beach, with the women and children veering off to hide in the nearby bush. An Aboriginal man entered the water, beckoning the Frenchmen to him. Two sailors volunteered to be the first ashore, though before they left the boat Dufresne ordered them to strip naked so they would appear less alien to the inhabitants. The French commander had learnt quite a lot about the people of the Pacific from his compatriot, Bougainville, who had circumnavigated the globe between 1766 and 1769. Bougainville published an account of his expedition which depicted Tahiti as an earthly paradise where both men and women lived in happiness and innocence, their lives untrammelled by the corruptive influences of Western civilisation. Bougainville nevertheless challenged prevailing philosophical thought by questioning whether it was beneficial to bring this essential goodness into contact with the outside world. His musings were subject to trenchant criticism, with Denis Diderot moved to publish a fictional tale of the Bougainville expedition which referred to the Tahitians as 'noble savages'. It was a savage critique of contemporary European society,[7] with Diderot's mockery having particular relevance in France where widespread unrest was soon to explode into revolution before imploding into the 'reign of terror'.

The idealised image of the 'noble savage' was firmly etched in Marion Dufresne's mind as he set out on his voyage into the vast expanse of the Indian and Pacific Oceans. In Van Diemen's Land his two volunteers reached the shore and were met by an elderly man who presented them with a firestick, accepted by the sailors as a token of friendship. They reciprocated with a glass mirror, astonishing the Aboriginal people as it was passed around. The Aborigines were also fascinated by their visitors' pale skins, and with the formalities dispensed with they laid down their spears and commenced to dance. At this point Dufresne's two boats grounded on the beach, with the complement presented with more firesticks and the French handing out knives and strips of cloth in return.[8]

This peaceful scene was suddenly shattered when a third boat pulled towards the shore from the anchored ships. The Aborigines became agitated, perhaps wondering just how many of these strange beings there really were. They outnumbered the two boat crews, but the third was about to tip the scales against them. Another reason for their concern, however, may have been due to the third boat crew openly displaying their firearms, whereas the first two had kept theirs out of sight. Appreciating their anxiety, Marion Dufresne ordered the boat to heave-to. It was already too late; the impetus brought it ashore, and as soon as the craft touched the beach the French were showered with stones and spears. The visitors temporarily withdrew, and a second attempt to land brought a similar response. Dufresne was struck on the shoulder and one of his crewmen speared in the leg, with the French firing several volleys of gunfire in return. Assisting their wounded the Aborigines fled as the French set out in pursuit. All but one escaped, the French recovering the body of a young man who had been killed by their retaliatory fire.[9] They examined the corpse and after washing it discovered that it was only dirt and smoke which made the man appear so dark. The unfortunate victim was a 'noble savage' no more; now he had been reduced to a scientific curiosity, a nexus between the philosophical thought and the scientific rationalism of the 'Age of Enlightenment'.[10]

With his idealistic beliefs shaken, Dufresne lost further interest in the inhabitants of Van Diemen's Land and sailed off to New Zealand. Worse was in store. After three months at the Bay of Islands where the French repaired and reprovisioned their ships the Maoris launched a sudden attack, killing Dufresne and 24 members of his crew.[11] Second-in-command Jules Crozet took charge and the ships eventually returned to France where Crozet detailed the shocking events to Jean-Jacques Rousseau. The philosopher could scarcely believe that these 'children of nature' in Van Diemen's Land and New Zealand could be so wicked. Although both clashes were accepted as being partly due to misunderstandings on the part of the French, they proved to be a pivotal point in philosophical thought. Thereafter the concept of the 'noble savage' was tainted with that of the 'ignoble savage'.[12] At all levels, from the seemingly most primitive to the advanced, humankind was henceforth considered to have an inherent 'evil streak' in its psychological makeup.

It was an Englishman, Tobias Furneaux, captain of HMS *Adventure* and second-in-command of James Cook's 1772–75 Pacific expedition, who next cruised the waters of Van Diemen's Land. After leaving Cape Town, Cook and Furneaux became separated in heavy fog, a possibility already foreseen by Cook, who made for the appointed rendezvous at Queen Charlotte Sound on the north-east tip of New Zealand's North Island. Furneaux also made his way thither, deciding to investigate the coast of Van Diemen's Land on the way.[13] He spent five days at Adventure Bay on Bruny Island, which he named after his ship, and while there Furneaux's crewmen examined an Aboriginal campsite with 'pearl scallop' shells (almost certainly abalone shells) close by. They also found a few mussel shells and the remains of crayfish, but of the Indigenous people themselves they saw nothing.[14] Furneaux left behind gifts in the way of 'medals, gun-flints, a few nails and an old empty barrel with the iron hoops on it', before sailing along the east coast of Tasmania as far north as the Furneaux Islands, which Cook later named in his honour.[15]

James Cook himself arrived at Adventure Bay with HM ships *Resolution* and *Discovery* on his third Pacific expedition in January 1777, and it is conceivable that the gifts left behind by Furneaux contributed to the cordial relations enjoyed with the local Aboriginal people. It was just as well, as Adventure Bay was beginning to become an important anchorage for mariners in these southern climes, a convenient location to take on wood and water. Yet, despite the presence of smoke, it was two days before the Aboriginal people made their appearance. A party of sailors cutting wood on shore was suddenly confronted by nine or 10 Aboriginal men, only one of whom was armed. They observed the sailors at work before taking up the saw themselves, appearing to accept the presence of the British as an everyday occurrence. They showed no sign of fear, and nor did they regard their uninvited visitors in any way superior.[16]

The following day men, women and children joined Cook's crewmen when they went ashore, the sailors distributing gifts amongst them. All went well until they were joined by Omai, a Tahitian interpreter on the expedition. One of the Tasmanian men had been encouraged to throw his spear at a target; when he missed, the disgusted Omai decided to display his superiority — with a fowling piece. The blast of the gun terrified the Aborigines, who fled into the bush. Cook lamented that all contact had now been lost, but the following morning 20 Aborigines were encountered on the beach and again showered with gifts, including a number of bronze medallions. In 1914 one of those medallions was uncovered at the northern end of Bruny Island. Amongst this group was the red-haired hunchback mentioned in the previous chapter, with friendly relations maintained for the duration of Cook's stay.[17] Although the Aborigines readily accepted the gifts bestowed on them, it was noticed that they did not keep them. Even the scraps of iron which might have proved useful were discarded. And, of course, they refused any fish that were offered. All that can be said of Cook's visit is that the British saw the Tasmanians in a very positive light. In the words of assistant surgeon William Anderson the Aboriginal people were 'mild and chearful [*sic*] without reserve or jealousy of strangers'. He added that 'their features are not at all disagreeable',[18] perceptions that were not destined to endure.

At this time William Bligh was master of HMS *Resolution* and it was Bligh who returned to Adventure Bay as captain of HMS *Bounty* in 1788 en route to Tahiti to collect breadfruit trees for transhipment to the West Indies. It was not a successful venture; mutiny erupted after their sojourn at Tahiti and Bligh was forced to make an epic journey by open boat across the Pacific to Koepang in Timor. In August 1788, however, hints of later mutiny were not apparent at Adventure Bay, where Fletcher Christian led an armed party ashore in search of food and water.[19] It was 11 days before the Aborigines appeared on the shore, and by then Bligh was unable to make close contact because of turbulent weather conditions. From behind the breakers he threw gifts wrapped in paper onto the beach, where they were collected by a group of Aborigines which included the red-haired hunchback Bligh had met eleven years before.[20]

After mutiny and further adventures, Bligh returned to Adventure Bay for a third time in February 1792 in command of HMS *Providence*. He was once again headed for Tahiti to take on breadfruit trees, an enterprise which on this occasion was accomplished successfully. While no contact was made with the Aboriginal people, Bligh did find time to closely examine one of their campsites where he noticed a complete absence of fish bones in the refuse.[21] He then sailed off, to be followed into these southern waters by Lieutenant John Hayes of the Bombay Marine, who had taken leave of absence to embark on a private trading expedition. Hayes sailed from Calcutta with two ships, arriving at Storm Bay in April 1793. Although there is no record of this expedition encountering any Aborigines, Hayes explored a river which the French had called the Rivière du Nord, renaming it the Derwent. Continuing upstream he came upon 'a beautiful cove' which he chose to name Risdon, after William Risdon, second officer of the *Duke of Clarence*, one of his vessels.[22] While Hayes has often been overlooked in the early history of Van Diemen's Land, the Derwent River and Risdon Cove were to achieve significance when the British decided to colonise the island in 1803. Until that time the British mariners learnt remarkably little about the Indigenous inhabitants. The French, on the other hand, were motivated by a higher level of scientific curiosity, and it was they who gained the first real insights into Aboriginal culture and society. At the same time, however, their understanding of indigenous cultures continued to be filtered through the narrow prism of the noble, and at times ignoble 'savage', which meant that all interpretations were measured against their own supposedly superior standards.

This was evident when Bruny d'Entrecasteaux's expedition departed France in 1791 in search of the missing La Perouse, whose two vessels had last been seen at Botany Bay in March 1788.[23] With two 350-tonne frigates, the *Espérance* and *Recherche*, d'Entrecasteaux was instructed to sail along the southern coast of Australia before entering the Pacific, orders that he interpreted to include a detailed survey of Van Diemen's Land. Like every other French expedition there were also important scientific aims,[24] and given that the voyagers spent a total of nine weeks in Tasmanian waters on two separate occasions, it is not surprising that they eventually made contact with the Indigenous inhabitants.

But it took time. On arrival in Tasmania the d'Entrecasteaux expedition anchored in Recherche Bay, where a survey was made of the channel named in honour of the commander. The French examined an Aboriginal campsite and, finding only woven baskets and an absence of weaponry, they concluded that the local Aborigines were an inoffensive people who lived in harmony with nature and lacked any industry. Piles of shells led members of the expedition to believe the Aborigines subsisted solely on molluscs. Before sailing off to continue their search for La Perouse the French also discovered a number of bundled canoes, though they were unimpressed with their sea-going qualities.[25]

A very different scenario unfolded when d'Entrecasteaux's vessels returned to Tasmanian waters in January 1793. The botanists were the first to fall in with a group of Aborigines, both sides laying down their arms to parley. At this point it dawned on the French that the Aborigines might not be so inoffensive after all, though their concerns were quickly allayed when the Aboriginal men made signs that they had come across their visitors the previous night in their bivouac and had left them undisturbed. They later led a French party through the bush in search of natural history specimens, with both sides rapidly warming to each other.[26] One young Tasmanian man also played a trick on one of the sailors. The Frenchman had collected a number of unusual shells which he deposited in a bag and hid in the bush, intending to collect it later. When he returned the bag had disappeared and after searching in vain for some time the sailor re-joined his companions. By signs the young Aboriginal man later let him know the bag was lying where it had originally been left — and so it was, with the Aborigines laughing at the sailor's expense.[27]

After showing another Tasmanian man how to use an axe the French marvelled at his precision. He proved equally adept with a saw, but after demonstrating how to light a fire with a magnifying glass and some bark tinder, the joke was on the Tasmanians when their eager pupil directed the sunlight onto his own thigh.[28] Both sides were confused when it came to the issue of gender. For their part, the Tasmanians could not understand why no women were to be found amongst their visitors, carefully examining the most effeminate-looking Frenchmen to see if they were possibly mistaken. The French, on the other hand, had expectations of their own regarding the role of women in society. They were appalled that Tasmanian women were the main providers of food and virtually everything else, their lives apparently one of sheer drudgery.[29] That said, it needs to be borne in mind that these recorders of Indigenous life were from the higher echelons of French society. For all their ideals, the lives of many lower-class French women would not have been all that different from their Aboriginal counterparts.

Regardless of class, the French were certainly fascinated by the Aborigines, who had once again reverted to 'noble savages'. A basic vocabulary of the Aboriginal language was compiled and there was a determined effort to understand social and political structures. As usual, they showered their Indigenous hosts with gifts, failing to understand why the only item sought by the Aborigines was strips of red cloth to adorn their bodies. The Tasmanians were satisfied with their own material culture and had little interest in the trappings of a supposedly advanced civilisation.[30] Nor did they appreciate French musical tastes. When an officer took up a violin and began to play, the Aborigines immediately made signs that the noise was hurting their ears.[31] Conversely, the French found Aboriginal singing to be quite melodic, noting how they achieved almost perfect harmony. Although unable to ascertain whether the Tasmanians had any religious beliefs, the French appreciated that their acquaintance was much too brief to dismiss its existence altogether.[32]

Yet, despite all the goodwill and apparent mutual respect, senior members of the d'Entrecasteaux expedition were never in doubt of their own superiority. While the Tasmanian Aborigines may have been a fine example of the initial state of human society, and appeared to be uncorrupted by passions, vice and material acquisition, it still meant that they were on a lower, more 'primitive' level. French observers showed surprise when there was any evidence of intelligence, such as the joke played on the sailor and another man's skill with the axe and saw. They were appalled by the treatment of women and disgusted when they saw parents grooming their children and eating lice. Jacques Labillardière, the expedition's naturalist, compared such traits to the habits of monkeys. They also considered the Tasmanians to be child-like in their innocence and trust, French writings peppered with judgemental statements.[33] For all their idealistic restraints, members of the d'Entrecasteaux expedition nonetheless gained valuable insights into customary Tasmanian Aboriginal society. In sheer scope, however, even these efforts were surpassed by observations made by the Baudin expedition in 1802.

Led by Nicolas Baudin, the expedition consisted of two corvettes, the *Géographe* and the *Naturaliste*, and it was their particular interest in Tasmania which convinced Governor King in Sydney that the French intended to establish a colony on the island. Formal British possession of Van Diemen's Land was undertaken while the French were surveying King Island in Bass Strait,[34] with permanent settlement of the Tasmanian landmass following soon after. This was ultimately to have tragic consequences for the Indigenous inhabitants, and in reality the Baudin expedition was totally focused on scientific inquiry not territorial expansion. The French ships had been fitted out with the most up-to-date scientific equipment available, with the complement including 23 scientific personnel: astronomers, geographers, mineralogists, botanists, horticulturalists, zoologists and draughtsmen. Among their number was Francois Péron, one of the first people to be formally trained in the budding discipline of anthropology.[35]

The Baudin voyage was one of the greatest scientific expeditions of the nineteenth century, from which the Museum of Natural History in Paris gained 100 000 animal specimens, 2500 of them new to science. When dried seeds and plants are included the entire collection exceeded 200 000 specimens. Artist Charles Lesueur prepared 1500 drawings and paintings, all of which were presented to French public institutions.[36] Péron's observations of the Tasmanian Aborigines continue to provide insights into a way of life that was just decades away from destruction. The expedition also came at great cost for the savants — the scientific personnel — only three of whom survived the voyage.

The original plan emanated from the prestigious Institut de France and was drawn up by a committee comprising leading scientific figures of the day, including de Fleurieu, Laplace, Bougainville, Cuvier and Lacépède. Baudin was chosen as leader, with Emmanuel Hamelin as his second-in-command and captain of the *Naturaliste*.[37] A wide gulf existed at this time between the British and French pursuit of scientific knowledge. By and large the British left scientific matters in the hands of individuals — a prime example being the wealthy Sir Joseph Banks — with the collections they amassed remaining their personal property. Although many British scientists donated their collections to public institutions, they invariably did so to promote and advance their own interests. The French state, on the other hand, appointed, financed and equipped scientific expeditions with the sole aim of enriching public institutions and therefore public knowledge.[38] There was a slight variation from this expected outcome with the return of the Baudin expedition in 1803, when the Empress Josephine was given first choice of all plant and animal specimens.[39]

In accordance with established protocols the French government applied to the British Admiralty for passports, duly granted to both vessels prior to their departure from Le Havre. This was a necessary precaution as Britain and France were so frequently at war that ships could leave their home ports and be captured or destroyed by naval vessels of one side or the other without knowing that hostilities had even broken out. Passports guaranteed a safe passage, and while question marks would later arise over their real intent, the British appear to have been thoroughly convinced that the Baudin expedition was solely engaged in scientific endeavour.[40]

In January 1802 Baudin established a base in the d'Entrecasteaux Channel, where the French spent four weeks collecting specimens and conducting surveys before moving north. During that time Francois Péron gathered information on the Aborigines. Born in 1775, Péron had joined the Revolutionary Army as an ordinary soldier in 1792. He was wounded and captured by royalist forces, returning to civilian life as part of a prisoner exchange. Despite losing an eye, Péron studied medicine for three years and became fascinated with the developing discipline of anthropology. Before completing his medical degree he managed to secure a position on the Baudin expedition as 'physician-anthropologist' with the assistance of powerful patrons, particularly Antoine Laurent de Jussieu, professor of botany at the Jardin des

Plantes in Paris.[41] Many latter-day anthropologists condemn Péron as judgemental and ethnocentric — as he undoubtedly was — but he was also capable of critical analysis, if not always for the right reasons. Péron was influenced by the prevailing philosophical climate, taking with him on the voyage an instrument known as a dynamometer to test Rousseau's claim that 'natural man' was physically superior to 'civilised man'.[42] He was pre-empted on Bruny Island by a burly midshipman named Jean Marouard, whose own test of strength could well have cost him his life.

While netting fish, Marouard and his companions were joined by a number of Tasmanian Aboriginal men. Marouard indicated to the most robust among them that he wished to test his strength; placing his feet firmly on the sand, the Frenchman took hold of the man's wrists and assuming that he understood his intention Marouard threw him to the ground. These antics went on for some time, with Marouard not surprisingly winning every round. Finally tiring of this one-sided contest the Frenchmen decided to return to the ships, and after saying their goodbyes and distributing a few gifts they began pushing their boat into the water. Marouard's back was turned when a spear suddenly lodged in his shoulder. A sub-lieutenant drew his pistol and with the seemingly unstoppable midshipman beside him the pair charged up the rise to find the culprit. Instead, they found seven or eight armed Aboriginal men who displayed no interest in the proceedings and the Frenchmen prudently withdrew.[43] Péron portrayed this incident as an example of inherent cowardice and treachery, although he did accept that the spearing could have been triggered by humiliation on the part of Marouard's opponent. As historian Shino Konishi has argued, however, this could just as easily have been a demonstration by the Aborigines of their own game of skill — spear-dodging — in which case the French midshipman failed miserably. Again, they might have either tired of the French or perhaps even wanted them to stay. The problem is that the only record of this incident is totally one-sided.[44]

Péron also found it difficult to accept the reversal of gender roles. While the French Revolution had provided an opportunity for Frenchwomen to gain a greater measure of self-determination, with many entering the public domain, the Napoleonic agenda which dominated gender discourse just prior to the departure of the expedition aimed to force women back into the paternalistic, dependent and obedient private sphere.[45] That was not what Péron found in Van Diemen's Land, when he and a few companions made contact with a group of women on Bruny Island. Right from the outset it was the women who had full control. After allowing the Frenchmen to approach, they were then instructed to sit down. Although Péron's party might not have understood the language, it was quite clear that questions were being directed at them and from the women's laughter they were obviously being mocked. When the surgeon, Jerome Bellifin, commenced to sing it appeared to be appreciated by their hosts until one of the women began to mimic him and then rose to perform an erotic dance which Péron considered to be bordering on the indecent. The Frenchmen were also forced to submit to having their faces painted with powdered charcoal, and while Péron understood that this may have been done to hide their pale skin and make them appear less disdainful, he could not hide his humiliation. Thereafter his writings tend to highlight the degradation of Tasmanian women.[46]

It was not just women who had the best of this supposedly 'superior' Frenchman. On one occasion a Tasmanian man forcefully demanded Péron's jacket, which he only managed to retain by pointing to his companion's firearm and murmuring *mata*, the Aboriginal word for dead. Another Aborigine ripped out an earring, and when Péron finally had an opportunity to test the strength of his Indigenous hosts with his dynamometer an elderly man appeared to grasp its purpose and refused to allow the others to use it. Péron also commented that while the Aborigines readily accepted gifts they immediately treated them with suspicion or simply discarded them. There were a few positive moments. On Maria Island the proto-anthropologist was able to compile a basic vocabulary of the local Tyreddeme language, finding the men extremely patient when teaching their pupil the correct pronunciation of the words. Péron considered the men both intelligent and good-natured; little was said about the women.[47]

Yet, as much as he might have appreciated the intellectual powers of the Aboriginal men, Péron's journals are liberally sprinkled with the superlatives 'blackness', 'ugliness', 'brutishness' and 'primitiveness'. In common with the commander and his officers, Péron never doubted French superiority, even when he was frightened or humiliated by the Aborigines.[48] He was also very fortunate. Péron was one of the three savants to survive the expedition, and through patronage he was given the task of writing a full account of the voyage. His luck, however, eventually ran out: only the first volume had been completed by the time Péron succumbed to tuberculosis in 1810, a work which is notable for the omission of any direct reference to Nicolas Baudin, with whom the physician-turned-anthropologist clashed before Baudin's death at Mauritius.[49] The remaining two volumes of the expedition were completed by Louis Freycinet, who shared Pèron's dislike for their commander and thus virtually ignored Baudin in his own work.[50]

But this was all in the future. After completing their survey in southern Van Diemen's Land the French ships sailed up the east coast where they became separated. Baudin and Freycinet in the *Géographe* crossed Bass Strait and charted the south coast of the Australian mainland from Wilson's Promontory westwards to Encounter Bay, where they fell in with Matthew Flinders who was completing the first circumnavigation of the Australian landmass.[51] With his crew ill from both scurvy and dysentery and desperately short of water, Baudin sailed for Sydney, surprisingly returning first to southern Van Diemen's Land where further survey work was conducted before continuing on to the British outpost.[52] By the time the *Géographe* reached Sydney the crew was so debilitated from illness that it was necessary for British sailors to board the vessel and bring it to its mooring. In the meantime, Emmanuel Hamelin in the *Naturaliste* charted the north coast of Van Diemen's Land, including Port Dalrymple, before sailing across to Westernport and then on to Sydney. Hamelin reprovisioned the *Naturaliste* and headed out to sea, only to be forced back by adverse weather conditions. It was only then that he found the *Géographe* at anchor and the expedition was finally reunited.[53]

After the recovery of his men, Baudin purchased a 20-tonne schooner, the *Casuarina*, to accompany the *Géographe* and *Naturaliste* back to Tasmanian waters, where a new base was established at Sea Elephant Bay on King Island. From there the *Naturaliste* returned to France with the bulk of the scientific collections,[54] but soon after the departure of the small French flotilla from Sydney innuendo and rumour began to run rife. During their stay French officers had been observed mapping the settlement's fortifications, and hints dropped in casual conversation convinced Governor King that the French were planning to establish a colony in Van Diemen's Land. The rumours appear to have emanated from Captain Anthony Fenn Kemp of the New South Wales Corps, who had falsely accused the French of smuggling alcohol ashore and been forced to apologise. Be that as it may, Lieutenant Charles Robbins in the armed schooner *Cumberland* was instructed to locate the French encampment and hand Baudin a strongly-worded letter from the governor outlining his suspicions as well as his intention of annexing Van Diemen's Land as British territory. Robbins duly found Baudin on King Island, where he raised the Union Jack, amusing the French by flying it upside down. To add to this comic farce, Robbins had departed Sydney in such haste that he was forced to borrow provisions and ammunition.[55] Baudin, however, was outraged by King's letter, handing Robbins an indignant protest of his own for conveyance to the governor:

> … To my way of thinking, I have never been able to conceive that there was justice or even fairness on the part of Europeans in seizing, in the name of their governments, a land seen for the first time, when it is inhabited by men who have not always deserved the title of savages or cannibals that has been freely given them … From this it appears to me that it would be infinitely more glorious for your nation, as for mine, to mould for society the inhabitants of its own country over whom it has rights, rather than wishing to occupy itself with the improvement of those who are very far removed from it by beginning with seizing the soil which belongs to them and which saw their birth. These remarks are no doubt impolitic, but at least reasonable from the facts; and had this principle been generally adopted you would not have been obliged to form a colony by means of men branded by the law and made criminals by the fault of a government which has neglected them and abandoned them to themselves. It follows therefore that not only have you to reproach yourselves with an injustice in having seized their land, but also in having transported on to a soil where the crimes and diseases of Europeans were unknown all that could retard the progress of civilization, which has served as a pretext to your Government … I have no knowledge of the claims which the French Government may have upon Van Diemen's Land, or of its designs for the future; but I think that its title will not be any better grounded than yours …[56]

Amidst the denial, the reproach regarding the convict origins of New South Wales, and question marks over the legality of British possession, lay a plea for the Aboriginal people which unfortunately fell on deaf ears. One week later the French sailed for home and Baudin to his premature death on Mauritius. Governor King shared none of the French commander's reservations and proceeded to deploy his forces to pre-empt a potential French claim to Van Diemen's Land. King had a number of secondary motives as well. One was to disperse his growing convict population; another was to exploit known reserves of timber and any other natural resources that might be discovered on the island.[57] There was also a need for a British outpost to protect colonial sealing gangs operating in Bass Strait, where American incursions had already resulted in violent confrontations.[58]

On 31 August 1803 a small expeditionary force consisting of two vessels, the *Lady Nelson* and the *Albion*, with a total complement of 49 under the command of Lieutenant John Bowen, sailed from Sydney to establish a settlement in the Derwent estuary of southern Van Diemen's Land. Bowen selected Risdon Cove on the east bank of the river as the site for this new British outpost.[59] In the meantime, David Collins had sailed from England to establish a settlement at Port Phillip Bay near present-day Sorrento in Victoria. Lack of water and timber quickly led to disillusionment, and a party led by William Collins (no relation) was sent to investigate the Tamar estuary in northern Van Diemen's Land.[60]

Port Dalrymple, as it was then known, had first been surveyed by Matthew Flinders and George Bass in November 1798 during their circumnavigation of Van Diemen's Land in the *Norfolk*. Sixteen days had been spent exploring the Tamar River, and when Flinders went ashore in search of water he found numerous tracks of the Indigenous people. Aboriginal men were also observed burning grass on the west bank of the Tamar and a family of three was seen on Middle Island.[61]

George Bass examined a number of Aboriginal shelters, and Flinders recorded in his journal that the estuary appeared to be as densely populated as the coast of New South Wales.[62]

Unlike Bass and Flinders, one of Collins's landing parties made contact with the Aboriginal people three days after their arrival in the Tamar River on 1 January 1804. Botanist Robert Brown and his companions distributed some biscuits among a group of Aboriginal men who approached, and showed them how to use a hatchet. The biscuits were discarded, but the men showed obvious interest in the hatchet, which Brown was loath to part with as they were in short supply. That was probably the reason why the Aborigines suddenly became aggressive and levelled their spears at Brown's party. While none were thrown, the British were sufficiently concerned to discharge a musket over the heads of the men. They retreated, but as Brown and his companions reached their boat, the Aboriginal men closed again and a round of buckshot was fired directly at one of their antagonists.[63]

The victim did not appear to have been seriously injured and the blast was sufficient to scatter his companions.[64] For two days they avoided the British, and it was only when Collins weighed anchor for the return to Port Phillip that an estimated 30 Aborigines, including women, appeared on the opposite shore. By signs they encouraged the visitors to approach them, the women began to dance while the men kept time with their waddies. Unbeknown to Collins's party this was a preliminary challenge to fight. So it was that as a boat drew towards the bank the women were hurriedly sent away and the men commenced shouting and throwing stones at the boat crew. Two shots were fired over their heads and the Tasmanian men withdrew to a discrete distance. When the boat grounded the entire group disappeared into the bush.[65]

It is not clear whether it was Aboriginal aggression that influenced David Collins's decision to forego the Tamar and relocate to the Derwent estuary. On arrival he took over command from Lieutenant Bowen and established the main settlement on the opposite bank of the river at Sullivan's Cove, an outpost that was destined to grow into the modern city of Hobart.[66] Governor King was nevertheless still intent on establishing a British settlement in northern Van Diemen's Land to control the waters of Bass Strait. The task fell to Colonel William Paterson. With a detachment of the New South Wales Corps and 74 convicts, Paterson initially set up his headquarters at Outer Cove (today's George Town) in early November 1804. His decision was influenced by the presence of fresh water even though Paterson had doubts about its reliability. His concerns were soon justified, and in April 1805 the settlement was shifted to the west bank of the Tamar and named Yorktown.[67] By then, conflict with the Aboriginal people was well underway.

Indeed, just seven days after Paterson's initial arrival, an estimated 80 Aborigines — almost certainly the entire local band — descended on the British camp at Outer Cove. One prominent individual, assumed to be the chief, was presented with a looking-glass, a hatchet and two handkerchiefs. But access rights to customary territory required much more than this and the Aborigines attempted to remove everything from the first tent they came across. When a sergeant of the guard intervened he was seized by some Aboriginal men and would have been hurled over a rock into the sea had not two privates opened fire. One Aboriginal man fell dead and a second was wounded, the Aborigines responding by hurling a few spears and stones without effect, obviously shaken by this sudden turn of events.[68]

Paterson did make at least one attempt to restore amicable relations. While exploring the Tamar River later the same month his party came across 'about forty natives, including men, women and children'. Paterson sent a soldier forward with a handkerchief held out as a gift, only to be repulsed by stones. The emissary withdrew after placing the material on the ground with a hatchet, and with distance between them the Aborigines recovered the items and evinced their delight. Paterson remained wary, positioning a guard to cover the party's withdrawal. At that point an Aboriginal man came forward and presented one of the soldiers with a necklace that included a white metal button among the strung shells. When the boat turned back towards the shore, however, the Aborigines disappeared into the bush.[69]

There were apparently no more British attempts at pacification. Although details are sketchy, it is known that Paterson later mounted a series of punitive expeditions against the Indigenous people from his Yorktown base.[70] Not that this was surprising; before redeployment to Van Diemen's Land Paterson had organised reprisals against the Aboriginal people of the Hawkesbury River district in New South Wales.[71] By early 1805 then, the British had firmly established themselves in both northern and southern Van Diemen's Land, well aware that the island was anything but uninhabited, a territorial acquisition largely motivated by European rivalry. As Baudin had earlier pointed out, the legality of the acquisition was highly questionable. Under existing international law there were only three ways that new colonies could be created: through conquest, cession by treaty or purchase, or occupation of an uninhabited land.[72] It was under the pretext of occupation that Van Diemen's Land became a British possession.[73]

The Aboriginal people were not cultivating the soil, and were deemed to be unsettled without any form of government. While the French might express indignation against this unlawful occupation, they were militarily too weak to oppose it. So, too, were the Indigenous inhabitants, who suddenly became subjects of a distant English Crown and therefore answerable to English law. At the same time they were denied the rights normally bestowed on a subject people. The wholesale acquisition of Van Diemen's Land by Britain also meant that any attempt on the part of the Aborigines to protect hunting grounds and resist the dispossession of their territories could only be seen in the eyes of English law as a criminal activity. Rendered powerless without the protection of a treaty or genuine rights, the interests of the Aborigines were simply cast aside.[74]

Confusion as to whether Van Diemen's Land had actually been a peaceful occupation rather than an invasion was nonetheless to persist well into the future and create problems for colonial administrations in their dealings with the all-too-present Aboriginal people. Claiming that the land was uninhabited or inhabited by an unsettled people became difficult to reconcile with the reality faced by British settlers on the frontier, who were later engaged in a conflict with people resisting dispossession — a struggle that stiffened into all-out war from 1826. The anomalous position that confronted Lieutenant-Governor George Arthur from 1824 was also recognised by Lord Bathurst, Britain's Secretary of State for the Colonies, whose instructions to Sir Ralph Darling (soon to take up the post of governor in Sydney) and by extension Arthur in Van Diemen's Land, was that if hostile incursions by the Aboriginal people could not be prevented it would be necessary to oppose them by force just as if they were subjects of an accredited state.[75]

Lacking any clear guidelines as well as an opportunity to negotiate a formal treaty, Arthur's administration soon became enmeshed in public controversy following a number of ineffective and contradictory policy decisions. They engendered considerable debate, much of it acrimonious, particularly when the colonial press hammered out the obvious injustices. A case in point was to arise in 1826 when two Aborigines — Jack and Black Dick — were executed following the fatal spearing of Thomas Colley, a stock-keeper at Oyster Bay. Arthur issued a government notice stating that the executions were intended as a warning to prevent further atrocities and would thus lead to conciliation with the Aborigines. More than a few colonists wondered how an execution could possibly be regarded as conciliatory.[76] Andrew Bent, proprietor of the *Colonial Times* in Hobart, drew on this incident to highlight the charade of treating Aborigines clearly involved in a war of resistance as if they were civilians committing acts of domestic crime. Warming to the topic, Bent insisted that if the Aborigines had resisted the initial British settlers with overwhelming violence then a legitimate claim could be made that Van Diemen's Land had been acquired by right of conquest. That had not been the case, and he hypothesised that if the Aborigines had won the war the British settlers would have found themselves subject to Aboriginal law.[77] Many years later the Reverend John West recalled the high level of support for Bent's arguments, with many colonists questioning whether the Aborigines could legally be accountable for their actions — or that any punishment inflicted upon them was just.[78]

The clergy, on the other hand, invoked divine right to justify the British colonisation of Van Diemen's Land. In 1837 the Reverend Thomas Atkins argued it was a universal law that when 'savage tribes' collided with 'civilised races' the former disappeared. Why should that be? Well, according to Atkins (and numerous others) 'savage tribes' had not complied with the divine conditions for survival. God had commanded 'man' to go forth and multiply, to replenish the earth, and to subdue it. Quite simply, the Indigenous hunter-gatherers had not obeyed God's command. What Atkins was saying really had more to do with nineteenth century attitudes to race rather than theological posturing. It was those very same attitudes which contributed to the brutality and indifference that often accompanied the eviction of the Van Diemen's Land Aborigines from their customary land. The prevailing views on race in the early part of the century were at least partly based on the justification of Britain's involvement in the slave trade. Although slavery in Britain (as distinct from the British Empire) was soon to end, it was very much alive and well when Van Diemen's Land formally became a British possession. It therefore comes as no surprise that the island's first commercial industry — sealing — was at least partly underpinned by the labour of Aboriginal women, so often victims of coercion.[79]

There were many ways in which the British attempted to justify their acquisition of Van Diemen's Land, which itself suggests that they were none too comfortable with the legality of their claim. Baudin was essentially correct, the British seizure of the island (and by extension the Australian mainland) was built on very shaky grounds indeed. Perhaps more importantly, though, they also had the strength to subdue it, the first test of might over right coming soon after Lieutenant Bowen established the initial British settlement at Risdon Cove on the Derwent River.

4

RISDON COVE AND THE LONG MARCH TO WAR

When Lieutenant John Bowen sailed from Sydney to establish a permanent British presence in Van Diemen's Land he was accompanied by 49 others, the majority of whom were either convicts or soldiers of the New South Wales Corps commanded by Lieutenant William Moore. Bowen, of course, selected Risdon Cove on the east bank of the Derwent River to set up his headquarters, and almost from the outset he was plagued by dissension among the military personnel. From all accounts Lieutenant Moore was a rather fractious character who spent much of his time at Risdon Cove undermining Bowen's authority, and in April 1804 his troops came perilously close to mutiny after complaining of too many duties to perform.[1] In some ways Van Diemen's Land mirrored the situation at Sydney, where officers of the New South Wales Corps were constantly challenging the vice-regal powers of the early governors. In January 1808 the struggle in Sydney was to erupt into the infamous 'Rum Rebellion' and the overthrow of Governor William Bligh, the same naval officer who had thrice visited Adventure Bay and attempted with mixed results to establish cordial relations with the Indigenous Tasmanians. Lieutenant William Moore was destined to play a significant role in the 'Rum Rebellion' after his return to Sydney, for it was he who handed Bligh the letter demanding that he relinquish his authority and submit to arrest.[2]

While this bloodless *coup d'etat* in Sydney still lay in the future, Moore was the major player in a bloody incident involving the Aboriginal people at Risdon Cove in May 1804. David Collins had by then established the main British settlement at Sullivan's Cove on the west bank of the Derwent approximately 8 kilometres downstream from Risdon. From the diaries of the Reverend Robert Knopwood it is known that the Aborigines occasionally visited Sullivan's Cove and fraternised with the British colonists. This came to an end when a young Aboriginal boy was forcibly detained, and although he later escaped the Aboriginal people thereafter tended to shy away from further contact with the settlement.[3]

But there had already been at least two retaliatory actions by the Aborigines prior to the clash at Risdon Cove. In February 1804 convict huntsman Henry Hacking, accompanied by the New South Wales Aborigine known as Salamander, shot a kangaroo and while returning to Sullivan's Cove were 'intercepted by a tribe of the sooty inhabitants of that neighbourhood' who used 'every policy to wheedle Hacking out of his booty'. There was no threat of violence, with the Aboriginal people reportedly treating Hacking 'with much affability and POLITENESS'. Salamander, however, was regarded 'with jealousy and indignation; and the poor fellow, sensible of his critical and precarious situation, appeared very thankful when delivered from their unwelcome presence'. Despite the concern, Hacking and Salamander managed to keep their kangaroo.[4] A more serious incident occurred the same month when a convict survey party led by assistant colonial surveyor James Meehan was attacked by Aborigines hurling stones near the present town of Pelham, approximately 40 kilometres north-west of Risdon Cove. The attackers temporarily retreated when Meehan discharged his musket, but at dusk they were discovered quietly closing in on the survey party's camp. This time they were dispersed by concentrated musket fire, and when the Aborigines were observed the following morning on a nearby hill armed with spears Meehan's party prudently withdrew from the area. There was no pursuit.[5]

By contrast, only one Aborigine had appeared at Risdon Cove. According to the Reverend John West, an armed Aboriginal man had entered the camp shortly after its establishment and was cordially received. He accepted gifts and by signs appeared to have accepted this trespass on customary territory. When an attempt was made to follow the Aboriginal emissary as he retired into the bush, however, he adopted a menacing stance with his spear poised until the British withdrew.[6] Collins had intended closing the Risdon settlement shortly after his arrival in Van Diemen's Land in February 1804, but delayed taking any action.[7] In fact, by May 1804 the Risdon population had actually increased to about 74–80.[8] Having been superseded by Collins in seniority, Bowen remained in command of the settlement, but he was absent in early May on an exploring expedition in the Huon River district, leaving Lieutenant Moore in charge.[9]

Around 2 pm on 3 May the residents of Sullivan's Cove heard what sounded like a cannon being fired upstream at Risdon. Collins sent a messenger to find out what had taken place, and at 8 pm that evening Lieutenant Moore arrived at Sullivan's Cove in person. Yet rather than reporting directly to the Lieutenant Governor, Moore first made his way to the residence of the Reverend Robert Knopwood.[10] It was not until four days later — 7 May — that the acting commandant at Risdon furnished Collins with a written report.[11] Moore claimed that on 3 May a large body of Aborigines armed with spears had descended on the British camp and forcibly taken a kangaroo from his convict servant. With five soldiers Moore had gone out to confront the transgressors, at which point he received information that a free settler named William Birt and his wife had been assaulted by another group of Aborigines. Moore despatched two soldiers to their assistance with orders not to shoot unless absolutely necessary. Whether these soldiers were detached from Moore's squad of five was not made clear, but on reaching Birt's farm they opened fire, shooting one Aboriginal man dead and mortally wounding another. The second body was later recovered further up the valley.[12]

There is no question that the soldiers remaining with Moore also opened fire, and that a carronade was discharged. Whether this artillery piece was actually fired at the Aborigines is another matter again. Moore insisted that he had acted on the suggestion of the settlement's resident surgeon, Jacob Mountgarrett, to fire one of the carronades as a means of intimidating the Aborigines.[13] There were two carronades at Risdon, more as a precaution against a possible convict uprising than protection against an external force. Importantly, on that fateful day only one was fired — and it was only fired once.[14] Apart from the two Aborigines killed near Birt's house, the British observed another Aborigine being led away bleeding and suspected that several others had been wounded. The official report thus counted the known casualties at two dead and one wounded.[15]

Collins had reservations regarding the veracity of Moore's account. He finally accepted it, largely because it concurred with statements made by Mountgarrett, whose only significant discrepancy was that there had been three fatalities.[16] A young boy aged between two and three years had also been taken into the surgeon's care, reputedly left behind when the Aborigines hurriedly fled the scene.[17] Mountgarrett begged to differ. On the evening of 3 May the Reverend Knopwood received a message from Mountgarrett requesting that he come to Risdon the following day to baptise the boy, whose parents had been killed, and that he should contact surgeon Matthew Bowden and ask whether the latter wished to accompany Knopwood and assist in the dissection of one of the victims.[18] Knopwood was unable to obtain a boat, and it was not until a week later that he finally reached Risdon Cove and baptised the Aboriginal boy as Robert Hobart May.[19] After the child was brought to Sullivan's Cove, Collins ordered that he be returned to his own people so they would know that no harm had befallen him.[20] The Lieutenant Governor was ignored, and the boy remained at Sullivan's Cove.[21]

This is the basic account of what has been called the 'Risdon Massacre' according to the two principal British participants, a clash that has been portrayed as a seminal moment in Tasmanian history. Some have viewed it as the genesis of a conflict that eventually overwhelmed the Indigenous population. Others, particularly the modern Tasmanian Aboriginal community, have used it as a political instrument. It remains a divisive issue, and for that reason it is important to reconstruct what may have actually taken place at Risdon Cove on 3 May 1804.

Apart from the difference in the number of fatalities — either two or three — Moore was not explicit about the number of Aborigines present. Mountgarrett, on the other hand, estimated there were between 500 and 600, clearly a wildly inflated figure.[22] They did agree that the Aborigines appeared to have hostile intentions. A little needs to be said about Jacob Mountgarrett, as his subsequent career reveals him to have been anything but a reliable witness. He was also a very unhappy man at the time of the clash between two cultures at Risdon Cove. When Collins arrived in the Derwent with his own medical team, Mountgarrett was informed that his services were no longer required. His request to establish himself as a free settler was refused and Collins arranged for his return to Sydney in August 1804. Within months Mountgarrett had attached himself as surgeon to Colonel William Paterson's party which sailed for Port Dalrymple in October to form a new settlement in northern Van Diemen's Land. On arrival the irrepressible Mountgarrett embarked on a number of short exploring expeditions before consolidating his position and prospering with the aid of generous land grants.[23] For 10 years all went well until he was accused of assisting the former harbourmaster and deputy surveyor, Peter Mills, whose slide into bankruptcy led to a brief career as a bushranger. Mills eventually surrendered and was lodged in custody, only to escape when his wife plied the guards with rum alleged to have been obtained from Mountgarrett.[24] More damning was the fact that Mills was recaptured while hiding in the surgeon's stables.[25]

Both men were sent to Sydney to stand trial, only to be acquitted owing to a lack of evidence: it was widely believed that the witnesses had been bribed. Surprisingly, both Mills and Mountgarrett were permitted to return to Port Dalrymple.[26] Mills later moved to Hobart and in 1816 sailed for England on a vessel that was lost at sea with all hands.[27] Mountgarrett's demise was considerably slower. An arm had been amputated during his brief sojourn in Sydney, and Mountgarrett's application for a pension was refused. This incapacity made it extremely difficult to continue working as a surgeon as well as conducting his wide-ranging business interests at Port Dalrymple. At the same time he was ostracised by the small community, and turning to alcohol only served to compound his problems. Mountgarrett was then suspected of involvement in the theft of cattle and the misappropriation of stores and medical supplies in his charge. In 1821 he was dismissed from all official positions and died penniless and childless seven years later. His wife Bridget, who Mountgarrett had married in 1811, died in poverty just a year after her husband.[28] During his time in Van Diemen's Land Mountgarrett had also displayed a penchant for collecting Aboriginal children, first begun with Robert Hobart May at Risdon Cove. Among others who lived with the Mountgarretts was Dolly Dalrymple, whose descendants form a significant segment of the modern Tasmanian Aboriginal community.[29]

The point of all this digression, however, is that Mountgarrett's reliability as a witness must be seriously questioned, particularly as there was another eyewitness to the events at Risdon Cove who gave a very different account of proceedings. Edward White was an Irish convict who had been transported to Sydney in 1802 and attached to Bowen's party the following year.[30] At Risdon Cove he was assigned to the free settler, Richard Clark. White was still in Van Diemen's Land in 1830 when he gave evidence to the Aborigines Committee which, among other things, was investigating the cause of the 'Black War'. The committee was inclined to believe that the incident at Risdon Cove 26 years before could have been the catalyst for the violence that was raging at the time.[31]

White's testimony is all the more remarkable as he had every reason to side with the majority of colonists who placed all responsibility for the violence directly on the Aborigines. White cast all blame for the Risdon Cove clash on Lieutenant Moore and the military. According to White, on the morning in question he was quietly hoeing Clark's land near a creek when he saw what he estimated to be 300 Aborigines coming towards the settlement with a mob of kangaroos hemmed in between them. There were men, women and children, all apparently surprised to see anyone there: in White's words, 'they looked at me with all their eyes'. He reported their presence to some soldiers further down the creek and returned to his work. He was neither harmed nor threatened by the Aborigines, who were solely focused on hunting the kangaroos. White was also adamant that they went no closer than 'half a quarter of a mile' (ie 200 metres) from William Birt's residence, and on the opposite side of the creek.[32]

But was White really there? After examining all the available documentation, Michael Asten was unable to discover any record of a convict named Edward White at Risdon Cove in May 1804. In fact, there is no mention of any convict of that name in Van Diemen's Land until 1818, and Asten has suggested that White was attempting to curry favour with the authorities in 1830 on account of his infirmity. If such was indeed the case it was blatant perjury.[33]

Be that as it may, however, the Aborigines definitely did not approach the settlement 'singing and carrying boughs as a symbol of peace' as one recent historian would have it.[34] They were actively engaged in the kangaroo hunt and did not venture near Birt and his wife or attack the soldiers. On the contrary, Moore's men commenced firing on the Aborigines some time around 11 am by White's suspect reckoning, 'when a great many of the Natives [were] slaughtered and wounded'. When asked to be more specific about the number of casualties, White replied that he did not know, but added that surgeon Mountgarrett had later sent some of the bones in two casks to Sydney. He was aware that 'a young boy' had been taken from the Aborigines who, he said, were only armed with waddies; they carried no spears.[35] A few days later the Aborigines drove off a party of convicts gathering oysters on the bank of the Derwent opposite Risdon Cove with stones and waddies, but thereafter they avoided any contact with the British settlement.[36]

If, as White claimed, the soldiers began firing on the Aborigines around 11 am and the carronade was not discharged until 2 pm — when it was heard at Sullivan's Cove — it suggests that Moore's troops had been engaged with the Aborigines for at least three hours. That was clearly not the case. Having recovered from their initial surprise the Aborigines fled the scene. They did not retaliate, and nor did they stand stock still waiting for the soldiers to shoot them down. There were fatalities, and the question of how many Aborigines actually fell has loomed large in all subsequent accounts of the 'Risdon Massacre'. Indeed, the number of casualties began to escalate from 1830 when other 'witnesses' testified to the Aborigines Committee. Unlike White, none of them claimed to have been present at Risdon Cove, and although they were close by at Sullivan's Cove their evidence can be considered nothing more than hearsay.

One of them was the Reverend Robert Knopwood, who entertained Lieutenant Moore on the evening of the clash at Risdon Cove and had met with Mountgarrett a week later. Knopwood 'supposed' that five or six Aborigines had been killed,[37] a figure that may be remarkably accurate. The evidence of the Hobart harbourmaster, James Kelly, diverged considerably, with Kelly contending that between 400 and 500 Aborigines had descended on the British encampment and that 'forty or fifty' had been killed.[38] While Kelly was certainly living at Sullivan's Cove on 3 May 1804, he was only 12 years of age at the time and as later events would show his reliability was highly questionable. The committee certainly placed little weight on his testimony, though members did concede it was possible that Aboriginal casualties could have been as high as Kelly claimed, albeit, with the qualifier that the number had probably been overstated.[39] In 26 years casualty figures had thus risen from two or three to possibly 40 or 50, and the following century they escalated dramatically.

With the resurgence of Tasmanian Aboriginal activism around the time of the Australian Bicentenary in 1988, it comes as no surprise that events such as that at Risdon Cove would be seized on as an example of past maltreatment of the Aboriginal people. Without a shred of evidence Aboriginal activists argued that over 200 men, women and children had been 'slaughtered' by the British on 3 May 1804.[40] Such a death toll suggests that the Aboriginal people had lined themselves up as stationary targets, with the activists apparently denying their Aboriginal forebears the intelligence they clearly possessed. Four years later Greg Lehman reduced the casualties to 'close to a hundred', insisting that the victims had been 'dragged back to the settlement, butchered and boiled down so the bones could be packed in lime and sent to Sydney'. When the survivors returned to bury their dead, continued Lehman, 'many could not be found'. The Aborigines avoided Risdon Cove in the aftermath of that fatal clash: there was no return to 'bury' any dead, and nor could there be. The usual burial practice among the Tasmanian Aborigines was cremation. Lehman identified the victims as members of the Moomairremener band,[41] which is a good place to start with the reconstruction of events.

Risdon Cove definitely lay within the territory of the Moomairrenemer, one of 10 identified bands comprising the Oyster Bay people whose total population has been estimated between 700 and 800.[42] The Oyster Bay people also maintained cordial relations with their inland neighbours, the Big River people, comprising five bands with a total population in the vicinity of 400–500 people.[43] The bands of both the Oyster Bay and Big River peoples were therefore quite large by Tasmanian standards, with the Moomairremener numbering around 80 individuals. Their home base lay around Pitt Water, and the seasonal movements of the Moomairremener differed from the other Oyster Bay bands with whom they had only limited contact. They tended to move inland later than the others, usually in September though sometimes as late as October, returning to their territory in February or March and wintering on the coast by June.[44]

Knowledge of the seasonal movements of the Big River people is less well understood. It is believed that four Big River bands had access to Oyster Bay territory, particularly that of the Moomairrenemer, as they came down the Derwent. WF Refshauge has pointed out that it is likely the Big River people entered Moomairrenemer territory around May, when their hosts would have returned from inland areas.

This was also the time when kangaroos were in prime condition.[45] On 3 May 1804 it appears that at least two bands of Aborigines were involved in the kangaroo chase at Risdon Cove, and it is likely that one of them was the Moomairrenemer, whose resource was being exploited.

Whether there was more than one band of Big River people involved cannot be determined with any certainty. Two bands with men, women and children present would have numbered somewhere between 160 and 200 people, certainly fewer than the estimated 300 of Edward White, but a considerable number of people congregated at any one time in the Tasmanian context. Mountgarrett's estimate of 500–600 can be accepted as an attempt to magnify the apparent emergency. Given that there was probably somewhere between 4500–5000 Aboriginal people at first contact, a figure of 300 would represent a substantial proportion of the island's entire Indigenous population. That would have been an exceptional gathering indeed, and a figure of 160–200 is far more likely. With Risdon Cove's European population somewhere between 74–80, there were certainly enough Indigenous people to engender fear amongst the colonists.

At least two bands were therefore heading towards the British encampment with a mob of kangaroos between them and, although they were shocked to see anyone there, the hunt had to progress. White claimed that the soldiers began firing around 11 am, though how many soldiers could have been involved is not clear. Moore said that he confronted the Aborigines with a squad of five, two of whom might have been dispatched to Birt's assistance. They were armed with standard issue Brown Bess muskets, ideal weapons for conventional European warfare with closed ranks facing each other at close quarters. They were considerably less effective in frontier situations.[46]

Muskets were heavy and cumbersome, weighing up to 6 kilograms, and they misfired at least once every six rounds. If the powder was damp they would not fire at all, and they were also slow to reload. While an experienced soldier from an elite unit could fire up to two rounds per minute,[47] New South Wales Corps personnel were not frontline troops. Muskets were only accurate up to 50 metres, and even at that range subsequent shots were deflected to a greater or lesser degree depending on the amount of slag left behind in the barrel. For all their limitations, these firearms remained in widespread use as late as the American Civil War of the 1860s (albeit, advanced smooth-bore weapons fitted with percussion caps) when they were in turn rapidly superseded by powerful repeating rifles. During that war, the Union General, William Rosecrans, was far from satisfied with the performance of his troops armed with the latest smooth-bore muskets, which fired two million rounds to account for 13 832 casualties. To put it another way, they fired 145 rounds to inflict just one casualty, and by that Rosecrans meant killed or wounded.[48] Of course, injuries from either a 0.69-inch or 0.75-inch lead ball travelling at 300 metres per second and which flattened on impact were horrendous.[49] But the target had to be struck first.

As the aggressors, Lieutenant Moore's soldiers had the element of surprise, and a number of rounds could have been fired before the Aborigines grasped what was happening. That does not mean that all rounds took effect. Nor is it known how close the soldiers were: the distance between the two groups could well have been in excess of 50 metres. That there were some casualties suggests the distance was less than 100 metres, as musket balls were unlikely to cause a fatal injury beyond that distance.[50] Musketry fire would also have left more Aborigines wounded than dead, the usual ratio being in the order of two or three to one.[51]

There is no indication that dead and wounded littered the field at Risdon Cove. No wounded were brought in, and nor did Angela McGowan's detailed archaeological work at this location uncover any large grave or signs of mass cremation.[52] When the Reverend Knopwood finally reached Risdon Cove a week after the clash he asked to be shown where the fighting had taken place. As Keith Windschuttle has rightly remarked, Knopwood was fascinated by morbid events, regularly recording hangings, murders and burials in his private diaries. Decaying bodies, a mass grave or even a funeral pyre would have drawn Knopwood like a moth to a flame. Instead, after inspecting the site he recorded nothing at all.[53] Quite clearly there was nothing to be seen.

Moore was arguably more intent on keeping the Aborigines away after his men had shed the first blood. By Moore's own admission the soldiers (and Mountgarrett) had pursued the Aborigines, but they would have been quickly outpaced. All of this brings us back to the two carronades, one of which was fired three hours after the initial clash. Moore acted on Mountgarrett's suggestion to discharge the weapon for the purpose of intimidating the Aborigines. Mountgarrett had previously been a naval surgeon and was presumably familiar with these artillery pieces,[54] but it is the timing that is of significance. It is possible that the Aborigines later regrouped with the intention of counter-attacking, though whether the report of the carronade was sufficient to disperse them or that they were injured by its fire can only be conjectured. What is clear is that after the carronade's discharge the Aborigines never returned.

Carronades were first developed in the 1770s by the Carron Iron Company in Scotland for the British Admiralty, and they continued to be used on British naval vessels with mixed success until the 1850s. They were small cannons light enough to mount on the forecastle or poop deck where conventional cannons would have made the vessels top-heavy. Their weakness was a shorter range, and to be used effectively any ship armed with these weapons had to close with its adversary. If that could be achieved the results were devastating. Firing a round shot the ball literally smashed its way through an enemy vessel's timbers causing deadly splinters to fly out and kill or maim the crew. When loaded with grapeshot they were used to shred an opponent's sails and cut any sharpshooters in the rigging to pieces. At a lower elevation along the deck they could rip apart the gun and sailing crews.[55] However, if the opponent was armed with conventional long cannon and remained outside the range of the carronades — as many did — they could easily destroy a ship equipped solely with these artillery pieces. The French were never able to replicate this British naval weapon, and during the War of 1812 American vessels armed solely with conventional weaponry proved more than a match for British ships armed with carronades.[56]

They came in a range of calibres. The two at Risdon Cove were 12-pounders, approximately 70 centimetres in length and weighed around 300 kilograms. Both had been removed from the *Investigator*, the ship in which Matthew Flinders completed the first circumnavigation of the Australian mainland.[57] As an anti-personnel weapon they were capable of discharging 42 4-ounce lead balls in a single shot. While this would have been lethal if fired directly into a mass of people, the ability to do so required highly skilled artillerymen who could adjust the elevation between one and two degrees for maximum effect. As far as is known there were no specialist artillery personnel at Risdon Cove, and an unskilled crew would have taken quite some time to load and fire the weapon. Calibrating the correct elevation was another matter again,[58] and it needs to be added that carronades had a violent recoil. If not adequately restrained by heavy ropes they had the potential to seriously injure the firing crew.[59] It is quite clear that on 3 May 1804 the carronade at Risdon Cove had not been discharged in the heat of battle.

That still leaves the two casks of bones that Mountgarrett forwarded to Sydney. Keith Windschuttle dismissed White's testimony regarding the casks on two grounds. First, that as a convict White would have had no knowledge of the dealings of Mountgarrett or any other member of the settlement's elite. Second, that no lime was available at the settlement for preserving the bones.[60] To take the first point, owing to the small size of the settlement practically everybody would have known everyone else's business, and there is no suggestion that Mountgarrett attempted to hide what he was doing.[61] It was a normal practice at that time to collect unusual specimens, be they plant, animal or human. If anything, the interest in Aboriginal skeletal material was destined to increase.[62] Windschuttle's second point that no lime was available is simply incorrect. Shells were already being burnt at Ralph's Bay to produce lime as mortar for building work at both Risdon and Sullivan Coves.[63] However, it is unlikely that bones, or perhaps human remains which had not been defleshed (notwithstanding Mountgarrett's dissection of at least one body), were sent away in lime. The usual preservative was alcohol,[64] and there was a ready supply of alcohol at Risdon Cove, Sullivan's Cove and on the *Ocean*, the vessel which carried them away.[65] Casks come in a variety of sizes, and the two that Mountgarrett forwarded to Sydney were not necessarily the largest ones available. Two small casks could easily have accommodated the bones from just two or three individuals, though none of this is even relevant if White's testimony was completely fabricated.

On the other hand, consideration does need to be given to the actions of the acting commandant at Risdon Cove on 3 May 1804. In 1870 historian James Bonwick published his account of the frontier violence in Van Diemen's Land as *The Last of the Tasmanians*. In this work Bonwick made the first claim that Lieutenant Moore was suffering 'from an over-dose of rations' rum' at the time the Aborigines approached the settlement.[66] That statement has tarnished Moore's reputation ever since, repeated in many subsequent accounts.[67]

Bonwick insisted that he received his information from 'a settler of 1804',[68] a source dismissed by Keith Windschuttle who believed that anyone who could have been called an original settler had departed Tasmanian shores long before 1870.[69] There was one person he overlooked, and that was Lieutenant Bowen's mistress Martha Hayes, who remained in Van Diemen's Land after Bowen left and later became a settler in her own right. Hayes died in 1871 at the age of 84, and it is likely that she was Bonwick's informant.[70]

The New South Wales Corps certainly had a reputation for hard drinking,[71] as did virtually all of Britain's military units.[72] For a detachment in a remote outpost such as Risdon Cove it is not entirely unrealistic that Moore and his men imbibed more freely than usual, which could also account for Moore's exceptional bravery. After being informed of the approach of a large number of armed Aborigines Moore confronted them with just five soldiers equipped with single-shot muskets — three men if two had gone to Birt's assistance — definitely not the actions of a coward.[73] Another oft-repeated allegation against Moore (again stemming from Bonwick) was that he reputedly fired on the Aborigines from 'a desire to see the niggers run'.[74] Used as an example of brutal callousness,[75] Moore's remarks (if indeed he made them) held a deeper meaning. The terminology allegedly used is only offensive by modern standards, and from Moore's perspective he faced a military threat with potentially disastrous consequences for the settlement he was temporarily commanding. He wanted to see the Aborigines run — to retreat — and thus remove the danger. To discourage, or perhaps even thwart an impending counter-attack the carronade was subsequently discharged and the settlement briefly returned to its slumber before its complete abandonment just months later.

Owing to limited evidence the events which occurred at Risdon Cove on 3 May 1804 are, of course, open to various interpretations.

It has also become an important Tasmanian foundation story, particularly unusual in that right from the outset blame was firmly attached to the British colonisers.[76] There can be no doubt that it was the result of a terrible misunderstanding and that the Aboriginal people were the innocent victims. Yet it still took some time for those Aboriginal voices to be heard. In February 1904 several thousand people, including the premier and governor, made their way to Risdon Cove for the unveiling of a monument to the settlement's founder, Lieutenant John Bowen. In the speeches that followed there was no mention of the blood that was shed on 3 May 1804, and as far as is known there were no descendants of the Aboriginal people in attendance. But nor was there any reference to the convicts whose labour had underwritten the success of Tasmania's first British settlement. In effect, it was an elitist non-Indigenous foundation story.[77]

Then, between 1978 and 1980, Angela McGowan conducted the first detailed archaeological investigation of the site, findings that were published in 1985. Not only did she uncover traces of the original buildings, McGowan also found evidence of Aboriginal occupation pre-dating the contact period.[78] This meant that Risdon Cove could now be seen as a foundation site for both Indigenous and non-Indigenous Tasmanians. That was graphically demonstrated three years later, Australia's bicentennial year, when a local drama group staged a re-enactment of Bowen's landing. The actors were bombarded with flour bombs and eggs hurled by some of the estimated 100 Tasmanian Aboriginal descendants,[79] and just one month later — on the anniversary of the 'Risdon Massacre' — the Tasmanian Aboriginal Centre (TAC) began agitating for total control of the former Risdon Cove site.[80]

That was achieved in November 1995, when Risdon Cove was proclaimed an Aboriginal Historic Site, with control of the land vested in the TAC.[81] It should have become a focal point for Aboriginal unity.

Instead, Risdon Cove once again literally became a bone of contention. In that very same year a Federal Court judgment held that it was 'impossible' to determine who was actually a Tasmanian Aborigine, a decision which prompted a number of self-identified Aboriginal groups to break away from the TAC's monopolistic control. One of them was the Lia Pootah, who claimed — without any evidence — to be direct descendants of the Moomairrenemer people whose customary territory embraced Risdon Cove.[82] They argued that they were the legitimate custodians, not the TAC. That struggle for control has continued, with the result that the site, significant in different ways for all Tasmanians, has been increasingly neglected, awaiting the outcome of an ongoing contest between possession and dispossession.

The violence at Risdon Cove on 3 May 1804 was also to continue intermittently until the mid-1820s, when it exploded into the Black War. Yet, remarkably little is known about frontier relations between 1804 and the early 1820s. It is generally agreed that while violent clashes definitely occurred they were by and large fragmented and limited in scope. The Aboriginal people certainly experienced considerable brutality at the hands of sealers and bushrangers, the first social group predating British colonisation. From the earliest days of settlement, in both north and south Van Diemen's Land, there was a heavy demand for meat which could not be met by the limited number of imported livestock. It was not long before the kangaroos and emus within easy reach of Hobart and Launceston had become extremely scarce. This resulted in convicts being sent into the bush with dogs to hunt wild game for sale in both settlements, a trade nominally controlled by military officers and wealthy free settlers.[83] The convicts were initially unarmed, relying on dogs alone to bring down the prey, but after a series of clashes with Aborigines they began to be issued with firearms.[84] Many of these convict huntsmen adapted well to the frontier lifestyle and the freedom that came with it, and it was not surprising that quite a few refused to return to disciplined servitude. The problem they faced was that while they could successfully hunt animals for food and hides to fashion clothing and footwear, they were bereft of other necessary items as well as luxuries such as tobacco and alcohol. This resulted in the waylaying of travellers and raids on isolated farmsteads beyond the immediate protection of the military. Thus was born the Australian outlaw — the bushranger — who appeared in every Australian colony and New Zealand. It was in Van Diemen's Land, however, that they reached the peak of their influence.[85]

Between 1805 when the first organised bushranging gang of Lemon and Brown was formed, until the mid-1820s, Van Diemen's Land was virtually a divided society. The military held sway in the settled districts, the bushrangers on the edges, and the Aborigines beyond.[86] There was, of course, extensive overlap, particularly between the bushrangers and Aborigines, and there are many apocryphal tales of great brutality inflicted on the latter. With the exception of Michael Howe, who kept a diary made from kangaroo hide and used animal blood as ink,[87] there are no first-hand written accounts of bushranger–Aborigine interactions, and many of the second-hand reports revolve around the murder of Aboriginal men for access to their women.[88]

Before Richard Lemon was shot dead and John Brown captured and executed in early 1808, they are said to have killed at least five Aborigines — two men and three women — and wounded another four. Between 1808 and 1810 William Russell and George Getley are reputed to have tortured and slain an unspecified number of Aboriginal people, almost certainly supported by the fact that both men were eventually killed by Aborigines. Lieutenant Governor Collins was in no doubt that their deaths were revenge killings.[89] Before he was bludgeoned to death in 1817 Michael Howe acquired a formidable reputation for murdering Aborigines, and he kept an Aboriginal mistress named Mary Cockerell, or 'Black Mary'. They were eventually surprised by soldiers, and although Howe eluded his pursuers Mary fell behind. To prevent her capture Howe unsuccessfully attempted to shoot his erstwhile paramour dead, a close encounter that convinced Mary to turn informant. She subsequently led troops to a number of Howe's hideouts where considerable quantities of stolen goods were recovered,[90] and was later taken to Sydney as a Crown witness in the trial of three of Howe's associates. On her return to Hobart Mary was victualled by the government 'and received indulgences in clothing'.[91] Howe's failure to shoot his female partner was the beginning of the end of his bushranging career.

In the north sealers had a particularly devastating impact on the Aborigines, while elsewhere convict stock-keepers and legitimate frontiersmen were no better. Lieutenant Governor Thomas Davey, who replaced Collins following the latter's sudden death in 1810, was quick to realise that as the flocks and herds of settlers spread into new country they devastated the natural resources of the Aboriginal people. In June 1813 Davey issued a general proclamation warning against the abuse of Aborigines,[92] an unenforceable order that was repeated by his own successor, William Sorell, in March 1819. Both Davey and Sorell also condemned the widespread kidnapping of Aboriginal children.[93] It has been claimed that by 1817 some 50 Aboriginal children were living in the homes of settlers,[94] a situation far from unique to Van Diemen's Land. Right across Australia during the nineteenth century Aboriginal children were kept as unpaid labour — girls often as sexual chattels.[95]

Examples of brutality abounded. James Hobbs gave testimony to the Aborigines Committee in 1830 regarding an assigned convict named James Carrett, otherwise known as Carrotts, who had openly boasted to Hobbs of killing an Aboriginal man from Oyster Bay to take possession of his wife. The corpse was decapitated, with the head hung around the neck of Carrett's captive as she was led back to his camp.[96] There are literally scores of such examples of inherent savagery against the Indigenous inhabitants of Van Diemen's Land, far too many to be dismissed out of hand.[97] The Aborigines, however, were not merely passive victims in these encounters: when an opportunity presented itself to strike back at their tormentors they seized it. In early 1818 an entire flock of 500 sheep was reported to have been destroyed by Aboriginal raiders at Salt Pan Plains, while around the same time a party of 13 armed settlers were besieged on a hill for three days. They finally managed to escape under cover of dark.[98]

But this was only one side of the frontier experience. In 1814 there were reports of Aborigines bartering kangaroo tails for mutton, and in 1819 Aborigines assisted in the harvesting of a potato crop on the farm of a Mr Bonner. In exchange for their labour the Aborigines received a portion of the crop as well as damper. On a farm owned by James Ross a campfire lit by the Aborigines briefly raged out of control, threatening the entire harvest. They joined with Ross and his men to extinguish the blaze and then shifted their camp to a safer part of the property.[99] So while there was certainly confrontation, it was tempered by a degree of collaboration. That delicate balance was nevertheless set to change from 1826 as the majority of the Indigenous population took up arms to challenge British domination, and one of the supposed sparks that ignited the Black War was said to have involved an Aboriginal man from New South Wales known as Musquito.

Probably born around 1780, Musquito's customary territory stretched from Broken Bay south to Manly on the north shore of Sydney Harbour in New South Wales. Musquito is known to have been involved in the conflict between British settlers and Aborigines in the Hawkesbury River district, where the former were repelled from Aboriginal land before making a second successful attempt backed by the firepower of the New South Wales Corps. By June 1805 nine prominent Aboriginal leaders had been captured and lodged in Parramatta Gaol; the tenth, Musquito, was taken by other Aborigines early the following month and handed over to the British.[100]

Neither Musquito nor his close associate Bull Dog took their incarceration quietly. Musquito constantly threatened to burn down the prison, and on one occasion the pair came close to escaping after working some of the mortar loose from the stonework. Their bid for freedom was thwarted by a non-Indigenous prisoner who alerted the guards. Musquito and Bull Dog nonetheless presented Governor King with a legal conundrum. While he was convinced that both men had been directly involved in the killing of four settlers, he was also aware that many Aborigines had been murdered by British civilians acting outside the law. His solution was to transport the pair to Norfolk Island as convicts, where they were put to work burning charcoal. Bull Dog was eventually returned to Sydney, but Musquito was forced to endure his exile for eight years until the penal settlement was closed down and the remaining prisoners sent to Launceston in northern Van Diemen's Land. Musquito went with them, arriving in March 1813 fully conversant in English and technically a free man.[101]

His brother Phillip in Sydney agitated for Musquito's repatriation, a plea finally acted upon by Governor Macquarie in August the following year. Lieutenant Governor Davey was instructed to make the necessary arrangements for Musquito's return to Sydney, but by then the Van Diemen's Land authorities had found his tracking skills so useful in the pursuit of bushrangers that he remained in the colony. In October 1817 Lieutenant Governor Sorell returned to the repatriation issue when he informed Macquarie that Musquito still wanted to return home. Although Sorell once again made arrangements for Musquito's repatriation it remains unclear why they were not followed through. In order to survive, Musquito found employment with the wealthy settler, Edward Lord.[102]

It was then that he found himself in a real dilemma, labouring with convicts and ex-convicts who deeply resented Musquito's role in the pursuit of bushrangers, people who were drawn from the same social group as themselves. Ostracised, Musquito abandoned Lord's property in 1818 and headed south. He finally joined a group of displaced Aborigines known as the 'Tame Mob', fringe-dwellers numbering at various times between 20 and 30 men, women and children, who lived on the outskirts of British settlements in south-eastern Van Diemen's Land, particularly in the territory of the Oyster Bay people. Unlike other Aboriginal groups, they were regarded by the settlers as inoffensive and harmless. While they still hunted animals, gathered plant foods and harvested oysters on the coast, members of the 'Tame Mob' had also developed a liking for tobacco, alcohol and introduced foodstuffs, including potatoes. They avoided working for settlers, preferring to accept irregular handouts, and by June 1823 Musquito had emerged as their nominal leader.[103] The Wesleyan missionary, Reverend William Horton, called on the 'Tame Mob' at Pitt Water in June 1823, his sensibilities offended by their mode of existence. Horton later wrote that he had asked Musquito whether he would prefer living like the settlers rather than in his current circumstances. Musquito reputedly answered in the affirmative, but added that his companions would not accept it.[104] Choice did not enter into the equation. Later the same year the world to which Musquito had grown accustomed exploded with tragic consequences.

In November 1823 Musquito and another member of the 'Tame Mob', Black Dick, arrived at the hut of stock-keeper John Radford near the present-day town of Swansea. They were accompanied by an estimated 65 Oyster Bay Aboriginal people — men, women and children — who normally avoided the settlers. Radford had with him a Tahitian stock-keeper named Mammoa and an invalid traveller, William Hollyoak, who was on his way to Little Swanport. Musquito, Black Dick and the Oyster Bay Aborigines camped close to Radford's hut for three days, hunting and generally entertaining themselves. Musquito spent much of his time with the stock-keepers, liberally feasting on his hosts' provisions. Then it all turned sour. The sole survivor, John Radford, later denied that he or his companions had interfered with the Aboriginal women,[105] but there is evidence to the contrary. The assault, however, was not of a sexual nature. Also present among the Oyster Bay Aborigines was a young man called Kickerterpoller, otherwise known as 'Tom Birch' or 'Black Tom', who had been raised by the wealthy Hobart merchant and shipowner, Thomas Birch and his wife Sarah. While it is often been stated that 'Black Tom' entered the Birch household at a tender age, he may in fact have been an initiated teenager.[106] Be that as it may, he later abandoned colonial society and he was certainly with Musquito and the 'Tame Mob' when they arrived at Radford's hut. Importantly, Black Tom later told George Augustus Robinson that the stock-keepers 'fired a quantity of small shot' into the back of an Aboriginal woman who 'was walking away' — presumably from the hut — causing 'a wound as broad as his hand'. According to Robinson, 'Tom said it was as cruel a thing as he ever saw done',[107] and it may have been this malicious act which triggered the attack on Radford and his companions.

Radford said that a number of the Oyster Bay men appeared outside the hut and he and Mammoa went out to see them. Before leaving the hut he advised Hollyoak to bring the firearms, but they were left inside when the latter emerged to join his companions. Musquito was on the opposite side of a creek with a few other armed Oyster Bay men and called for Mammoa to join him. Musquito held a waddy and a stick. After talking to Mammoa the group walked towards the hut and sensing their purpose Radford went back inside to retrieve the guns only to find they had disappeared. At the hut Musquito untied the stock-keepers' dogs and led them away, and it was then the Oyster Bay men levelled their spears at Radford and his companions. The three men ran for their lives, and notwithstanding being injured in the side and thigh Radford still managed to outpace his pursuers. He heard the screams of Mammoa and Hollyoak behind him, and while it is certainly questionable whether Musquito or Black Dick took part in the actual killings, press reports focused almost exclusively on their involvement in the double murder.[108] Surprisingly, even though he was well-known to the stock-keepers, 'Black Tom' was never mentioned as a participant.[109] As will later be shown, this young Aboriginal man walked a tightrope between two societies and lived an extraordinarily charmed life until his death from dysentery in 1832.

Musquito was not so fortunate; he was implicated in a series of attacks on settlers between November 1823 and August 1824, some of which resulted in the loss of life. Only in one incident, however, is there definite evidence of Musquito's presence. That occurred in August 1824 when he cooed a settler at Pitt Water to draw him from the hut and then wounded the man with a spear. By then Musquito was already living on borrowed time; less than a week later he was captured by a Tasmanian Aborigine named Teague (or Tegg), who had been raised in the household of surgeon Edward Luttrell. Accompanied by two of Luttrell's assigned convicts, Teague caught up with Musquito and two Aboriginal women on the east coast. Musquito was unarmed and attempted to escape, only to be shot and wounded by Teague.[110]

It was perhaps no coincidence that the Luttrell family was involved in Musquito's capture. Edward Luttrell had previously been a land-owner in the Hawkesbury River district when Musquito was active in the resistance campaign. In 1810 one of Luttrell's sons, Edward

Jnr, had been charged in Sydney with shooting and wounding the Aboriginal resistance leader, Tedbury, and the following year another of Luttrell's sons was killed by Aborigines — possibly in revenge. Luttrell Snr died in Van Diemen's Land in June 1824, so it was almost certainly Edward Jnr who sent Teague and his assigned convicts to hunt down Musquito. He certainly attempted to claim credit for the renegade's capture.[111]

Black Dick was taken soon after and the pair stood trial in Hobart's Supreme Court on a charge of aiding and abetting in the murder of William Hollyoak. The court refused permission for the defendants to brief counsel, speak in their own defence or call witnesses. The prosecution's case rested heavily on the circumstantial evidence of John Radford, who was running for his life and did not actually witness the death of the invalid traveller.[112] It mattered little. Musquito was found guilty, and while Black Dick managed to secure an acquittal, both men were then tried as 'principals in the second degree for aiding and abetting in the wilful murder of Mammoa'. Musquito was again found guilty and Black Dick acquitted,[113] but the latter could not escape the gallows. A few weeks later Black Dick stood trial for the murder of hut-keeper Patrick Macarthy and on this occasion he was found guilty.[114] Along with five non-Indigenous offenders, Musquito and Black Dick were hanged at Hobart on 25 February 1825.[115] They were followed to the grave in September the following year by Jack and Dick, executed for the murder of stock-keeper Thomas Colley. By then, however, the Black War was already well underway.

The first concerted attack on British settlers took place in January 1826, when 'about 150' Aborigines descended on a property at Western Creek and seriously wounded a convict servant before they were repulsed.[116] The following May five Aborigines, all conversant in English, broke into a farmhouse in the Macquarie River district and beat a settler to death with waddies. The convict servant was also seriously injured and the farmhouse ransacked before the raiders withdrew.[117] In September, Mary Smith's two stock-keepers, Perry and Hallan, were 'brutally murdered' by Aborigines,[118] while two months later '300' Aborigines are said to have attacked George Simpson's property on Penny-royal Creek and speared one of his employees to death. In the Lake River district George Taylor's body was found transfixed by spears and his head savagely shattered by blows inflicted by either waddies or stones.[119] Before the month was out four sawyers at Cockatoo Valley in the Macquarie River district shared some of their provisions with 50 Aborigines who then turned on their hosts, killing one and seriously wounding another.[120] In December another stock-keeper was found dead near Piper's Lagoon: 'A more shocking spectacle was never seen. His body, especially his head, was literally beaten to a mummy. His throat was cut and his lower extremities cut off. Indeed he was cut to atoms.'[121]

These were the initial rounds in the Black War that engulfed the island colony of Van Diemen's Land, and the timing suggested to more than a few colonists that the violence had been triggered by the executions of Musquito and the three Tasmanian Aborigines. Up until this time the Indigenous people had shown little signs of aggression beyond local retaliatory measures, so much of the blame for the outbreak of violence was cast on Musquito. After all, he was an Aboriginal man from New South Wales, supposedly more 'advanced' than his Van Diemen's Land counterparts, and familiar with the ways of the British.[122] That argument can still occasionally be heard today, but the reality was very different.

At the conclusion of the Napoleonic Wars in 1815 there was a marked increase in the number of settlers entering Van Diemen's Land. Many received extensive land grants along the Midlands corridor between Hobart and Launceston, thereby severing the seasonal migration routes of the Aboriginal people of the southern and eastern regions — and seriously depleting their natural resources. The scale of this influx was considerable. In 1817 there were only 2000 non-Indigenous people in Van Diemen's Land, mostly congregated in and around Hobart and Launceston. By 1824, just seven years later, the non-Indigenous population had risen to 12 643, including some 4000 free settlers. By then they had completely altered the balance of the economy through pastoral enterprises. In 1823 alone the government granted 175 000 hectares of land to free settlers. Another way of looking at this impact is through the increase of livestock. In 1816 there were 54 000 sheep in the colony; by 1823 sheep numbers had increased to 200 000, and by 1826 they had more than doubled again to 553 698.[123] As Sharon Morgan explained, the key period of expansion occurred from 1823 when:

> Settlement had now spread throughout most of the previously explored and accessible parts of the island. From the two 'beach-heads', Hobart Town and Launceston, settlers had penetrated along the major river systems — the Tamar, North Esk and South Esk, Lake and Western Rivers in the north; the Derwent, Coal, Clyde, and Shannon Rivers in the south; the Elizabeth and Macquarie Rivers in the midlands — as well as along the route between the northern and southern settlements, along the shores of the Derwent Estuary and Pitt Water, and at Great Swan Port.[124]

It was this massive encroachment and accompanying destabilisation of their own economies that finally forced the Aboriginal people of eastern Van Diemen's Land to respond in the mid-1820s. The situation by then had clearly become intolerable, and with nowhere to go the Aborigines had little choice except to fight back. The Black

War was a struggle for basic survival, with all the odds stacked heavily against the Indigenous inhabitants. Despite that, and to the surprise of many colonists, their resistance proved to be extremely effective. But the Aboriginal people were unable to present a united front. The Black War was in effect a series of frontier wars dependent on spatial location and timing, and it was in the north that the impact of the British presence was felt first.

5

THE SEALING FRATERNITY AND THE 'BLACK WAR'

The north-east occupies a significant place in Tasmanian Aboriginal history as it was there that the process of devastation began, and it can be rightly argued that it was in this geographic region that the struggle for control of the entire island had its genesis. Pivotal in that development were the sealers, men who were bent on the accumulation of riches or at least a fair semblance of living through the exploitation of marine mammals. The sealing saga began in 1797 when the *Sydney Cove* sailing to Sydney from India was forced to run aground on Preservation Island in eastern Bass Strait to save the crew and its valuable speculative cargo. Serious leaks had plagued the vessel throughout the voyage, and after encountering a series of fierce gales the pumps had failed to cope with the increasing influx of water. Seventeen crewmen subsequently set out from Preservation Island in the ship's longboat to seek assistance from Sydney, only to be wrecked at the northern end of Ninety Mile Beach in today's Victoria. The survivors continued their journey overland, but through privations and violent clashes with Aboriginal people along the way only three men finally reached the British outpost on Sydney Harbour. One of two vessels sent to the aid of their marooned captain and crewmates disappeared without trace, though the survivors and much of the *Sydney Cove's* cargo were eventually retrieved.[1] While they had been waiting for help to arrive the seamen had observed immense colonies of seals on the surrounding islands, news that was well received in Sydney, where there was a desperate need for a viable export commodity.[2]

So it was that when Matthew Flinders and George Bass sailed from Sydney in the *Norfolk* the following year to confirm the existence of the passage separating Van Diemen's Land from the Australian mainland they were accompanied as far as the Furneaux Islands by Captain Charles Bishop and the *Nautilus*, a vessel specially-fitted out to harvest the seals which were said to be so abundant.[3] Bishop established his base at Kent Bay on Cape Barren Island, where his men set a standard of exploitation and greed that was to become the hallmark of the industry. They killed an average 200 seals a day and after less than two months the *Nautilus* was able to return to Sydney with 5000 sealskins and 350 gallons of oil in its hold. Fourteen men were left behind to continue the slaughter.[4] When Flinders and Bass returned from their circumnavigation of Van Diemen's Land they reported huge numbers of seals on the western islands of Bass Strait as well as an estimated 150 million shearwaters — mutton-birds — flying in formation near Three Hummock Island.[5] Along with Flinders's charts, their observations provided signposts for further penetration of Bass Strait by sealers and for the future colonisation of Van Diemen's Land.

The early sealers were a diverse group of men representing many countries, later described as 'a hotchpotch of beachcombers, deserters from ships and escaped convicts': they were all that and more. Many were skilled seamen, some of whom possessed unusual capabilities.[6]

Others were violent and dangerous, a reflection of their brutal and bloody calling. Sealing was nevertheless of crucial importance to the early Australian colonial economy, providing employment for shipwrights, coopers, blacksmiths and a host of other artisans and labourers aside from those whose job was to kill and butcher the basic resource.[7]

By the mid-eighteenth century the Chinese had discovered a technique for removing the coarse outer hair of sealskins which left only the soft under-fur, ideal for the manufacture of hats, coats and footwear. In 1798 Englishman Thomas Chapman developed an even more sophisticated process for treating sealskins which quickly led to London becoming the chief international market for the industry. Nor was it just sealskins that provided financial incentives. Prolific numbers of giant elephant seals in western Bass Strait were rich in oil used for lighting and lubrication. Seal oil, in fact, was superior to widely used whale oil as a light source as it burnt with a pure flame and lacked the smoke and offensive smell characteristic of the cetacean product.[8] Such was the pattern of exploitation, however, that within four years the Bass Strait seal colonies had been decimated, with many sealers forced to venture as far afield as New Zealand and further south to the sub-Antarctic islands in search of their quarry. The elephant seal colonies on King Island were completely wiped out: today the nearest breeding colonies of this huge marine mammal are on sub-Antarctic Macquarie Island.[9]

Sealing gangs were paid a percentage of the catch known as a lay. Depending on their experience and ability a lay could vary from 1/60th to 1/100th of the total. That was not a percentage of the profits. If a sealer was entitled to a lay of 1/100th it meant that on his return he received ten skins for every 1000 taken, and in the first few years it was not unusual for sealing gangs to accumulate tens of thousands of skins in a single season. The problem for individual sealers was to covert their skins into cash, which they generally did by selling them to the entrepreneur who had outfitted the expedition for a price well below their true market value. The cost of clothing and rations was also deducted by the outfitter on a per capita basis,[10] and the provision of rations to sealing gangs was anything but generous, mostly consisting of salt meat and flour. Lack of vegetables ensured that many sealers were afflicted with scurvy, alleviated only by the presence in some localities of native green foods.[11]

Outfitters in Sydney were usually ex-convicts, notably Simeon Lord, Henry Kable and James Underwood, men who had made good through exceptional business acumen and more than their fair share of luck.[12] Despite the predatory dealings of the outfitters, in the early years of the industry it was possible for sealers to establish a business of their own or even purchase a small farm on the proceeds of just two or three seasons.[13] But they had to be tough. Along with their provisions the sealing gangs were landed on islands known to contain seal colonies, with the mother ship then sailing off to engage in other commercial ventures until it was time to collect the men. Their work involved clubbing or stabbing the animals to death while they were either asleep or coming ashore — in other words, when the seals were most vulnerable. Depending on the species they were either skinned or butchered, the blubber boiled down in try-pots to obtain the oil.[14] One of the major concerns of the sealing gangs was that the mother ship might not return. Many disappeared without trace, in some cases leaving their gangs marooned for years on sub-Antarctic islands.[15]

For various reasons, though, numbers of sealers chose to remain permanently on the Bass Strait islands, particularly in the Furneaux Group at the eastern entrance, eking out a living hunting the remaining seals, snaring wallabies for their pelts and harvesting mutton-birds for oil and feathers. They traded these commodities for sugar, tea, tobacco and alcohol.[16] The sealers also needed women, and this led to raids on Aboriginal bands right along the north and east coasts of Van Diemen's Land as well as the southern coast of the Australian mainland. There can be no doubt that the abduction of women contributed significantly to the demographic collapse of the Aboriginal population in north-eastern Van Diemen's Land from a very early period. Quite a few of the sealers acquired multiple 'wives', some of whom were later sold or traded to other members of the sealing fraternity. In more extreme cases they were killed when considered unmanageable or simply of no further use.[17]

Although it has been argued that Aboriginal people actively participated in this perverse trade it is based on the flimsiest evidence,[18] allowing one recent and uncritical revisionist to take it to fanciful heights.[19] To do so ignores the strict moral codes and kinship obligations governing Aboriginal societies. While this is not to deny the possibility that some Aboriginal bands may have conducted raids on others to obtain women, virtually all the available evidence points directly at the sealers, who came ashore and seized Aboriginal women by force. William Stewart, a Sydney trader who visited the Bass Strait islands, informed the colonial secretary of New South Wales in 1815 that the sealers routinely obtained Aboriginal women by this means and kept them as virtual slaves. Stewart noted that they were then expected to hunt and forage for their captors and were transferred or disposed of as if they were personal property. Very few ever returned to their homeland, and failure to comply with the wishes of their masters invariably resulted in the women being half-hung, beaten with clubs or flogged with whips made from kangaroo sinews.[20] The horrendous testimony of women such as Buller (Jumbo), Tibb (Sarah), Bullrub and Wattecowwidyer (Wot) was recorded by George Augustus Robinson and should not be glibly ignored. Nor should the testimony of some of the sealers themselves be disregarded,[21] and as Keryn James has cautioned:

> Naturally, all the nuances of human relationships occurred after the initial act of kidnapping. There is evidence of negotiation, resistance and accommodation resulting either in abandonment for some, or liberation or marriage and family life for others. What must be acknowledged is the use of Indigenous women as 'unfree' and forced labour for the sealing industry ...[22]

In their quest for both women and seals these wild men of the southern waters covered extraordinary distances. In 1827 Major Edmund Lockyer of the 57th Regiment was sent to King George Sound in the brig *Amity* to establish the first British settlement in today's Western Australia. The expedition arrived on Christmas day to find four Aboriginal men, one badly injured, marooned on Michaelmas Island by sealers. If it had not been for the fortuitous arrival of the *Amity* they would have perished there. After returning the men to the mainland Lockyer began investigating the activities of the sealers along this stretch of coast. One of them was a New Zealand Maori, William Hook, a former seaman who claimed to have joined the sealing fraternity under duress.[23] Hook, in fact, had been involved with the sealers from a very young age,[24] but his statements provide valuable insights into the tactics used by the sealers to obtain women.

Shortly after landing in King George Sound the sealers were visited by local Aboriginal men, and although relations were friendly the locals refused to bring their women to the sealers' camp. To gain their confidence the sealers began taking the Aboriginal men on fishing excursions until the occasion finally arrived when five of the Aborigines requested to be taken to Green Island to hunt birds. John Randell and James Everett directed the boat crew to abandon their unsuspecting passengers as soon as they had gone ashore — a precursor for the stranding of Aboriginal men on Michaelmas Island. Once they were out of the way the sealers raided the Aboriginal camp and abducted four women, two of whom managed to escape the same night despite being tightly bound together. The other two remained in the hands of the sealers until they were rescued by Lockyer's men, by which time one of the captives had been severely injured by Samuel Bailey who was duly arrested. Further searches uncovered another three Aboriginal women, two from Van Diemen's Land and one from South Australia, who were first sent to Sydney and then repatriated home.[25] A number of Van Diemen's Land women also lived with sealers on Kangaroo Island off the coast of South Australia, where some of their descendants were among the pioneer settlers.[26]

The story that the Aborigines bartered women appears to have emanated from the sealers themselves, particularly through their able advocate James Kelly, a master mariner and harbourmaster. With his close personal and professional interest in the sealing industry Kelly was anything but an impartial witness, and it is a single incident recorded in the journal of his 1815–16 circumnavigation of Van Diemen's Land that is often cited as evidence of Aboriginal involvement in the barter of women. Kelly related a conversation between George Briggs, a sealer who accompanied him on the whaleboat voyage, and Mannalargenna, leader of the Cape Portland band in the north-east. Mannalargenna is said to have requested Briggs and the rest of Kelly's party to provide support with firearms in a planned attack on a neighbouring band at Eddystone Point led by Tolobunganah, who had allegedly formed an alliance with Michael Howe's bushranging gang. When Briggs refused assistance, Mannalargenna angrily retorted that Briggs had sided with the Cape Portland people in the past when the sealers wanted women. Immediately after Kelly related this conversation he added that Briggs had purchased his wife from the Cape Portland band, a statement that is not borne out by the facts. Briggs actually had two Aboriginal women, both of whom had been abducted by force. One was Woretemoeteryenner (otherwise known as Pung and a daughter of Mannalargenna). After bearing three of Briggs's children he sold her to fellow sealer John Thomas for one guinea. The second woman, Dumpe, later lived with the sealer Thomas Tucker.[27]

The testimony of fellow adventurer, Captain James Hobbs, who agreed with Kelly that Aboriginal men were heavily involved in the barter of women, is similarly highly questionable. Hobbs claimed that 'four or five carcasses of seals' were sufficient to acquire 'a native woman'.[28] Kelly was less specific, simply informing Commissioner John Thomas Bigge in 1820 that the sealers often purchased women from Aboriginal groups with skinned seal carcases. It is often overlooked that Kelly did admit the sealers 'sometimes carry them [Aboriginal women] off by force and employ them in hunting kangaroos for their skins and also in killing seals, at which the women are very expert'.[29] They certainly were.

The incident Kelly related in his journal of the 1815–16 circumnavigation of Van Diemen's Land also proved to be highly profitable. Through the services of the Aboriginal women Kelly and his companions accumulated 122 sealskins in addition to a large stock of kangaroo pelts, netting them the considerable sum of £180 when later sold at Hobart. On this occasion it was strictly a commercial arrangement: in return for kangaroo pelts Briggs provided the Cape Portland women with access to seals on offshore islands normally inaccessible. The Aborigines feasted on the carcases after they had been skinned. It is also of interest to note that while the women were working offshore they maintained contact with, and were nominally under the control of, their own menfolk through smoke signals.

It is difficult to accept that the Aboriginal bands of north-east Van Diemen's Land, in particular, would have continued bartering women over decades without any visible return and until there were virtually no women left. By November 1830 there were 74 Aborigines remaining in the north-east, only three of them women.[30] The following year George Augustus Robinson recorded that all the Aboriginal women living with the sealers were aged in their early twenties or younger. As the sealers had actively been raiding the coast before 1810 this further suggests a high mortality rate among the captives. The mobility of the sealers and their predatory behaviour was clearly a major factor in the decimation of north-east Van Diemen's Land's Indigenous population.[31]

The impact of the sealing fraternity on Aboriginal groups along the central north and north-west coasts was far less destructive than in the north-east. The central north is also a useful entry point into the Black War, a series of fragmented conflicts fought at various times in different places. The Western Plains and the Meander Valley in the central north of Van Diemen's Land was just one of those theatres, with the actions of the female renegade known as Walyer also serving as a timely reminder that there was anything but a uniform resistance to British incursion. A Tommeginner woman from Table Cape, Walyer is often said to have been abducted by Aborigines and sold to sealers.[32] The available evidence, however, suggests that she and her siblings were banished by the Tommeginner and willingly joined the sealers.[33] Banishment was extremely rare among Aboriginal societies anywhere in Australia, a form of punishment for only the most heinous offences. In pre-contact Australia it was also a virtual death sentence, but with Aboriginal societies on the north coast of Van Diemen's Land in complete disarray Walyer and her siblings not only survived their ordeal, they were able to return to the north-west with firearms and a determination to use them. They were joined by other displaced Aboriginal people, with Walyer soon emerging as their leader — the only female Aboriginal leader ever recorded in Van Diemen's Land. But she was certainly not the resistance fighter as is so often stated.[34] Although Walyer's band reputedly attacked

European huts,[35] they mostly preyed on other Aboriginal people.[36] Her reign of terror did not go unchallenged. On at least one occasion she and one of her confederates known as Jenny narrowly escaped death after being speared by the Big River people.[37]

Indeed, internecine conflict between the large socio-economic groups and often between bands continued even at the very height of the Black War,[38] an absence of pan-Aboriginality considerably weakening the overall effectiveness of Aboriginal resistance. The war in eastern Van Diemen's Land lasted from 1826 to early 1832, though conflict continued in the far north-west until as late as February 1842. Those 16 years of armed confrontation claimed the lives of hundreds of British colonists and effectively destroyed the Aboriginal people. Yet, while it may have ended in defeat, given the relatively small geographic size of the island and recognising the strong Aboriginal attachment to place as well as the continuation of internecine conflict, the Aboriginal people still managed to put up an extremely stout defence. On quite a number of occasions it was the Aborigines who were actually on the offensive.

The Meander Valley and Western Plains also provide an important snapshot of the wider conflict which erupted throughout southern and eastern Van Diemen's Land from 1826. In essence, the central north of Van Diemen's Land stretches from the Asbestos Range, just east of Port Sorell, westward of Emu Bay (Burnie), south to the Surrey Hills and Middlesex Plains, and east again to Quamby Bluff.[39] This was the customary territory of four bands of Aboriginal people with a combined population of between two and three hundred. The homeland of the Punnilepanner lay around Port Sorell while that of the Noeteeler was in the Hampshire Hills. The Quamby Bluff district, where much of the fighting took place, was home to the Pallittorre people, while the Plairhekechillerplue, occupied the area around Emu Bay.[40] The experience of the Pallittorre people of Quamby Bluff was at variance from elsewhere in Van Diemen's Land during the post-contact period. Until the early 1820s their territory was largely inaccessible to the British colonists owing to the dense forests which surrounded it, with encroachment only commencing when all other readily available grazing land had been alienated. Rather than sheep, cattle were the dominant livestock in this district, and the wealthy individuals who concentrated on beef production largely left control of their herds in the hands of overseers and assigned convicts who were already well-versed in the ways of frontier life. Importantly, these men also had access to horses, and because it was a new frontier they were heavily armed and mostly beyond reach of the law. They were men who had either been brutalised by the convict system or had gained sufficient bush skills to have complete faith in their own ability to deal with any violent situation.[41]

Some of them were equipped with Indian Pattern Smooth Bore muskets that were as lethal as modern shotguns. Others were weighed down by a brace of pistols and bayonets. Paddy Heagon, overseer of William Field's property near Deloraine, is alleged to have armed himself with a swivel gun which he had learnt to use while harpooning whales.[42] Swivel guns were the smallest type of cannon, largely used on ships and land as anti-personnel weapons as they were less than a metre long and could be quickly mounted almost anywhere. They had a wide arc of fire and their 1¼-inch bore allowed them to fire grapeshot with deadly effect. Heagon is said to have killed 19 Aborigines with the swivel gun charged with nails,[43] an action which Lyndall Ryan has described as a 'massacre'.[44] Keith Windschuttle noted, however, that mystery surrounds not only the identity of Paddy Heagon but how he could have obtained such a weapon.[45] The story was told to George Augustus Robinson by surveyor Henry Hellyer, who was certainly a credible informant, but given its second-hand basis and the uncertainty of Heagon's very existence, the particulars need to be handled with extreme caution. It could well have been an idle boast. After examining all the available evidence, as well as the range, calibre and other characteristics of swivel guns, WF Refshauge was adamant that while individuals could be killed in this manner it was physically and technically impossible to commit a multiple murder. In other words: 'there was no swivel gun massacre'.[46]

By 1826 the trickle of hooves west from the Norfolk Plains had become a veritable stampede, and early the following year there were at least 20 stock-keepers in the Meander Valley alone, their huts forming a line of fortified outposts bisecting Pallittorre territory. Relations had initially been friendly, and as elsewhere in Van Diemen's Land many of the stock-keepers acquired Aboriginal partners. How many were taken by force is unknown, but it was certainly a contributing factor in the development of hostilities.[47] One Aboriginal woman who was not forced into a relationship was Dolly Dalrymple, who had been raised in the household of the errant surgeon, Jacob Mountgarrett. The daughter of sealer George Briggs and Woretemoeteryenner, Dolly Dalrymple lived in the Meander Valley with the convict stock-keeper Thomas Johnson.[48] She was destined to play her own role in the Black War in the years ahead.

Another major factor in the breakdown of friendly relations was the stock-keepers' habit of shooting kangaroos to supplement their meagre rations. When the kangaroos disappeared, cattle, and in some cases sheep, filled the void. In December 1825 the Pallittorre expressed their displeasure at the hunting of kangaroos to stock-keeper James Cubitt, who responded by shooting at them. While Lyndall Ryan insisted that the Aborigines retaliated a few days later by surrounding Cubitt's hut, only to suffer 14 casualties from a 'shotgun' wielded by Dolly Dalrymple, she is badly mistaken.[49] That incident took place nearly six years later and involved the Big River people from south-eastern Van Diemen's Land — not the local Pallittorre — whose numbers by then had been seriously depleted.

With the influx of livestock the stock-keepers in the Meander Valley and on the Western Plains were at open war with the Aborigines by the middle of 1826. That many of the latter were killed is beyond question, but the two years 1827 and 1828 were particularly violent. It is also of interest that much of the fighting occurred during the winter months of both years, a time when the Pallittorre were usually on the coast to avoid the extreme cold of the high country and the associated difficulties of eking out a living.[50] In June 1827 the Pallittorre plundered a stock-keeper's hut at Daisy Plains and attempted to spear the overseer. He escaped to raise the alarm, with a party of stock-keepers tracking the raiders to their camp which they attacked at dawn. Aboriginal casualties are said to have been anywhere from one to nine.[51] The gravity of the situation resulted in a field police constable and two non-commissioned officers of the 40th Regiment being stationed at Daisy Plains. Later the same month the Pallittorre succeeded in killing overseer William Knight, though an assigned servant managed to reach Daisy Plains where a punitive expedition consisting of five men was quickly organised. Led by Corporal Shiners, they espied smoke near Laycock Falls (now known as Lobster Falls, and not Liffey Falls as Lyndall Ryan contends, which is on the opposite side of the Meander Valley).[52] There were six campfires, and as Shiners and his men approached at dusk they were detected by the Aborigines' dogs and began firing their guns from a distance of between 30 and 40 metres. One, a pistol, failed to discharge and the Aborigines immediately fled. While the attackers had every reason to inflate the number of casualties there was, in fact, only one. Both John Skinner and Thomas Williams agreed that the following morning they found one trail of blood but no sign of any deceased.[53] Despite that, an anonymous correspondent in Launceston

— far removed from the scene — later claimed that 60 Aborigines had been killed or wounded in this affray,[54] a figure far too high to be taken seriously. Indeed, such a catastrophic result from four firearms (possibly muskets) firing at an extended distance on dusk is an utter absurdity.

The Aborigines struck back the following day when another stock-keeper was killed at Quamby Bluff and the constable, soldiers and at least two stock-keepers again set out in pursuit. They returned to Daisy Plains with spears and other spoils of war; rumour had it that up to 30 Aborigines had been killed. A week later the Aborigines replied in force by killing two shepherds at Quamby Bluff, with 'nine or ten' Aborigines dying in the subsequent reprisal.[55] The fact that this conflict continued into the following winter makes it clear that while Aboriginal casualties may have been considerable they were nowhere near as high as Ryan insisted. The Pallittorre were a single band, with their total number unlikely to have exceeded 80 individuals. There is no evidence of involvement by up to 400 Aborigines as Ryan argued,[56] as it is our belief that this was purely a local struggle between the stock-keepers and the customary landowners. That is not to deny that by the end of 1828 the Pallittorre people had been seriously decimated, but the fact that they continued to return to their territory until as late as 1834 suggests that casualties have been considerably overstated.[57] It also proved to be a pyrrhic victory for the stock-keepers, as the crushing of Pallittorre resistance created a vacuum that was later exploited by the Big River people from the south.

Violence at this level was beyond the comprehension of Lieutenant Governor Arthur, who initially believed there was very little to fear from the Indigenous population following his arrival in 1824. An efficient administrator, Arthur divided the settled areas of eastern Van Diemen's Land into military districts in May 1826, where a resident magistrate was supported by field police — often ex-convicts — and a squad of soldiers. Rather than Aborigines, however, this was largely a response to the depredations of bushrangers, who remained a significant menace.[58] Arthur was confident that the Aboriginal people would welcome civilising influences and readily abandon their hunter-gatherer lifestyle. Notwithstanding the deaths of 13 colonists at the hands of Aborigines in 1824, the Lieutenant Governor warned the non-Indigenous population that the Aborigines were British subjects and therefore entitled to the full protection of English law. Stock-keepers and other rural workers on the frontier were advised that if their attacks on the Aborigines continued they would be prosecuted. Only one ever was. In 1824 convict William Tibbs was found guilty of manslaughter after killing an Aborigine, but the conviction was subsequently quashed and he was discharged.[59] With the execution of Musquito and the three Tasmanian Aborigines in 1825 and 1826 respectively, Arthur was confident that all animosity had now been laid to rest.

He was wrong. In response to the continuing dispossession of their land and the concomitant destruction of natural resources the Aborigines in the south-east launched at least 15 separate raids between September and December 1826 that left 19 settlers and stock-keepers dead and another five wounded. The Oyster Bay man, Kickerterpoller or 'Black Tom', was responsible for some of this violence, although his activities and those of his compatriots regularly overlapped. Occasionally they worked in collusion. 'Black Tom' became leader of the 'Tame Mob' following the execution of Musquito. They were tame no longer. As early as April 1826 'Black Tom' was identified as heading a raiding party at Dromedary Mountain between Hobart and New Norfolk which left a settler named Browning dead and his assigned servant injured.[60] The following June 'Black Tom's' close associates assaulted and robbed three stock-keepers near Jerusalem.[61] In November–December 1826 he was also involved in at least five separate incidents at Millers Bluff on the Macquarie River, Liffey Creek, Cross Marsh near Kempton (then Green Ponds), the Macquarie Plains south of Abyssinia and at Brown Mountain north of Pitt Water. Their depredations were thus wide-ranging, leaving in their wake another four settlers and stock-keepers dead.[62]

'Black Tom' was finally captured by soldiers led by the chief constable of Sorell, Alexander Laing. He was spared the noose and sentenced to incarceration at Macquarie Harbour on the west coast, though it is unlikely that he was sent to that forbidding institution of secondary punishment. Either through petitioning by his foster mother (who had remarried following the death of her husband Thomas Birch in 1821), or intervention by the Pitt Water magistrate, James Gordon, 'Black Tom' was released into Sarah Hodgson's care in early 1827.[63] By then, however, his habits had become too ingrained. Shortly afterwards he committed a spate of robberies and assaults in the southern Midlands.[64] 'Black Tom' was recaptured in November 1827 and released again in July 1828 to work as a guide for the roving parties which George Arthur had organised to hunt down and capture Aborigines in the settled districts. He later joined George Augustus Robinson's 'Friendly Mission' and died after contracting dysentery at Emu Bay (Burnie) in May 1832.[65]

His compatriots, the Oyster Bay people, had been increasingly unhappy with their changed circumstances from early 1824. In March of that year they killed stock-keeper James Doyle just north of Bagdad and burned down his hut.[66] Between July and August they killed another five stock-keepers, but it was their raid on the farm of James Hobbs at York Plains which best illustrates the reason for much of this aggression. As well as plundering Hobbs's hut and driving off cattle, they dug up and carried away a large quantity of potatoes.[67] Drought prevailed during 1824 and 1825, placing great stress on the

Aboriginal people,[68] though their well-orchestrated attacks further suggest that they were deliberately attempting to undermine the economic base of the colonists. In April 1825, for instance, they raided the property of Temple Pearson and drove his flock of sheep into the Elizabeth River.[69] Again, much of the violence was concentrated in the southern Midlands, with Aboriginal women often used as decoys and scouts before attacks were launched.[70]

In early 1825 a stock-keeper was speared west of Oatlands and two others killed on the upper Macquarie River.[71] While there were no attacks on the Central Plateau to the end of 1825 that was soon to change, and by early 1826 the Big River people had also become firmly embroiled in the developing hostilities. They were the most formidable of all the Van Diemen's Land Aboriginal groups, and their involvement resulted in at least 13 settlers and servants being killed during 1826.[72] Faced with this escalating violence, George Arthur altered his approach. In late November 1826 he issued a new proclamation which allowed the settlers to use force to repel any Aborigines who appeared to have hostile intentions. If they were unable to undertake this measure themselves they could now call on assistance from the nearest field police and military detachment.[73]

As the Aborigines were technically British subjects there could be no declaration of war. This was a counter-insurgency campaign, and one in which the soldiers were only of minimal advantage. The British Army was based on harsh discipline and blind obedience, with any sign of initiative quickly stifled. Their training and expertise was ideal for counter-insurgency campaigns in urban areas but hopelessly ineffectual in frontier situations.[74] The field police were a different matter, as many of the ex-convict constables had extensive bush experience and they were nominally in charge.[75] Although resented by the soldiers, Arthur's proclamation soon showed its worth when a party of police and soldiers clashed with the Oyster Bay people near Pitt

Water. Fourteen Aborigines were killed and 10 captured. Another action near Abyssinia left two Big River men dead.[76]

The following year, however, 30 colonists were killed by either the Big River people or their Oyster Bay neighbours. Their raids were conducted so skilfully and with such daring that many colonists feared a major offensive. Finally coming to the realisation that the Aborigines were responding to the alienation of their land and the destruction of natural resources, George Arthur briefly toyed with the idea of setting aside an Aboriginal reserve in the largely untouched north-east of Van Diemen's Land.[77] This had actually been mooted in the press as early as February 1826, but by the time Arthur seized on it as a possible solution the attitudes of the colonists had hardened considerably. From late 1826 the press was baying for one of two alternatives: removal of the Aborigines from the Tasmanian mainland — or their complete extermination.[78]

In the summer of 1828 elements of the Oyster Bay and Big River peoples descended on the settled districts from the high country west of the River Ouse. In January a convict working in a road gang was killed and two others wounded by the Oyster Bay people near Kempton. They remained in the area for at least four weeks, hunting kangaroos and burning off large tracts of grassland. At every opportunity they also harassed the settlers' flocks. By March the Oyster Bay people were in the Eastern Marshes, burning huts and haystacks, before moving to the coast where they camped over winter.[79] The Big River people, on the other hand, concentrated most of their attacks in the southern Midlands between Oatlands and Bothwell, an area particularly suited for hit-and-run raids, with isolated huts and farmhouses proving irresistible targets. The southern Midlands consists of a series of narrow river valleys along which the farms of settlers were surrounded by pockets of cleared land and separated from their neighbours by ridges that were then covered in dense forest. The high ground thus provided ideal cover for the Aborigines, while the narrow confines of the valleys made it easier to descend and cross exposed areas near the farms before their occupants were able to react. Many farms in the southern Midlands were attacked multiple times, forcing considerable numbers of the settlers to abandon their properties and seek land in safer localities.[80]

John Sherwin's farm on the Clyde River was struck four times between August 1829 and May 1830. In February 1830 the Big River people waited until Sherwin and his assigned servants had finished their lunch and were either inside or close by the buildings. At an opportune moment an Aborigine sprinted across the cleared ground with a firestick and after reaching the back of the buildings undetected quickly set fire to the thatch on the roof of Sherwin's house before running across to the servants' quarters and repeating the operation. The arsonist had safely returned to his colleagues before Sherwin's men noticed the flames and all hands began fighting the fire. Realising the building was lost, Sherwin directed his men to salvage his possessions inside. While all this was going on another two Aboriginal men descended from the ridge with firesticks and calmly walked along the wooden fences setting fires at intervals. It was not until the fences were ablaze that Sherwin finally noticed the Aborigines dancing on the opposite side of the river. They reputedly yelled in English: 'Go away you white buggers — what business have you here?' When Sherwin prevented one of his men from going towards the raiders with a gun they called him a coward and continued their dancing. Regardless of the actual dialogue, this was a typical surprise raid on an isolated farmstead that was carried out so effectively by the Aborigines at the height of the Black War. Sherwin, though, was made of tougher fibre than many others: he soon rebuilt.[81]

In January 1828 the Ben Lomond people from the high country of north-east Van Diemen's Land moved into the Eastern Tiers where they attempted to kill stock-keeper Daniel Cubitt who had a reputation for murdering Aborigines. Although Cubitt escaped, his attackers warned that 'they would have him yet'. They never did. On separate occasions Cubitt was speared at least six times but managed to survive his wounds. The Ben Lomond people continued past Campbell Town towards the Lake River, plundering huts for provisions and terrifying local settlers. By the time they reached Lake River they were raiding several huts every day.[82] The following April they returned to their own territory and chased a stock-keeper working for settler John Batman from one of their favourite hunting grounds. Batman and four of his men, supported by three field police constables and two soldiers, set out in pursuit. They surprised the Aborigines at their campfires and although Batman later claimed to have wounded one man and captured a teenage boy (who escaped the following day),[83] it is likely that Aboriginal casualties were considerably higher. The future co-founder of Melbourne was an accomplished bushman who — like Cubitt — gained a notorious reputation for killing Aborigines.[84]

On 15 April 1828 Lieutenant Governor Arthur issued yet another proclamation which effectively divided Van Diemen's Land into 'settled' and 'unsettled' districts. Troops were deployed across wide areas to prevent Aborigines from passing through the designated settled areas.[85] Arthur was confident that this arrangement would be successful, and to ensure that the Aborigines were aware of his new policy he later accepted the advice of Surveyor General George Frankland and created a series of picture boards illustrating the benefits of harmonious relations which were nailed to trees along the frontier.[86] This was a ridiculous gesture, with the depictions of right and wrong having little meaning for the Aborigines, particularly in view of the fact that settlers regularly fired on them whenever they were seen. Even more bizarre was Arthur's plan to issue Aboriginal leaders with passes to enter the settled areas if they could guarantee peaceful intentions. To obtain their pass, however, the Aborigines had to apply directly to the Lieutenant Governor.[87] The idea was laughable.

Yet, when the Aborigines failed to appear in the settled districts during the winter of 1828 Arthur felt assured that his new policy was having the desired effect. Nor had any Aborigines been sighted along the frontier. High hopes were rudely shattered with the coming of warmer weather. Spring saw the Oyster Bay and Big River peoples launch a series of raids on stock-keepers and farmhouses in the Eastern Marshes, the Midlands and along the Clyde River. At the same time the Ben Lomond people began burning down the huts of stock-keepers along the Nile River further north.[88] Despite his best attempts, Arthur was forced to concede that the settled districts themselves were now under siege. Settlers across a wide swathe of eastern Van Diemen's Land clamoured for military protection to repel this new threat, and after consultation with the Executive Council Arthur declared martial law on 1 November 1828. By this measure the military were empowered to arrest without warrant or shoot on sight any Aborigine found within the settled districts.[89] This was not the first time that martial law had been invoked in Van Diemen's Land, the precedent established in April 1815 by then Lieutenant Governor Thomas Davey to counter the bushranging epidemic. On that occasion martial law had remained in force for six months:[90] in this instance it was to remain in place for three whole years.

Following the proclamation of martial law Arthur acted on the advice of the experienced Oatlands police magistrate, Thomas Anstey, and created two different mobile patrols to operate against Aboriginal insurgents. Pursuing parties consisted of eight to 10 men, mostly soldiers and field police, whose task was to prevent attacks on settlers. They were rarely in the right place at the right time,[91] and the pursuing parties were certainly less successful than the six official roving parties which combed the settled districts in a bid to capture Aborigines. The roving parties were usually led by a field police constable and comprised (where possible) an Aboriginal guide in addition to four or five assigned convicts with a good knowledge of the frontier. Other roving parties consisted of field police and soldiers.[92] Jorgen Jorgenson was typical of the leaders: literate and bush-wise — though in his case one of the least successful.[93] Another roving party was led by the black West Indian, Gilbert Robertson, at that time chief constable at Richmond, and he had a particularly useful guide in 'Black Tom'. Robertson's party quickly achieved results. In early November 1828 they captured five Aborigines from the Campbell Town district in the northern Midlands near Great Swanport. One of them was the accomplished leader, Umarrah. After a year's confinement in Richmond gaol Umarrah was released to join George Augustus Robinson's 'Friendly Mission', but his days of fighting the colonists were still far from over.[94]

A number of free settlers, notably John Batman in the north-east, formed their own roving parties. The problem was that they tended to kill more Aborigines than they ever captured, mostly through campfire ambush.[95] In August 1829 Batman also raised the idea of recruiting Aboriginal trackers from New South Wales to pursue the Tasmanians. George Arthur tentatively agreed with the suggestion and nine Aboriginal men, the majority from the south coast of New South Wales, were eventually brought to Van Diemen's Land.[96] Led by Batman they played a decisive role in the capture of 11 Oyster Bay people, mostly women and children, near Great Swanport in September 1829. The captives were lodged in the Campbell Town gaol.[97] Convinced of the effectiveness of this new strategy, Batman tried a slightly different ploy in April 1830. Four of the captured women were released on the proviso that they assist Batman's two most trusted mainland recruits, Crook and Pigeon, to bring in their compatriots. The plan went awry when the women escaped and the New South Wales Aborigines returned to Batman's property near Ben Lomond empty-handed. Three of the women were later recaptured near the Piper River in the far north, while the fourth is believed to have been shot and killed.[98] The New South Wales Aborigines served with at least one other roving party and a few of them also joined George Augustus Robinson's 'Friendly Mission'. Always keen to keep the credit for himself, Robinson played down their contribution, which was probably far more significant than he cared to admit.[99]

Between November 1828 and November 1830 the various roving parties captured between 20–30 Aborigines. At the same time, however, another 60 were reputedly killed.[100] To encourage more live captives George Arthur introduced a bounty of £5 for adults and £2 for children in February 1830;[101] it had little effect as the killing continued. By that time the roving parties as well as many settlers were also beginning to exploit their knowledge of Aboriginal seasonal movements. In January 1829 a group of Oyster Bay people arrived at Moulting Lagoon to find settlers waiting in ambush. In the clash which followed 10 Aborigines were shot dead and three captured. Similarly, when a group of Big River people arrived in the Eastern Marshes on their way to the coast two months later they were surprised by Gilbert Robertson's roving party. In this encounter five Aborigines were slain and only one captured alive. The death toll was not all one-sided. Between January and June 1829 the Oyster Bay people killed eight assigned convicts in the Pitt Water district.[102]

Notwithstanding Robertson's lethal action in the Eastern Marshes, he had considerable empathy for the Aborigines. While Robertson recognised they were fighting for their territory and survival he was equally aware that the chances of capturing them alive were slim. It was Robertson who first raised the idea of appointing a 'conciliator' to travel throughout Van Diemen's Land with Aboriginal guides to induce the Aborigines to lay down their arms by peaceful means. He naturally envisaged himself undertaking that role, but when the scheme was finally approved by George Arthur the man chosen was George Augustus Robinson, who had been thinking along similar lines.[103]

In the winter of 1829 nine roving parties and perhaps 100 soldiers were actively patrolling the settled districts searching for Aboriginal infiltrators.[104] While none were found, with the coming of spring the colonists once more found themselves under attack. In September a settler and three servants were killed on the east coast and in the southern Midlands.[105] The following month a settler and a soldier were wounded in separate incidents in the New Norfolk and Kempton districts. A shepherd named John Brown was killed near Jerusalem and two stock-keepers harassed with spears in the same district. Near the Ouse River another shepherd was beaten to death with waddies and a stock-keeper wounded by spears. A settler by the name of Thomson was injured near the Shannon River. November proved to be even more lethal. Thomas Clark was burned to death after the Aborigines set fire to his master's house near Bothwell and a female servant was killed at Green Valley. James Halliday was slain near Kempton and at least 10 other settlers and servants were wounded in a series of wide-ranging attacks.[106]

In December 1829 settler James Doran was speared near the Sorell Rivulet and died from his injuries,[107] but how many Aborigines were killed in encounters with the roving parties, settlers and stock-keepers will never be known. Under martial law only military personnel were authorised to shoot on sight, and yet this was a common practice among settlers and their servants both within and without the settled districts.[108] John Batman's roving party offers a good example of what went on outside the government's purview. In September

1829 they tracked a group of Ben Lomond people to their camp one evening and closed in with the intention of rushing in at first light and capturing as many Aborigines as possible. According to Batman, a member of his party inadvertently struck the barrel of his musket against another and alerted the dogs in the Aboriginal camp which attacked the ambushers. The Aborigines fled and Batman ordered his men to open fire. They managed to catch a woman and a child around two years of age in the camp, and then followed trails of blood to discover two men who had been seriously wounded. They told the roving party that at least 10 other men and two women had also been seriously wounded by the gunfire. As it turned out, both men were so badly injured they were unable to complete the long trek back to Batman's property. In the circumstances Batman felt obliged — so he said — to end their suffering by summary execution. For the capture of one woman and a child anywhere from two to 16 adults had thus been slain. And this was a rare instance of the action being reported. The captured woman, Luggenemenener, was afterwards confined in Campbell Town gaol: Batman kept her son.[109]

Constantly on the run, many other Aborigines succumbed to privations and illness. Birth rates plummeted, so there was never any chance of resistance being sustained in the longer term. By the summer of 1829–30 there is reason to believe that the Indigenous population of south-eastern Van Diemen's Land had fallen to just a few hundred, possibly even less.[110] Despite that, the colonists once again panicked after another series of deadly raids were launched against them. In January 1830 a ticket-of-leave convict (ie a transported felon who had earned limited freedom through good behaviour) was killed near the Ouse River and the following month the violence escalated.[111] A settler named Brodie was wounded by spears at Berriedale and an assigned servant, Lawrence Deening, killed at Black Marsh. At Great Jordan Lagoon a servant of Thomas Betts was wounded by spears and James McCarty battered by waddies. Both men survived. Not so William Hepley at Hollow Tree Bottom, who was fatally injured by spears and waddies. A servant was also killed on the Clyde River, as were two others near Kempton. In the same district a settler by the name of Blundle survived after being speared, but a 10-year-old boy tending his father's sheep at Constitution Hill near Bagdad was speared to death by Aboriginal raiders.[112] The police magistrate at Bothwell, who already had 30 soldiers at his command, maintained that he required three times that number to guarantee the safety of settlers in the surrounding district.[113]

The presence of troops made little difference to the Big River and Oyster Bay peoples, and the elaborate defensive works created by some of the wealthier settlers offer clear evidence of a siege mentality. After Captain Torlesse took possession of a property called Montacute between Bothwell and Hamilton, he encircled the house and outbuildings with a high brick and stone wall for protection, installing firing positions at intervals to repulse any raiders. Despite these extensive measures the Aborigines attacked Montacute on six separate occasions, the last time with firesticks in February 1830.[114] Following the destruction of John Sherwin's house on the Clyde River for the fourth time settlers in the Bothwell district warned the Lieutenant Governor that if military protection was not substantially increased their occupancy of the contested land would no longer be tenable.[115]

Arthur called on the Aborigines Committee, which had been formed in November 1829, to develop an effective means of dealing with captured Aborigines and to determine what measures could be implemented to safeguard the lives and properties of the settlers. Apart from condoning Arthur's existing policies, the Committee recommended that all operations against the Aborigines should be placed in the hands of resident police magistrates and that every police station should be reinforced with a detachment of mounted police to respond quickly to every emergency. It was further suggested that the number of field police should be increased.[116]

In the winter of 1830 the Big River and Oyster Bay people appear to have largely remained in the high country west of the Ouse River, well aware of the fate that was likely to befall them if they attempted to reach the coast. Their strategy was to attack and plunder outlying stock huts for provisions and by August four of the settlers' servants had been killed in a series of well-executed raids.[117] Although Arthur was completely unaware of how few Aborigines actually remained, he realised that if the initiative was not seized the Indigenous people were likely to be exterminated by the settlers. On 27 August 1830 the Executive Council supported his call for a *levée en masse*, the mobilisation of the civilian population, who would join with the military and police in a large-scale operation against the Aborigines within the settled districts. This was the famous — or infamous — 'Black Line', a human cordon formed outside the northern and western extremities of the settled districts. The intention was to drive the remaining Big River and Oyster Bay people through the Forestier Peninsula and Eaglehawk Neck into the natural trap of Tasman Peninsula where they could be captured.[118] By this means Lieutenant Governor Arthur hoped that the frontier conflict which had cost so many lives on both sides of the frontier in eastern Van Diemen's Land could be finally brought to an end. The effectiveness of this extraordinary measure was soon to be put to the test.

6

THE 'BLACK LINE' AND 'FRIENDLY MISSION'

On a theoretical level the 'Black Line' may have appeared sound. On a practical level it presented Lieutenant Governor Arthur with a logistical nightmare, particularly in view of the inhospitable terrain and climatic conditions. As it transpired, the Black Line rapidly descended into haphazard chaos, with never any chance of accomplishing its stated aim of driving the Oyster Bay and Big River peoples into the confines of the Tasman Peninsula. This, however, was not immediately apparent. On 1 October 1830 Arthur extended martial law throughout the island colony as participants in the human cordon gathered at their starting positions.[1] In total some 2200 colonists, roughly 10 per cent of the non-Indigenous population, was directly involved. Of that number 550 were soldiers from the 63rd, 57th and 17th Regiments, more than half the available troops in Van Diemen's Land. Apart from field police the remainder were either volunteer civilians or ticket-of-leave convicts, the latter compelled to join the Black Line unless they could provide a substitute in their place. Although a few settlers and merchants also took part, most could not spare the time away from their farms and businesses. Quite a number of their sons participated, but in many instances they sent their assigned servants to join the line.[2] To free the troops, temporary militias were formed in Hobart and Launceston.[3]

The Black Line was staggered in sectors extending from St Patrick's Head on the east coast, westwards in an approximate U-shape to the South Esk River, south to Campbell Town in the northern Midlands, and north-west along the Meander, Macquarie and Lake Rivers.[4] Arthur organised supplies, clothing and weapons for his mighty force, most of which proved to be inadequate for the task. Each man was allocated a daily ration of 900 grams of flour, 680 grams of meat, 85 grams of sugar and 15 grams of tea. On commencement every participant was issued with rations for seven days which, it was believed, would be sufficient until they reached one of the thirty-odd ration depots established at key locations in advance of the line.[5]

Tea and sugar came from the government commissariat stores, while meat and flour were purchased from farmers and storekeepers, not infrequently at grossly inflated prices. Jackets and shoes were also supplied from the commissariat stores, while women convicts at the Female Factory — a prison on the outskirts of Hobart — manufactured 640 pairs of trousers.[6] Firearms were limited to just 900 muskets (and 30 000 cartridges), which meant that only two in every five men on the line were armed. The unarmed provided logistical support to maintain the momentum, but the shortage of firearms created a degree of dissatisfaction among those engaged in the operation, who expected to be at least armed for self-defence.[7] Optimistically, 300 sets of handcuffs were available to restrain captives,[8] perhaps ten times more than the number of Aborigines actually within the settled districts when the Black Line began.

Arthur's grand force was divided into three divisions, each under the direct control of Major Sholto Douglas and Captains Wentworth and Donaldson, the latter two respectively from the 63rd and 57th Regiments. Douglas commanded the northern division which slowly pushed south, while Wentworth advanced east from a line extending from New Norfolk to Lake Echo. With 300 men from Launceston and the Norfolk Plains, Donaldson's division extended over the Central Plateau.[9] These divisions were further sub-divided into corps — again under the control of military officers. Local magistrates organised civilians into the smallest units comprising parties of 10, with section leaders issued with maps to enable them to maintain their correct position in the line.[10] Unfortunately, most of the maps were highly inaccurate and often incomplete. It was not surprising, then, that many sections became hopelessly lost in the inhospitable terrain in which they soon found themselves.[11]

Following preliminary sorties the Black Line commenced moving forward on 7 October 1830 across a 195-kilometre front. There was no attempt at stealth, the idea being to frighten the Aborigines into moving ahead of the cordon.[12] Right from the outset there were obvious gaps, particularly in the elevated western areas, where snow and icy winds soon separated the various sections: shouting a designated number, blowing bugles and firing muskets were the only means of ensuring at least some contact, tenuous though it often was.[13] As the Black Line advanced into rugged, often unexplored terrain, desertions commenced and many sections soon lost their way. Rations, which were at best of indeterminate quality, had to be supplemented by hunting and foraging, necessitating unplanned halts by sections right along the Black Line.[14] The conditions were also hard on footwear, with Arthur forced to order a continual supply from Hobart and Launceston. It was never sufficient, with many participants reduced to walking bare-footed.[15] Given the circumstances, it was rather remarkable that after almost three weeks in the field the northern and western divisions were finally able to come together on 20 October. This, in fact, was the first time that a close cordon had actually been effected since the operation began.[16]

How many Aborigines had already slipped through the line will never be known. The worry was that hostilities continued behind the advancing human cordon. Even before participants in the Black Line took a step forward, three assigned servants were killed and another grievously wounded on the South Esk River.[17] Umarrah, leader of the Tyerernotepanner band of the north Midlands who had been liberated from Richmond gaol to join George Augustus Robinson's 'Friendly Mission', was heavily involved in actions further north. After absconding from the 'Friendly Mission' near Trial Harbour on the west coast, Umarrah had displayed uncanny ability by making his way back to the Campbell Town district. In October 1830 he presented himself to military authorities in Launceston, and at George Arthur's request joined the Black Line. Absconding yet again, he led a series of raids against the settlers in the Tamar and South Esk River valleys, extending his sphere of operations into the north-east.[18]

On 14 October 1830 Captain Stewart was wounded by spears within five kilometres of Launceston.[19] Three days later a settler named Gildas was killed on the West Tamar and his hut plundered.[20] More huts were raided along the South Esk River, a series of actions which culminated in the spearing of shepherds Murray and Davis. They survived, unlike the assigned servant Peter McCasker, who was killed at Retreat near Westbury.[21] This attack almost certainly involved a separate Aboriginal group. Umarrah was finally recaptured by Robinson's 'Friendly Mission' in August 1831,[22] and he was spared the indignity and suffering of forced exile by succumbing to dysentery at Launceston in March the following year.[23] Umarrah's brief campaign in the north is nevertheless a reminder of the ongoing conflict to the rear of Arthur's massive operation, and it is often overlooked that the Black War also continued in advance of the Black Line. On 16 October 1830 the assigned servant, Thomas Pratt, was killed by spears and waddies near Sorell. Two days later settler William Gangell was wounded by spears near Pitt Water and his 11-year-old son beaten with waddies. On the very same day another Pitt Water settler, Thomas Coffin, was also speared and fortuitously survived his injuries.[24]

Be that as it may, the divisions under Douglas and Wentworth continued south in an ever-tightening line. Donaldson's division remained behind the main front in a bid to catch any Aborigines who managed to slip through the cordon.[25] On 25 October Arthur received reports of an Aboriginal band trapped ahead and halted the line between Sorell and Prosser Bay for three weeks.[26] It was too late. The previous day a civilian advance party led by Edward Walpole had inadvertently stumbled on an Aboriginal camp towards dusk. Rather than requesting assistance they waited until dawn before rushing in to capture their human quarry, an action that was only partly successful. Although one man and a boy were taken, two other Aborigines were shot dead. It later emerged that 26 men and 15 women and children from the camp made their escape through the Black Line to safety.[27] This proved to be the only tangible result of the entire campaign.

During the enforced bivouac Arthur kept his force occupied by constructing abattis, a rudimentary form of fencing, to strengthen the human cordon.[28] Sentries and dogs patrolled constantly along the entire line. Such was the rugged terrain, the monotonous (and often non-existent) provisions, the constant fear of an Aboriginal spear hurtling through the air, and the continual drenching rain that morale plummeted to a new low. One settler who attempted to arouse discontent among his companions was sent home in disgrace, while three convicts had their ticket-of-leave revoked through desertion.[29] They were particularly unfortunate, as desertions had been common almost from the outset. Arthur attempted to raise the morale of his force by adding tobacco and soap to the rations,[30] while establishing depots immediately behind the line where purchased livestock was slaughtered and butchered by ten convicts to provide fresh meat on a regular basis. Local farmers again pushed up their prices to cash in on this golden opportunity. Flour was at this time retailing in Hobart at 2½d per pound; Arthur's administration paid farmers in the Pitt Water district 4d per pound to supply the Black Line.[31]

By 28 October Donaldson's western division had converged on the township of Bothwell, where the men briefly socialised and enjoyed the fruits of civilisation after enduring often horrendous conditions. The following day they were mustered and marched south-east along the existing road system to Richmond. Apart from this forced march rapidly disintegrating into a 'shambles' as individuals chose to walk at their own pace, it also makes a mockery of any claim that a tight cordon was maintained throughout the Black Line operation. In this instance Donaldson's men skirted huge chunks of the countryside in a bid to strengthen the southern perimeter.[32]

When Arthur's now unified force finally lurched forward to slowly close on the neck of the Forestier Peninsula on 17 November, there were high hopes that the remaining Aborigines would soon be trapped in the natural penitentiary of Tasman Peninsula. A sweep of East Bay Neck was completed on 25 November and only served to confirm the worst: there was no sign of any Aborigines ahead. Arthur was no longer under any illusions that his campaign had been successful. The following day the men were issued with rations for three days and ordered to disperse. The civilians returned to their homes and the soldiers to their usual stations scattered throughout the settled districts.[33]

For all its faults the Black Line had briefly stimulated the economy of Van Diemen's Land,[34] but it had also come at an enormous cost. The final tally was in the order of £30 000 — almost half the colonial revenue for an entire year — so expensive that it was finally paid by the British government from its annual funding for the Convict Department.[35] Arthur's brainchild was the largest single military operation ever undertaken on Australian soil until the Second World War,[36] but it also proved to be a total failure, ultimately defeated by a whole raft of factors. One was the exceptional bushcraft of the Aboriginal people, though it needs to be added that if their numbers had been greater than they actually were perhaps a modicum of success might have been achieved. That, of course, still leaves open the question of whether live captures would have exceeded fatalities. Possibly of even greater import was the terrain, which ensured that many areas were unable to be searched at all owing to the difficulty of access. Frigid conditions and torrential rain further compounded the problems, but it should not be overlooked that local commanders made more than their fair share of errors. This was exemplified by Captain Donaldson choosing to march his entire division from Bothwell to Richmond while abandoning any pretext of searching the countryside for Aboriginal fugitives. Nor was it ever possible to effectively seal the gaps which existed along the cordon, no less so than at night. Sentries and blazing bonfires made little difference, and it was almost certainly during the twilight hours that most of the Aborigines managed to flee to safety.

One year later, in October 1831, a smaller version of the Black Line was organised to catch approximately 20 Aborigines who had been harassing local settlers further north. This operation involved 74 civilians and 10 soldiers sweeping across a narrow front of 1.5 kilometres towards the Freycinet Peninsula on the mid-east coast. Sentries and bonfires were again used at night even though the gaps on this occasion were almost non-existent. Yet, for all the precautions, the majority of the Aborigines reached safety through an 80 metre breach in the very centre of the cordon during the night. There were no captives or casualties.[37]

Contemporary critics of the Black Line — and there were many — considered the operation to have been a complete farce which squandered a huge sum of money for no apparent purpose. More recent commentators have nevertheless argued that the sheer scale of the campaign awed the Aborigines into submission.[38] It is certainly true that this was the first time they would have understood the enormous resources which the colonists could amass against them. Moreover, elements of bands from the north-east of Van Diemen's Land who managed to escape through the Black Line later sought refuge with Robinson's 'Friendly Mission', and Robinson himself was not above threatening that a similar action would be launched again if they did not accept his protection.[39] But this was not the case with the Oyster Bay and Big River people who were the express targets of Arthur's campaign. Their fight continued until almost the bitter end, although it is relevant that much of the remaining fighting took place in the north of Van Diemen's Land, rather than the severely contested south-east.

Summer was usually a quiet time in the on-going conflict as the Big River and Oyster Bay peoples hunted in the interior. The warmer months of 1830–31 were particularly quiet, with the colonists apparently having good reason to believe that the Black Line had been far more effectual than its critics allowed. But those hopes were again dashed when a series of fatal clashes occurred in the north. In late January 1831 a man and child were speared on the West Tamar River, while Mary McCasker, already widowed by the Black War, was killed by Aborigines at Retreat on the Dairy Plains. Two months later the sawyers, John Taylor and Edward Sharpe, were wounded near Ben

Lomond. Later the same month Mrs Cunningham was mortally wounded by spears on the East Tamar River, and two soldiers were injured on the Norfolk Plains, near today's Longford. The pressure was maintained. Thomas Rattan, a servant of Captain Stewart, was wounded by spears at Ivory's Bend on the Tamar River in April, while further south the assigned servants, Carter and Boss, were killed near Lake Sorell in May.[40]

The fighting was at times considerably widespread. The daughter of settler Bassett Dickson was injured near Ellenthorpe and two servants wounded by spears at Morven. Jane Kennedy was battered to death by waddies near the Ouse River in June and the wife of a settler named Triffitt was wounded by spears. In many instances huts were plundered for provisions.[41] It was in the north, however, that a well-known incident involving Dolly Dalrymple and the Big River people took place on 22 August. Living at the time with convict stock-keeper Thomas Johnson, whom she would later marry, Dolly Dalrymple was alone with her two children, six-year-old Jane and two-year-old Sarah when the Big River people attacked Johnson's hut. Jane sustained a spear wound in the leg, but her mother held off the raiders with a musket for six hours until Johnson arrived back at the hut on horseback and the Big River people withdrew. This incident has often been grossly exaggerated, with Dalrymple held to have killed up to 14 Aborigines; in fact, there were probably no fatalities.[42] For her stoic defence, however, Dolly Dalrymple was rewarded by Arthur's administration with 20 acres (eight hectares) of land near Perth, where Johnson erected a new home and established himself as a carter after gaining his ticket-of leave.[43] The couple were to prosper.

Just nine days after they were repulsed by Dolly Dalrymple, the Big River people exacted revenge in an action which sent shockwaves reverberating throughout Van Diemen's Land. On 31 August 1831 they killed Bartholomew Thomas and his overseer, William Parker, near Port Sorrell. The first landowner in the district, Bartholomew Thomas's brother Jocelyn was at that time the colonial treasurer of Van Diemen's Land and a member of the Executive Council. Bartholomew was a former military officer and veteran of the Napoleonic Wars who later served with Simon Bolivar when he liberated South America from Spanish domination. On taking up his land near Port Sorell Thomas had also established friendly relations with the local Punnilerpanner band, a relationship which meant nothing to the Big River warriors.[44]

Further violent actions took place in both the northern and southern regions of eastern Van Diemen's Land as the year 1831 slowly drew to a close. In September a cook was wounded by spears near Pitt Water and an assigned servant named Charles Hughes beaten with waddies at Brushy Plains.[45] The following month one of William Archer's servants was wounded by spears near Westbury — again in the north — and in December another cook was similarly wounded near Botherton's Marsh.[46] Huts were continually looted as the Aborigines sought desperately needed provisions, but the end was already in sight. With their numbers depleted, the surviving Oyster Bay and Big River peoples knew their resistance campaign could no longer be sustained. In January 1832 they were contacted by Aboriginal envoys of George Augustus Robinson's 'Friendly Mission' near Lake Echo on the Central Plateau, and after giving Robinson's terms serious consideration they finally agreed to lay down their arms. There were just 16 men, nine women and one child left alive.[47] Whether they were actually the last of the Big River people is nonetheless debatable. In December 1840 surveyor James Erskine Calder (later Surveyor General) was instructed to cut a track to Macquarie Harbour:

> When I had proceeded about 20 miles from Lake St Clair, I came to a small plain where I found a native encampment comprising

> two wigwams (sufficient for 6 or 8 persons) which had evidently been deserted only a few days … The footprints about them, though lately obliterated by recent rains left no doubt of their being those of persons not troubled by boots. That they had lately been occupied was also to be inferred from the appearance of a fire place, from pieces of kangaroo flesh which were lying about only partly decayed etc.[48]

Calder later observed Aborigines on the lower ridges of Frenchman's Cap, but they disappeared as night closed in. Who these people were and what happened to them is not known: there is no record of them having been seen again, and their fate thus remains a mystery. They were never sighted by George Augustus Robinson, whose 'Friendly Mission' was the second string in Lieutenant Governor Arthur's bow and the one which ultimately achieved the results so desperately sought. On the other hand, while conciliation was a creditable means of ending hostilities (at least in eastern Van Diemen's Land) the overall effect of the 'Friendly Mission' in enticing the Aborigines into exile on a Bass Strait island was to bring them perilously close to extinction. That said, there can be no denying that the man who brought it to fulfilment was an extraordinary individual whose travels throughout the length and breadth of Van Diemen's Land would surely have destroyed lesser souls.

George Augustus Robinson was born in 1791 — probably in London — the son of a builder. Although he received little formal education Robinson was an avid reader who immersed himself in religion from an early age. He followed in his father's footsteps and became a builder, but in 1822 Robinson planned to join a utopian settlement in Nicaragua. On the eve of his departure news filtered back that the scheme was fraudulent, and it was only then that he turned his attention to Van Diemen's Land. Leaving his wife and five young children, Robinson sailed from England and arrived in Hobart in January 1824, quickly establishing himself as a building contractor. Within a year of his arrival Robinson's fortunes were already on the rise. He employed several men and had accumulated the substantial sum of £400, yet despite this success it was two years before Robinson's wife and children finally decided to join him. Almost certainly through his involvement with local religious groups Robinson also became interested in the Aboriginal people, particularly after the outbreak of the Black War in 1826 which coincided with the deterioration of his financial circumstances. While Gilbert Robertson had been among those who first raised the idea of ending hostilities through conciliation, Lieutenant Governor Arthur had done little about it, and it was not until May 1828 that he finally began providing rations to the Bruny Islanders and other Aborigines who had avoided confrontation. In March the following year Arthur advertised for 'a steady man of good character to effect an intercourse with the natives'.[49]

By now convinced he had been chosen by God to save the Aborigines from the brutalities being inflicted upon them, Robinson successfully applied for the position. Having read accounts of missionary endeavours in the Pacific Islands, he soon went beyond the task of distributing government rations to construct a village of huts, each with its own garden, to wean his Aboriginal charges into European ways. Robinson intended to teach them agriculture, to clothe them and to educate their children in a school. Education for Robinson was based solely on the bible, but he quickly realised that the first step in his plan to 'civilise' the Aborigines was to learn the local Aboriginal language and as much as possible of their cultural life.[50]

Robinson set out to complete that task with gusto, at the same time recognising the close cultural ties which existed between the Bruny Islanders and Aboriginal bands in the remote south-west. In June 1829 he suggested to Arthur that he should travel to that region with some Bruny Islanders to acquaint them of the government's humane intentions. Robinson's plan, however, was at least partly motivated by the rapidly looming prospect of his own failure. His model settlement on Bruny Island had a population of just 19, and not only did the Aborigines disagree with his policy of separating children from parents, they were often ill from wearing wet clothing and their dependence on the convict rations Robinson had substituted for their customary fare. Salt meat, bread, biscuit, potatoes and tea contained considerably less protein, while the tobacco Robinson provided merely served to exacerbate the growing health problems.[51]

With illness running rampant the adults relocated to other parts of the island, too late to prevent four deaths, and the situation only became worse. When nine Ninene people from Port Davey visited Bruny Island in July 1829 for cultural reasons, their brief time at Robinson's establishment was sufficient to kill two-thirds of their number.[52] Growing desperation led Robinson to broaden his plan by travelling the full length of the west coast to bring the message of peace to all Aborigines he encountered. It was certainly sweeping in its scope, for much of this region was formidable terrain where no colonist had ever ventured before, and even today large areas remain untouched by the human presence. Robinson had the confidence, fortitude and stamina to accomplish his aim, but there was little to go back to. The exceptional mortality rate at the Bruny Island establishment ensured its closure as soon as Robinson had taken his leave with the remaining Aborigines.[53]

In December 1829 Arthur authorised Robinson to put his plan into effect, with instructions to establish cordial relations with the Aboriginal people on the west coast and through them with the bands of the interior. He was accompanied by 12 Aborigines, including 'Black Tom' and Umarrah who had already played their own roles in the Black War and were transferred to Robinson from Gilbert

Robertson's roving party. The three surviving Ninene people were expected to facilitate intercourse with their compatriots. Fourteen convicts were also attached to the first 'Friendly Mission', which was split into three groups. Robinson led an overland party, which was shadowed along the coast by a whaleboat crew, both of which rendezvoused with a schooner at Port Davey. Thereafter the whaleboat carried the bulk of the supplies north, meeting with Robinson's party at various points along the coast, while the schooner returned to Hobart.[54] This procedure was roughly followed in all of Robinson's subsequent peregrinations.

Notwithstanding that they were among the most isolated Aboriginal people in Van Diemen's Land, the four bands of the south-west had already been decimated by introduced viral infections which had spread through their ranks like wildfire. By the time Robinson set out on his first mission the Indigenous population of this region had plummeted from two or three hundred to around 60.[55] Through his guides, notably Dray whose brother belonged to the Ninene band, Robinson made contact with 26 people in March 1830. Willingly camping with the mission, they became suspicious during the night and only three women, a girl and infant remained by morning.[56]

Robinson fell in with them again a few weeks later, and on this occasion they accompanied the 'Friendly Mission' for four days as they travelled north. By mid-April Robinson had contacted nearly all the Aboriginal people of the south-west, and he had also learnt a number of valuable lessons which would later stand him in good stead. The Ninene people, for instance, became aware that Robinson's knapsack contained three pistols, and it had taken all their owner's powers of persuasion to convince them that he intended no harm.[57] Until the later stages of his conciliatory journeys Robinson refrained from carrying firearms. He also learnt that by reducing the size of his overland party and relying on the hunting skills of his guides the mobility of the mission was considerably increased, and it was of no mean importance that one of Robinson's great aptitudes was his willingness to eat almost anything. Although there were few recruits, he believed that if this first venture into the south-west was followed up within a year circumstances would be more favourable for inducing the Aborigines to 'voluntarily surrender'.[58] What he really meant was capture. Robinson was convinced that if the Aborigines remained in their ancestral lands they would increasingly become vulnerable to attack from colonial freebooters. At the same time, however, their forced removal would allow new areas to be settled.[59] This supposedly win-win situation nevertheless overlooked two very important issues: if the Aborigines were to be removed where would they go, and what would happen to them in the longer term? The solutions would only be learned through bitter experience, by which time it was too late to avoid a disastrous outcome.

In the meantime the 'Friendly Mission' continued working its way north along the rugged west coast until, at Trial Harbour, there was an unexpected setback when Umarrah and two other men from the north Midlands suddenly decamped to make their way home. This was a serious blow, as all three had been of great assistance in effecting communication with the Aborigines of the south-west, and Robinson was relying heavily on them to continue their work in the north-west.[60] While Umarrah and his companions had no affinities with the bands of the south-west, they were mortal enemies of those to the north and understandably feared for their lives. Moreover, as Robinson and Arthur already suspected, the Aboriginal bands of the north-west were engaged in a violent struggle with the employees of the Van Diemen's Land Company, a state of affairs which could only serve to exacerbate customary enmity.

Eleven days after the disappearance of Umarrah and his companions Robinson's mission encountered the Peternidic people at the mouth of the Pieman River. They were in no mood to parley, and shadowed Robinson's party as they continued their trek north to Cape Grim. All Robinson could do was place gifts at any campsites he came across as a means of conveying his peaceful intentions.[61] Robinson's concerns were highlighted when the mission reached Cape Grim, where he gathered considerable evidence of atrocities which had been committed against the local Pennemuker band, including information obtained from north-east Aboriginal women accompanying a party of sealers near Woolnorth.[62] At the end of June 1830 the mission located two Aborigines — a man and a woman — on Robbins Island, and after being informed through correspondence that Arthur had introduced a bounty for captives, Robinson directed his boat crew back to Robbins Island where another two men were taken.[63] All four were despatched to Launceston, with orders from Robinson to forward the female captive, Narrucker, to Hobart. In fact, it was one of the men, Nicermenic, who was sent south,[64] but any expectation Robinson had of collecting the £20 bounty was soon shattered.

After travelling through the inland areas controlled by the Van Diemen's Land Company, the mission reached Emu Bay where Robinson learned that Arthur had authorised the release of three of his captives with instructions to repatriate them back to Cape Grim. At this stage the Lieutenant Governor could see no valid reason why Aborigines outside the settled districts should be incarcerated, as he still held to the belief that if the Aboriginal people could be persuaded to avoid the settled districts the frontier conflict could finally be brought to an end. Robinson, on the other hand, was outraged that his work had been undermined and that he had been deprived of his bounty. Of lesser consideration was the safety of the three repatriated Aborigines, who were first returned to the headquarters of the Van Diemen's Land Company at Circular Head, today's Stanley.[65]

There was no alternative for the mission except to continue east to Launceston. In the Mersey River district a party of Aborigines was sighted on three separate occasions — almost certainly renegades led by the female leader Walyer — and Robinson was under the distinct impression they were shadowing his mission with the aim of attacking at the first opportunity. Although Robinson could have pre-empted Walyer, there seemed little point in capturing this group if they were only going to be set free, and the mission reached George Town without incident. Robinson expected to be greeted with great acclaim for his remarkable feat of travelling halfway around Van Diemen's Land and contacting such a large number of Aboriginal people. Instead, he was virtually ignored.[66] The reception was no better in Launceston, where preparations were underway for the Black Line. These were early days, and it was not until frontier conflict had finally been brought to an end — at least in eastern Van Diemen's Land — that Robinson finally received the accolades which he so desperately sought. In Launceston during October 1830 it was a very different matter, with the settlement's commandant, Major Abbott, simply informing the 'conciliator' that there was no further work for his mission. Captain Donaldson, soon to command the western division of the Black Line, proved more receptive, advising Robinson to confer with George Arthur who was believed to be at Campbell Town. He hurried south and finally caught up with the Lieutenant Governor at Ross in the southern Midlands on 6 October 1830.[67]

Robinson was able to convince Arthur that there could be no peace while the Aborigines remained beyond the settled districts, and that his mission should attempt to persuade the Aborigines to voluntarily surrender for their own protection. Where to put them was another matter again. For his part, Arthur wanted Robinson's 'Friendly Mission' to participate in the Black Line, a course of action which Robinson successfully argued against on two grounds. The obvious one was the very real possibility of his Aboriginal guides being shot by trigger-happy colonists. He was also concerned that if his mission was identified with the Black Line it would seriously compromise its objective, with the Aboriginal people almost certain to reject any peaceful overtures. Robinson's alternative was for the mission to continue into the north-east of Van Diemen's Land where there was a good chance of encountering Aborigines who had slipped through Arthur's cordon. At the same time he would be well-placed to 'rescue' Aboriginal women from the sealers in the Furneaux Islands.[68] This was a cunning ploy. The removal of women from the sealers would be appreciated by the Aboriginal men, who would then be more willing to assist in tracking down other Aborigines. Arthur concurred with Robinson's plan.

The north-east leg of the mission commenced the same month across country that Robinson noted was well-stocked with natural resources and would have been ideal for the Aboriginal Reserve briefly envisaged by Lieutenant Governor Arthur — except that the concept completely ignored Aboriginal affinity to ancestral land: a reserve in the north-east would only have benefited the existing custodians. Be that as it may, Robinson's 'Friendly Mission' made exceptionally rapid progress across the coastal heathlands east of the Piper River without sighting one Aborigine. It was not until 1 November 1830, when the mission was inland from the Bay of Fires on the east coast, that contact was finally made.[69] This was a party of seven Cape Portland Aborigines who had recently witnessed the operations of the Black Line after joining with the Ben Lomond band to attack the Big River people further south. On their return they were intercepted by a military patrol and three Aborigines were shot dead. They claimed that their Ben Lomond allies had exacted revenge by tracking the soldiers to their campsite and killing two of the despised redcoats. To reduce the risk of further casualties both bands then split into smaller groups as they continued north to their homelands.[70]

Robinson warned that the Black Line would soon converge on the north-eastern districts, a threat that soon persuaded the Aborigines to accompany Robinson and his guides further north, where the mission was to rendezvous with the accompanying boat crew. Once that had been accomplished, Robinson was able to cajole the Aborigines into being taken across to Swan Island on the pretext they would be safe from the advancing soldiers.[71] Subterfuge was beginning to bring results, and with the Aborigines effectively marooned on Swan Island, Robinson turned his attention to the Aboriginal women living with the sealers. At that time there were around 20 sealers residing in the Furneaux Islands and perhaps as many as 25 Aboriginal women scattered throughout the length and breadth of Bass Strait,[72] but to be forewarned is to be forearmed. The sealers had taken a number of women to Flinders Island and others were hidden on the smaller islands after being told that the approaching strangers intended to kill them. Robinson took away one of two women found on Woody Island, and on Gun Carriage Island another four were contacted by Robinson's female envoys. The women had been unaware of the mission's presence. Robinson again permitted two of them — known to the sealers as Poll and Dumpe — to remain on the island; the other two returned with his party to Swan Island. His entire catch therefore amounted to just four.[73]

While Robinson had been prowling the Furneaux Islands in the second boat now attached to his mission, another seven Aborigines had arrived on the coast opposite Swan Island and been taken into 'protective custody' by Robinson's assigned convict Alexander McKay. Among the new arrivals was Mannalargenna, leader of the Cape Portland band, who would become one of the conciliator's most trusted and successful guides.[74] In just two short weeks the 'Friendly Mission' had thus gathered nineteen Aborigines, forcing Robinson to improve the existing facilities on Swan Island. At the same time his coxswain, James Parish, made two further sweeps of the islands. He returned from the first trip on 11 December with six Aboriginal women,[75] and after setting out again discovered another five women on Penguin Island.[76] Along with the mission guides this now brought the total number of Aborigines to over 40, but Robinson's attempts to house them in huts and attend his Sunday sermons were shunned by the captives. Instead, the Aborigines organised new social relationships and re-immersed themselves in cultural activities. The women who had been removed from the sealers soon proved to be Robinson's greatest headache, actively opposing all his efforts to curtail their new-found freedom.[77]

One of them was Walyer, who had attempted to liquidate the 'Friendly Mission' west of Port Sorell. Soon after Robinson had safely passed through the area Walyer had been captured by two sealers and taken to the Furneaux Islands, where the men soon found they had bitten off far more than they could chew. When Walyer refused to work they decided to maroon her for a time on Penguin Island. On the way to their destination, however, Walyer attacked the two men and may well have killed them had not James Parish and his boat crew fortuitously arrived on the scene. The sealers willingly handed Walyer over to the mission, but once on Swan Island she attempted to incite rebellion by telling the others that soldiers were on their way from Launceston to shoot them or place them in irons. To restore some semblance of order, Robinson sent Walyer with Parish's boat crew on another search of the Furneaux Islands. On her return an unsubdued Walyer continued to cause unrest,[78] and there was no obvious sorrow when Robinson recorded her death from what was possibly influenza in early May 1831.[79]

As the resources of Swan Island were limited it was never meant to be more than a temporary place of exile, and Robinson's captives were soon transferred to Gun Carriage Island. That, too, was only intended as a stop-gap measure and in January 1831 Robinson travelled to Hobart for discussions with Arthur regarding the long-term future of his captives — and to renegotiate his official position. Robinson wanted his salary increased, and in this he succeeded well beyond all expectations with Arthur raising his annual pay from £100 to £250. On top of that Robinson also received a £100 gratuity payment and a land grant of just over 2500 acres (1036 hectares). But Arthur wanted quick results, particularly the capture of the Big River people who were clearly the most aggressive of Van Diemen's Land's Indigenous inhabitants. Robinson managed to delay taking action against the Big River people, proposing instead to make more permanent arrangements for the Aborigines already in his care and to remove the remaining Aboriginal women from the sealers.[80] As it was abundantly clear that the majority of colonists were totally opposed to the Aborigines remaining on the mainland of Van Diemen's Land, an offshore island was the only viable alternative. This solution was nevertheless vigorously opposed by Chief Justice John Pedder, who countered that Arthur's administration needed to negotiate a treaty with the Aboriginal people, even if it was to limit them within clearly designated areas. As Pedder saw it, exile on an offshore island could only lead to their rapid demise: they would 'pine away', he insisted.[81] Pedder's arguments were unfortunately ignored, his wisdom only recognised in hindsight.

Robinson, on the other hand, had a number of issues to deal with in the here and now. Apart from the Big River people there were other Aboriginal bands to conciliate, and he still had to follow up on his west coast mission and somehow induce the Aborigines to abandon their customary lands. And there were even more pressing problems. The sealers had complained to Arthur about Robinson's removal of their 'wives', with the conciliator ordered to return a number of women to the Furneaux Islands. If this was a bitter pill to swallow it was made even worse by Arthur's instructions for Robinson to accept the assistance of the sealers in rounding up the remaining Aborigines in north-east Van Diemen's Land.[82] As Robinson was only too aware, reliance on the sealers would diminish his growing prestige, but in this instance he need not have worried. None of the sealers showed any enthusiasm for assisting him, and the last of the north-east people were eventually located at Oyster Bay in January 1832 by the free settler Anthony Cottrell, who had recently been employed by the government to track down the Aborigines.[83]

This was still in the future when Robinson returned to Swan Island from Hobart, and directed the next stage of the 'Friendly Mission' towards the pursuit and capture of Umarrah and his companions who had wreaked havoc behind the Black Line and were still waging their resistance campaign along the Tamar and South Esk River valleys and into the north-east. The mission spent two months ranging between the Piper and Little Mussel Roe Rivers before Robinson realised that his guides had no intention of leading him to Umarrah. They were replaced by Mannalargenna and Pevay, a young man from Robbins Island in the north-west, though it is relevant that Robinson only gained Mannalargenna's assistance by promising that when the Aborigines finally laid down their arms they would be allowed to remain in their respective territories and issued with government rations. In August 1831 Mannalargenna finally tracked Umarrah and his 15 followers to the mouth of the Piper River where they peacefully surrendered to the mission.[84] This was particularly significant as it finally ended the frontier conflict near Launceston, and from Robinson's perspective he had re-acquired the services of a skilled guide who had displayed his formidable talents before absconding on the west coast. Indeed, when Arthur again pressured Robinson to pursue the Big River people he made sure to include both Umarrah and Mannalargenna in his party.[85]

As the mission headed south from Campbell Town the remaining Big River and Oyster Bay people were moving into the high country. What Robinson did not count on was that Umarrah and Mannalargenna, from the north Midlands and north-east respectively, were sworn enemies of his quarry — and had no great desire to find them.[86] The mission meandered throughout the settled districts, north to south and east to west, with the guides frequently leading Robinson well astray. One of them, known as Richard, deserted on the Norfolk Plains, and Robinson had a difficult time preventing the women from slipping away to join the Big River and Oyster Bay people. Persistence finally paid off, however, and Robinson caught up with the remaining resistance fighters west of Lake Echo on 31 December 1831.[87] It was only accomplished after Robinson promised they would have an interview with the Lieutenant Governor, who would redress their grievances. To capitalise on publicity he organised for them to be paraded through the streets of Hobart where they attracted the attention of virtually the entire population. Rather than having their wrongs righted, however, the proud Big River and Oyster Bay people soon found themselves exiled to Bass Strait.[88]

The way was now clear for Robinson to undertake his second mission to the west coast, with the initial aim of contacting and removing the Aboriginal people from land controlled by the Van Diemen's Land Company in the north-west. The 'Friendly Mission' was considerably strengthened by the addition of Anthony Cottrell and four New South Wales Aborigines along with Robinson's son George Jnr and a Hawaiian assigned convict named John Maclaine. Among the 12 Tasmanian Aboriginal guides were Mannalargenna, Woorrady and Truganini, the latter two having been with Robinson from the very beginning.[89] Leaving Launceston in early April 1832 they headed west, and the mentality of the Van Diemen's Land Company was amply demonstrated in an incident which took place not far from the company's headquarters at Circular Head. The mission camped one evening on the bank of the Black River, and the following day the guides went off to hunt game. Woorrady fell in with two company servants and explained that all the Aborigines thereabouts belonged to Robinson's 'Friendly Mission'. Cottrell was absent with the New South Wales Aborigines that night when 'thirteen or fourteen' company servants descended on the mission's camp. Robinson challenged the men, who hurled abuse and levelled their firearms at the Aboriginal guides. They eventually left, and Robinson believed that his mission had only been saved from disaster by the fact of it being a moonlit night;[90] it is more likely that killing was not the company's intention.

From their contact with Woorrady the company servants were well aware who they were dealing with, and they also knew that Robinson's earlier investigation of a series of incidents at Cape Grim had brought them unwanted attention. Their purpose was clearly to intimidate Robinson and his mission, and although the removal of local Aborigines was to their advantage it mattered little. The company was bent on a war of extermination which would guarantee the disappearance of the Aborigines for all time. Nor can there be any doubt that Edward Curr, manager of the Van Diemen's Land Company, was behind this surprise raid. For 13 or 14 employees (some of whom were assigned convicts) to leave the company's headquarters at night fully armed without someone in authority being aware of it requires too great a stretch of the imagination. Although Robinson and Curr were outwardly on amicable terms it is known that there was simmering tension between the two men.[91] But threats by the Van Diemen's Land Company were the least of Robinson's worries in the north-west.

Like many other Tasmanian Aboriginal leaders, Mannalargenna was held to have the gift of prophesy, and while he was by now one of Robinson's most trusted guides the depth of his allegiance is questionable. As the mission advanced further west Mannalargenna suddenly prophesised that Robinson would be speared to death when they reached the Arthur River. Robinson recorded Mannalargenna's 'ridiculous' prediction in his journal,[92] ignoring the dire warning and concentrating on the removal of Aboriginal people in the north-west. The signs were initially auspicious. At the Welcome River Pevay proved instrumental in effecting communication with a group of his own people from the Parperloihener band, including two of his brothers and their leader, Wymurick. Constantly under threat from the Van Diemen's Land Company, the Parperloihener readily accepted Robinson's protection, though Mannalargenna was wary of these west coast people and attempted to hide Wymurick's spears. He was caught in the act and would have been killed by Wymurick had not Pevay and Robinson quickly intervened.[93] Relations took some time to be restored, and to ensure that the advantage was not lost the mission returned to the coast with Wymurick's group, who were taken across to Hunter Island. Unbeknown to the Parperloihener this soon became a temporary prison; the mission continued south and the Parperloihener were trapped until Robinson could make arrangements to have them shipped east.[94]

A base camp was established roughly a day's trek north of the Arthur River where Mannalargenna remained with the assigned servants after the bulk of the mission advanced to the waterway. A small party including Timme, Woorrady and Truganini swam across the Arthur River while Robinson (a non-swimmer) waited for his remaining guides to construct a raft. No sooner were they across than the advance party returned with 29 Aborigines. Most of them were local Tarkiner people, led by Wyne, but there was also a small sprinkling of Ninene people from the south-west, who already knew Robinson and his mission and appeared less than enthusiastic to see him.[95]

Robinson organised a temporary camp, intending to recross the Arthur River and take the Aborigines back to his base the following day. Among the new arrivals was Pevay's sister, whose husband warned Pevay that an attack was imminent. The information was relayed to Robinson. One can expect that he slept very little that night, and he had good cause for concern as the following morning the Tarkiner suddenly rose with their weapons poised. The mission Aborigines fled, with Robinson close behind. As it turned out he made a wise decision in following Truganini, and the fact that he managed to keep pace with her speaks volumes for his level of fitness.[96]

Completely unaware that Robinson was close behind Truganini made for the Arthur River; before plunging into the water she turned back to find Robinson virtually breathing down her neck. As Robinson noted, she showed 'much agitation', no doubt expecting that he had been killed by the Tarkiner at the camp. Truganini lied to Robinson that the mission Aborigines were dead, and suggested that he hide in the bush while she swam across the river to seek help at the base camp. Robinson knew that trying to hide from the Tarkiner people in their own country was tantamount to suicide, and quickly binding some pieces of wood together for flotation he instructed Truganini to push him across the river. Robinson later wrote that she 'wanted encouraging' to comply with his wishes.[97] Once safely across the pair walked down to the original crossing place where they discovered the rest of the mission Aborigines unharmed and looking at Robinson 'with amazement'. In his own dramatic account of the incident Robinson emphasised his calmness and bravery in the face of almost certain death, though he did find room to praise Truganini — 'the woman' — for saving his life.[98]

That was probably the last thing she wanted to do. Although it can only be conjectured, it appears that the mission Aborigines had planned to join with the Tarkiner people in this remote region of Van

Diemen's Land well before any contact was made. Unlike the bands further north the Tarkiner were not threatened by the Van Diemen's Land Company, and it also provided a wonderful opportunity to be rid of Robinson without the risk of drawing blame if anything went wrong. The advance party almost certainly made some arrangement with the Tarkiner and Ninene people before returning to Robinson. Such a plan can account for Mannalargenna's uncanny prophesy of Robinson's death as well as his reluctance to leave the base camp.[99]

With the plot foiled, however, the mission Aborigines returned north to Hunter Island with Robinson, who now had 50 Aborigines under his control and limited resources to keep them content. He arranged with Edward Curr to charter a vessel and convey his captives east, after which Anthony Cottrell and George Robinson Jnr were to take the mission Aborigines south to Macquarie Harbour. Robinson departed immediately for Hobart, re-joining the mission at its destination in March 1833. In the interim the mission captured seven Aborigines who were confined on Grummet Island.[100]

After arriving at Macquarie Harbour, Cottrell was instructed to take his captives north to the coast, where they could be deported to Flinders Island, while Robinson headed to the south-west of Van Diemen's Land. Following his experience on the Arthur River the previous year there was no longer any pretence of gentle persuasion. Robinson's assigned servants now openly displayed their firearms and force was used to bring in the remaining Aborigines. Within 12 days a group of Ninene people were captured and sent back to Macquarie Harbour for deportation to Bass Strait. Robinson continued south and by June 1833 his mission in this region had been completed, with the last Aboriginal people of the south-west finally secured.[101]

After returning to Macquarie Harbour Robinson directed his attention northwards to the Tarkiner people. In July the mission came across nine Tarkiner led by Wyne, who was overpowered by

Mannalargenna and Timme. Unlike the other west coast people, Wyne's group was incarcerated on the lower floor of the convict gaol at Macquarie Harbour where they were subjected to gross abuse. Convicts on the floor above shouted obscenities, banged constantly on the ceiling and poured water and urine on the frightened Aborigines below. Disease broke out, and within 18 days seven of the Tarkiner were dead. Wyne succumbed on 31 July after using his last remaining reserves of strength in a fruitless bid to break down the door. His wife Naydip gave birth to their child on 10 August with the infant dying the same day. Naydip lasted only 24 hours longer,[102] and it is difficult to avoid the conclusion that the exceptional treatment of these people was revenge for Robinson's narrow escape the previous year. Robinson had a number of redeeming qualities, but forgiveness was certainly not one of them.

The work of the 'Friendly Mission' was now drawing to a close. After a fruitless search for Aborigines reported near Circular Head, Robinson returned again to the north-west during March and April 1834 and succeeded in capturing another 20 Tarkiner people. His attempt to track down a group of Tommeginer from Table Cape was nevertheless frustrated after the mission guides were warned off by sharpened stakes projecting along a pathway.[103] It was probably just as well, as the mission Aborigines were by then close to rebellion. Many of them — notably Mannalargenna — were beginning to have grave doubts about Robinson's sincerity. They had witnessed captive after captive placed aboard vessels bound for the islands of Bass Strait, and it was becoming increasingly clear that exile was likely to be their own fate. For that reason they lit fires to alert their quarry, adopted 'go-slow' tactics and often led Robinson away from the fugitives.[104]

Robinson's sons, George Jnr and Charles, sporadically continued the search for Aborigines in the north-west with mixed results until June 1837.[105] Despite knowing full well there was still active resistance in this region, Robinson lodged a claim on Arthur's administration in February 1835 for having removed all the Aborigines of Van Diemen's Land.[106] Arthur was clearly satisfied with what Robinson had accomplished, though he lamented that exile in Bass Strait was not the outcome he had hoped for. The Lieutenant Governor also regretted not having accepted the advice of Chief Justice Pedder and attempted to make a treaty with the Aboriginal people.[107] While that might have been possible on the west coast, it is doubtful if a treaty could have been effected anywhere else, and certainly not in the south-east. There was no concept of pan-Aboriginality in Van Diemen's Land, with such terms as 'Palawah' (one people) created in the late twentieth century by modern descendants for political purposes. In the nineteenth century an entire series of treaties would have been necessary.

George Augustus Robinson understood the diversity of Aboriginal societies in Van Diemen's Land, and although his association with the Aboriginal people was still far from over, perhaps it is opportune to make an assessment of his character. His was a complex personality, a man who was either despised or praised by his contemporaries. Unlike so many of them, however, Robinson was genuinely interested in the Aborigines and their culture, and it is fortunate that he was. Without his copious observations our knowledge of Aboriginal societies in the first decades of the nineteenth century would be seriously diminished. While considering himself a missionary who had been chosen by God to save the Aboriginal people of Van Diemen's Land, he went further than most by learning their languages (limited though it may have been) and essential aspects of their cultures. He was happy to live with the Aborigines for extended periods of time and he appreciated their knowledge and intellect. In that respect Robinson distinguished little difference between the Indigenous people and members of his own society.[108] He was also acutely aware of the direct relationship between racial contempt and frontier violence. Robinson recognised that attempts to dehumanise the Aborigines were designed to justify their dispossession and destruction. He never doubted that the Aboriginal people were the true possessors of the soil, and although his was a plan of exile he believed they were entitled to full compensation for their loss. Robinson was quite vocal in his condemnation of the brutal treatment of the Aborigines, an outspokenness that often drew the vehemence of his fellow colonists.[109]

For himself Robinson wanted wealth, status and respect, and his journals are liberally sprinkled with the slights he received at the hands of prominent landowners who refused to treat him as an equal. At the same time, Robinson was quite capable of dealing out harsh punishments to his assigned servants who did not show him the respect that he felt he rightly deserved.[110] Robinson was exceptionally fit, and he had extraordinary powers of endurance and fortitude. There can be no denying his courage, and if Robinson's name had not become inextricably linked with the Aboriginal people he could well be remembered today as one of Van Diemen's Land's greatest explorers. Instead, he is usually associated with the destruction of the island's Indigenous inhabitants, a purveyor of death who continued to inflict pain and suffering well beyond the final 'Friendly Mission'. Robinson was a flawed figure, whose attempts to bring conflict to an end were defeated on the north-west frontier.

7

THE NORTH-WEST FRONTIER

The north-west of Van Diemen's Land, a region stretching from Table Cape in the east to Cape Grim in the west and south to Macquarie Harbour, supported at least eight Aboriginal bands with a combined Indigenous population of four or five hundred. The territory of the Tommeginer lay around Table Cape, while that of the Parperloihener was centred on Robbins Island. Cape Grim was home to the Pennemuker and Studland Bay was the ancestral land of the Pendowte. The territory of the Peerapper lay around West Point and the mouth of the Arthur River was homeland to the Manegin. The Tarkiner were based around Sandy Cape and their southern neighbours, the Peternidic, were custodians of the land near the mouth of the Pieman River. With an overall coastline stretching over some 550 kilometres, the economy of all these bands leaned heavily towards the exploitation of maritime resources.[1]

When Bass and Flinders circumnavigated Van Diemen's Land in 1798 they did not observe any Aborigines along the north-west coast, though Bass came across 'several deserted fireplaces, strewed round with the shells of the sea ear [abalone]' on Three Hummock Island.[2] Similarly, Louis Freycinet recorded smoke from Aboriginal fires on Hunter Island while surveying the region in 1802.[3] The following year sealing master James Chace made a reconnaissance of the north-west and found Hunter Island to be 'well peopled with natives'.[4] As Hunter Island had ample quantities of water and wood it is likely to have been visited by other gangs of sealers during subsequent years. Raids along the nearby coast for Aboriginal women would almost inevitably have followed.

On 3 January 1816 James Kelly and his four crewmen landed on the coast south of Cape Grim during their circumnavigation of Van Diemen's Land. Their fire attracted an estimated 50 Aborigines, who were initially friendly, but when George Briggs brought two swans from the whaleboat to present as gifts events took a nasty turn. The Aboriginal leader attempted to seize Briggs while directing his companions to hurl stones at the other three Europeans. Kelly and his men responded by discharging their firearms, wounding 'several natives' according to Kelly. Yet even as they fled two men tried unsuccessfully to drag Briggs along with them. Kelly believed that the altercation arose over the swans, but it seems more likely that it was Briggs they were after.[5] An experienced sealer who had operated for many years along the northern coast of Van Diemen's Land, it is likely that Briggs had ventured into this region before, possibly for the purpose of abducting Aboriginal women as he certainly did on a number of occasions in the north-east.[6]

Until the early 1820s the Aborigines of the north-west were only occasionally disturbed by these transient maritime visitations, violent though some of them might have been. But there had been no permanent encroachment on their territories, a course of action which began to shift from 1823 when Lieutenant Governor William

Sorell sent Captain John Hardwicke to report on the potential of this region for settlement. Although Hardwicke described the Indigenous people around Circular Head as 'extremely wild', he managed to establish friendly relations with the Aborigines south of West Point. While Hardwicke was not particularly impressed by the north-west as a viable region for development,[7] the Lieutenant Governor was not so easily discouraged and engaged John Hobbs to search for pastoral land. In February 1824 Hobbs departed Hobart with 12 carefully selected convicts in two open boats, one of his crewmen being James Carretts, whose brutality towards the Aboriginal people was to be brought to the notice of the Aborigines Committee six years later. There is no indication that Hobbs had any contact with the Aboriginal people of the north-west on this exploratory survey, and he was just as unimpressed with the quality of the landscape as Hardwicke — except for the area around Circular Head, where 'the soil is all of the best quality'.[8]

That finding was to have serious repercussions, especially for the Pennemuker band of Cape Grim. While there is no record of when sealers first visited the Cape Grim area, a gang certainly landed sometime around 1820 for the express purpose of abducting Aboriginal women. There are two versions of what transpired on that fateful day. A Pennemuker man named Penderoin witnessed the incident and later told George Augustus Robinson that his band had camped opposite the offshore islets known as the Doughboys, where mutton-birds were supposedly plentiful. While the men went inland to hunt kangaroos the women and children remained in the camp with a few older men. Some of the women swam out to the Doughboys for mutton-birds, and when they arrived back at the camp nine sealers rushed out from a cavern where they had been hiding. Trapped by the cliffs there was no escape, and Penderoin claimed that 12–14 women were taken away by force. His brother, Tunnerminnerwait (Pevay), another eyewitness, corroborated Penderoin's information, adding that two of the sealers were from 'Owyhee' (Hawaii).[9] Robinson heard yet another account from the assigned convict and bushman Alexander McKay, whose informant was one of the sealers directly involved. As the raiders descended on the camp an elderly Aboriginal man climbed into a banksia bush and hurled a spear which narrowly missed its target, tangling in one of the sealer's garments. The sealers then shot both this man and another elderly defender before dragging away seven women.[10] Cape Grim was to become the scene of considerable bloodshed in the years to come, a consequence of land acquisition by the Van Diemen's Land Company. Mutton-birds, however, are not common on the Doughboys, with Robinson apparently confusing mutton-birds with muttonfish, the common name for abalone at that time, shellfish which are plentiful in these waters.

A joint stock company with a royal charter (essentially a grant from the British regent allowing it to operate), the Van Diemen's Land Company was a beneficiary of the recommendations made by John Thomas Bigge, the commissioner sent out to New South Wales and Van Diemen's Land by the British government in 1819. Bigge's harsh criticism of Governor Lachlan Macquarie's administration in Sydney led to the latter's recall in 1821, and the British government also acted on the commissioner's advice that convicts should be assigned as cheap labour to private landholders on the basis of the number of livestock they owned. The Van Diemen's Land Company was founded in 1824, the same year that another joint stock company, the Australian Agricultural Company, had been granted one million acres of land in New South Wales. Under the terms of that extremely generous gift no other joint stock company could take up land in New South Wales, which is why the directors of the new rival turned their attention to Van Diemen's Land and named their company accordingly. Unlike their competitor on the Australian mainland they had no interest in agriculture as all 11 directors were London merchants closely associated with the wool industry. Their plan was to breed Merino and Saxon sheep on an extensive scale to meet the demands of burgeoning British textile manufacturers.[11]

In May 1824 they applied to the British Secretary of State for the Colonies, Lord Bathurst, for half a million acres of land in Van Diemen's Land, and Bathurst sought the advice of William Sorell, who had recently returned to London following the expiration of his term as Lieutenant Governor of the island colony. Sorell confirmed that Van Diemen's Land was desperately short of capital, and agreed that the presence of a joint stock company would go a considerable way towards boosting the economy. The problem was that the bulk of the land suitable for pastoralism had already been taken up, and Bathurst was adamant that he would only allow the company to operate if its activities were sufficiently remote from the settled districts. Admitting that he had no real knowledge of the north-west, Sorell suggested that it could prove suitable for the for the company's operations.[12]

By the 'north-west' he meant the entire region from Port Sorell to Cape Grim, with the former Lieutenant Governor unaware that 2000 acres (809 hectares) of land had already been granted to Captain Malcolm Laing Smith near Port Sorell. Bathurst knew, and while agreeing with the company's request he limited their grant to 250 000 acres — half of what had been asked for. After the Van Diemen's Land Company received its royal charter on 10 November 1825 Bathurst instructed Sorell's successor, George Arthur, to arrange for suitable land to be made available in the north-west of the colony and for convicts to be assigned to the company's officials.[13] For his part, Sorell also introduced the company directors to Edward Curr,[14] who would subsequently become a central figure in their operations and, by extension, conflict with the Aborigines.

The son of a civil engineer, Edward Curr was born at Sheffield, England, in 1798 and after graduating from college (rather than university) he rejected his father's assistance to study for a profession or establish his own business and travelled to Brazil. His stay in South America was only brief, however, and on returning to England Curr accepted financial help from his father to form a partnership with John Raine, a London merchant on the verge of departing for Van Diemen's Land. Curr and his wife Elizabeth followed, arriving at Hobart in February 1820, but the venture was short-lived as Curr could not agree with Raine's business practices. After visiting Sydney he formed a new partnership with Horatio Mason, and on his return to Hobart Curr gained the acquaintance of Lieutenant Governor Sorell, became active in church affairs, and served in the Deputy Judge Advocate's Court.[15]

Networking quickly paid off when Sorell granted Curr 1500 acres (607 hectares) of land at Cross Marsh. When his father died in 1823 and the partnership with Mason was dissolved, Curr returned to England, where he published a book the following year entitled *An Account of the Colony of Van Diemen's Land, Primarily Designed for the Use of Emigrants*. He hoped that his publication would bear fruit;[16] Curr, in fact, reaped a veritable harvest. He praised the climate as ideal for the production of quality wool, and although Curr's knowledge extended little beyond Hobart he outlined the potential of northern Van Diemen's Land for pastoral activities. The Aborigines received no mention whatsoever.

Following his meeting with the directors of the Van Diemen's Land Company, Curr was appointed their chief agent on a comfortable salary of £800 per annum. By the time all arrangements had been made to commence operations in Van Diemen's Land, he had been promoted to company manager and, with his second-in-command Stephen Adey and their respective families, sailed for Hobart, where they arrived in March 1826.[17] Stores, livestock and indentured labourers followed, with the workforce boosted by the addition of assigned convicts. Lieutenant Governor Arthur was under the impression that the company would confine itself to the Cape Grim area, but by devious means Curr attempted to shift the company's land grant closer to Port Sorrell.[18] It mattered little. A survey of the north coast between George Town and Cape Grim was conducted by the company's agricultural superintendent Alexander Goldie and surveyor Joseph Fossey under the guidance of Richard Frederick in July and August 1826. They found that the only land suitable for the company's purpose lay around Circular Head, though after walking overland to Cape Grim Goldie and Fossey noted additional 'good sheep land', the area marred only by 'a low plain' which Goldie believed 'would make a good run for cattle'.[19]

Circular Head, which would eventually blossom into the town of Stanley, also possessed a reasonable anchorage and a good supply of fresh water, so it was finally chosen by Curr as the company's headquarters.[20] It was not until January 1827 that Curr finally arrived at Circular Head and viewed the prospects for himself. He was not particularly impressed, quickly realising that the available land was not sufficient to satisfy the company's long-term aspirations. A small party led by Henry Hellyer, who had been hired in England as surveyor and architect, was dispatched inland to search for more grazing land. From the summit of St Valentine's Peak Hellyer gazed down on grassy plains he believed eminently suitable for the company's requirements. Hellyer descended and examined both areas at close quarters, naming them the Surrey and Hampshire Hills. Even though he noticed the grass of the former 'had recently been burned by the natives', limited colonial experience prevented Hellyer from recognising these open pasturelands as artificially constructed Aboriginal hunting grounds. His optimistic report was nevertheless endorsed by Joseph Fossey,[21] both men blithely unaware that these extensive tracts of land were also bitterly cold sub-alpine uplands where sheep had no hope of surviving.[22] The Surrey and Hampshire Hills were ultimately to prove a costly mistake for the Van Diemen's Land Company, but when Hellyer and Fossey reported back to Curr preparations began in earnest to establish a stock and supply route to link and integrate these new discoveries with the holdings at Circular Head and eastwards towards the settled districts. Hellyer remained with the company until, in May 1832, he was appointed to the government survey department. He did not take up the position, committing suicide in controversial circumstances at Circular Head the following September.[23]

Curr was to live a lot longer, and he was also appointed as a magistrate.[24] With the stroke of a pen the Aborigines of north-west Van Diemen's Land had not only been dispossessed of their land, they also became British subjects under the protection of Edward Curr, the only government representative in the entire region. In just eight years fewer than one hundred of the original four or five hundred Aboriginal people can be accounted for; the remainder simply disappeared,[25] and given that the region was under the total control of Edward Curr and the Van Diemen's Land Company during those years the activities and policies of the manager deserve close scrutiny. First, though, it is necessary to consider the state of affairs from an Aboriginal perspective.

As elsewhere in Van Diemen's Land, the Aboriginal bands of the north-west undertook regular seasonal movements for economic and cultural purposes. In early September they tended to congregate around the mouths of the northern rivers and coastal lagoons to harvest swan and duck eggs. They then gradually moved towards the far north-west and offshore islands to exploit mutton-birds and seals.[26] By early March they were inland on important hunting grounds such as the Hampshire and Surrey Hills, returning to the coast with the onset of cooler weather.[27] As the Van Diemen's Land Company occupied Aboriginal land both on the coast and inland where there were vital economic resources it was inevitable that conflict would arise, particularly as Edward Curr ignored the instructions of his London-based directors to avoid confrontation.[28] Elitist and arrogant, Curr ruled with an iron fist, using violence when necessary to control his convict and indentured workforce. It could hardly be anything else when it came to the Aboriginal people,[29] although Curr initially believed they posed little threat. In a report to the directors he advised that while the Aboriginal people were numerous around Cape Grim they were not associated with those involved in the escalating conflict of eastern Van Diemen's Land.[30] Curr's sentiments were soon to experience a dramatic shift.

The first known clash occurred in December 1827, when a shepherd named Thomas John was speared in the thigh at Cape Grim, a customary punishment for breaching Aboriginal law. Three years later George Augustus Robinson was able to confirm that this had indeed been the case when he was told by Aboriginal women that company shepherds had been in the habit of taking them into their huts for sex. Their men had retaliated by spearing John as a warning, but the shepherds struck back by shooting at least one Aboriginal man dead.[31] Unfortunately, this triggered a chain of events that was to culminate in the 'Cape Grim Massacre' the following February. Four weeks later Aboriginal raiders, possibly led by Wymurick, returned to Cape Grim and destroyed 118 of the company's prized ewes. Some of the sheep were speared; others were driven into the sea and drowned.[32]

Curr sent an armed party in the supply vessel *Fanny* from Circular Head to exact revenge. Led by Richard Frederick who knew the far north-west as well as any other colonist at that time, they located a large camp of Aborigines just on dusk and decided to delay their attack until first light. Heavy rain during the night intervened. With damp powder the muskets were useless and the party withdrew without the Aborigines even being aware of their presence. That, at least, was the official version.[33] There was another one. Rosalie Hare, the wife of a ship's captain, visited Circular Head in January 1828. She was told by company employees that Frederick's party, supported by four shepherds permanently stationed at Woolnorth, had actually carried out a reprisal. According to Hare's informants 12 Aborigines had been killed and the rest fled, but it did not end there. The Aborigines quickly regrouped and pursued Frederick and his men back to the *Fanny*, which they were fortunate to reach without any casualties to themselves.[34] This version certainly has a ring of truth. Having located the Aborigines in their camp at dusk Frederick's party had the element of surprise, especially with their intended victims silhouetted against campfires. It is hardly credible that they would have waited through a cold rainy night knowing full well that their firearms had been rendered useless.

There was also an interesting side issue in this growing conflict. With Curr constantly agitating for more suitable land, Lieutenant Governor Arthur sent Assistant Surveyor John Helder Wedge to the north-west in a bid to locate enough grazing land to satisfy the company manager and to ensure their activities were kept well clear of the settled districts.[35] Wedge began his survey in January 1828 and by the following May he and his men were approaching West Point when they noticed an Aboriginal man keeping them under close observation. Realising he had been seen, the man walked quickly behind a small sand dune and Wedge's party gave chase. As they rounded the dune they came face-to-face with 16 armed Aborigines, the surprise causing one of Wedge's men to panic and discharge his gun. The Aborigines, one of whom was almost certainly wounded, fled with the survey party again in pursuit. One Aborigine separated from his companions and ran into the sea, ignoring Wedge's entreaties to come ashore. He remained in the water for more than 30 minutes before being washed ashore apparently lifeless,[36] a mere boy aged between nine and 10 years of age. After being placed near a fire and rubbed vigorously the child's circulation was restored and he fully recovered.[37] Teetoreric (otherwise known as May Day) remained with Wedge until his death two years later, at which time there were three other Aboriginal boys sharing the Assistant Surveyor's household at Launceston.[38]

In view of his later marriage there was probably nothing sinister in Wedge's motives,[39] and while Teetoreric was living out the remainder of his short life in Launceston, events were continuing to unfold in the north-west. Roughly six weeks after Frederick's aborted or successful attack at Cape Grim the company servants struck again, an incident that has come down to posterity as the 'Cape Grim Massacre'. As with the clash at Risdon Cove in May 1804, this incident has also sparked considerable debate over what actually took place, and no information was forthcoming at all until 18 months after the event. It could well have remained hidden forever had not Agricultural Superintendent Alexander Goldie been implicated in another killing at Cooee Point, just a few kilometres from the fledgling settlement at Emu Bay — or Burnie as it is now known.

Unlike all other indiscriminate murders of Aborigines in the north-west, the incident at Cooee Point in August 1829 took place close to a free settlement, incurring the very real risk of coming to the notice of authorities in Hobart. What comes through all of this is a powerful indication of the Van Diemen's Land Company's unofficial policy of extermination. It was a state within a state, and with his magisterial powers Edward Curr possessed absolute authority. Isolated, faced with a growing crisis which included the loss of valuable livestock on which the company's future prospects were totally dependent, Curr was determined to succeed at any cost. Yet, as the appointed official of George Arthur's administration, the company manager also had to be extremely circumspect to ensure that nothing leaked out. This is what makes the so-called 'Goldie Incident' so important.

On 21 August 1829 employees of the company were erecting sheep sheds at Cooee Point under the supervision of Alexander Goldie. Two Aboriginal women, one with a child aged around six years, were seen by the men who downed tools and attempted to trap them on the beach. One of the women broke through the closing cordon and fled into the scrub, at which point Alexander Goldie mounted a horse and successfully gave chase. In his absence the second woman was shot and wounded before being killed by a blow from an axe which severed her jugular vein. Goldie reported the incident to Curr, relating all the information in a matter-of-fact tone as he had almost certainly done on previous occasions. Goldie was clearly taken aback by his superior's exceptional response, for Curr replied that he had never read 'a more revolting detail than that contained in your letter and the manner in which this barbarous transaction is related without one word of disapprobation'.[40]

This was news to Goldie, who was later to claim that shooting Aborigines was company policy, and it is relevant that in Curr's reply to Goldie he made no comment regarding the surviving Aboriginal woman, suggesting that a form of slavery was also practised by the company. As Goldie reported to Curr:

> The woman is in irons I make her wash potatoes for the horses and intend taking her to the hills and making her work … the woman will not speak and is often very sulky. She broke the irons once and was nearly getting away I think she is about 20 or 22 years old. I have no doubt she will work.[41]

Nor was anything said, or questions asked, concerning the fate of the child whose mother had been murdered. Killing and slavery thus appear to have been the norm, and Curr's supposed horror was seemingly quite out of character. Goldie certainly recognised it as such, and he also knew why. The murder had taken place too close to the Emu Bay settlement and Curr was already attempting to distance himself, and by extension the company, from any involvement. Knowing that his superior could no longer be trusted Goldie acted first by writing directly to Lieutenant Governor Arthur with his own account of the incident. He did so without Curr's knowledge, and Goldie took the matter a good deal further, documenting a number of other lethal actions perpetrated by the company servants against the Aboriginal people. His list included a mass killing at Cape Grim in February the previous year.[42]

George Arthur responded by ordering Curr to conduct a magisterial inquiry into the murder at Cooee Point. Curr, however, was suddenly stricken by 'illness', so ill in fact that he was confined to his residence and unable to make the journey to Emu Bay and investigate the affair. Not to be thwarted, Arthur suggested that if he was too ill to travel Curr should issue warrants and bring all the witnesses back to Circular Head.[43] At this point the company manager wrote to his directors, advising that he could no longer avoid conducting an inquiry into the murder of an Aboriginal woman as he had hoped. It was his 'painful duty' he said,[44] so painful that he had delayed taking action for four months.

It was not until the middle of December 1829 that Curr finally arrived at Emu Bay, and the subsequent inquiry was of little consequence. He simply took a statement from Thomas Watson, the local storekeeper, though this alone would have caused some concern as Watson's information came directly from the company servants involved. News of the murder had obviously been leaked almost immediately and Watson corroborated Goldie's report, adding that it was Nathaniel Russell who fired the shot which severely wounded the victim. Russell had previously been injured by Aborigines and had vowed vengeance.[45] He had been fortunate to survive an Aboriginal attack at Burghley Hut at the Surrey Hills in September 1828, when four company servants had been left for dead. They eventually reached Emu Bay, where Henry Hellyer was shocked at their 'most deplorable state'.[46]

Curr could well understand the motivation, and later explained to Arthur that little more could be done as he was stranded at Emu Bay for two days without a horse. Goldie had left the settlement for Burghley Hut following another Aboriginal raid, and Richard Sweetling, the servant responsible for striking the woman with an axe, had since been speared and was recuperating at the Hampshire Hills. If anything, Curr was slightly twisting the truth. Goldie did not leave Emu Bay until 18 December, the day after Curr had interviewed Watson, and he had done so to warn the men in the stock camps that if they continued killing Aborigines they could no longer count on Curr's support and might well be charged with murder.[47]

Curr finally obtained a horse and visited Burghley Hut on 22 December. The following day he was at another stock camp further south known as the Racecourse, where he confronted Goldie and Henry Hellyer regarding their attempts to undermine his authority. While there, Curr personally led an armed party of company employees against the Aborigines in a bid to reassert his authority and reinspire confidence. His men were promised spirits if they could bring back an Aboriginal head so that it could be mounted on the roof of a stock hut to serve as a grisly warning. The company employees apparently lacked their usual vigour as the attack was aborted, a fact that is known from Goldie's public disclosure. Indeed, Curr was forced to explain his actions to the company directors, though he did so without showing any remorse. Claiming to 'have a perfect loathing of shedding blood', Curr insisted that he was protecting the company's interests by teaching the Aborigines a lesson they would not forget, an exercise that was to be reinforced by the decapitated head.[48] In 1831 an Aboriginal head was finally obtained at Surrey Hills by one of Curr's men following an attack on a company hut. Said to belong to a young man 'aged about twenty-four', the skull was passed to the company's surgeon, Dr Joseph Milligan, later superintendent and medical officer of the Aboriginal Establishments at Wybalenna on Flinders Island and Oyster Cove, south of Hobart. Mulligan eventually sold the cranium to a voracious collector of skeletal remains named Joseph Barnard Davis.[49]

After his own unsuccessful head-hunting expedition Curr returned to Circular Head and completed his magisterial inquiry into the Cooee Point killing. All he had was Watson's statement and Goldie's report, but he noted that as Arthur had declared martial law in the settled districts of Van Diemen's Land in November 1828 the killing could not be construed as murder.[50] Curr stood on very shaky legal grounds. Arthur sought advice from Alfred Stephen, the Solicitor General, who reasoned that the issue rested on whether the woman had died from the gunshot wound or the blow of the axe. If it had been the latter then it would depend on how long she had been a prisoner before being struck.[51] All sense of humanity evaporated in this tangled legal logic.

In subsequent correspondence Curr's emphasis dwelt on the gunshot, the death-dealing strike of the axe steadily trivialised until it became a minor wound similar to a 'lancet cut'. Arthur failed to question any of this, probably because Stephen had pointed out that if the killing of the woman at Cooee Point was acknowledged as homicide it would undermine the effectiveness of Arthur's declaration of martial law: the colonists would be discouraged from hunting down

Aborigines if there was a good chance of being charged with murder.[52] But perhaps the real question in all this was whether the land controlled by the Van Diemen's Land Company actually constituted part of the settled districts where martial law applied. Technically it did not.

This was an issue that was never raised and the case was effectively closed. But it was not quite over. News of what might have been considered a minor issue in the Black War eventually reached the British government in faraway London, possibly through the directors of the company. Sir George Murray, then Secretary of State for the Colonies, requested full details of the incident from Lieutenant Governor Arthur. Usually forthright when it came to dealing with his London superiors, Arthur's replies in this instance were remarkably evasive. As it transpired, however, his explanations were eventually accepted and no mention of the Cooee Point murder was included in the despatches published in the 1831 parliamentary papers dealing with the Aborigines of Van Diemen's Land.[53] It was, after all, an isolated incident in the midst of full-scale warfare; the affray at Cape Grim, on the other hand, was something else again.

George Arthur had by now become extremely curious as to what was taking place in the remote north-west, and with the 'Friendly Mission' heading into the region George Augustus Robinson was instructed to investigate the affray at Cape Grim.[54] Robinson regarded his task as an official inquiry, and when the mission arrived at Woolnorth in June 1830 he wasted little time in carrying out his perceived duty. He spent two days examining the property with Joseph Fossey, by then station overseer, who took him to Mount Victory and explained that its name commemorated 'an encounter with the natives'. There was no mention of casualties or the circumstances which led to the clash. At the time four shepherds had been permanently stationed at Cape Grim. One of them was Charles Chamberlain, who was still working on the property and duly interrogated by Robinson.

Chamberlain stated that 30 Aborigines — all men — had been killed, and their bodies thrown over a cliff into the sea. When Robinson pointed out that there were conflicting opinions regarding the death toll, Chamberlain insisted that he and his companions were afraid that their actions might come to the attention of outside authorities and result in serious trouble.[55] He was unaware that Robinson was an agent for George Arthur's administration.

When Keith Windschuttle examined the 'Cape Grim Massacre' he discredited Chamberlain's testimony on the basis of his character. There can be no doubt that the assigned servant was a dangerous man who had been further brutalised by the convict system. Sentenced to transportation for 14 years in 1825 when he was 22 years of age, Chamberlain's subsequent record in Van Diemen's Land was marked by a string of serious offences. He had been regularly flogged and spent time in chain gangs. Later, in 1835, he received an additional seven year sentence.[56] While Chamberlain may not have been a reliable witness his character profile was that of a violent criminal, an ideal match for a situation where killing Aboriginal people was actively condoned if not actually encouraged.

Two months later Robinson also had the opportunity to interrogate another participant in the 'Cape Grim Massacre'. Unlike Chamberlain, William Gunshannon was initially evasive. Eventually conceding his involvement, Gunshannon refused to be drawn on the number of Aborigines he and his companions had killed on that fateful day, claiming that he only saw some 'traces of blood afterwards'. He nevertheless disclosed that women had been among the victims, and bluntly told Robinson that he was prepared to shoot any Aborigines he came across.[57] The Aborigines had similarly marked out Gunshannon for special treatment. After the affair at Cape Grim the shepherd was lucky to survive spear wounds inflicted at the Surrey Hills.[58]

During the intervening period the convict and accomplished bushman, Alexander McKay, guided Robinson to Cape Grim so that he could personally examine the site. At the base of the cliff Robinson gathered 'several human bones' and 'a piece of the bloody cliff', the latter often misconstrued as bloodstained stone.[59] The presence of human bone is probably the weakest evidence of the incident, as Robinson's investigation took place more than two years after it occurred. Cape Grim is one of the wildest stretches of coastline in Australia, lashed by the winds of the Roaring Forties. During severe gales waves can reach more than 10 metres in height,[60] and Robinson admitted that he had to scurry away from the bottom of the cliff as the tide was on its way in.[61] It is beyond the realm of credibility that human bones or, for that matter, bloodstains could still be found so long after the event — unless, of course, they were from a more recent killing.[62]

Robinson also spoke with Aboriginal women accompanying a party of sealers, all of whom roughly confirmed the sequence of events which began with the spearing of Thomas John and culminated in the 'Cape Grim Massacre'. They said that 30 Aborigines had been killed. Only one of the women was from the north-west; the others were from the north-east and had been living with the sealers for years.[63] Keith Windschuttle has argued that the women were obviously led by Robinson's questioning as they did not have the ability to count to 30.[64] That may well be correct, though it is possible that the women from the north-east had acquired that ability after their lengthy association with sealers. The problem is that they were not eyewitnesses, so their evidence was at best nothing more than hearsay.

From all the information available to him Robinson reconstructed the events at Cape Grim. As he saw it, a band of Aborigines had made camp opposite the Doughboys so they could exploit the mutton-birds. They were favoured by the fair weather which was essential for the women to be able to swim across to the rookeries. Having harvested the birds and tied them together with grass they then returned to the mainland. While the band was feasting on their avian prey they were ambushed by the shepherds from the heights above. Some of them found refuge in the sea, while others managed to escape around the cliffs at the water's edge. A number sought shelter in a cleft of the cliff. All those exposed to the shepherd's guns were killed, and after descending to the campsite the shepherds discovered and executed those hiding in the fissure.[65] There is one technical problem with Robinson's reconstruction. The incident occurred in February, when the women were probably gathering abalone rather than mutton-birds. It was too late in the season for eggs, too early for decent-sized chicks and the adults would have been foraging for food at sea. As mentioned earlier, mutton-birds are not particularly common on the Doughboys, but 'muttonfish' — abalone — certainly are in the surrounding waters. The confusion is the same as with the incident around 1820, albeit, without Robinson's informants providing any details of the women's activities.[66]

This is roughly the version which has found its way into the secondary sources and, as Keith Windschuttle pondered, it is remarkable that the incident did not give rise to a local legend or story.[67] One reason for that is the relative isolation of Cape Grim, which meant that nobody outside the Van Diemen's Land Company knew of the affray until Alexander Goldie informed Lieutenant Governor Arthur. Even then, information was limited until the company's records began to be deposited in the government archives from the late 1950s. None of the nineteenth century chroniclers mentioned the 'Cape Grim Massacre', not even Jorgen Jorgenson who was in the north-west both before and after the event. The first recognised historian to stumble on it was Archibald Meston, who published his history of the Van Diemen's Land Company in 1958 after gaining access to some of the records. Additional information did not come to light until 1966, when Brian Plomley completed his mammoth task of transcribing and publishing George Augustus Robinson's journals of the 'Friendly Mission'.[68] Both works became the basis for all subsequent accounts, notwithstanding that a cult of denial persisted among local historians of the north-west until recent years. The latter looked upon Edward Curr as the region's unblemished 'founding father'.[69]

There has also been considerable confusion over where the incident actually took place. Cape Grim is a small promontory facing west and adjacent to, and just south of, the Doughboys. The cape is on a larger peninsula, the most northerly extremity of which is known as Woolnorth Point. Over time the name 'Cape Grim' has been applied rather loosely. In 1798 Bass and Flinders named the entire peninsula Cape Grim, while in 1824 surveyor Thomas Scott referred to Cape Grim as a point immediately to the north of the Doughboys. The location known as Cape Grim today first appeared on a map in 1872 as Slaughter Hill, and was not renamed until 1975. At the same time a location known as Suicide Bay suddenly appeared on maps just to the south of the Doughboys and slightly north of present-day Cape Grim.[70]

All of this topographical uncertainty has understandably made it difficult to pinpoint exactly where the shepherds attacked the Aborigines in February 1828 — except that it was approximately opposite the Doughboys. Then there is the logistical problem of how four shepherds armed only with muskets could wreak such havoc without being counter-attacked and possibly killed themselves. For one thing, they had the advantage of height, and they certainly had sufficient firepower, as muskets had come a long way from the standard-issue Brown Bess used by the soldiers at Risdon Cove in May 1804. By the late 1820s the most commonly available weapon was the Indian Pattern Smooth Bore musket which could discharge rounds of shot without damaging the barrel. With a calibre of 0.75-inch, it was slightly larger than modern 12-gauge shotguns and at close range equally lethal. Like the earlier Brown Bess, wounds inflicted by this weapon often caused death. At least one of the shepherds stationed near Cape Grim, John Weavis, was also an experienced soldier, having served in two British regiments and undertaken a tour of duty in the West Indies from 1815 to 1817, where he may have been involved in the suppression of slave revolts. If his companions had not already been proficient in the use of firearms, they had ample time to learn from John Weavis.[71]

As Keith Windschuttle has rightly pointed out, however, we may never know exactly how many Aboriginal people were slain by the company shepherds at Cape Grim. He suspects the figure could have been as low as six,[72] though if wounded are taken into account the potential casualties immediately rise into double figures. While Chamberlain was adamant that 30 Aborigines were killed he was not necessarily referring to a single action. There were three known attacks by company servants in the Cape Grim area that are known — and there may have been more. Nor did it end there.

To prevent the Aborigines from plundering company stock huts Curr resorted to a number of devious strategies. In 1841 he advised police magistrate John Lee Archer that he had tried spring-loaded guns which fired when the huts were entered; man-traps capable of severing an arm or leg had also been concealed in huts, while on at least one occasion an armed company servant had been hidden inside an isolated outpost to ambush raiders.[73] Curr did not mention to Archer that his men had a more subtle means of ridding the company's lands of Aborigines. In 1830 the superintendent at the Surrey Hills, George Robson, told George Augustus Robinson that when he had offered his men strychnine to kill 'hyaenas' (thylacines) the men replied that while they had no immediate use for it they would certainly require it during the summer months 'to poison the natives' dogs'. Summer, of course, was the time when the Aborigines returned to these uplands to hunt kangaroos. Robson took the strychnine away with him, believing that it would be used to lace flour and poison the Aborigines themselves. Robinson accepted that hundreds of Aborigines had been killed in this manner in the north-west,[74] but the evidence remains entirely circumstantial. The subject nevertheless re-emerged in 1841 when Edward Curr sent an anxious note to company superintendent Adophus Schayer in response to a rumour that company servants were indeed poisoning the Aboriginal people.[75] He had cause for concern as government officials had begun making discreet inquiries into the matter, an investigation that ultimately came to nought. It appears that no-one was willing to provide information.[76]

In his report to Lieutenant Governor Arthur prior to resigning from the Van Diemen's Land Company, Alexander Goldie had also alleged that Aborigines who posed no threat had been hunted down in organised punitive expeditions.[77] To some extent violence had the tacit support of the London directors. Although urging Curr to find a means of incorporating the Aborigines into the company's workforce, they were 'aware that a knowledge of the strength and power of the Company must first be proved to exist and fully impressed upon the natives'. To accomplish that directive they shipped out 'Fire Arms, particularly pistols which they conceive will be more use than muskets because they can be carried about the person'.[78] As is clear from the treatment of the surviving Aboriginal woman from Cooee Point, the closest Curr came to incorporating the Aboriginal people into his workforce was to condone a form of slavery. Curr's actions finally left him with two choices: either to physically remove the Aboriginal people of the north-west as Robinson's 'Friendly Mission' partly accomplished, or to eliminate them altogether. By taking the latter course it became an act of genocide, and while genocidal intent is not necessarily applicable elsewhere in Van Diemen's Land it can certainly be applied to the north-west. Curr offered no assistance to Robinson's 'Friendly Mission', and his malevolent attitude towards the Aboriginal people was shown again in 1831, when Alexander McKay, working on behalf of Arthur's administration, captured four men and a woman who had been attacking the company's livestock and huts at the Surrey Hills. The colonial government requested Curr to cover the cost of McKay's supplies, rightly reasoning that his work had benefitted the Van Diemen's Land Company. Curr refused.[79]

Yet, despite his best efforts, Aboriginal resistance in the north-west continued long after the cessation of hostilities in all other regions of Van Diemen's Land. In November 1836 Robinson was forced to mount another mission to the north-west, with nine Aboriginal envoys on this occasion led by his sons George Jnr and Charles. They managed to contact a family group comprising a 'husband, wife and four children, including a boy of about fifteen' near Cradle Mountain. The Aborigines refused the overtures of the mission and escaped into the bush. Further searches were made by Robinson's sons between January and June 1837 without success.[80] Conflict in the north-west erupted again in 1839 and persisted until February 1842. In September 1839 two unarmed company servants were attacked by Aboriginal men and a boy at the Surrey Hills and climbed trees in a bid to escape. The Aborigines hurled spears at the men 'for upwards of two hours', one of the men receiving multiple wounds in his arm from fending off the missiles before the Aborigines finally departed.[81] It was probably this group who attempted to steal blankets from a stock-keeper's hut in the same area. The following month two men, a youth and a woman attacked company servant Neil McDonnell, who survived five spear wounds. In December 1840 a company servant stationed at the Surrey Hills, James Lucas, was chased into his hut after being speared. The Aborigines showered the building with stones, only desisting from the attack when another armed company servant arrived on the scene.[82]

Fighting occasionally spread slightly beyond the Van Diemen's Land Company grants. In April 1841 a free settler named Thomas Field, who farmed on Middlesex Plains just outside the company's eastern boundary, had a narrow escape after being chased into his hut by hostile Aborigines. His attackers attempted to pull the building down, threatening Field with all manner of violence, and were on the point of achieving their aim when two armed colonists appeared on the scene and the Aborigines fled.[83] Three months later Aborigines plundered company huts at West Bay, Circular Head, on four separate occasions, removing blankets, clothing and ammunition.[84] Curr warned the colonial government that if assistance was not forthcoming blood would soon be shed,[85] a strange appeal from a man whose policy from the outset had been the total destruction of the Aboriginal population.

Whether Aborigines were responsible for all the raids reported by Curr is debatable. For instance, he complained of a hut being plundered at Woolnorth on 13 September 1841 when three convict servants were present,[86] but the fact that the latter offered no resistance suggests they may have cast blame on non-existent raiders to obtain extra supplies for themselves. On other occasions, though, the circumstances are beyond contention. The following month 'eight or nine' Aborigines, equipped with firearms, twice struck a property run by former company servant James King at Rocky Cape, removing goods and slaughtering sheep.[87] King had earlier been refused a firearm for protection by police magistrate John Lee Archer on the grounds that killing Aborigines was illegal. He subsequently obtained a pistol courtesy of Edward Curr.[88] Three weeks later the farm of John King at Table Cape (James King's employer) was also attacked by Aborigines. King's two employees were driven off and the farmhouse plundered of flour, blankets, sugar and two guns. Flour that could not be carried away was wantonly destroyed, and before leaving the Aborigines dispersed the livestock and drove two bullocks over a cliff. King is said to have known the local Aborigines, and was adamant the raiders were from further west.[89] The theft of guns is also of interest, even though it occurred many times and in many parts of Van Diemen's Land. It is known that the Aborigines could dismantle and clean firearms as well as any colonist. They knew how to keep the powder dry and could even fashion flints from natural stone. The incident at Rocky Cape was exceptional, however, as the Aborigines preferred to rely on their own technology.[90] Firearms were usually only stolen to deprive the colonists of their use.

On 1 January 1842 the Aborigines attacked another company servant at the Surrey Hills, and later the same month repeated attempts were made to plunder company huts at Studland Bay, just south of Cape Grim. The Aborigines set their dogs onto the sheep, killing some and maiming others. On 16 February the Aborigines succeeded in plundering a hut close to the company's headquarters at Circular Head and speared several valuable horses. Eleven days later they attempted to spear two company servants at a place known as The Patch near Table Cape.[91] The servants escaped, and this was the last recorded act of resistance by the Aboriginal people of north-west Van Diemen's Land. The fate of the raiders remains unknown.

Edward Curr regarded these attacks as a very serious matter indeed. Although dismissed from his position by the directors in 1839 Curr remained at Circular Head until his successor, James Gibson, finally arrived in February 1842. The last Aboriginal attack occurred just days before Curr's departure for the Port Phillip district, an apparent coincidence which suggests two possibilities: either the Aborigines were hunted down and killed by his men or they fled the region. Given the powerful Aboriginal affinity for home soil it is unlikely that their homeland was abandoned. It is more likely that they were liquidated.[92] But unbeknown to Curr a few Aboriginal people still managed to remain at large in the north-west.

It was not until October 1842 that the Lanne family was finally captured by sealers and Aboriginal women from the Australian mainland near the Arthur River. This had been at the instigation of James Gibson, who offered a £50 reward if they could be taken alive (as they were).[93] The Lanne family's origins almost certainly lay outside the north-west, and there is no certainty that they were the same family group which had been contacted by George Augustus Robinson's sons near Cradle Mountain in November 1836. At the time of their capture the Lanne parents, John and Nabrunga, were aged 'about fifty', while their five sons were from 'about thirty' to 'two or rather more'.[94] The gender of three of the children near Cradle Mountain was unspecified; the exception was a boy aged 'about fifteen'.[95] The Lanne family was destined for exile on Flinders Island, and one of the sons, William, would have the dubious distinction of becoming the 'last full-blooded Tasmanian Aboriginal male'.[96] With the capture of the Lanne family James Gibson was able to confidently inform his directors that Van Diemen's Land was now completely free of its original inhabitants.[97] Like Curr, Gibson may have been mistaken.

Surveyor James Erskine Calder definitely thought otherwise, claiming that Aborigines had been reported near the headwaters of the Forth River in 1845 and 1846. According to Calder the colonial government deliberately chose to ignore these sightings.[98] Of the four or five hundred people of the north-west around one hundred were removed to the islands of Bass Strait, and their fate was already sealed. Only six of the 47 Aborigines repatriated back to the mainland from Flinders Island in 1847 were from the north-west. Nicermenic, whose home territory lay around Circular Head, died at Oyster Cove, south of Hobart, in May 1849. His son Adam, who was born at Wybalenna on Flinders Island in August 1838, followed his father to the grave at Oyster Cove in October 1857. He was the last representative of the eight Aboriginal bands of the north-west.[99]

The frontier conflict throughout Van Diemen's Land had cost both sides dearly. Between 1803 and 1832 at least 437 colonists had been killed or wounded.[100] Aboriginal casualties are more shadowy as they were seldom recorded, and the claim made by Keith Windschuttle in 2002 that plausible evidence only exists to account for 118 deaths should be regarded as errant nonsense.[101] Recent research by Nicholas Clements has more than trebled that figure, with Clements insisting that around 600 Aborigines were killed by violence in eastern Van Diemen's Land alone.[102] Coupled with the obvious deaths in the north-west that figure can be increased to over 1000, but even then it only accounts for perhaps 25 per cent of all Aboriginal deaths between 1803 and the 1840s. The only evidence of large-scale loss of life was at Cape Grim in the north-west, and attempts to portray frontier conflict in the island colony as a series of 'massacres' are misguided at best. The killing fields of Van Diemen's Land were far more subtle. Aboriginal people were eliminated in ones and twos, threes and fours, a family here and a small group there. As Clements has convincingly argued, the isolated ambuscade was a very effective means of destroying the Aboriginal people.[103] This was a secretive war where no tallies were kept and few questions were asked, exemplified by the actions of the Van Diemen's Land Company in the north-west. It was this steady process of elimination (aided to some extent by internecine warfare) which dramatically reduced the Aboriginal population of Van Diemen's Land between 1803 and the early 1840s.

With the exception of the far south-west, disease was definitely not a major factor in the post-1803 period as Keith Windschuttle insisted.[104] There are no records of ailing and helpless Aboriginal people anywhere else — except when they had been captured and incarcerated (with Windschuttle highlighting the Bruny Island Aboriginal Station in 1829). The fate of Wyne and the Tarkiner from the west coast offer another graphic example. These people were in fine physical condition until George Augustus Robinson exacted his revenge by locking them within the grim confines of the Macquarie Harbour penal settlement. Within weeks they had succumbed to disease. Nor is there any evidence that disease ever escaped from this penal settlement to decimate the west coast Aborigines. Limited contact with military personnel was usually violent, and absconding convicts were either slain or shunned.[105] There was no social interaction of any consequence which could have led to the transfer of lethal microbes. Robinson recorded the extinction of the nearest Aboriginal band, the Peternidic,[106] an unsubstantiated claim which has led at least one historian to surmise that it could have resulted from the spread of disease.[107] Robinson's journals need to be treated with caution: there was no extinction. Members of the Peternidic band were among the later exiles on Flinders Island.[108] Rather than germs it was muskets, pistols and sabres which impacted disastrously on the Aboriginal population of Van Diemen's Land. Even this was not enough to totally eliminate them as many colonists wished. On the contrary, there were numerous survivors, and the problem which next confronted colonial authorities was what to do with them.

8

CAPTIVITY AND EXILE

Although the idea of exiling the Aborigines on an offshore island was not exclusively his, George Augustus Robinson certainly pushed for it to become a reality. Even at the height of the Black War Lieutenant Governor Arthur consistently advanced policies specifically designed to retain the Aboriginal people on the mainland of Van Diemen's Land.[1] Had Robinson not disregarded Arthur's wishes and given serious consideration to the Aborigines remaining on the mainland, the tragedy of Wybalenna would at least have been minimised if not avoided altogether. Robinson's desire to bring in the last of the Aborigines from the west coast and thereby secure the £1000 which had been offered when his 'Friendly Mission's' work had been completed,[2] led him to disregard the advice he had given the Executive Council four years earlier that it might be possible to leave the west coast Aborigines alone and have government agents reside among them.[3] Alexander McGeary, a convict bushman who accompanied Robinson on many of his journeys, later publicly condemned his former master for his decision to capture the 'peaceable and harmless creatures' living near Macquarie Harbour because — so McGeary said — 'they were of no annoyance to any person' and lived in a region where there was no-one to disturb.[4] Robinson's decision to incarcerate Wyne and his fellow Tarkiner in the convict gaol at Macquarie Harbour is all the more tragic given that much of their customary territory still lies vacant today. Just months after the Tarkiner had experienced hideous brutality and death the penal settlement was permanently closed and the convicts and guards transferred south.[5]

Robinson further showed his disdain for the Executive Council by resorting to the use of armed convicts to capture the Aborigines on his last foray to the west coast. This in itself was a flagrant breach of Lieutenant Governor Arthur's orders that the Aborigines should only accept the protection of the 'Friendly Mission' through their own volition.[6] Robinson's devotion to self-interest was nothing new. He had regularly used his very public displays of evangelical zeal as a means of cloaking his activities and, at the same time, to cultivate influential allies. In 1829 when the alarming mortality rate on Bruny Island made it clear that the days of Robinson's first Aboriginal Establishment were numbered, he was quick to make use of his evangelical contacts so he could move on to the next stage of his chosen career.

Taking note of Gilbert Robertson's early success in capturing Aboriginal people by using other Aborigines as both trackers and mediators, Robinson adapted the idea for himself. Through his brief experience on Bruny Island he gained some familiarity with the Ninene people of Port Davey in the remote south-west, which is why he deliberately chose to launch the first 'Friendly Mission' in their direction even though the Ninene had largely remained aloof from the conflict engulfing the settled districts of Van Diemen's Land.[7] Robinson claimed otherwise,[8] and also made sure that he was accompanied by Bruny Islanders who had a close relationship with the Ninene. With the Aborigines at his establishment rapidly succumbing to disease Robinson had little to lose and much to gain, and to that end he cultivated the support of two influential churchmen — Colonial Chaplain William Bedford and the Anglican chaplain, James Norman.[9]

In September 1836, on the eve of his departure for England, George Arthur closely interrogated Robinson as to who had originated the plan to conciliate with the Aborigines. Arthur was sure that he had first heard of it long before Robinson had put it into operation and that it might have come from Gilbert Robertson. Robinson denied that was the case, insisting that his rival had 'no definite plans'.[10] He lied, but his position had never really been under threat owing to his staunch allies, Bedford and Norman, who served him particularly well after their appointment to the Aborigines Committee. They lobbied Arthur to support Robinson's plan to travel right along the west coast, and Bedford went so far as to recommend the transfer of the Aborigines in Gilbert Robertson's roving party to Robinson's 'Friendly Mission'.[11] Alexander McGeary later recalled that he had been involved in the selection of Aborigines for Robinson's first mission and that some of them had indeed been taken directly out of Gilbert Robertson's hands.[12]

Robertson understandably complained,[13] but the authorities took little notice. After all, he had vociferously spoken out against the execution of Musquito and Black Dick in February 1825, and following the capture of Umarrah, Robertson had successfully prevented his execution by arguing that the North Midlands leader was technically a prisoner of war, not a common criminal.[14] These confrontations with the authorities over Aboriginal rights eroded what little official sympathy Robertson had, placing him in a position that George Augustus Robinson was able to exploit for his own ends. By the time

Robinson's first mission was underway his main rival was thus in a particularly weak position, and within a year his two most powerful supporters were strategically placed on the Aborigines Committee. Even on his journeys, Robinson managed to maintain contact with the seat of power through his correspondence with Bedford. At the same time he was able to develop and implement his own policies away from the scrutiny of the Lieutenant Governor. Robinson always believed that what was in his best interest applied equally to the Aborigines, which itself justified everything he did.[15] There was no room for the opinion of anyone in authority.

When the four Aborigines he captured in the north-west had been sent to Launceston and three repatriated back to Circular Head in 1830 on Arthur's instructions, Robinson unleashed his venom in his journal, railing against the no-nothing 'wiseacres at their parlour fireside at Hobart Town'. In his own words, Robinson was 'the only person that can judge what is best to be done'.[16] Two people who could have provided a credible alternative account of Robinson's activities were the experienced convict bushmen Alexander McGeary and Alexander McKay. They had no chance of doing so, for after making good use of their services Robinson had dismissed both men and then gone to great lengths to play down their contribution while simultaneously discrediting their characters.[17]

In 1831 Robinson had another good reason to call on the assistance of the Reverend Bedford when John Batman emerged as a potential rival after being placed in charge of the Aboriginal trackers from New South Wales. Robinson appealed to Bedford to have his authority as head of the Aboriginal Service confirmed. Bedford readily acquiesced, informing Robinson that any matters relating to the service would henceforth be placed solely under his direction. The following year Bedford was behind the move to offer Robinson an extremely generous remunerative package for his final mission to the west coast of Van Diemen's Land. At the same time Alexander McGeary was dismissed and replaced by two of Robinson's sons, George Jnr and Charles.[18] Although a teenager with virtually no bush experience, George Jnr received McGeary's full wage in addition to two convict servants: one to carry his bedding and personal effects, the other to care for the pet possums he took on the journey. At the conclusion of the west coast mission George Augustus Robinson received a 3000 acre (1214 hectare) land grant while George Jnr and Charles were the recipients of 1000 (400 hectare) and 500 acre (200 hectare) grants respectively.[19] This was a splendid outcome for the Robinson family — and a very disastrous one for the Aborigines.

Among McGeary's later complaints was his use as a personal messenger to maintain contact between Robinson and the Reverend Bedford in Hobart. During the 'Friendly Mission's' sojourn in the north-east of Van Diemen's Land in late 1830–early 1831 McGeary had been sent to Hobart on three separate occasions seeking Bedford's assistance to have Robinson appointed as a magistrate. He was with Bedford in the Lieutenant Governor's office when the request was denied,[20] a temporary setback for Robinson as he was finally appointed as a magistrate after securing the superintendency of the Aboriginal Establishment at Wybalenna on Flinders Island.[21] There can be no denying that Robinson used his contacts well and took advantage of every opportunity to promote himself. He treated people like pawns in a game of high stakes which he eventually won.

That was yet another reason why he was despised by many colonists, and Robinson made a particularly bitter enemy after Alexander McGeary was replaced by his sons. McGeary denigrated Robinson on a number of occasions, claiming that his former master had greatly exaggerated the perils he supposedly faced on the 'Friendly Mission'.[22] The only time that Robinson's life had been seriously threatened was at the Arthur River in September 1832, though Robinson insisted that he was in constant danger during the pursuit of the Big River and Oyster Bay peoples.[23] When he finally caught up with them near Lake Echo there were only 26 utterly exhausted and demoralised survivors. There had, in fact, been little to fear.

It is nonetheless relevant that these survivors only agreed to lay down their arms on the understanding that the Lieutenant Governor would redress their grievances. They were not. After a short stay in Hobart they were shuffled aboard a vessel and whisked into exile.[24] In the north Robinson had promised both Mannalargenna and Umarrah they would remain in their respective homelands.[25] When exile was unavoidable it is clear that Robinson assured the Aboriginal people of the east, including the mission guides, that it would only be a temporary measure.[26] Those unfulfilled promises rebounded after his appointment as superintendent at Wybalenna in 1835, when a 'rumour' began circulating among the Aboriginal people that his arrival on Flinders Island would mark their return home. According to Henry Reynolds, Robinson 'temporized, postponed his departure date, proposed that the [Aborigines] be moved to southern Victoria and wrote to the Colonial Secretary suggesting that he should not take command at Wybalenna'.[27] The Aboriginal understanding that banishment was temporary could only have come from Robinson himself. There was never any contact with the colonial government; all negotiations had been strictly conducted by the 'conciliator', and all of them proved false. By the time the 'Friendly Mission' had begun its work many of the Aboriginal groups were fragmented and demoralised, their numbers seriously depleted through frontier conflict. The Aboriginal people had every reason to be receptive to the overtures of a skilled negotiator offering terms of peace. Robinson betrayed their trust.

He had also grasped the advantage of using offshore islands as at least temporary holding pens where the Aborigines could be secured before transhipment. In the north-west he had lured Wymurrick and his people to Hunter Island, while in the north-east Swan Island had fulfilled the same purpose. Given Robinson's ambition to dictate policy initiatives relating to Aboriginal affairs, a strong case can be mounted that it was largely through his efforts that the idea of permanent exile in Bass Strait was finally adopted. It was certainly through Robinson that it was subsequently accomplished. As noted earlier, however, he was not the originator of this final solution. As early as December 1826 the colonial press had given serious consideration to banishing the Aboriginal people to an offshore island, suggesting that King Island at the western entrance to Bass Strait might prove suitable.[28] It was certainly large enough and at that time unoccupied, so it perhaps comes as no surprise that early the following year Arthur's administration sent surveyor George Barnard to examine the island. Barnard's report was published in March 1827, the surveyor producing a glowing account of the moderate climate, plentiful supplies of fresh water, fine stands of timber suitable for building materials, and an abundance of native game. He also reported the presence of an ideal harbour,[29] but when King Island was again proposed as a place of banishment for the Aboriginal people in 1831, it was rejected on the grounds that it had no suitable anchorage for supply vessels.[30]

By then Arthur's administration had tested a number of other islands off the coast of Van Diemen's Land. The initial choice, in fact, fell on Maria Island in the south-east, where Robinson was instructed to conduct a survey of the southern section in October 1829.[31] Maria Island was endowed with a moderate climate, a relatively large size — approximately 20 kilometres in length and 13 kilometres wide — and like King Island it abounded with native game. Moreover, as the island was the customary territory of the Tyreddeme band of the Oyster Bay people, it was familiar to many of the Aborigines who were intended to be placed there.[32] However, the northern section of the island, separated from the south by a narrow isthmus, was the site of a penal settlement, thus severely limiting its potential. Robinson was unimpressed, considering the soil in the south sterile and the topography too rugged. The only arable land he found was on the western side of the island and restricted to roughly 200 acres (80 hectares). Robinson considered the isthmus too wide to be effectively guarded, which would make intercourse between the convicts and Aborigines a probability. Above all, the island's close proximity to the mainland made escape almost a certainty.[33] His mind was already focused on a final solution.

Despite Robinson's pessimistic report others favoured Maria Island. One of them was Captain George Jackson, master of the cutter *Charlotte*, who had extensive knowledge of the islands around Van Diemen's Land. Jackson wrote to the Board of Enquiry established by Arthur in 1829, arguing that Maria Island was superior in that it could easily be supplied from Hobart and was less exposed than the islands in Bass Strait. Jackson pointed out that escape could easily be prevented by stationing a military detachment with a boat on nearby Lachlan Island, but his suggestions fell on deaf ears and the island was ruled out of contention.[34] Lieutenant Governor Arthur had a number of significant issues to consider. For one thing, he wanted to ensure safety for the Aborigines (and by extension the colonists). Once that had been achieved he intended inculcating the Indigenous people in European ways through dress codes, education and farming. While his motives may have been admirable, it does not appear to have occurred to Arthur — or many other colonists — that the Aborigines might actively resist those imposed alien measures. The Lieutenant Governor had clearly bowed to the inevitable: exile was the only means of ensuring peace. And as the numbers of Aborigines captured by the 'Friendly Mission' and others steadily increased through 1830 the problem of finding a place of banishment became particularly urgent. When the Board of Enquiry was reconstituted as the Aborigines Committee in that year, one of its first tasks was to solve the deportation crisis.[35]

In the meantime Robinson began experimenting with his own temporary refuges. Neither Hunter Island in the north-west nor Swan Island in the north-east offered feasible long-term solutions. The first trial was Swan Island, approximately 3.5 kilometres in length and less than a kilometre wide. The island has a number of open plains but the soil is mostly sandy and low shrubs dominate the vegetation.[36] It is not known where Robinson established his initial settlement except that it was almost certainly close to a beach where he and his boat crews erected their tents. The Aborigines constructed their own windbreaks. After three weeks the camp was shifted to a more sheltered location where rough huts were built. Water was obtained by sinking a well, while rations were shipped in from Launceston. Supplies were nevertheless erratic, forcing Robinson's men as well as the Aborigines to rely heavily on natural resources. Penguin and mutton-bird rookeries were exploited, women dived for abalone and crayfish, and the men were regularly rowed across to the mainland to hunt kangaroos and wallabies.[37]

Alexander McKay was left in charge of the settlement when Robinson and his coxswain James Parish were absent on their forays to the Furneaux Islands in search of Aboriginal women living with the sealers. The Aborigines, including the mission guides, were apparently content with their situation, probably because they knew it was only a temporary arrangement. For the mission Aborigines it was a welcome interlude from constant trekking, while the Cape Portland Aborigines were on a safe haven immediately adjacent to their homeland which, of course, the men regularly visited. The only thing lacking was a gender balance, with men greatly outnumbering women, and for all his prudery Robinson was well aware that without restoring that balance the period of contentment could not last.[38] Nor was he able to prevent the women from having sexual relations with his boat crews and it may have been during his excursions to the Furneaux Islands that Robinson first considered their potential as a permanent place of exile. In January 1831 he sailed to Hobart for discussions with Arthur's administration, again leaving McKay in charge. During his absence the sealers raided Swan Island, and despite McKay's later protestations that he did all he could to prevent them taking liberties with the Aboriginal women Robinson was unconvinced. In fact, Robinson came to believe that McKay had acted in collusion with the sealers and had sexual relations with some of the women himself. Notwithstanding that Robinson seized every opportunity to downplay McKay's contribution to the 'Friendly Mission' for self-aggrandisement, there is evidence that McKay was a rather unsavoury and violent character who definitely had the blood of Aborigines on his hands.[39]

During their sojourn on Swan Island the general health of the Aboriginal people was reasonably good. There was only one case of serious illness and no deaths in the four-and-a-half months until their transfer to the Furneaux Islands in March 1831. One of the women rescued from the sealers had been 'infected with a loathsome disease' — almost certainly venereal disease — and owing to the westerly winds and sandy soil many of the Aborigines and some of Robinson's men were afflicted with ophthalmia.[40] This was a far better outcome than anywhere else the Aborigines were lodged in Bass Strait, but their fate was sealed in January–February 1831 when the Aborigines Committee in Hobart made the decision to deport the Aboriginal people to the Furneaux Islands. The decision was not taken lightly. Both Maria and King Islands were carefully reconsidered before they were definitely ruled out, and some thought was given to using Hunter Island in the far north-west. This was rejected owing to the

Van Diemen's Land Company holding proprietary rights over the island. On the best information available the unanimous decision of the Aborigines Committee was that Gun Carriage Island would be the site of the permanent Aboriginal Establishment. Now known as Vansittart Island, Gun Carriage was said to have a good anchorage, abundant supplies of wood, water, abalone and mutton-birds. Native game abounded on nearby Cape Barren Island, which was readily accessible.[41] The committee had been swayed by the arguments put forward by Robinson:

> Mr. Robinson is of [the] opinion that if the Natives were placed on an island in Basses Straits they would not feel themselves imprisoned there, or pine away in consequence of restraint, nor would they wish to return to the main land, or regret their inability to hunt and roam about in the manner they had previously done on this island. They would be enabled to fish, dance, sing, and throw spears, and amuse themselves in their usual way.[42]

It was almost as if Robinson had learnt nothing from the Aboriginal people. Of all the Furneaux Islands Robinson preferred Gun Carriage, and its relatively small size does not seem to have entered into any calculation. It is only three kilometres long and 2.5 kilometres wide, and in early 1831 a number of sealers were in residence. But it was escape-proof, with 57 kilometres of water separating the island from the mainland.[43] Despite the obvious failure of the Bruny Island settlement Robinson was appointed superintendent. In a surprising move contrary to the wishes of the Aborigines Committee, the colonial secretary instructed Robinson to investigate the potential of Clarke Island. If that proved unsuitable then he could direct his attention to Gun Carriage Island, and with that eventuality in mind Robinson was furnished with authorisation to evict the sealers.[44]

George Jackson sailed from Hobart in March 1831 to tranship the Aborigines on Swan Island. He was met there by Robinson, who had earlier travelled up the east coast of Van Diemen's Land and called in at the Maria Island penal settlement in an attempt to secure the services of the resident surgeon, Dr Thomas Brownell. The medical officer refused to relinquish his post, so the convict dispenser, Archibald Maclachlan, either volunteered or was ordered to accompany Robinson to Bass Strait. Maclachlan had been sentenced to transportation for 14 years at Edinburgh in May 1821 for committing the rather unusual crime of 'sinking a ship'. After arriving at Hobart he was appointed medical dispenser of the Colonial Hospital until sent to Maria Island in the same capacity. As it transpired, Maclachlan was a reasonably good choice, treating the Aborigines well and doing the best he could to alleviate their medical problems.[45]

After the closure of the Swan Island settlement and embarking the Aborigines on the *Charlotte*, Robinson established a temporary camp at Horseshoe Bay on the eastern shore of Preservation Island. The following morning he sent two boats across to Gun Carriage, probably as a show of force to intimidate the sealers. Already aware of what was taking place they had taken their Aboriginal women to other islands where they could not be found.[46] Robinson spent the next four days examining Clarke and Cape Barren Islands, neither of which were considered suitable for an Aboriginal Establishment, particularly Clarke Island which lacked a reliable source of fresh water.[47]

After a quick reconnaissance of the Kent Group, where the approaches were too dangerous for supply vessels, Robinson finally decided on Gun Carriage. Arriving in person he gave the sealers notice to quit and demanded they surrender the Aboriginal women. The only two he managed to get his hands on were Emerenna (Bet Smith) and Lucy, respectively partner and daughter of Thomas Beedon. He did not have them for long. The most influential sealer, James

Munro, travelled to Hobart and had an audience with George Arthur, protesting against Robinson's removal of the Aboriginal women. He also produced a petition from Thomas Beedon, his efforts achieving the desired result. Robinson was instructed to return a number of women to the sealers, including Emerenna and Lucy. Other resident sealers told Robinson they either had no women or they had run away and were nowhere to be found.[48] While this was not the last time the sealers outwitted Robinson, there was no avoiding their eviction. The majority shifted to Woody Island, where the conciliator sent a corporal and two soldiers to keep them under observation. It was a futile exercise and the detachment was withdrawn the very next day.[49]

On 24 March 1831 the temporary huts on Preservation Island were dismantled and the *Charlotte* sailed with the Aborigines for Gun Carriage. A fierce gale sprang up and the vessel was almost lost, necessitating the landing of the Aborigines on Great Dog Island where the huts and stores were unloaded yet again. It was four days before Robinson could reach Gun Carriage Island, and then it was only to purchase potatoes and pigs from the sealers. The carpenter subsequently rowed across from Great Dog Island and erected a store before the Aborigines were brought over in batches during the following week.[50] Two of the original 13 sealers remained. One was an invalid; the other, John Smith, owned a boat that was hired by Robinson for general duties related to his Aboriginal Establishment. Smith's Aboriginal partner, Pleenperrenner (otherwise known as 'Mother Brown'), was appointed overseer of the women, a position she evidently enjoyed. The real bonus was the eight substantial huts built by the sealers, each with its own large garden. Three were occupied by Aborigines who had accompanied Robinson on the 'Friendly Mission'.[51] At this stage Robinson is said to have had a total of 53 Aborigines in his charge.[52]

Having organised the new settlement Robinson then set out in the *Charlotte* to make yet another unsuccessful sweep of the Furneaux Islands in search of Aboriginal women cohabiting with the sealers. Adverse winds prevented his return to Gun Carriage Island and the *Charlotte* continued on to George Town. The vessel finally arrived back at Gun Carriage with additional supplies (including 10 sheep) at the end of April 1831. Also on board were Aborigines who had been held in Launceston Gaol and a small number taken from the colonists.[53] The vessel arrived just in time. Due to an oversight, supplies had not been shipped to Gun Carriage Island as expected and the settlement was gripped by famine. At the same time 'a violent diarrhea [sic]' had caused the death of two Aborigines, while a number of others were gravely ill.[54] Apart from the shortage of provisions, Archibald Maclachlan attributed the deteriorating condition of the Aborigines to the bleak environment, inadequate housing and poor water supply. Robinson thought otherwise, blaming the deaths and illness on Maclachlan's incompetence.[55] Yet in June 1831 he was quite prepared to leave Maclachlan temporarily in charge again when he resumed the 'Friendly Mission', and Maclachlan's employment continued through the transfer to The Lagoons and then Wybalenna on Flinders Island. He was not replaced until December 1833.[56]

When George Jackson returned to Hobart in the *Charlotte* he notified the Aborigines Committee of the island's defects, offering the suggestion that the settlement should be relocated to the south-western side of Flinders Island, opposite Green Island, at a place known as The Lagoons. The committee agreed,[57] although it was not until November 1831 that the transfer finally took place. Another problem which existed on Gun Carriage Island — and did not come to the attention of the Aborigines Committee — was that neither Robinson nor Maclachlan had been able to prevent sexual liaisons between the Aboriginal women and the convict servants. The situation did not improve in July, when Sergeant Alexander Wight of the 63rd Regiment arrived as temporary superintendent. He was accompanied by a corporal and five privates.[58] Wight was around 48 years of age and had served with the regiment for 22 years. He would remain a non-commissioned officer in the 63rd for a further three years before taking his discharge in 1834. Wight was anything but inspirational, a product of the mind-numbing obedience which characterised the rank and file of the British Army until beyond the First World War. His official military record described him as 'indifferent', so why he was chosen as superintendent of the Aboriginal Establishment is very strange indeed — except that it was only intended as a temporary measure. When Robinson returned from the 'Friendly Mission' Wight's duties would be confined solely to the distribution of rations.[59]

Wight was still in charge in November 1831 when Jackson arrived in the *Charlotte* to undertake the transfer of the settlement to The Lagoons on Flinders Island. During the sojourn on Gun Carriage Island at least 10 Aborigines had died, apparently from respiratory infections, a mortality rate of roughly 20 per cent.[60] Unfortunately, The Lagoons offered no improvement. The site chosen was exposed to cold westerly winds which penetrated the flimsy wooden huts built on an unstable sand dune only 45 metres from the water's edge. The soil was poor and the only available drinking water was obtained from holes dug in the sand just above the high-tide mark. Not surprisingly, it was brackish and unpleasant. The fresh-water lagoon from which the location takes its name dried up during the summer months, and the settlement was also difficult to access, with the nearest anchorage at Green Island, 5 kilometres away.[61]

Contrary to his orders Wight employed three sealers, and he had little compassion for his charges, treating the Aborigines as if they were prisoners of war and freely using coercion to have his commands obeyed.[62] While the Aborigines most definitely were not prisoners of war they were certainly being captured in numbers as Robinson's 'Friendly Mission' pursued its course through the Midlands and more northerly areas of Van Diemen's Land. When the 26 Big River and Oyster Bay people arrived in January 1832 the Aboriginal residents divided themselves into three separate groups based on customary alliances. The Big River and Oyster Bay people remained together, while the north-eastern and Ben Lomond bands formed their own camp and the north, north Midlands and western Aborigines coalesced. Whether Aboriginal men offered the women to the assigned convicts and sealers in exchange for flour and dogs as claimed by one historian is problematic.[63] Rather than the women being offered they were simply taken by the European staff, though many of those who had lived with the sealers showed an obvious preference for European men. Notwithstanding the occasional food shortages the Aborigines usually had ample rations (supplemented on occasion by native game), and an incident which occurred in January 1832 reveals that the Aboriginal men were anything but willing participants in an exchange system involving their women. There are two versions of what took place.

According to Sergeant Wight he had been advised that 16 Aboriginal men, 12 of them recent arrivals, had orchestrated a plan to kill the Europeans, commandeer the boats and escape to the mainland. Wight's informant remains unknown, but to thwart the attempt he placed an armed sentry on duty in the hut where most of the Europeans slept. The Aborigines struck one night in late January and were challenged by the sentry who they attempted to disarm. Failing in their purpose they fled into the bush. Returning next morning Wight confined the men under an armed guard and two days later had them marooned on three small islands — Little Kangaroo, Mile and Chalky. Those on Little Kangaroo and Mile Islands were provided with a little food in addition to water, but those placed on

Chalky Island were only given water. The exiles somehow managed to survive until Robinson returned a few weeks later and had all of them brought back to the settlement. It was then that he heard a very different story. The Aboriginal men claimed that they had become incensed at the Europeans taking liberties with their women and had gone to the hut to retrieve them.[64] Their account certainly rings true, particularly as the men only attempted to disarm the sentry and fled when that failed.

Wight was certainly quick to jump to conclusions. Just prior to Robinson's return 42 Aborigines had left the settlement on a hunting trip which lasted three days. When they returned one of the men was missing and two women who had been living with the sealers told Wight he had been killed by the Ben Lomond men. Wight interviewed the two suspects, who denied that anyone had been harmed. Unconvinced, he had the men handcuffed and ordered Maclachlan and two of the sealers, Edward Mansell and Robert Gamble, to take them back to where the missing man had last been seen. A search of the area revealed nothing and at this point Mansell apparently threatened to shoot the men if they did not reveal the location of the body. Despite the handcuffs the terrified captives tried to escape and in the ensuing struggle both men were shot and wounded by Mansell. When they were returned to the settlement Wight prepared to restrain them more securely with iron hoops, only dissuaded from doing so by Maclachlan, who insisted on tending their injuries. Roughly five hours later the missing man strode into the settlement claiming that he had been lost.[65] The Ben Lomond men had obviously been framed. The separate divisions which the Aboriginal people formed at the settlement, and this unfortunate incident, highlight again the strength of customary enmity which has never been fully reconciled.

Robinson arrived at The Lagoons in February 1832, and early the following month he swore in Maclachlan as a special constable and sent him to Woody Island to apprehend Mansell for wounding the two Aboriginal men. Maclachlan returned with his prisoner and after interrogation by Robinson no further action appears to have been taken.[66] A violent individual known to have killed Aborigines, Mansell was never brought to justice. Fortunately for the Aboriginal people, Wight was replaced in March 1832 by Ensign William Darling, who brought eight of his own troops. Darling proved to be an enlightened choice as superintendent. Like Wight, he had come out to New South Wales with the 63rd Regiment, but that was all they had in common. Darling was a young humanitarian who quickly gained the respect of the Aborigines without the use of force, and while he could initially do little about the site chosen for the Aboriginal Establishment, he did manage to implement a number of vital improvements.[67]

Robinson remained only a brief time at The Lagoons, and keeping with his strong Christian convictions he introduced religious services on Sundays. Even God could not prevent the illnesses which steadily attacked the Aboriginal incarcerates, and nor were the mission Aborigines immune. When Robinson left Flinders Island he was accompanied by 16 Aborigines, two of whom — Umarrah and Robert — were almost immediately hospitalised in Launceston. Both men had been with Robinson from the very beginning. Discovered in the bush when he was around 18 months old, Robert had been raised by the colonist Mary Busby. In 1829, however, he was sent to Bruny Island at Lieutenant Governor Arthur's request and accompanied Robinson's first mission along the west coast. Robert died at Launceston on 23 March from 'an inflammation in the chest', and Umarrah succumbed the following day from dysentery.[68] When Robinson left Launceston for his second mission to the west coast, it is possible that the prevailing situation at The Lagoons and the increasing mortality rate played on the minds of at least some of his remaining Aboriginal envoys and contributed in no small measure to the plot with the Tarkiner people to be rid of the conciliator once and for all.

Be that as it may, with Robinson gone Darling implemented his own civilising program on Flinders Island that was partly based on bribery. Those women who agreed to wash clothes, bake bread and clean the huts were rewarded with extra food or a generous ration of tobacco, while those who refused went without. By the same means Darling persuaded the Aborigines to wear clothing and refrain from coating their heads and upper bodies with ochre. At the same time, though, he tolerated many cultural activities, including ceremonies, as long as designated tasks had been completed.[69]

Ochre remained a prized commodity on the settlement, the more so as there were no natural deposits on the island and the authorities never contemplated shipping any in. After all, the intention was to slowly wean the Aborigines off their cultural practices as the first step to becoming 'civilised'. Ochre still managed to find its way to the Aboriginal Establishment via Aboriginal people sent from the mainland, and substitutes were available in the form of rust scraped from old steel bolts or by pounding soft red bricks to a powder.[70] Song and dance also arrived as part of the newcomers' cultural baggage and was quickly copied by the resident Aborigines. To facilitate communication between different speakers they developed their own unique *lingua franca*, or creole, a combination of English and Aboriginal words and phrases.[71]

When the Quakers, George Washington Walker and James Backhouse, visited The Lagoons in October 1832 they described the settlement as consisting of a number of small huts for the European officers and three large huts for the Aborigines. The latter were A-frames 6–7 metres in length and 3 metres in width, the interior partitioned into separate rooms with walls made from boughs thatched with grass or rushes. The floors were dirt. The Aboriginal population at the time of their visit numbered 78: 44 men, 29 women and five children, which suggests that each hut accommodated approximately 26 people. It also meant that the gender imbalance had not been overcome. A brush fence built around three sides of the settlement offered some protection from cold westerly winds.[72]

Darling's hut was around 7 metres long and 4 metres wide with two sliding windows. The storekeeper's abode was roughly the same size, while the huts of the civilian officers were about 4 metres square. Some of them had weatherboard walls, while others were constructed from boughs and thatched in a similar manner to the Aboriginal huts. Despite the brush fence they were all draughty, with Backhouse noting that Darling lined the walls of his hut with blankets. The soldiers and assigned convicts were housed similarly to the Aborigines, and while there was a separate kitchen where food was prepared for all, this was 'merely a place protected on one end and side by a sloping fence, with a table and a fire on the ground'. The chapel was even more primitive, with Backhouse referring to it as 'a place formed of branches'.[73]

On the other hand, Darling improved the water supply by tapping into a freshwater spring in the middle of the lagoon, and he removed the armed guards which had characterised Wight's regime. He also took active steps to keep the sealers away from the settlement. Apart from his system of rewards, Darling taught the Aborigines how to use implements and domestic utensils, and whether or not they appreciated these relatively benign attempts at social control, they were certainly far less rebellious than they had been under his predecessor. Darling maintained regular correspondence with Lieutenant Governor Arthur in Hobart so the latter was kept fully informed about conditions on Flinders Island. Ever the efficient administrator, Arthur was burdened with costs, but he was not prepared to limit expenditure if it meant depriving the Aboriginal exiles. He was genuinely interested in their welfare and only too well aware they had been grievously wronged. Arthur made obvious mistakes, particularly in his expectation that they could be transformed into black Europeans and embrace Christianity. But he was a product of his age, and was simply unable to grasp that the Aborigines did not necessarily want to become part of the dominant society. At the same time, though, they made a very good show of pretending that they did.[74]

George Washington Walker recorded that every day Darling invited a number of Aboriginal men to his table for either breakfast or tea. They waited patiently outside until permitted to enter, and sat on the stools around the table and ate whatever food was on offer with their knives and forks. According to the Quaker, the Aboriginal people looked forward to the day they would have their own individual huts, sleep in their own beds and sit in their own chairs. The prospect of having their own small garden where they could grow potatoes was, he said, 'highly pleasing to them'.[75]

Potatoes appear to have been the only vegetable included in the rations, the remainder usually comprising salt meat, biscuit, possibly a small amount of rice, tea and sugar. The Quakers were aware that it had taken Darling quite some time to prevent his guests throwing away the cutlery and crockery as soon as they had finished their meals, all of which were prepared by a European member of staff. The Aborigines were willing to cut wood for the fire and even bring it in, and eventually one of them assisted the cook in a number of ways.[76] That was as far as it went. Nor did the Aborigines acquire any fondness for salt meat, though they did enjoy strong sweet tea and milk.[77]

While beef and mutton was occasionally available, the Aborigines were fortunate in being able to supplement their rations with native game, including abalone and mutton-birds, all of which were prepared in the customary fashion.[78] As a means of subsidising expenses, Darling encouraged the Aborigines to gather wallaby skins for sale, again rewarding those who complied. This proved to be a difficult task as the Aboriginal method of cooking these animals was to simply throw them on a fire to singe off the fur.[79] He had more success encouraging the Aborigines to wear clothing, but even here there were limitations. Possibly owing to the effort required to undress, the women tended to present themselves fully clothed. Not so the men, partly because trousers were in short supply, and most of them refused to wear convict-issue trousers which had been dyed yellow. Their main clothing consisted of nothing more than a frock coat, and even this was regularly shed during the excitement of a ceremony.[80]

Although they regularly attended religious services on Sunday, the Aborigines similarly refused to abandon their own spiritual beliefs, continuing to regard relics of the dead as a means of curing sickness.[81] The important thing to note, however, is that Darling's term as superintendent was the best the Aborigines ever experienced. Like Arthur, the young commissioned officer was genuinely concerned for their welfare, and that was why he came to the conclusion that an alternative location would have to be found for the Aboriginal Establishment. After examining the report of surveyor George Woodward, who had been sent to Flinders Island in January 1832 to report on the topography and natural resources, Darling believed that he had found what he was looking for at a place known as Pea Jacket Point, 24 kilometres north of The Lagoons.[82]

In early May he reported to George Arthur on the apparent advantages, and the following month Darling 'very minutely' investigated the location, considering 150 acres (60 hectares) of surrounding land suitable for cultivation with ample pasture for sheep and cattle. So keen was Darling to transfer the Aboriginal Establishment that he immediately stationed two soldiers at Pea Jacket Point to prepare a garden. At the same time a well was dug to provide fresh water. The main drawback was the lack of a safe anchorage, which meant that supply vessels would have to continue using Green Island, thereby adding to the distance from the proposed settlement. To overcome this problem Darling suggested that a transit store could be erected on Green Island and a launch used to bring supplies directly to Pea Jacket Point by water.[83]

His choice of site received favourable support from the Quakers, Backhouse and Walker, both men impressed with the richness of the soil. By then an elderly soldier and two assistants were in the process of erecting turf and wattle huts lined with grass which the Quakers considered superior to the accommodation at The Lagoons. Housing was increasingly becoming urgent owing to the steady influx of Aboriginal people. For this reason Darling also requested the appointment of a full-time storekeeper to relieve himself of the onerous duty of distributing rations. Arthur responded by sending William Budds from the Commissariat Department in Hobart. Budds was accompanied by his wife and two children as well as his brother, who had been granted permission to go to Flinders Island owing to his skills as a carpenter.[84] William Budds was later to become a considerable nuisance on the settlement, though quarrelling and feuding among the European staff was a regular part of life at the Aboriginal Establishment regardless of where it was located.[85]

In October 1832 Darling and four Aborigines sailed from Flinders Island with Backhouse and Walker in the *Charlotte* to retrieve Wymurick and his people from Hunter Island where they had been left by Robinson. While he was in the north-west Darling removed another four Aboriginal women living with sealers. Early the following month, and with Arthur's full consent, he began the task of relocating the settlement to Pea Jacket Point, placing Maclachlan in charge while he sailed to Hobart to confer with the Lieutenant Governor. Within three weeks of his return on 10 January 1833 the relocation had been completed and The Lagoons permanently abandoned.[86] Pea

Jacket Point was soon to be renamed Wybalenna, an Aboriginal term meaning 'black man's houses',[87] and unlike The Lagoons it was to acquire a sinister reputation after Darling's term as superintendent came to an end around July 1834. At this point it is worth considering the experience of the Van Diemen's Land Aborigines as this new phase was about to begin.

On Swan and even Hunter Island there had been no real problems. The Aboriginal people were able to maintain their customary lifestyle, and appear to have been relatively comfortable with their altered circumstances. The same cannot be said about the period spent on Gun Carriage Island or during Sergeant Wight's term as superintendent at The Lagoons. In both instances the settlements were run as veritable concentration camps and the Aborigines treated as if they were little more than common criminals. At The Lagoons they were able to gain a brief respite from the discipline by going on hunting expeditions, but return was always inevitable.

Then there is the issue of housing, the standard of which was not particularly high. Robinson believed that the respiratory infections which decimated the Aboriginal people on the islands of Bass Strait were a direct consequence of poor accommodation, and he later did the best he could to ensure the buildings erected at Wybalenna were as warm and comfortable as possible.[88] While that was not always achieved, the effort was at least made. It appears that the huts erected on Preservation and Great Dog Islands were prefabricated structures and extremely basic. The sealers' huts commandeered on Gun Carriage Island were a far better proposition, but they were largely used to accommodate the European staff. During Robinson's brief time on the island three of the sealers' huts were allocated specifically to his loyal guides on the 'Friendly Mission' — Mannalargenna, Woorrady, Kickerterpoller and their wives. There is no evidence that they were given over to the resident Aborigines when Robinson resumed his mission. Nor is it clear when the A-frames were erected at The Lagoons on Flinders Island; it was probably after the arrival of Ensign Darling. So it can be accepted that right up until March 1832 the Aborigines were largely dependent on customary shelters, though there is one other factor which enters into this equation. The Aboriginal people themselves did not welcome the use of European-style accommodation, considering it the cause of all their illnesses.[89] For the Aborigines it was healthier to continue using customary shelters, and they actively resisted being coerced into accepting European alternatives.

Food was also important. By the time the Aborigines were settled on Gun Carriage Island they were already becoming dependent on government rations, none of which was healthy. The rations were nevertheless supplemented by native game, especially from neighbouring Cape Barren Island, but the hunting excursions were strictly controlled and of limited duration.[90] By the time the Aborigines had been transferred to Flinders Island where hunting was less restricted their dependence on rations had intensified, and it soon become even greater after local resources were decimated. As George Washington Walker noted:

> In hunting, they destroyed the game recklessly, and could not be restrained from killing the kangaroo as long as their dogs would run. On an adjoining island where there were large numbers of wallaby, the blacks, in three or four hunting excursions, killed over a thousand head. By this kind of wholesale destruction, kangaroo, once very abundant in the neighbourhood of the Flinders Settlement, soon became extremely scarce.[91]

One of the most remarkable aspects of the Aboriginal exile was that they showed little of the previous aggression towards Europeans which had marked the frontier conflict. Aboriginal resistance in captivity was passive rather than overt, almost certainly indicative of their utter demoralisation. Simmering resentment, on the other hand, continued to underlie behaviour between different Aboriginal groups, occasionally erupting into fights or even brawls. While they did reach the stage of living together, hunting excursions remained a separate affair based on customary alliances. At the same time, however, there is no record of an Aboriginal person being killed by another during their lengthy expulsion from Van Diemen's Land. Taken as a whole, Robinson was accurate in his assessment of Aboriginal behaviour at the various Bass Strait settlements as 'peaceable'.[92]

The problem with the sealers was never fully overcome. Irrespective of where the Aboriginal Establishment was located, the sealers were seldom far away — forever lurking with intent. Sexual liaisons between the Aboriginal women and the sealers were not the only concern of the superintendents. There were numerous occasions where the European staff, whether assigned convicts, soldiers and even at times storekeepers and tradesmen, sought out the Aboriginal women for sexual favours. Importantly, while the Aborigines had willingly laid down their arms to end the violence, they did not expect to be treated as criminals and constantly under armed guard. Military detachments served at the various Aboriginal Establishments from the very beginning to almost the end — 1831 to 1845. When the Aboriginal people first went ashore on Gun Carriage Island they were under the watchful eyes of a corporal and three soldiers. The detachments varied in size thereafter, with their duties never clearly defined. That they were guards can be taken as a given, but that can also mean any number of things. They were there to prevent the Aborigines from escaping; they were there to prevent them attacking the European staff; and they were there to prevent them from harming each other. Yet, there were never any Aboriginal escapes; apart from

Gleebooks

9660 2333 books@gleebooks.com.au

A.B.N. 87 000 357 317

TAX INVOICE

Van Diemen's Land: An Abori	40.00
Total less GST	36.36
Total GST	3.64
Total Sale	40.00
MachineEFT or Clender Amount	40.00
Change	0.00

Reg: Nancy Tr# 6/1401

Operator: BJ

Ph: 61 2 9660 2333 21/03/2015 17:11:39

a half-hearted attempt to disarm the sentry at The Lagoons, there were no attacks on the European staff; and while the Aborigines occasionally fought each other, there is no evidence that the soldiers ever intervened.[93]

Not that it was all about the Aborigines. The soldiers protected the stores which were vital to the survival of the Aboriginal Establishments, all the more so when supplies were almost depleted. The military was also there to stop the convicts from escaping. Generally speaking, they were totally inefficient. There were times when they failed to protect the Aborigines, particularly the women, from the staff and sealers. There were times when they failed to support the civil officers, and they certainly did not prevent a number of convicts from escaping.[94] Moreover, they were not above taking liberties with the Aboriginal women themselves. It was only during William Darling's time on Flinders Island that the military detachments can be said to have been at least reasonably efficient, and that was only because Darling was a regular military officer who could wield real authority.[95]

From the Aboriginal perspective the soldiers were a sinister omniscient presence, complete with their detested red coats and military accoutrements, a constant reminder of all the violence they had already experienced. They served as a warning that it could all so easily happen again if the Aborigines were to make one wrong move. Having the military stationed at the Aboriginal Establishments can itself be seen as an act of coercion, even though the focus shifted over time. From guarding the Aborigines in the initial stages their main duty became one of guarding the convicts.[96] That was paralleled by the government policy relating to the Aborigines. At first the emphasis fell on 'civilising' the Aboriginal people to transform them into inferior black colonists. That period largely ended in 1834 when Ensign Darling left Flinders Island. Although George Augustus Robinson made out that he was pursuing the same course, the reality was very different. Robinson knew that Wybalenna was never going to succeed, and slowly — ever so slowly — the settlement became a depot where Aboriginal pensioners were destined to end their days. While it did not quite end that way it came very close indeed, and to understand that evolutionary transformation it is necessary to closely examine the Wybalenna Aboriginal Establishment on Flinders Island.

9

WYBALENNA

The renaming of the Aboriginal Establishment to Wybalenna by William Darling only three weeks after being transferred from The Lagoons was an exercise in toponymy not only endorsed by Lieutenant Governor Arthur, but probably originated with him.[1] The idea of naming places for psychological reasons is an area of study which has been largely neglected even though it has profound significance. In the aftermath of the First World War, for example, many Australian soldiers were offered small farms as a reward for their service and as a means of assisting their transition back to civilian life. Soldier settlements where farms were clustered together were regularly named after battlefields on the Western Front and the Middle East, thus providing the returned warriors with a sense of familiarity in an otherwise alien environment.[2] It was no different for the Van Diemen's Land Aborigines exiled on Flinders Island.

The move north to Wybalenna involved a major building project, with Darling doing his utmost to ensure not only that the Aboriginal people were housed comfortably, but that they would also be more inclined to occupy the new dwellings. It was precisely for this reason that they were of wattle-and-daub construction, each measuring approximately 8 by 4 metres, with a double fireplace in the centre. They mirrored customary Aboriginal camps with their open fires, and were large enough to allow communal living. Divided into two compartments, they could accommodate up to six people in each, and it appears the Aborigines appreciated the superintendent's efforts as they willingly cut the wattle boughs and gathered the grass for thatching the roofs of their new homes.[3]

The added bonus was that these dwellings were inexpensive to build and required only minimal skilled labour. George Arthur was concerned with keeping the number of assigned convicts to the lowest number possible, though he was not averse to providing skilled tradesmen if and when required. In April 1833 there were 15 convicts at the settlement. Apart from four boatmen overseen by the free coxswain, the convict labour force consisted of a cook, tailor, baker, two brick-makers and one bricklayer, a carpenter, clerk and three general labourers. Anticipating rain during the coming winter months, Darling made certain that all major building work had been completed by May, and the huts seem to have contributed to a marked improvement in the overall Aboriginal health profile. In the winter of 1832, 10 Aborigines had fallen ill from pulmonary complaints at The Lagoons; the winter of 1833 saw only two convalescents,[4] though it needs to be added that this relatively healthy situation came to an abrupt end when Robinson and Anthony Cottrell began forwarding their captives from the west coast to Flinders Island.

Of the 32 deaths at Wybalenna during the calendar year 1833, virtually all were recent arrivals from the west coast. When the 'Friendly Mission' had largely completed its work the following year there were only seven deaths on the settlement up to July, when Darling re-joined his regiment.[5] Thereafter the mortality rate began climbing once again, particularly after Robinson took over as superintendent in November 1835. Prior to their incarceration the Aboriginal people had been able to alleviate the impact of contagious disease by regularly dispersing into smaller family groups. At Wybalenna and the previous Aboriginal Establishments they were congregated together, thereby intensifying detrimental health problems.

While it is easy to condemn Robinson and others in hindsight, it is worth bearing in mind that they did not have access to the medical knowledge available today. The same can be said about the state of medicine generally in the early nineteenth century. Even in Britain doctors were often best avoided, and many people relied on traditional herbal remedies to cure their ills.[6] Resident surgeons at Wybalenna certainly did the best they could to combat the rampant respiratory infections, but the solution to these issues was well out of reach in that day and age. Not even improvements to Aboriginal housing could hope to stem the rising mortality rate.

That only became a major problem when William Darling left Flinders Island. The young ensign nevertheless had his hands full trying to overcome the irregularity of supplies from Hobart, resulting as much from bureaucratic bungling and the tardiness of staff at the Commissariat Store as the shipping service itself. A good example occurred in January 1833 when Darling returned to Flinders Island to find two supply vessels riding at anchor off Green Island. With the settlement on the verge of starvation one of them had arrived almost empty, prompting Darling to complain to the colonial secretary. In this instance there was a rapid response because his complaint was immediately passed to George Arthur who personally intervened. The Lieutenant Governor attempted to prevent a similar emergency by directing the storekeeper at the Aboriginal Establishment to furnish the commissary with regular returns so that the settlement's requirements could be anticipated in advance. Although the storekeeper complied, it did little to improve the regularity of supplies and shortages continued.[7]

Apart from considering Wybalenna to be a healthier location, Darling had also been impressed by its agricultural potential. From a very early period gardens were cultivated to produce an array of vegetables to supplement the ubiquitous potatoes, but large-scale agriculture was not to be a success. Darling intended to grow enough wheat at Wybalenna to make the settlement self-sufficient in flour, an almost impossible undertaking without the benefit of a plough. Despite repeated requests a plough was never shipped to Flinders Island, and while Arthur agreed with Darling that an experienced agriculturalist would be of great benefit to the Aboriginal Establishment, the colonial government was unable to find a suitable person willing to work on remote Flinders Island. Men were eventually sent, but none of them had sufficient knowledge to make farming a successful venture. Animal husbandry fared no better. The flock of sheep and a few head of cattle shipped in from Launceston were too few in number to be maintained in the longer term owing to the continual demand for fresh meat.[8] To make matters worse, only 18 months after the establishment of Wybalenna the Aborigines had almost exterminated the native game through overhunting.[9]

Darling maintained his program of 'civilising' the Aborigines by pressing them to wear European garments, keep their huts clean and tidy and to cultivate the small gardens. It was either Darling or Arthur who took this one step further by removing the Aboriginal children to the Queen's Orphan School in Hobart, where they were inculcated with British learning. There is no record of the parents ever protesting against the separation of the children, so whether Darling was able to convince them of its merits or, as Brian Plomley suggested, they had resigned themselves to the fact that their future lay in fully accepting the European way of life, can only be conjectured. It is difficult to believe that there were not at least some occasions when the parents protested vigorously. To his credit Robinson reversed this policy and had the children returned to Wybalenna, though he continued to segregate them on the settlement.[10]

There was little for the adults to do at Wybalenna, and as to their cultural activities the record is largely silent. With their household 'duties' the women would have had less time on their hands than the men, but the boredom must have often been overwhelming. Gardening and a limited amount of hunting was probably the extent of male activities until they became infatuated with the game of marbles and, later, cricket.[11] When the opportunity arose there can be little doubt that cultural issues rose to the fore. Surprisingly, the one non-cultural activity which did have some appeal was gardening, and in many ways it was unfortunate that farming did not succeed at the settlement. This would have been a useful means of giving the men, in particular, a degree of direction and purpose which, in turn, could have improved their general health.[12] European staff, on the other hand, spent much of their free time bickering and feuding with each other.

William Budds had not been long in his position as storekeeper before he fell foul of the superintendent. William Darling had ordered Budds to accommodate the convict clerk in his house during working hours until a separate office could be built, as he was concerned that other convicts could gain access to the settlement's records in the communal hut. Budds wanted nothing to do with it, telling the superintendent in no uncertain terms that it was beneath his dignity to house a convicted felon for any amount of time in his own household. The storekeeper was reprimanded for using insulting language, and shortly afterwards one of the Aboriginal men asked Darling for some rum. When questioned as to why he wanted the alcohol the man replied that Budds often gave it to him to relieve the pain in his bowels. Darling then went to Maclachlan who, after all, was the medical officer. Maclachlan was aware that Budds was issuing alcohol for medicinal purposes, but as he was a convict there was little that he could do to stop the practice. Nor was that all. Maclachlan also informed Darling that Budds regularly gave the Aboriginal women fishing tackle so they could supply him with fish. Maclachlan was concerned, as he had tried to minimise the interaction between the Aborigines and Europeans on the settlement.[13]

Budds's explanations failed to satisfy Darling, who was on the point of lodging an official complaint against the storekeeper when he was offered a full apology and the matter was held in abeyance. Tension between Darling and Budds clearly continued because in March 1833 the storekeeper requested the commissariat officer in Hobart to relieve him of his post. Protocol demanded that Budds should have first approached Darling, and when the superintendent was asked for his opinion Darling had no hesitation in stating that he no longer had any need for a storekeeper as Maclachlan had taken over the duty of distributing rations. Although Budds was recalled the colonial government appointed a new storekeeper, Loftus Dickenson, who arrived the following August and somehow managed to avoid much of the perpetual squabbling among his fellow staff.[14]

Not that this was the end of William Darling's personnel problems. As an evangelist, George Arthur never deviated from his belief that the best way to 'civilise' the Aborigines was through embracing Christianity. To that end he appointed Thomas Wilkinson as catechist at Wybalenna. Wilkinson and his wife Louisa arrived at Flinders Island with their four children in late June 1833, and like Darling and Maclachlan he soon became deeply concerned with the welfare of the Aboriginal people. Yet, like Budds, he soon clashed with the superintendent and was destined to leave the Aboriginal Establishment before he had time to make any real impact. Not a great deal is known about Wilkinson except that he was born in England and arrived in Van Diemen's Land only three months before his appointment to Wybalenna. He later had a distinguished career in journalism and politics in Victoria, and Wilkinson shared George Augustus Robinson's belief that the only way to win the minds of the Aboriginal people was to understand them first. He went further than the conciliator, however, by negotiating the middle ground,[15] and it was rather unfortunate that his efforts in that direction were not appreciated by others, least of all by George Arthur.

By September 1833 Wilkinson was able to report that he had translated the first four chapters of Genesis into the Ben Lomond language, and although the Aborigines themselves could not grasp all that much of it they still found Wilkinson's efforts of some interest. The catechist also opened a school for the adult Aborigines, with three of the pupils held to be capable of reading what he called 'easy lessons', while nine 'fine youths' were learning the alphabet. The Lieutenant Governor applauded the school, while condemning Wilkinson's translation of the bible into an Aboriginal language.[16] With the intention being to inculcate the Aborigines into European ways it meant the abandonment of all aspects of their own culture, including language.

Wilkinson's strict and unwavering adherence to the righteousness of religion also meant that he placed himself morally above everyone else at Wybalenna, and the superintendent was no exception. Brian Plomley suggested that he was consumed by 'religious bigotry', which seems a fair assessment.[17] The catechist certainly detested Maclachlan, and his stream of complaints regarding the medical officer's alleged improprieties with Aboriginal women quickly set him at odds with Darling, who had considerable faith in Maclachlan's abilities — so much so that he had recommended him for a full pardon in January 1833. It soon reached a point where Darling suspended Wilkinson from his duties and called on George Arthur to conduct an investigation.[18] The Lieutenant Governor sought the assistance of the Quakers, Backhouse and Walker, to sort out the affairs at Wybalenna.[19] They arrived at Flinders Island in December 1833 and although they succeeded in reducing some of the friction, full reconciliation was entirely out of the question. The Quakers simply felt that Wilkinson lacked sufficient tact in dealing with others, but Arthur decided to recall him in April 1834.[20] He was replaced by Robert Clark the following August — and Clark soon proved to be an even more disruptive influence on the settlement.[21]

While Backhouse and Walker were engaged in their inquiry, the colonial surgeon made the decision to replace Maclachlan for reasons that are not entirely clear. With a growing number of Aborigines to attend Maclachlan had asked for an increase of his salary, and in this he received the full support of Darling. It is unlikely that this was the reason behind Maclachlan being relieved of his duties, and nor would it have been any personal failing. Even though Darling mounted a strong case for his retention at Wybalenna, the authorities in Hobart remained unmoved and, accepting the inevitable, Maclachlan tendered his resignation in December 1833. Cronyism probably played a role in Maclachlan's removal, for he was replaced by James Allen, a young surgeon who was a protégé of the colonial surgeon in Hobart. Allen was said to possess considerable talent, expectations which were never quite fulfilled on Flinders Island. There is no denying that he was competent and did not neglect his medical duties. It was just that Allen did only what he had to do and nothing more.[22]

It was rather unfortunate that the three men who shared a genuine concern for the welfare of the Aborigines were unable to act in concert and, more importantly, all three left Wybalenna within the space of eight months. Darling's program was continued for just over a year by his successor, Henry Nickolls, before it was slowly undone by George Augustus Robinson and his own successors. Notwithstanding that the figures are somewhat fudged, there were around 126 Aborigines at Wybalenna when Darling left in July 1834. From the time of his arrival at The Lagoons in March 1832 there had been a total of 39 deaths, the majority in 1833 and mostly among new arrivals from the west coast who were already suffering from serious respiratory illnesses. Compared to the later mortality rate, Darling had achieved at least satisfactory results and can certainly not be blamed for the tragedy that was still waiting to unfold.[23]

Nor can the disastrous outcome be attributed to Darling's successor, who arrived with his wife and five children in September 1834. For a number of reasons Henry Nickolls had little option but to follow the policies of his predecessor. For one thing, he knew that his appointment was only a stop-gap measure until George Augustus Robinson took over the superintendency. Unlike Darling, who was given a relatively free hand when it came to the general administration of the Aboriginal Establishment, any initiative shown by Nickolls was quickly called into question by George Arthur.[24] That was made even worse later when Nickolls had the audacity to query the Lieutenant Governor's views on the correct way to 'civilise' the Aborigines.

The building program definitely had to be pushed ahead, for when Nickolls arrived the state of the huts accommodating the Aborigines were in a poor state of repair. While Darling's idea of constructing the huts using a wattle-and-daub technique was admirable, it proved impossible to maintain them in an adequate condition. Nickolls also saw the need for a more secure storehouse, a separate hospital and a decent chapel for the catechist, who was still conducting services behind a windbreak. The colonial secretary responded by granting Nickolls permission to build the three public buildings, but surprisingly made no comment on improving the Aboriginal accommodation.[25]

The new superintendent was not spared the perpetual problem of irregular supplies. When he first arrived at Wybalenna there was only sufficient flour for four weeks and it was not known when more would be received. On three separate occasions Nickolls was forced to send the Aborigines out on extended hunting expeditions to avert famine. With native game already seriously depleted, the settlement was only saved from complete starvation in the last instance by the fortuitous arrival of the mutton-birds. In December 1834 Loftus Dickenson tried to surmount the problem by ordering supplies six months in advance, only to find that while the order was received in Hobart the required stores were never sent. The quality of those which did arrive also left much to be desired. Flour was frequently riddled with weevils and hard biscuit often had to be soaked in water until it was soft enough to eat.[26] At that time daily rations for adult Aborigines consisted of 450 grams of salt meat, 450 grams of flour, 250 grams of biscuit, seven grams of sugar and the same amount of salt. Children received half the adult ration, and all recipients received seven grams of soap.[27] Cleanliness was apparently just as important as a basic diet.

Nickolls persevered with the cultivation of wheat and attempted to increase the available livestock, both measures doomed to failure. By the time he left Wybalenna the best he could claim was that 5 acres of land had been cleared, fenced and planted with potatoes. An additional two acres were planted with turnips and small quantities of barley and cabbages were also grown. This had only been possible through the contribution of Aboriginal labour,[28] the latter fully aware that these crops were potentially the only thing standing between themselves and complete starvation.

The assigned convicts continued to represent a problem through their efforts to have sexual relations with the Aboriginal women.

There was an added dimension in that they detested being sent to the isolation of Flinders Island and invariably caused trouble in the hope of being sent back to the mainland.[29] Then there was the new catechist, Robert Clark. By early 1835 Nickolls was being swamped by an avalanche of complaints from Clark, everything from cattle trampling his garden to the negligence of convicts. All of it appears to have been done with the object of undermining Nickolls's authority, reaching a new level when the superintendent allowed the Aborigines to fetch water on the Sabbath. Clark reported this heinous crime to the colonial secretary, who demanded an explanation from Nickolls. The latter insisted that it was due to the improvidence of the Aborigines, who could not be prevented from using all their available water on Saturdays.[30]

When the Nickolls tried to strike back at the catechist by suggesting that he should place more emphasis on teaching the Aborigines writing, reading and arithmetic rather than religious instruction, he drew the Lieutenant Governor's wrath. Arthur's reprimand questioned the superintendent's knowledge of missionary endeavour around the world, with Arthur claiming that any success at 'civilising' Indigenous people had only been accomplished after they had first been converted the Christianity. Nickolls was told in no uncertain terms that in future he was to give Clark his full support and restrict himself to the day-to-day running of the Aboriginal Establishment.[31]

In that respect Nickolls did achieve some measure of success. While the general health of the Aboriginal people did not show any marked improvement, it was no worse than under Darling's administration. The Aboriginal women were also instructed by the wives of the civil and military officers, including Nickolls's own wife, in a range of domestic duties. For the first time they began cooking meat and vegetables in a non-customary fashion, and when the baker left the settlement and was not replaced they were taught how to bake damper. Henceforth, one of the women in each hut baked damper for the others, and they soon began competing amongst themselves to see who could produce the best damper. The women were also instructed in needlework, becoming so proficient that they began manufacturing much of the settlement's clothing requirements under the supervision of the tailor.[32]

The Aboriginal men, on the other hand, did as little as possible and even then only when the superintendent was prepared to work alongside them. Those from the west coast as well as the Big River and Ben Lomond people were particularly recalcitrant, but there was a clear reason for their reluctance to engage in manual labour. Nickolls was advised that they had been induced to lay down their arms and leave their homelands only after being promised that the 'King' would provide everything they wanted. They expected that promise to be honoured, and saw no reason why they should learn about the acquisition of material possessions, or supply labour, or even procure such things as wallaby skins in exchange for food. Everything was theirs by right. They did not mind doing a little gardening or a minimal amount of labour as long as they were not expected to do it and were treated properly. As they understood it, the convicts were there to do all the work.[33] This provides an insight into the tactics applied by George Augustus Robinson and his 'Friendly Mission'. Totally demoralised, their societies ripped apart and themselves hunted down like wild animals, the Aborigines readily welcomed a promise that they would be looked after and left in peace.

They also reminded Nickolls that there was something else involved in Robinson's deal, and were anxious to know when they would be allowed to return to their homelands. That anxiety was increased with every death on the settlement, as they expected to end their days on their home soil — not in a place of exile that was only meant to be temporary. Nickolls sympathised with the Aborigines to the extent of relaying their concerns to the colonial secretary, making it clear in his correspondence that someone had wilfully deluded them.[34] That someone, of course, was Robinson, though Nickolls refrained from mentioning his name. It was also a matter of some urgency as their growing impatience was beginning to manifest itself in a resurgence of customary enmity towards each other. The Big River and Ben Lomond people were already at loggerheads, the situation further inflamed by the west coast Aborigines, who tended to shift their allegiance to whichever group suited them.[35]

Nickolls's concerns over the growing unrest, and the reasons for it, were duly passed on to George Augustus Robinson by George Arthur. It was then that Robinson became evasive about accepting his appointment as superintendent. He had clearly told the Aborigines that his arrival on Flinders Island would mark the beginning of their repatriation, and now he had to face the people who had been lied to and somehow convey the message that there would be no homecoming. Judgement day was on hand, and after having his every move closely scrutinised by George Arthur it may have been with some relief that Henry Nickolls left Wybalenna in November 1835. His departure literally went off with a bang. Robinson, who had arrived the previous month, organised a gala affair where the Aborigines and European staff dined sumptuously on roast mutton and plum and rice pudding washed down with wine. Roles were reversed, with the civil and military officers waiting on the Aborigines and Robinson serving them in turn. In the afternoon the Aborigines played cricket and later took their tea with the Europeans. The highlight was a spectacular fireworks display in the evening, with rockets, sky serpents, Catherine-wheels and crackers lighting up the night sky. It was Robinson's flamboyant way of welcoming in his new regime as much as it was a send-off for Henry Nickolls.[36]

Robinson got straight down to business the very next day, calling on surgeon James Allen for a report on the existing state of affairs at Wybalenna. It was not good. Allen insisted that the Aboriginal huts had been placed in the worst possible location, their doorways open to the prevailing westerly winds, which meant they were uncomfortable and often cold. Allen elaborated on the irregularity of supplies, emphasising that the settlement required stores for six months in advance to overcome shortages. The Aborigines also required clothing and blankets, and the water supply was still far from satisfactory. The Aboriginal men were angry about the continuing relationships between the women and the convicts and, above all else, they were looking forward to returning to their homelands.[37]

It is not known how Robinson circumvented the question of repatriation. Unlike his predecessors, he knew many if not most of the Aborigines personally and had the ability to convince them of almost anything.[38] That they would have broached the subject is almost certain, and Robinson may well have fed them yet another lie. He knew only too well that the colonists would not tolerate the Aborigines on the mainland of Van Diemen's Land in the foreseeable future, though he did have plans to relocate them to the Australian mainland, an idea that was fully supported by Lieutenant Governor Arthur. It may have been this scheme that Robinson used to allay Aboriginal anxieties, but it too was doomed to failure. Governor Gipps in Sydney vetoed the plan, fearing a repetition of the frontier conflict which had engulfed the island colony.[39]

In the meantime Robinson made a number of improvements at Wybalenna, though it is difficult to assess what he actually accomplished as opposed to what he claimed to have done in his official reports.[40] He definitely set about replacing the huts used to accommodate the Aborigines as he was thoroughly convinced of a direct correlation between their failing health and inferior housing. While it is not known what materials went into their construction, the doorways were certainly repositioned away from the prevailing winds in a bid to make them warmer. They were otherwise unsophisticated, borne out by the necessity to undertake a major building project in March 1837, when 20 new brick huts were erected for the Aborigines with either brick or wooden flooring. Each hut accommodated two families, and they were fitted with a fireplace and built-in beds. The first of them was occupied in July that same year.[41]

Perhaps predictably, this second building program did not neglect the European staff, particularly the civil and military officers. Some of their dwellings were renovated while others were completely rebuilt from brick. A new residence was constructed for Robinson and his family, though only one building from this period has stood the test of time. That is the brick chapel, on which work commenced in December 1837 and the first service held within its walls in July 1838.[42] The chapel remains a powerful reminder of Robinson's direction when it came to 'civilising' the Aboriginal people. He was not interested in turning them into yeoman farmers like Darling and Nickolls. Although there was a secular school where reading, writing and arithmetic were supposedly taught, most of the curriculum was based on a primitive form of catechism where the Aborigines learnt a strange mix of church history and biblical stories. As it had no real meaning in the European sense, God only knows what the Aboriginal people thought of it, and all education, whether secular or religious, was based on rote learning with the Aborigines expected to commit everything to memory. While they were able to regurgitate some of the material at any one time, most of it was quickly forgotten during their extended hunting excursions. On their return the process would begin yet again.[43]

No qualified teacher was employed, the wives of the civil and military officers sufficing as instructors with the assistance of three of Robinson's children, Henry, William and Maria. A few of the younger Aborigines who had spent time at the Queen's Orphan School in Hobart, notably the three Brune brothers, David, Thomas and Peter, along with Walter Arthur, acted as teacher's aides. These four young men, as well as Mary Cochrane and Bessy Clark who had also attended the Queen's Orphan School,[44] were involved in another Robinson initiative which was essentially meaningless. In September 1836 they produced the first issue of the *Flinders Island Weekly Chronicle*, a hand-written newspaper that ran irregularly until December the following year. Under Robinson's guidance it was compiled solely for the settlement's Aboriginal population, but the reality was that the only ones who had any chance of reading and understanding the content were those who wrote it. Selling for twopence a copy, this publication has historical significance as Australia's first Aboriginal newspaper, but it can only be described as sub-standard by any measure.[45] It is also worth bearing in mind that the producers were the best educated Aborigines at Wybalenna. Robinson regularly waxed lyrical in his reports about how well the Aborigines were attending to their lessons, and it was not until years later that he came closer to the truth when he wrote in his journal that during his time at the settlement not one Aborigine had been able to read and write properly. In fact, very few of them could even speak English with any degree of confidence.[46]

Unlike Thomas Wilkinson, who had tried to capture the minds of the Aborigines through their own language, Robinson always spoke to them in English even though he had a grasp of at least some of their languages.[47] He agreed with George Arthur and others that the redundancy of customary language was an integral part of the 'civilising' process, and in many ways English was far better than the pidgin-type garble that Clark used to communicate his religious instruction. With his dull monotone and virtually incomprehensible pseudo-language it was little wonder that many of the Aborigines rapidly drifted off to sleep. Indeed, even Robinson became completely bored when he sat in on Clark's teaching, ordering the catechist to simplify his lessons and restrict them to no more than one hour in duration.[48] Another aspect of Robinson's 'civilising' was the tactic of renaming many of the Aborigines. By January 1836 he had come to regard their customary names as 'most barbarous and uncouth', so they were replaced in some cases by appellations drawn from history and the classics. Pevay, for instance, became Napoleon; Truganini was renamed Lalla Rookh; and Woorrady was henceforth known as Alpha. This was a common strategy adopted by slave-owners in the Americas as a means of breaking down tribal affinity and customary pride.[49] Ira Berlin has also made the point that the withholding of surnames (in most cases) also functioned to deny adult slaves their adulthood.[50] This was particularly applicable at Wybalenna, where the value of adult customary skills and knowledge was set at nought. The process of learning, whether sewing, farming, Christianity or the English language thus consigned the Aborigines to a state of permanent childhood. On a more positive note, however, Robinson did have additional motives for renaming some of his charges. Many of the women, for instance, had been given demeaning and often masculine names by their sealer captors, and Robinson claimed that the Aborigines themselves were 'highly pleased' with the new names he had bestowed.[51] We can only take Robinson's word for that. At the same time it is possible if not probable that the Aboriginal people continued to use their customary names outside of his hearing.

In August 1836 Robinson also organised an open market, ostensibly to introduce the Aborigines to the capitalist economic system. Who the major beneficiary was is questionable. To his credit, Robinson never compelled the Aborigines to undertake work, and those who volunteered their services were paid monetarily. Road-building, for example, attracted a daily pay rate of between one shilling and one shilling and sixpence. Yet, while they received wages there was nowhere to spend it, and the accumulation of wealth was a totally alien concept. At the same time basic rations were provided at no cost, so the creation of a public market gave the recipients a chance to purchase items not supplied by the government.[52]

According to Robinson the market was so successful that it had to be held weekly. The Aborigines sold wallaby skins, mutton-bird feathers, salted mutton-birds, poultry, fish, shell necklaces, spears and waddies. As the civil and military officers tended to shun the market the main purchaser appears to have been Robinson. The Aborigines used their profits to buy fresh fruit such as plums, fishing tackle, crockery, tobacco pipes, steel tomahawks, beads, marbles and straw hats. More problematic was that they also purchased shirts, buckled belts, women's dresses, needle and thread and soap,[53] commodities which either were, or should have been, supplied by the government. Robinson also sold the Aboriginal people produce from his own garden, and some of the items were relatively expensive, particularly when compared with the rate of pay Aboriginal workers received. Fishing tackle (which was supplied by the Commissariat Store in Hobart) was sold for one shilling and sixpence, while a steel tomahawk cost two shillings. The village constable scheme will be discussed shortly, but suffice to say here that Aboriginal constables were paid at the rate of one shilling per week. Thus, a steel tomahawk equated to two weeks' labour.[54] In May 1837 Robinson did away with the legal tender by taking £20 worth of old English coinage and stamping the obverse 'F.I.' and the reverse 'A.E.' (Flinders Island Aboriginal Establishment), with its use restricted solely to Wybalenna. [55]

Vivienne Rae-Ellis has argued that Robinson was the one who befitted most from the weekly market. Although regular accounts of all transactions were kept to give it a semblance of legitimacy,

Robinson did not keep the books himself. Instead, he initially approached surgeon James Allen, who despite his affair with Maria Robinson refused to accede to his future father-in-law's request. Like the other officers, Allen avoided the market altogether. Storekeeper Loftus Dickenson was of the same mind, so it finally fell to the lot of catechist Robert Clark,[56] who Brian Plomley castigated as a 'toady'.[57] Clark, in fact, tried to avoid keeping the accounts as well, until ordered to do so by Robinson. The mutton-bird feathers, salted mutton-birds, wallaby skins, cultural artefacts and even wool from the settlement's sheep which passed through the market found a ready sale in Launceston. Profits should have gone into the government's coffers or directly into the Aboriginal Establishment. There is no evidence that they went into either; all of it apparently went into Robinson's pocket. This explains why the other officers avoided becoming involved, as the market was a thin veneer for a fraud which could easily have enmeshed them if it had been exposed.[58] It was not.

The spears, waddies and shell necklaces are worthy of further comment as Robinson did all he could to slowly wean the Aboriginal people away from their cultural practices in a bid to place them on the road to 'salvation'. These items were worth money, and it was therefore on non-material culture that Robinson focused his attention. Men were encouraged to cut their hair, and both sexes discouraged from using ochre. Ceremonies were said to have entirely disappeared and customary songs replaced by psalms and hymns.[59] Cultural practices were far too important to disappear in their entirety and were almost certainly engaged in when the Aborigines managed to slip away from the settlement for any length of time, particularly on extended hunting expeditions.[60] It is unlikely that Robinson really believed they had been made redundant. He knew the Aborigines too well, and it was his understanding of their social systems which led him to introduce a more positive initiative which directly involved the Aboriginal people in their own affairs. The entire Aboriginal community elected constables to keep order, but it was the senior men, the band leaders, who administered the pseudo-law as it applied to the community. While Robinson is certainly known to have exerted some influence over the election of the constables, he relied entirely on the authority of the senior men to make the scheme work.[61] A sceptic might see this as yet another divide and conquer strategy, which it undoubtedly was, though it must be admitted that it did provide the Aborigines with some responsibility as well as reinforcing their customary power structure.

Robinson was keen to put a stop to promiscuity, with men and women regularly changing partners. This was anything but a customary practice and clearly the product of the unnatural environment in which the Aborigines were now placed.[62] The same can be said in regard to theft, largely committed by children. The Aboriginal people had little concept of private ownership and to be charged with 'stealing' would have been virtually meaningless. An Aboriginal woman named Agnes was one such offender, having purloined a silver spoon from Robinson's own household. After being charged with theft, Robinson stopped her tobacco ration for a fortnight by way of penalty.[63] There was a separate gaol at Wybalenna,[64] so it can be assumed that at least some offenders spent varying periods in even more confined incarceration. In the majority of cases, though, as exemplified by Agnes, punishment largely revolved around the deprivation of privileges.

While the Aborigines were able to gain a limited degree of social control amongst themselves, they were not prepared to exert any control over their dogs, which became a serious nuisance. Virtually every adult Aborigine owned at least one dog, and many several, the animals allowed to roam the settlement at will. Half-starved and savage, Robinson was forced to step in when the dogs began devouring poultry and attacking the settlement's sheep. This was largely achieved through his high personal standing among the Aboriginal people, as well as his policy of paying the owner of any dog which had to be destroyed. By this means he was able to temporarily reduce their numbers. After Robinson left Wybalenna, however, the dogs once again became a menace, resulting in considerable friction between the Aborigines and succeeding superintendents, mostly from want of tact by the latter.[65]

In 1836 Lieutenant Governor Arthur appointed Robinson as a magistrate, one of his cherished ambitions. This was nevertheless a sensible move as it enabled him to effectively deal with the assigned convicts. At the same time Robinson was forced to chart a careful course. If a convict was charged with a serious offence they would have to be returned to the mainland and their labour lost. If Robinson was too lenient, on the other hand, he risked losing control. Somehow he managed to achieve a rather delicate balance, but it was a little different with the soldiers, who were reluctant to do anything beyond their specific military duties. Although Robinson's magistracy carried some weight, his ability to handle the military personnel was less effective than with the unfree labour force.[66]

It was the Aboriginal children who received the harshest treatment. Even after Robinson brought them back from the Queen's Orphan School in Hobart they were segregated from their parents and the rest of the Aboriginal community. They lived in a dormitory attached to Robert Clark's residence and were weighed down by strict regimentation. Rising from their beds at 6.30am, the children washed and said prayers until 7am when they gathered together with the Clark family to read from the bible. Following breakfast at 7.30am the children went to school, breaking for a two-hour lunch at noon before continuing their studies until 3.30pm. Tea followed, and between 6pm and 8pm they assisted the adult Aborigines at the evening school before returning to the dormitory for more worship.[67] Lights went out at 9pm — a very exciting schedule indeed — and from all accounts the catechist and his wife treated the children brutally.[68] This was no exaggeration. In 1835, 14 children aged between six and 15 years were under the control of the Clarks. The children later testified that they had been beaten, chained and forced to sleep in the poultry shed. One girl named Hannah was allegedly hung by her neck from a beam as punishment.[69]

When boys reached the age of around 15 Robinson endeavoured to have some of them taught trades. Peter Brune, for example, was apprenticed to the settlement's tailor, while his brother Thomas became an apprentice shoemaker. Yet, it is difficult to fathom what was going on in Robinson's mind when he decided to teach one of the brightest boys of all, Walter Arthur, how to look after the sheep. Both Walter and his brother Augustus became shepherds, while a number of other boys inferior in intellect and reading and writing skills were employed in the superintendent's office.[70] None of the children learnt anything of substance. They were denied parental love and affection, physically separated from the customary way of life, and they were not prepared for entry into colonial society even if it had been acceptable. In essence, the children were trapped between two worlds with escape almost entirely out of the question.

Death was one way out, and Robinson could do little to stem the rising mortality rate. Indeed, as deaths increased his attitude gradually swung from one of respect and genuine grievance to a detached acceptance that it was all due to the 'will of providence'.[71] When Mannalargenna lay dying in December 1835 Robinson rushed to the hut to commune with his old friend, and when the leader of the Cape Portland band breathed his last Robinson was so upset that he could not bring himself to view the body: he mourned in solitude.[72] Less than two years later, however, Robinson began collecting the bones of deceased Aborigines which their families kept as charms to ward off their own illnesses. From there it was a short step to keeping Aboriginal skulls, with Robinson becoming so keen to build a collection that many corpses were decapitated prior to burial.[73]

When George Arthur was recalled in 1836 he was replaced by Sir John Franklin, who visited Wybalenna in January 1838 with his wife Lady Jane, the latter expressing a desire to obtain an Aboriginal skull for her own natural history assemblage.[74] The death of Deborah two months later allowed Robinson to fulfil Lady Jane's request,[75] and in February the following year he forwarded a skull from a male Aborigine so that she could have an example from both sexes.[76] Robinson continued to keep many skulls for himself, including the cranium of Deborah's husband Rodney from the west coast, who passed away in August 1838.[77]

In November 1837 Robinson made a rough sketch of the burial ground, and the following year measured it with exactness, plotting the individual graves. When told by the Aborigines that a number of burials and cremations had taken place outside the burial ground before his arrival, Robinson carefully marked them on his diagram as well. Once the map had been completed Robinson began to systematically loot the graves. There is no record of what the Aborigines thought of this ghoulish behaviour, though it could be relevant that when Robinson embarked on a five-day exploratory journey across Flinders Island with six former mission Aborigines, including Woorrady and Truganini, he was shunned. Unlike earlier occasions the Aborigines refused to share food gathered in the hunt, so Robinson was forced to subsist on dry bread and tea. In the evenings they built their own shelters, leaving Robinson to huddle alone beside the fire in the open air.[78] For whatever reason the superintendent had lost much of the affection and respect he once had, and that was particularly noticeable with Truganini who may have shared Robinson's blanket on many 'Friendly Mission' journeys.[79]

Although extremely annoyed by their behaviour, perhaps it did not really matter. Robinson's time at Wybalenna was only meant to be temporary as he pursued his chosen career to higher levels. In August 1836 he was offered the position of Protector of Aborigines in the new colony of South Australia, only to turn it down when the salary offered was below what Robinson considered he was worth.[80] He remained at Wybalenna until the more lucrative appointment as Protector of Aborigines at Port Phillip (Victoria) became available in February 1839. For the Aboriginal people, in particular, they had been wasted years. Robinson's term as superintendent at Wybalenna had differed little from his initial experiment on Bruny Island, and the knowledge that he had gained in the interim was barely apparent. Deaths occurred with monotonous regularity, and many of his supposed improvements to benefit the Aboriginal people and make them more comfortable were completely fallacious.

A good indication of the discrepancy between the official reports and the reality became obvious in March 1836, when Robinson left the settlement to spend 13 weeks at Hobart. George Arthur was impressed by the superintendent's glowing accounts, but for some inexplicable reason he became convinced that all was not as well as Robinson claimed. While Robinson was absent the Lieutenant Governor instructed the commandant at Launceston, Major Thomas Ryan, to conduct an independent investigation into the Aboriginal Establishment.[81] Ryan arrived at Wybalenna in March 1836 to find the Aborigines suffering from malnutrition and a host of maladies. Robert Clark defended Robinson by insisting that all the settlement's defects were the result of previous administrations, but Ryan could not ignore the poor state of housing which had not been addressed since Robinson's arrival.[82]

Although the Aboriginal accommodation was later improved, at the time of Ryan's visit the huts were literally falling apart. On one occasion a violent storm swept across the settlement and Ryan found the Aborigines shivering around their fires with no blankets and rain pouring through gaping holes in the roofs. He raced across to Robinson's residence where he found several bales of new blankets which the superintendent had not bothered to distribute. The Launceston commandant did it himself, handing out more than a hundred blankets, while instructing the convicts to effect temporary repairs to the huts with brick and plaster before nightfall. As Vivienne Rae-Ellis sardonically commented, Ryan accomplished morein 12 hours than what Robinson had in five months.[83]

Ryan may have been fooled by Clark's defence of Robinson to some degree, but he still found it difficult not to accept that the Aboriginal people were being slowly and systematically exterminated. After receiving Ryan's report Arthur ordered Robinson to make immediate improvements, but little was actually done while Robinson remained as superintendent (officially commandant from May 1836 when Arthur acceded to Robinson's request for an official change to his title).[84] Perhaps the designation was in keeping with a veritable concentration camp where death constantly stalked the inmates. From mid-1836 to the beginning of 1839, when Robinson left Wybalenna to take up his appointment as Protector of Aborigines in the Port Phillip district, the Aboriginal death rate averaged one every three weeks. During Robinson's entire term as superintendent *cum* commandant the total number of Aboriginal deaths reached 59.[85]

Perhaps the only thing which prevented the Aborigines from losing all hope was Robinson's promise that they would be relocated to the Australian mainland. In August 1838 he sailed to Sydney where, *inter alia*, Robinson held discussions relating to his forthcoming appointment as Protector of Aborigines. He also learnt that he could take no more than eight Van Diemen's Land Aborigines to Melbourne. Returning to Flinders Island in January 1839 Robinson and his family packed their belongings and left Wybalenna the following month. Rather than eight Aborigines, Robinson actually took 15.[86] The remainder of the Aboriginal community were left to contemplate their fate, and at the very time Robinson sailed out into the waters of Bass Strait an influenza epidemic was sweeping through the settlement. The Aborigines abandoned their huts and fled into the bush in a bid to escape its deadly clutches, an evasive measure that was not completely successful.[87]

In a way this marked the twilight years of Wybalenna, with the Aborigines largely neglected and still gripped by the spectre of death. After taking over the reins of power from George Arthur, Sir John Franklin embarked on a major cost-cutting exercise which had a direct bearing on the Aboriginal Establishment. European staff was reduced to 16 and annual expenditure halved to £2000.[88] Until April 1839 the settlement was supervised by Robinson's eldest son, George Jnr, who appears to have been spectacularly inept.[89] He was replaced by former police magistrate Malcolm Laing Smith, the same Laing Smith whose land grant at Port Sorell had frustrated the aims of Edward Curr and the Van Diemen's Land Company. Laing Smith soon revealed that he was more interested in farming for himself than looking after the interests of the Aboriginal people, and Wybalenna was effectively managed by his sons who allowed the Aborigines to use ochre, perform ceremonies and go out on hunting expeditions whenever they felt so inclined. As a result of this new-found freedom their general health showed a marked improvement and a number of infants were born on the settlement.[90]

It all came to an end in May 1841 when another epidemic swept through Wybalenna, coinciding with an economic depression in the Australian colonies. Franklin was forced to slash expenditure on the

Aboriginal Establishment even further, cutting the European staff to just eight and replacing Laing Smith with Peter Fisher and, in 1842, Henry Jeanneret, both of whom were qualified medical men (though Jeanneret's sanity had previously been questioned).[91] At Franklin's direction eight of the children were removed to the Queen's Orphan School in Hobart and the Aboriginal adults were now expected to work for their keep.[92] For all but one of the Aboriginal residents the situation thus became even grimmer. The fortunate individual was Woretemoeteryenner, mother of Dolly Dalrymple, who managed to escape the confines of Flinders Island in 1841. With the exception of a few of the Aboriginal people Robinson took with him to the Port Phillip district, Woretemoeteryenner was the only Aborigine to be permanently released from Wybalenna.[93]

After gaining his conditional pardon in October 1836 Thomas Johnson had married Dolly Dalrymple at Longford. The couple experienced a major setback in August 1836, when Johnson received a seven year sentence after being convicted of having stolen wheat in his possession. Dolly Johnson's request for Thomas to be assigned to herself was officially refused, but there is strong evidence that Johnson remained in the Perth district where he continued working as a carter. At the time of his conviction the couple had four dependent children and Dolly had no independent income, yet she weathered the five years before Thomas was again free quite successfully. Indeed, three more Johnson children were born between 1836 and 1841, and having gained his freedom a second time the couple never looked back.[94]

In 1841 Dolly Johnson petitioned the colonial government for her mother to be released into her care from Wybalenna, and in an extraordinary gesture Woretemoeteryenner joined her daughter and son-in-law at Perth.[95] Four years later Thomas took over the tenancy of Frogmore Estate in the Mersey River district and prospered, purchasing 500 acres of land nearby where he erected an imposing new family home called Sherwood Hall. Commercial enterprises followed, with the Johnsons acquiring the Native Youth Inn at Sherwood, the Dalrymple Inn at Ballahoo, the Alfred Colliery and a timber export business. They were among the largest landholders in the Mersey River district and both were highly-respected. Little notice appears to have been taken of Dolly Johnson's Aboriginality. She died at Latrobe on 1 December 1864 at the age of 54, survived by 10 of the couple's 13 children. Thomas remarried the following year and died in December 1867.[96] Their descendants form part of the modern Tasmanian Aboriginal community. Dolly and Thomas were predeceased by Woretemoeteryenner, who died at her daughter's home on 13 October 1847 after enjoying almost six years of freedom.[97]

The people Woretemoeteryenner left behind at Wybalenna did not fare so well. When Henry Jeanneret arrived as commandant in August 1842 the Aboriginal population numbered only 52, comprising 12 couples, 11 single men, six single women and 11 children, none of whom were in the best state of health. Packs of dogs were again roaming wild, destroying gardens and livestock with impunity, and contributing to the poor health of their owners. Dogs wandered in and out of the huts at will and there was little attempt at cleanliness.[98] Aboriginal numbers received a slight boost during the year when seven of the Van Diemen's Land Aborigines were sent back from the Port Phillip district. As discussed in the following chapter, their interlude had been anything but peaceful. The Lanne family also arrived on Flinders Island in 1842, supposedly the last group of Aborigines on the mainland of Van Diemen's Land.

Some of those who had accompanied Robinson to Port Phillip, notably Walter Arthur, soon began causing Henry Jeanneret considerable difficulty as they had gained a good understanding of their basic rights while working for settlers on the Australian mainland and viewed themselves as a free people. Jeanneret tried to impose a semblance of order by following Franklin's instructions and compelling the Aborigines to work, but the Port Phillip group refused to have anything to do with forced labour. The women quickly re-established sexual relationships with the convicts and sealers, the latter having continued to loiter around the Aboriginal Establishment.[99] The more pressure Jeanneret placed on the returnees from Port Phillip the more they resisted, with his problems further compounded by relentless squabbles with the European staff. The main troublemaker appears to have been Robert Clark, and Jeanneret's constant stream of complaints to the colonial secretary regarding the difficulties he faced, and the government's neglect of the Aboriginal Establishment, led to accusations of incompetency. In December 1843 Jeanneret was suspended from his position.[100]

He was replaced by Joseph Milligan, who had a genuine humanitarian interest in the Aboriginal people. Milligan allowed them considerable freedom and actively encouraged the continuation of cultural practices, but the sterile environment of Wybalenna now acted against any improvement. In 1844 there were 57 Aborigines at the settlement,[101] their situation taking a turn for the worse in December 1845 when Jeanneret successfully appealed against his suspension and was reinstated as commandant.[102] With Joseph Milligan and Robert Clark working behind the scenes Walter Arthur prepared a petition to Queen Victoria in February 1846. This extraordinary document was passed to the British government and finally reached the monarch's hands in March 1847. Signed by Walter Arthur and several other Aboriginal men, the petition outlined their grievances against Henry Jeanneret, but went further by articulating their understanding of why they had been exiled. According to the petitioners the Aboriginal people were not captives who had been defeated in war; on the contrary, they were a free people who had laid down their arms as part of a negotiated settlement between themselves, George Augustus Robinson and Lieutenant Governor George Arthur. They contended that the Aborigines had fulfilled their part of the agreement and were still waiting for the colonial government to fulfil theirs.[103] What that part of the bargain was is open to speculation. Henry Reynolds has suggested that it may in fact have been a treaty which recognised the rights of the Aborigines as the true possessors of Van Diemen's Land.[104] The evidence for this, however, is rather slim. Any promise which had been made emanated solely from George Augustus Robinson, not necessarily with the sanction of George Arthur and the colonial government. Rather than any suggestion of a treaty the essence of the document was that as a free people the Aborigines had the right to reject the reappointment of Henry Jeanneret as commandant of Wybalenna. It was probably no more complex than that.

Nor did it matter. By the time the petition reached Queen Victoria Jeanneret had returned to Flinders Island, and the struggle against his authority was renewed. At one point Walter Arthur was imprisoned by the commandant for 17 days, almost certainly an act of revenge for his part in preparing the petition.[105] The Aboriginal people retaliated by unleashing a barrage of complaints against Jeanneret, prompting the colonial secretary to enquire into the management of Wybalenna. The investigation was conducted by the port officer at Launceston, Matthew Friend, who was unable to find evidence for many of the allegations, though he did condemn Jeanneret for the illegal imprisonment of Walter Arthur.[106] All correspondence relating to the affairs at Wybalenna was subsequently passed to the British government, where it came to the attention of James Stephen, Under-Secretary of State for the Colonies, who was deeply concerned by the plight of indigenous people throughout the British Empire. After consulting the available information Stephen recommended that Wybalenna should be closed down and the Aboriginal people repatriated to the mainland of Van Diemen's Land.[107]

Lieutenant Governor William Denison was of the same mind, but for a very different reason. For some time he had been concerned that sexual liaisons between Aboriginal women and the sealers could produce a 'hybrid' population and create problems for the colonial government in the not-too-distant future. To avoid that possible outcome Denison found what he believed to be a suitable location for the remnant Aboriginal people at Oyster Cove, an abandoned penal station south of Hobart.[108] In May 1847 he dismissed Jeanneret and reappointed Joseph Milligan to oversee the transfer from Flinders Island. Feelings amongst the colonists still ran deep, however, and there was considerable opposition to the intended repatriation.[109] Louisa Anne Meredith was among those appalled by the decision, summing up the feelings of many colonists who, unlike herself, had experienced the Black War:

> Of the charitable and humane feelings which actuated Sir W. Denison, but one opinion can be entertained. How far he was justified in gratifying them by making this change is a separate question, as the colonists, especially those who had formerly suffered such fearful experience of the aboriginal ferocity and cruelty, were strenuously opposed to the measure—on the grounds that every adult man among the natives had been actively engaged in many, some of them in hundreds, of most brutal and unprovoked murders, and that in all probability a return to their old haunts would lead to a renewal of the horrors which, since their removal, have been unknown, but which in former years rendered a residence in the colony one long series of alarms, suffering and loss, with the daily imminent peril of a frightful death.[110]

Those bigoted views were no longer justified, and Denison swept all opposition aside. In October 1847 the Aborigines at Wybalenna gathered up their belongings — including the dogs — and boarded a vessel bound for the south. There were no regrets: Wybalenna had been a place of suffering and death. The survivors numbered just 46: 14 men, 22 women and 10 children. One man died shortly after arrival,[111] and the remainder were blithely unaware that the pain and suffering was still far from over.

10

THE PORT PHILLIP INTERLUDE (1839–1842)

George Augustus Robinson's appointment as Protector of Aborigines in the Port Phillip district (future Victoria) was a lucrative one indeed, attracting an annual salary of £500. Robinson also had the support of four assistant protectors — Charles Sievwright, James Dredge, William Thomas and Edward Parker — all of whom received annual salaries of £250. Unlike Robinson, however, the assistant protectors were appointed directly by the British government and had no previous experience of Australian conditions or the Aboriginal people. Three of them were Methodist ministers, while the fourth, Charles Sievwright, was a former military officer who had been forced to sell his commission to pay off gambling debts.[1] These four men arrived from England via Sydney in advance of Robinson, and despite their lack of experience they were to prove more than worthy subordinates. Indeed, and notwithstanding the damning assessments by Superintendent Charles Joseph La Trobe and Governor George Gipps,[2] it would be fair to say that without their combined efforts

Robinson would have achieved very little during his 11 years at Port Phillip. Although he undertook a number of significant overland journeys to South Australia, New South Wales and the Western District of Port Phillip (in the latter case accompanied by Pevay from Van Diemen's Land) — as well as a few exploratory trips throughout the hinterland — the valuable information Robinson compiled was only of benefit to posterity: it had little resonance for his own contemporary society. And Robinson's attempts to 'civilise' the Indigenous people of the southern Australian mainland proved to be an abysmal failure. Unlike their Van Diemen's Land counterparts, the Victorian Aborigines were not confined to a relatively small island and usually not shot on sight. To a certain extent they were able to come and go as they pleased.[3]

When Robinson arrived in Melbourne there were very few Aborigines to be found as a serious epidemic of influenza had swept through the fledgling European settlement, claiming a number of Aboriginal victims and sending the survivors fleeing into the interior. Robinson was so ill himself that it was four days before he could step ashore, and bearing in mind that he may have become ill in Sydney before sailing south to pack his belongings at Wybalenna, it is possible that Robinson was the source of the fatal contagion which gripped the Aboriginal Establishment on Flinders Island in February 1839.[4] The Aboriginal absence from Melbourne was merely temporary, however, and by the time Robinson had regained his strength the Indigenous people had begun returning to the European settlement where they camped on an area of land that is now the site of the Royal Botanic Gardens. It was there that Robinson and his family occupied a small cottage while the Van Diemen's Land Aborigines were left to build their own shelters from grass. As soon as he had established himself, Robinson and the assistant protectors held a feast for the Victorian Aborigines, providing lavish quantities of beef, mutton and

Van Diemen's Land Map, Arrowsmith 1825

Francois Péron (1775–1810), the French proto-anthropologist who compiled valuable information on the Van Diemen's Land Aborigines

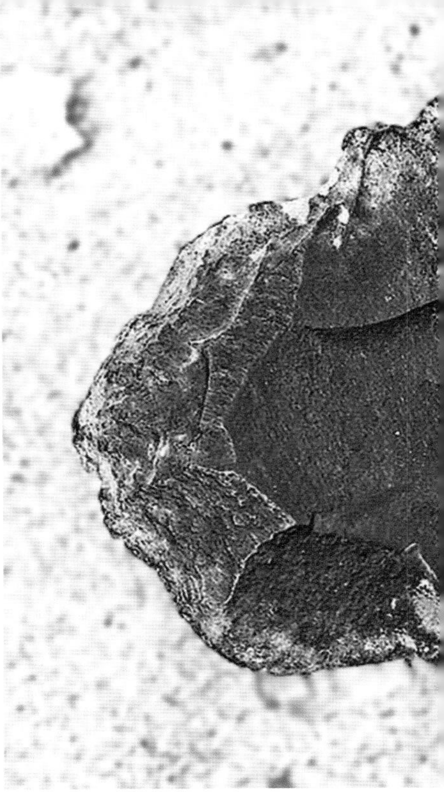

Stone Flake cutting tool from the north-west coast, a reminder of the depth of Aboriginal antiquity in Tasmania and the skill of their craftsmen (photography Ian McFarlane)

Petroglyphs at Sundown Point in north-west Tasmania (photography Ian McFarlane)

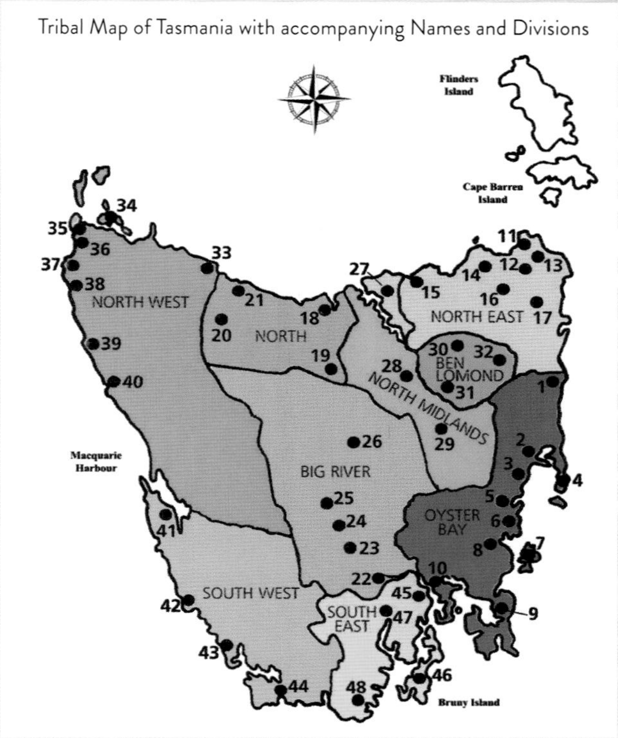

Swivel gun. The mysterious Paddy Heagon reputedly used such a weapon during the conflict in northern Van Diemen's Land

Van Diemen's Land Tribes and their Territories

Oyster Bay Tribes

1. Leeter.maire.mener : St Patricks Head
2. Linete.mairener : North Moulting Lagoon
3. Loon.titeter.maire.lehoinner : North Oyster Bay
4. Toorerno.maire.mener : Schouten Passage
5. Pore.dareme : Little Swanport
6. Lare.maire.mener : Grindstone Bay
7. Tyred.deme : Maria Island
8. Port.maire.mener : Prosser River
9. Pydai.rerme : Tasman Peninsula
10. Moo.maire.mener : Pittswater, Risdon

North East Tribes

11. Trawl.wool.way : Cape Portland
12. Leener.rerter : *uncertain*
13. Pinter.rairer : *uncertain*
14. Peeber.ranger : *uncertain*
15. Pyem.maire.nener.pairener : Pipers River
16. Leeneth.mairener : *uncertain*
17. Panpe.kanner : *uncertain*

North Tribes

18. Punniler.panner : Port Sorrell
19. Pallit.torre : Quamby Bluff
20. Noe.teller : Hampshire Hills
21. Plaire.heke.hiller.plue : Emu Bay:*uncertain*

Big River Tribes

22. Leenow.wenne : New Norfolk
23. Panger.ninghe : Clyde-Derwent junction
24. Brayl.wunyer : Ouse and Dee Rivers
25. Lar.mairene : West of Dee
26. Lugger.mairenerner.pairer : Great Lake

North Midlands Tribes

27. Leterre.mairener : Port Dalrymple
28. Pannin.her : Norfolk Plains
29. Tyerer.note.panner : Campbell Town

Ben Lomond Tribes

30. Planger.maire.enner : *uncertain*
31. Plinder.maire.mener : *uncertain*
32. Tonener.weener.laremenne : *uncertain*

North West Tribes

33. Tomme.ginner : Table Cape
34. Parper.loihener : Robbins Island
35. Pennemuker : Cape Grim
36. Pendowte : Studland bay
37. Pee.rapper : West Point
38. Manegin : Arthur River mouth
39. Tarkiner : Sandy Cape
40. Peternidic : Pieman River mouth

South West Tribes

41. Mimegin : Macquarie Harbour
42. Lowreene : Low Rocky Point
43. Ninene : Port Davey
44. Needwonee : Cox Bight

South East Tribes

45. Mouhe.neene : Hobart
46. Nuenone : Bruny Island
47. Melukerdee : Huon River
48. Lylue.quonny : Recherche Bay

Derived from Rhys Jones, 'Tasmanian Tribes', appendix to Norman Tindale, *Aboriginal Tribes of Australia: Their Terrain, Environmental Controls, Distribution, Limits and Proper Names*, Australian National University Press, Canberra, 1974, p.237

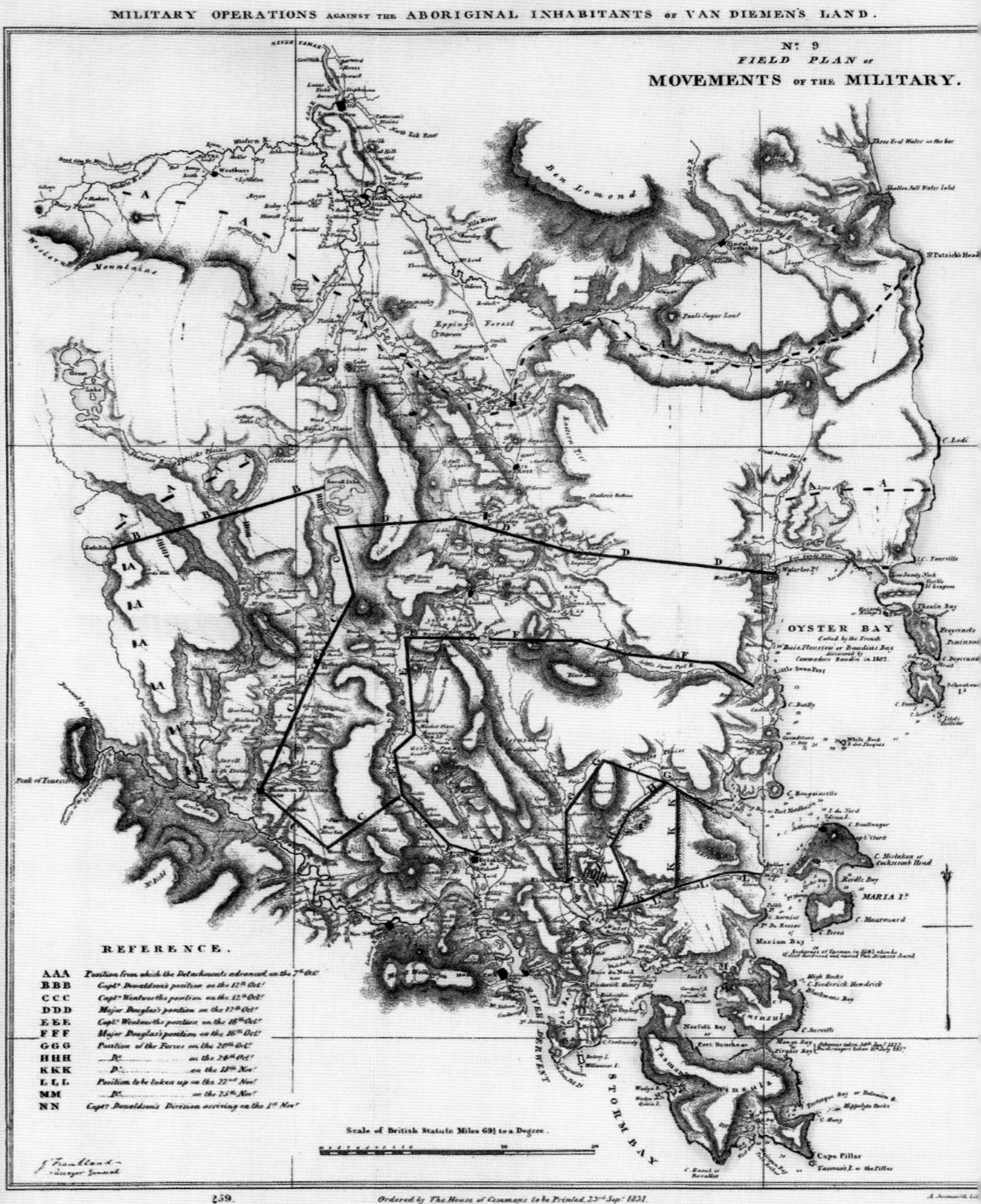

George Frankland's field plan of the 'Black Line' in 1830

Cape Grim Massacre Site (photography Ian McFarlane)

Van Diemen's Land Company Holdings, 1833

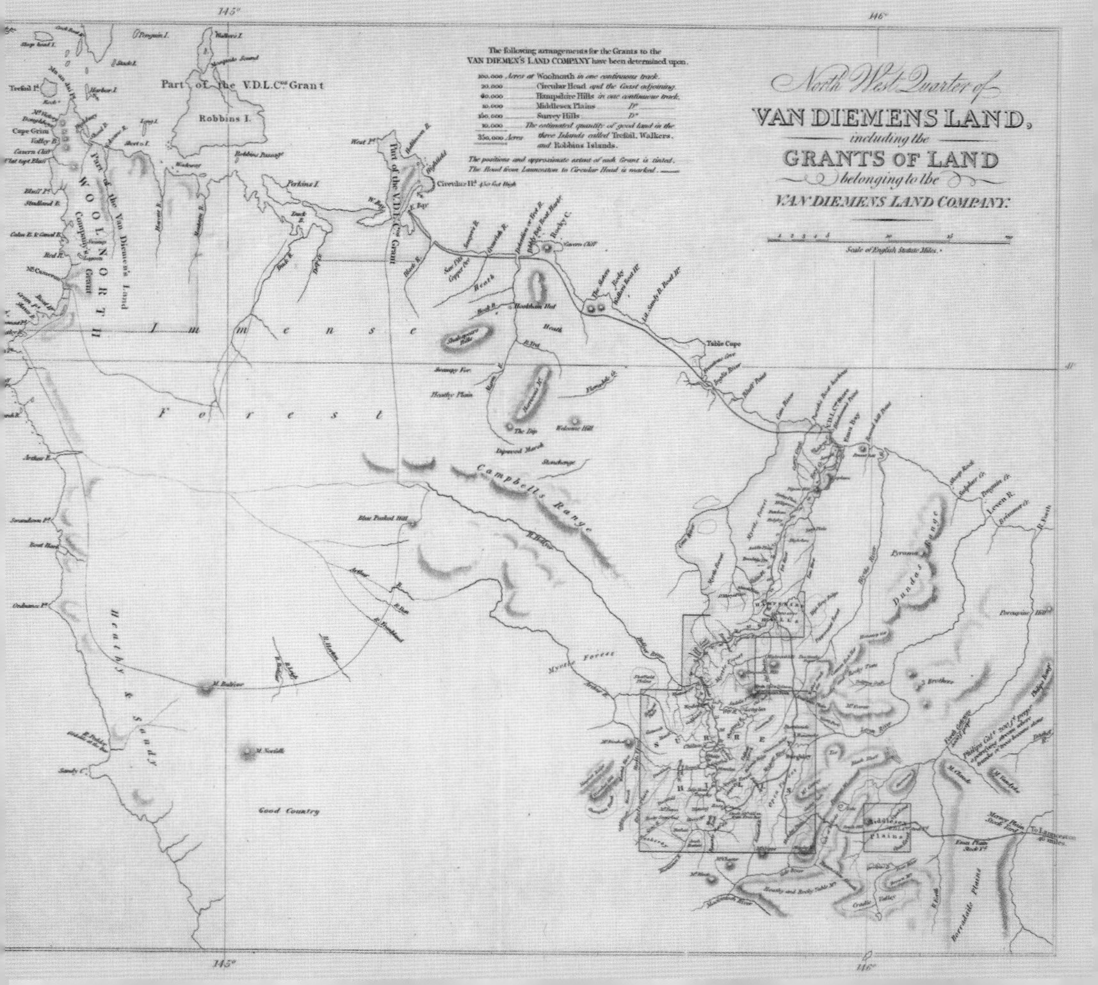

Mathinna (1835–1852): a tragic victim of colonisation

Aboriginal Station Oyster Cove (1900). Pencil and watercolour attributed to Annie Benbow (courtesy of the W.L. Crowther Library, Tasmanian Archives and Heritage Office)

Tasmanian Aborigines at Oyster Cove Aboriginal Establishment, April 1858. (photography by Bishop Nixon courtesy of the W.L. Crowther Library, Tasmanian Archives and Heritage Office)

Truganini (c.1812–1876), witness to the full horrors unleashed upon the Van Diemen's Land Aborigines by European colonists

William Lanne (c.1835–1869), whose body was mutilated after death

Poster released by the Tasmanian Aboriginal Centre as part of the protest against road works at the Jordan River levee north of Hobart which they claimed would destroy an ancient archaeological site

bread. Competitive games were held and the evening's entertainment was concluded with the usual Robinson touch by a spectacular fireworks display. Robinson also made a point of inviting Melbourne's European community to this day of festivities and by all accounts the majority responded, but his idea of the feast differed considerably from that of the Aborigines. Robinson intended it as a one-off gesture to convey his good intentions; the Aborigines understood it to be a new policy whereby they would be provided with regular provisions and other goods, an expectation which was quite understandable given that many of them had already been dispossessed of their land and natural resources.[5]

That was anything but the government's intention. In October 1839 Charles Joseph La Trobe replaced administrator William Lonsdale as Superintendent of the Port Phillip district,[6] with instructions from Governor Gipps in Sydney to distribute indigent rations sparingly to avoid the Aborigines becoming dependent on government handouts. After all, if the Aborigines were to be 'civilised' they would first have to learn to work for wages.[7] Tight fiscal restraints had a direct impact on George Augustus Robinson, who was forced to keep detailed accounts of everything he provided for his charges. La Trobe was also keen to have the Aboriginal presence entirely removed from the environs of Melbourne,[8] a task which fell to Assistant Protector William Thomas.

In March 1839 Robinson allocated separate spheres of influence for his subordinates. Sievwright was given responsibility for the Aboriginal people of the Western District; Parker took charge of the north-west and the Loddon River area; Dredge operated in the north-east and northern central regions (including the Goulburn River); while Thomas's interests lay in the south around Melbourne and Westernport. Owing to governmental lethargy it was six months before the assistant protectors were able to gather together sufficient resources to commence their allotted tasks.[9] Robinson spent all his time organising the new department and paid very little attention to the Aborigines himself. At the same time he neglected the Van Diemen's Land Aborigines he had brought to Port Phillip to such an extent that they were often short of provisions. A few of the older men, notably Woorrady, worked on properties purchased by Robinson's sons or were hired out to local settlers. Two of the Van Diemen's Land Aborigines, Timme (otherwise known as Bob) and Walter Arthur, made extended droving trips to the new colony of South Australia. Woorrady was ageing and in poor health, allowing Truganini and a few of the other women ample opportunity to mix freely with the Victorian Aborigines.[10] Truganini soon became a considerable source of annoyance to Robinson, who was regularly forced to send out search parties to bring her back to Melbourne. On one occasion Truganini and Kalloongoo (Charlotte) wandered as far afield as Port Nepean where they were discovered living with European shepherds,[11] but it seems clear that even by this early stage the Van Diemen's Land Aborigines were becoming aware that their close relationship with Robinson was rapidly drawing to a close. From Robinson's perspective they were becoming an unwanted liability.

In the meantime William Thomas had managed to establish an Aboriginal station on the Mornington Peninsula, where he was authorised to issue rations as a means of enticing the Victorian Aborigines away from Melbourne.[12] This was only partially successful owing to the significant ceremonial sites which lay along the Yarra River, attracting Aborigines from as far away as the Goulburn Valley in the north.[13] The assistant protectors also faced difficulties from other quarters, not the least of which were restrictions placed on their legal powers. Although appointed as magistrates, they were only authorised to take action in cases which directly involved the Aboriginal people and even then they could only do so with the consent of higher legal authorities.[14]

In the event of Aborigines being killed by Europeans the assistant protectors could only issue a summons if there were independent European witnesses willing to support a prosecution, as Aboriginal testimony was not accepted in courts of law. Sievwright, for instance, charged two shepherds with killing Aborigines 160 kilometres north-west of Melbourne only to find the Attorney General unwilling to proceed with a prosecution after the shepherds pleaded self-defence. As the bodies of the victims had been burnt and there were no other European witnesses Sievwright's hands were effectively tied. Sievwright was frustrated yet again in November 1839 when he received a report that between 20 and 30 Aborigines had been killed by Europeans in the Lake Corangamite district approximately 140 kilometres from Melbourne. After Superintendent La Trobe gave Sievwright permission to hire a horse to investigate the incident, he was unable to obtain one and was eventually forced to purchase a mount at his own expense. By the time he reached the scene of the alleged murders there was no longer any evidence to be found.[15]

From July 1839 reports began to filter in to Melbourne of Aborigines being issued with firearms by Europeans. There was some substance to these claims: settlers on the frontier occasionally armed their Aboriginal workers for defence against other Aborigines, while a few traders around Melbourne were in the habit of equipping Aborigines with firearms to obtain lyrebird tail feathers and possum skins, the demand for both commodities so great that fortunes could be made.[16] The authorities nevertheless expected the assistant protectors to disarm the Aborigines without providing them with any real legal backing. Moreover, William Thomas refused to carry arms himself, which made the task particularly dangerous, and there were a number of occasions when he came perilously close to being killed by

Aboriginal people who resented his attempts at intervention.[17] Unlike the Van Diemen's Land Aborigines, the Victorians were not averse to using firearms against the settlers, prompting legislation to be passed prohibiting all Aborigines from carrying firearms. Although a clause was inserted to allow exemptions under special circumstances, La Trobe instructed local magistrates not to make any exceptions.[18] This great fear of Aborigines bearing firearms is worth keeping in mind in view of the events which occurred in late 1841.

The Van Diemen's Land Aborigines regularly made the journey to the ration depot William Thomas had established on the Mornington Peninsula, and in their altered circumstances Pevay soon emerged as a new leader. Like Timme, he had been closely associated with George Augustus Robinson for 13 years, and even before he left Wybalenna Pevay had increasingly taken upon himself the burden of leadership as the older men either died or became too ill to play a proactive role.[19] It was Pevay who took matters into his own hands around September 1841, when he gathered together Timme and three Van Diemen's Land women — his wife Fanny, Truganini and Matilda — and fled into the bush. They had little reason to remain in Melbourne. Apart from the constant struggle to procure enough food, they were among alien Indigenous people who were already suffering from a host of introduced illnesses, particularly dysentery. The Port Phillip Aborigines had been reduced to living in conditions that Pevay's little band knew all too well, with death a regular companion. Rather than remain where they were and risk the likelihood of succumbing to a similar fate, they commenced a series of raids on the settlers which was remarkably similar to the ones conducted by Umarrah in Van Diemen's Land from late 1830 to August 1831.[20] There was a connection. Fanny, or more correctly Ploorenernooperner, was Umarrah's sister, who had been forcibly abducted by sealers.[21]

The eldest son of William Thomas recorded the circumstances surrounding the departure of Pevay and his compatriots from Melbourne. They were, so he said, tired of the monotony and restrictions placed on their movements. Thomas described Pevay as a natural-born leader of great dignity, who often talked about the injustices inflicted on his people in Van Diemen's Land, seldom failing to mention how they had been hunted down and killed like common criminals. Now was the time for revenge, as they were no longer 'cooped up in an island'; at Port Phillip they had an unlimited expanse of country in which to roam. According to William Thomas Jnr, Truganini actively encouraged Pevay and the others to exact retribution from the Europeans.[22] Pevay was also echoing threats of revenge which his wife Fanny frequently made to the sealers until she had finally been taken from them by Robinson's coxswain, James Parish, in 1830. A man named Turnbull who knew both Fanny and the sealers well warned that she would be troublesome if ever taken to the Australian mainland, as Fanny often said that if she ever reached there she would be able to teach other Aborigines how 'to kill plenty of white men'.[23] No doubt those sentiments were shared by Matilda, who had been forcibly abducted from her Oyster Bay people by the sealer John Starker.[24]

In early 1841 a Van Diemen's Land Aborigine named Probelattener (otherwise known as Lacklay or Isaac) began warning the settlers to arm themselves as they would soon be under attack.[25] The alarm was taken very seriously. Settlers on Mornington Peninsula and throughout the Westernport area more generally either armed themselves for defence or fled to the safety of Melbourne. Initial reports had it that the Van Diemen's Land Aborigines had joined with their Victorian counterparts,[26] an alliance that never eventuated. Robinson was publicly embarrassed when the *Port Phillip Herald* openly stated that all five Aborigines were skilled in the use of firearms and emphasised that they had been brought to Port Phillip by the Protector of Aborigines.[27]

Instead of the Mornington Peninsula, however, Pevay led his group into the Dandenong Ranges where they first armed themselves with a fowling piece stolen from a local settler named Horsefal. With this weapon they attacked the property of a Mr Ordon, firing several shots through the roof in an unsuccessful attempt to burn the homestead down. After noticing they were being observed through a keyhole, shots were directed at the door. The two men inside broke through the rear wall and fled into the bush, leaving the Van Diemen's Land Aborigines to enter the building by climbing down the chimney. They carried away a bag of sugar and 130 pounds (60 kilograms) of flour.[28]

They next struck the home of a Mr Mundy, where they obtained more firearms to attack the station of Mr Allen in the same district. Here they stole a large quantity of ammunition and also made off with three prized kangaroo dogs. The camp of a timber-cutter named Westaway was raided at night with the Europeans scattering into the bush to avoid a fusillade of bullets. This raid netted the Van Diemen's Land Aborigines more firearms as well as £22 in banknotes, which Pevay deliberately burnt in the campfire. Although it has been suggested that this may have been a symbolic gesture to mark their complete break with European culture,[29] the fact that Pevay's band was accumulating a considerable arsenal of European weaponry leaves the real meaning behind his action unclear.

The Van Diemen's Land Aborigines then left the Dandenong Ranges and slowly made their way back towards the coast. Armed parties of soldiers, police, civilians and Aboriginal trackers were already in half-hearted pursuit as up until this time the robberies had been little more than a nuisance. The situation radically altered when Lieutenant Samuel Rawson of the 28th Regiment received word from miners working a coal seam on the coast that two whalers had been killed near Cape Patterson. Pevay's little band had now become a serious matter indeed, and when Rawson's party was reinforced by an armed force led by Commissioner of Crown Lands Frederick Powlett the chase began in earnest.[30] When news of the murders reached Melbourne La Trobe ordered Robinson to join the pursuit. Robinson instead set out to inspect the Aboriginal stations where it was highly unlikely Pevay and the others would make an appearance. The protectorate's representative in the search was William Thomas, who was to play an instrumental role in the capture of the renegades.[31] But it took some time. Despite their undoubted expertise local Aboriginal trackers experienced considerable difficulty in following Pevay's band, with Pevay, in particular, exhibiting consummate skill in removing virtually all trace of their movements through the bush. There were a number of close calls, and on one occasion Pevay realised that their pursuers were close behind. Splitting into separate groups the Van Diemen's Land Aborigines managed to escape through a swamp.[32]

On 17 November they raided Anderson's station, shooting and seriously wounding one of the employees. In the homestead they found two women and a child who were assured by Pevay they would not be harmed. He kept his word, and the Aborigines made off with three muskets, three bags of shot and quantities of flour and sugar.[33] Thomas was close behind and was soon joined by Rawson and Powlett's enlarged force. On the evening of 19 November Aboriginal trackers finally located the camp of Pevay's band near Lady's Bay. The pursuers moved in quietly at first light the following morning, the element of surprise suddenly lost when they were attacked by the Aborigines' dogs and they were forced to fire randomly into the encampment. The Van Diemen's Land Aborigines were only saved from complete annihilation by the thickness of the undergrowth, with the only injury

— a minor scalp wound — sustained by Truganini. Both Pevay and Timme managed to escape, only to be called back by the women after Rawson and Powlett had given assurances that no harm would come if they surrendered peacefully. The men were thus swayed to give themselves up, with all five secured with handcuffs and guarded closely by Aboriginal troopers.[34]

In the camp Powlett's men found five single-barrelled and three double-barrelled guns, along with four pistols, one of which was equipped with a spring-loaded bayonet. All the firearms were loaded, and the Aborigines also had in their possession three bags of shot, seven canisters of powder and a copper bullet mould capable of making 50 musket balls at a time.[35] This represented a substantial armoury, and while it is possible that Pevay had entertained the hope of being joined by Victorian Aborigines in his campaign against the colonists, it is equally possible that his band was seeking to deprive their enemies of firearms to afford some measure of protection for themselves.

They openly admitted having committed nine robberies and shooting four Europeans, including the two whalers who were killed on 6 October approximately 5 kilometres from where they were finally captured. Pevay said they had mistaken the two men for miners who had fired on them after the Aborigines had been caught robbing their hut. Truganini led members of Rawson and Powlett's party to where the bodies had been buried, but who actually killed the whalers remains in some doubt. William Cook was apparently wounded and then bludgeoned to death, while the whaler known only as 'Yankey' was shot dead. Timme told Corporal William Johnson of the Border Police that Pevay had threatened to kill him if he refused to shoot,[36] later adding that Pevay and Truganini had been responsible for terminating the life of Cook. Truganini initially admitted to Powlett's men her role in the murder before suddenly changing her story, claiming that all three women were on a high bank some distance from the scene of the crime.[37] Along with Pevay's confession, it was this statement in particular which saved the women from the gallows. From the available evidence, however, it appears that Truganini was more than just a passive observer.

All five Aborigines were committed to stand trial for murder, the women before and after the fact. The trial commenced on 20 December 1841 and it received extensive press coverage and a great deal of public interest.[38] The trial judge was John Walpole Willis, a controversial figure who had previously served in Upper Canada and British Guiana before coming to Australia. He was amoved from the bench in Canada, passed over for the position of chief justice in British Guiana and later amoved from the bench in Melbourne, probably the only judge in British history to be amoved from the high bench twice. Soon after arriving in Sydney Willis had clashed with Chief Justice Sir James Dowling and was appointed resident judge of the Port Phillip district to distance him from the centre of legal power.[39]

The accused pleaded not guilty and were defended by a young Irish barrister named Redmond Barry, who had only recently been appointed standing counsel for Aborigines. Thirty-nine years later Barry was to preside over the trial of bushranger Ned Kelly. As there were no European eye-witnesses all those called by the prosecution gave evidence into the circumstances surrounding the murders. Some of them recalled the admissions of guilt made by Pevay and Timme at the time of their capture, and in a break from legal protocol Judge Willis accepted a statement from Truganini that Pevay and Timme had been the actual killers.[40]

Barry then called George Augustus Robinson as the chief witness for the defence. Three months previously Robinson had sat in this same courtroom before the very same judge watching a murder trial involving a Port Phillip Aboriginal man named Bonjon. In that instance the accused had killed Yammerween, another Aboriginal man. Judge Willis had gone to great lengths to ascertain whether Bonjon understood the significance of his actions according to British law and custom. After concluding that he did not, Willis directed the jury to find the accused not guilty. Bonjon was subsequently delivered into Robinson's care. As Willis said at the time, Aboriginal people could not be considered as foreigners in a kingdom which they actually owned.[41] Although his ruling raised serious concerns in Sydney as it questioned the entire legality of British colonisation,[42] it was nevertheless allowed to stand. Bonjon was not so fortunate. Incensed that the Europeans had released him, Yammerween's people waited for the chance to exact their own punishment by murdering the killer in turn.[43] While Judge Willis showed considerable empathy for Bonjon, his judgements certainly lacked the consistency of Aboriginal customary law. This was made explicit when a European pastoralist, Sandford George Bolden, later appeared before him charged with murdering an Aborigine and was discharged after Willis directed the jury to find Bolden not guilty. According to the Supreme Court judge, leaseholders had the right to prevent unlawful entry onto their land.[44] This ruling rightly brought a strong rebuke from Superintendent La Trobe, for under the terms of pastoral leasehold Aboriginal people had been granted the legal right to obtain sustenance on Crown land. Willis's decision was again allowed to stand, though much was made at the time of his close friendship with the brother of the accused.[45]

Despite Willis's legal juggling the acquittal of Bonjon had followed a precedent established in 1836, when a Sydney jury acquitted an Aborigine known as Jack Congo Murrell after he had been charged with killing another Aborigine named Jabbingee near Windsor. The press had generally agreed with the decision, pointing out that it was absurd to impose foreign laws on Aborigines who had no means of understanding them. It was further added that if true justice was to be achieved juries should rightly consist of Aborigines, though if they could not comprehend the legal processes the whole exercise was futile anyway.[46] While all this appeared well and good, Aboriginal people were anything but equal before the law. No European was convicted of murdering an Aborigine in the Port Phillip district until 1848, and even then they were sentenced to just two months imprisonment. By 1848 five Aborigines had been executed for killing Europeans.[47]

When Robinson gave evidence in the trial of the Van Diemen's Land Aborigines he effectively sent Pevay and Timme on their way to the gallows. Robinson quickly made it clear that all the Aborigines on trial had a good grasp of the principles of religion and were aware of the existence of a Supreme Being. They also knew the difference between right and wrong.[48] With that opening salvo there was no longer any possibility that Judge Willis could have used the legal precedent which saved the lives of Jack Congo Murrell and Bonjon. Having sealed the fate of the men, Robinson then made an impassioned plea on behalf of Truganini, telling the court how she had saved his life at the Arthur River on the west coast of Van Diemen's Land. He then went on to say that the women were unable to act on their own volition and entirely subject to the will of the men. Robinson knew full well that his statement was errant nonsense.[49]

Quite clearly, he had not forgotten his close brush with death involving the Tarkiner people in September 1832, and his later treatment of Wyne and his people at Macquarie Harbour revealed a vindictive streak which appears to have been in play at the trial in Melbourne. Although Robinson gave Pevay a reasonable character reference and said that he had been with him since he was little more than a child, Robinson was far more enthusiastic when it came to Timme. He had not forgotten Pevay's role in the affray at the Arthur River.[50] When Robinson and Truganini had made their escape and met up with the other 'Friendly Mission' Aborigines he had noted that Pevay was in possession of the knapsack from which Wyne had removed a blanket immediately before the Tarkiner people attacked. Robinson also knew that Pevay had lied when claiming to have protected him when he ran after Truganini.

Now was the time for revenge. Not so for Timme. Robinson elaborated on the assistance that Timme had rendered the 'Friendly Mission' and how he had made himself useful at Port Phillip. He went on to mention Timme's droving trip to Adelaide with Alfred Langhorne, and how he had been instrumental in saving the party when they were attacked by Aborigines on the Murray River.[51] The damage had nevertheless been done with his opening remarks, and Redmond Barry summed up the defence by telling the jury about the many injustices inflicted on the Aboriginal people in Van Diemen's Land, revealing his clear understanding of the connection between Aboriginal resistance in the island colony and Pevay's campaign against the colonists at Port Phillip.[52] This point was seized on by Judge Willis in his own lengthy address to the jury, but he did so to emphasise 'the extremely hostile nature' of the Van Diemen's Land Aborigines in their conflict with the colonists.[53] Perhaps influenced by Robinson's evidence, Willis was determined in this instance to have the Aborigines found guilty.

In this he was at least partly successful. The jury took just 30 minutes that night to find both Pevay and Timme guilty of murder, with the women acquitted. On account of the previous good character of both men and the 'peculiar circumstances' in which they were placed, the jury had arguably been swayed by Barry's defence to add a mercy plea.[54] Willis dutifully forwarded the plea for clemency to Sydney with the court transcripts, making it clear that it did not have his support. Nor was clemency encouraged by Superintendent La Trobe.[55] The Van Diemen's Land Aborigines appeared before the bench the following day for sentencing, and to Robinson's chagrin the women were released into his care with instructions that they were to be confined to his residence and prevented from roaming at will.[56]

Both men were sentenced to death, but owing to the jury's recommendation for mercy they were initially in high spirits. Despite the overcrowded conditions in Melbourne Gaol they were able to exercise regularly, often playing ball with a bundle of rags. To their horror, however, word finally reached Melbourne that the Executive Council in Sydney had rejected the mercy plea, and the date for their execution had been set down for 20 January 1842.[57] With the sudden realisation that their time on earth was now limited, Timme's demeanour underwent a complete transformation. He ate and slept little and wept often, and even on his last night he refused to eat or accept the tobacco which was offered. Pevay, on the other hand, accepted his fate with nonchalance and on the final night remained in high spirits, eating heartily.[58] This was to be Port Phillip's first public execution and it aroused considerable interest, attracting between four and five thousand spectators — roughly a quarter of the district's entire European population.[59] It also meant that an executioner had to be found, with John Davies selected from the 18 convicts who offered their services. Davies was granted his freedom and £10; some of the others wanted more, including the heads of the Aborigines before burial as they were worth good money in Britain.[60] Davies was more than satisfied with what he received, but his inexperience was to cause problems.

The two Van Diemen's Land Aborigines were taken from the gaol at seven in the morning and placed on Robinson's new cart for the journey to the gallows. Robinson did not attend the execution, electing to wait for the bodies at the burial ground which is now the location of the Victoria Market. Aborigines were interred just outside the consecrated ground. Assistant protector James Dredge attended the execution in Robinson's place. The temporary gallows were erected on a small rise to the east of Swanston Street, and having arrived at their destination Pevay mounted the scaffold with confidence. It was a very different matter with Timme, who commenced sobbing and was unable to move without assistance. He was literally dragged up the steps to have the noose placed around his neck. Had he known what was in store Timme would undoubtedly have been worse, for when the trapdoor opened both men failed to plummet the full length of the rope. They struggled and writhed convulsively as the assembled crowd hurled abuse at the executioner. An onlooker finally had the presence of mind to kick away a piece of timber obstructing the trap and the two men dropped the full descent. Pevay appears to have died almost instantly; Timme's noose had either been wrongly placed or been dislodged in the initial fall and he slowly strangled to death, a sight that was said to have horrified even the most hardened spectators. After the regulation hour the bodies were taken down and conveyed to the burial ground.[61]

There was a strange postscript to this terrible chapter in early Victorian history. Many years later a letter written by assistant protector William Thomas was discovered in which Thomas said that a report he had sent to the government had been returned by an unnamed person. Perhaps it was Robinson. Thomas was particularly disappointed as he claimed that it contained information which would almost certainly have saved the lives of Pevay and Timme. Until such time as the report itself comes to light (if it ever does) we have no way of knowing how it might have altered the final outcome.[62]

Almost six months after the execution — and to Robinson's great relief — Superintendent La Trobe offered to pay the cost of returning the remaining Van Diemen's Land Aborigines to Flinders Island. Four stayed behind. Thomas Thompson, Peter Brune and Johnny Franklin had taken up regular employment and were allowed to remain in the Port Phillip district. Franklin's mother, Kalloongoo (Charlotte), also settled permanently on the mainland. Another four, Meeterlatteenner (Rebecca), Probelattener (alias Lacklay or Isaac), Rolepana (Benny) and Thomas Brune, had died on foreign soil.[63] The rest sailed from Melbourne on 6 July 1842. Woorrady, who had been in poor health since his arrival at Port Phillip, succumbed during the voyage and was buried on Green Island. The seven survivors were delivered into the hands of Wybalenna commandant Henry Jeanneret on 16 July. As Jeanneret soon found, the experience at Port Phillip had strengthened rather than crushed the spirit of the sojourners.[64] Walter Arthur became a particular thorn in the commandant's side until Wybalenna was finally closed down in 1847 and the surviving Aborigines were repatriated to Oyster Cove, just to the south of Hobart.

11

THE TRAGEDY OF OYSTER COVE

While the Aboriginal exiles were only too pleased to leave Wybalenna they were fortunately spared the thought that Oyster Cove could ultimately prove even worse. The first hint came soon after their arrival when one of the men died. It was not surprising. Located roughly 30 kilometres south of Hobart, Oyster Cove was a former penal establishment which had been closed down after the accommodation failed to meet the minimum health requirements for convicted felons. The settlement, consisting of just over 16 hectares of land (with a separate reserve of some 688 hectares located 1.5 kilometres further west along the Little Oyster Cove Rivulet) was situated on low swampy ground with poor drainage. Although the establishment faced the sea, it was hemmed in by heavily-wooded slopes which encouraged mist to hug the ground for much of the year.[1] The buildings had been constructed of wood rather than brick, which meant they were constantly damp. They were also infested with vermin, exacerbated when the dogs accompanying their Aboriginal owners moved in to their new abodes. Nor did these wooden dwellings provide any protection from the bitterly cold southerly winds which regularly blew across the settlement.[2]

Although Joseph Milligan was superintendent he chose to live in Hobart and visit Oyster Cove on a regular basis.[3] Robert Clark was appointed Milligan's assistant as well as continuing as catechist, though there is no evidence that he provided any religious instruction at Oyster Cove, whatever its worth may have been. Clark soon reverted to his usual habit of meddling in everyone's affairs and generally making a nuisance of himself. He also took advantage of his new circumstances by purchasing land near the Aboriginal Establishment which he farmed with implements provided for the Aborigines. Clark was eventually dismissed from office in July 1848, but after pleading that he would be left destitute the government agreed to appoint him as the settlement's storekeeper on an annual salary of £100. Even this failed to curb his troublesome ways, with Clark continuing to cause problems until his death from heart disease in March 1850.[4]

For a brief period there was a resident shoemaker and, later, a teamster at Oyster Cove. The only assigned convict retained after the transfer from Flinders Island was John Russell, a former soldier, who continued as the settlement constable and general rouseabout.[5] Magistrate Thomas Manley visited Oyster Cove on a weekly basis, and in many ways it was Manley who did much of the actual supervision, including overseeing the renovations of the Aboriginal dwellings which had been completed by April 1848. Even then the accommodation was far from adequate.[6]

For his part, Clark regularly reported that the Aborigines were working industriously, all of them tending their gardens and the women actively engaged in sewing and needlework. The available evidence suggests they did nothing of the sort. The adults were largely left to their own devices, coming and going much as they pleased.[7] While they were expected to cook their own meals in large iron pots placed within each dwelling, the Aborigines preferred to light their fires and cook outside owing to the perpetually damp interiors. Government rations had been slightly increased, and these were supplemented by regular harvesting of the abundant shellfish in the d'Entrecasteaux Channel and wallabies, wombats and other small mammals hunted in the vicinity of the Aboriginal Establishment. As at Wybalenna, however, over-exploitation quickly eliminated all native game within easy reach.[8] The Aborigines also developed a fondness for fishing, often commandeering two of the three boats provided for their use.[9] As late as January 1867 Visiting Magistrate Henry Daldy commented that the Aborigines were forced to 'go out fishing' when the government meat ration failed to arrive,[10] though whether the Aborigines were taking scale-fish or molluscs remains in doubt. The third boat at Oyster Cove was used to bring in firewood.

Despite the damp conditions the general health of the Aboriginal residents was initially quite good, and at Christmas 14 Aborigines from Oyster Cove were invited to attend a feast at New Norfolk hosted by Lieutenant Governor William Denison. This may have been intended to placate the fears of the colonists, many of whom still held vivid memories of the violence of the 'Black War'. The following Christmas Denison entertained six Aboriginal men at Government House in Hobart,[11] but beneath the surface all was not well. The major downside of life at Oyster Cove was once again the forced removal of the children, with three boys and four girls sent to the Queen's Orphan School in Hobart.[12] One of the latter was Mathinna, who like so many others was to meet a tragic end. The relationship with surrounding colonists can only be described as ambivalent. On one hand, failure to keep their dogs under control resulted in the settlers' livestock being maimed and destroyed. Two of the dogs, which had been identified as killers, were shot on Milligan's orders, and he warned the Aborigines that any more trouble with their canine pets would lead to extensive culling. The attacks only ceased temporarily, generating considerable anger among neighbouring pastoralists for many years ahead.[13] Apart from the settlers, the environs of Oyster Cove were also home to timber-splitters and sawyers, many of whom obtained access to the Aboriginal women through the supply of alcohol. Addiction soon became one of the major health problems at the Aboriginal Establishment.[14] In the late 1840s a visiting American sailor, Robert Elwes, was unimpressed by what he saw:

> In a bay called Oyster Cove, towards Mount Wellington, are the miserable remains of the Aborigines of Tasmania. They are supported by Government, a commissioner being appointed to look after them, and do almost nothing, seeming to wait in apathy for their own extinction.[15]

In 1848 a number of deaths reduced the resident population to 36. No deaths were recorded in 1849 and only one in 1850, but from that time on death once again began to regularly stalk the survivors of Wybalenna. Ten Aborigines died in 1851,[16] and when George Augustus Robinson paid a brief visit to Oyster Cove in April of that year he counted only 30 residents, which by then included a number of younger people who had returned from the Queen's Orphan School. This was Robinson's one and only visit to Oyster Cove, for the following year he sailed to England and retired in comfortable circumstances. For a number of years he gravitated between Paris and Rome before finally settling at Bath in England, where he died in October 1866.[17] During his visit the Aborigines told Robinson that they wished to return to either Flinders or Cape Barren Island as the present location was too unhealthy. Clearly, they could see the writing on the wall, but nothing was ever done until it was far too late. Before leaving Oyster Cove, Robinson was presented with shell necklaces by Mary Ann Arthur and Fanny;[18] he was given nothing by Truganini, who was conspicuous by her absence when he took his final leave.[19] Robinson was never to see the Van Diemen's Land Aborigines again, and it is not likely that he really cared.

Another three Aborigines died in 1852,[20] most of the deaths resulting from influenza and pulmonary complaints — exacerbated in many instances by alcohol addiction. But there may have been at least one other factor involved. Peter Dowling has advanced the interesting hypothesis that many, if not most, of the Aboriginal people at Oyster Cove probably suffered from mercury poisoning. Mercury was widely used to treat a range of maladies until the 1940s, when its toxicity was finally understood. One particularly common treatment was mercury chloride in a powdered form known as calomel, which was regularly administered to the Aborigines at Oyster Cove just as it was to colonists elsewhere. Although mercury itself may not have been directly responsible for any deaths, it caused general debilitation which almost certainly had a serious impact on the overall health profile of the Aborigines.[21] It is also relevant that mercury poisoning can induce a range of psychotic disorders — depression, manic depression, personality change, panic attacks and hallucinations.[22] Mental illness was certainly evident at Oyster Cove. In 1859 Truganini's girlhood friend, Dray, held court with her dogs, while Caroline constantly cried and sobbed. One of the men, Tippo Saib, was senile,[23] and there were numerous other cases of psychotic disorder which may not have existed in customary Aboriginal society. Notwithstanding that there was much to be depressed about at Oyster Cove, mercury poisoning appears to have contributed to the prevalence of mental illness.

In October 1852 Joseph Milligan informed the colonial secretary that the Aboriginal dwellings were again in a state of disrepair. Although authorisation was readily granted to make the necessary improvements only £5 was allocated for the task. Three years later the cost of repair work was estimated at £300, and what readily becomes apparent from this is the increasing neglect of the Aboriginal people, who were largely out of sight and therefore out of mind. They may have only been too well aware of their obscurity, for by the mid-1850s many were losing touch with reality through their addiction to alcohol. In 1854 Milligan reported that three of the four remaining men were chronic alcoholics while the majority of the women were also drinking to excess. Given this state of affairs the community divided itself into two groups: the heavy imbibers who cared for little and those who at least attempted to retain some semblance of order and regularity in their lives. But there was little for them to do. The only work of any consequence being carried out at Oyster Cove was the collection of firewood.[24]

In October 1854 Fanny Cochrane, who had been living at Oyster Cove with her half-sister Mary Ann Arthur, made her escape by marrying the English ex-convict sawyer William Smith at Hobart. Fanny had been born at Wybalenna to Tanganuturra, otherwise known as Sarah or Tibb, though her paternity has been the subject of considerable debate.[25] As she is the only success story to emerge from the tragedy of Oyster Cove it will be necessary to return to Fanny Cochrane Smith later.

Further government economising occurred in 1855, when visiting magistrate James Kirwan reported on the extremely poor state of the buildings where only five males and 11 females remained. By then they were almost completely unsupervised and largely roamed at will, often to the nearest hostelries.[26] On 28 April the Aborigines had an unexpected visit from Governor Sir Henry Fox Young, the vice-regal entourage making a careful inspection of 'the whole of the establishment' before departing back to Hobart the same day.[27] Despite this first-hand observation of the deplorable conditions, funding cuts continued. So did the social problems. In May 1855 three of the women and one of the men visited an inn at Kingston, where they began fighting and exposing themselves after becoming inebriated. Police were called and all four were taken into protective custody until regaining their faculties. This incident prompted Kirwan to remind the colonial secretary of the fate which overtook Mathinna.[28]

The daughter of Toweterer (alias Romeo), leader of the Lowreene band of Low Rocky Point in south-west Van Diemen's Land, and his wife Wangeneep (or Evelyne as she was renamed by Robinson), Mathinna had been born at Wybalenna in 1835. When Sir John and Lady Jane Franklin visited Flinders Island three years later they were captivated by the young girl's beauty, intellect and spirit. In 1840 they had Mathinna brought to Hobart, where she lived with the Franklins in Government House and was educated with their daughter.[29] Mathinna was often seen riding in the vice-regal carriage dressed in a scarlet jacket and adorned with a shell necklace, invariably accompanied by a pet possum.[30] This privileged upbringing came to a sudden end in December 1843, when Lieutenant Governor Franklin was recalled to England and Mathinna was abandoned to the bleak rigours of the Queen's Orphan School. She remained only a year at the institution before being returned to Wybalenna, from where she was repatriated with the surviving Aborigines to Oyster Cove in 1847. Mathinna was never able to adjust to her altered circumstances and like so many others turned to alcohol in a bid to ease her pain and suffering.[31] One night in September 1852 she visited an inn at North West Bay and drank to excess. On her return home the inebriated young woman fell on her face in a puddle and drowned, her lifeless body discovered the following morning.[32]

Kirwan's scathing report on the existing conditions at Oyster Cove resulted in Milligan's dismissal and the appointment of John Strange Dandridge as Superintendent of Aborigines in July 1855.[33] This turned out to be an inspired choice, as Dandridge and his wife Matilda treated the Aborigines with great care and affection. Dandridge had only arrived in Van Diemen's Land in 1845, when he commenced his shaky rise through the ranks of the public service. Dismissed on one occasion, his continuing employment was due to the influence of his wife, daughter of the renowned artist John Skinner Prout.[34] The tragedy was that Dandridge's appointment as superintendent came too late to prevent the inexorable slide of the Aboriginal people into oblivion.

There was at least one ray of hope. In August 1855 Walter and Mary Ann Arthur left the Aboriginal Establishment to reside on an adjacent 15 acres (six hectares) of land which had been granted to them by the government.[35] Surprisingly, the idea of granting land to the Indigenous people who had been forcibly dispossessed of that very same land was nothing new in Van Diemen's Land. In 1829 Lieutenant Governor George Arthur granted 20 acres (eight hectares) of land to Robert, possibly to serve as a model for other Van Diemen's Land Aborigines prepared to lay down their arms. Robert also received 'a boat, cart, bullock and farm implements', though what eventually became of his grant remains unknown. While 'Black Tom' (Kickerterpoller) was to be similarly assisted, there is no evidence that he received any land,[36] and it was not until the following year that John Batman resurrected this novel idea when he suggested to Arthur that two Aboriginal men, Pigeon and John Crook, who had been brought from New South Wales to track down local Aborigines, should be rewarded with grants of land and government assistance to establish themselves as small farmers. As was usual with Batman, an ulterior motive was almost certainly at play. Both Pigeon and John Crook received their grants conveniently close to Batman's own holding near Ben Lomond in north-east Van Diemen's Land.[37]

There can be little doubt that Batman's intention was to eventually incorporate the blocks into his own landholding and reduce the two men to the status of agricultural labourers. It was perhaps with that same idea in mind that he proposed a similar reward should be extended to William Ponsonby (otherwise known as 'Black Bill'), a Van Diemen's Land Aborigine who had been raised since childhood by settler James Cox of Clarendon, near Evandale, just south of Launceston. Ponsonby was likewise assisting Batman to track down the remaining Indigenous people of the north-east, and in 1830 he married a Van Diemen's Land Aboriginal woman named Catherine Kennedy, who had been raised by another colonist family near Cross Marsh. Batman declared Ponsonby to be 'a good farming man' and his wife 'a good house servant', with Lieutenant Governor Arthur readily agreeing to grant 100 acres (forty hectares) of land to the couple. It was never taken up. By May 1830 Batman reported that William Ponsonby was 'very ill', so ill in fact that he died at Hobart the following December.[38] There was to be no repeat of this novel means of incorporating the Van Diemen's Land Aborigines into colonial society until 1855, when Walter and Mary Ann Arthur received their land grant near Oyster Cove. It came, of course, with the expectation that it would be cultivated in the European manner, but right from the start the Arthurs encountered difficulties which were entirely outside their control.

As perhaps could only be expected, they faced opposition from neighbouring white settlers, one of whom objected to the couple using the track which ran across his land to their grant. They had no alternative, and no sooner was this issue resolved than a colonist named Fitzgerald laid claim to their holding. With the help of Dandridge that problem was also overcome,[39] but although Walter and Mary Ann Arthur were expected to work their land like the British colonists there were clear limitations to what they could have. This became patently obvious when Dandridge assisted Walter Arthur to apply for the services of a ticket-of-leave convict to help with the cultivation. The application was rejected for unspecified reasons;[40] it was more than likely that the government objected to an Aboriginal man having a white servant, an inversion of what was considered proper in colonial society.

The small size of the Arthurs' grant meant that it was always going to be a struggle to become self-reliant, duly recognised by the government when it decided to pay Walter Arthur a small salary to assist with keeping the Aboriginal Establishment in order and to take charge of the three boats. Unfortunately, and perhaps not entirely unexpectedly considering his precarious position, Arthur turned to alcohol. His drinking reached a point where it began to affect his personality, and there were often violent scenes when he was intoxicated. Even Dandridge was forced to complain about his (and Mary Ann's) erratic behaviour.[41]

In 1858 Walter Arthur sought to exchange his grant for more productive land in the Huon Valley, which would have simultaneously provided an opportunity to escape from the temptations of the bottle. This was his own decision, but when Assistant Colonial Secretary Travers Solly, a keen temperance advocate, demanded that Arthur sign a pledge to abstain from alcohol, he rightly saw it as a denial of his basic rights. Arthur refused, and was forced to remain on the original grant. In September 1859 his salary was terminated when he failed to attend to his work at the Aboriginal Establishment, and following a domestic altercation with Mary Ann he made a final attempt to turn his life around by shipping aboard the 'dry' whaling barque *Sussex* for an 18-month voyage.[42] Walter Arthur returned to Oyster Cove in January 1861, purportedly 'looking much worse than before he left'.[43] On 11 May he accompanied the publican who supplied medicinal spirits, beer and eggs to the Aboriginal Establishment in an open rowing boat to Hobart. After drinking for a few hours in a waterfront tavern the two men set out on the return journey to Oyster Cove. Walter Arthur fell overboard, and despite his reputation as a strong swimmer he disappeared in the dark waters. Whether it was through the combined effects of alcohol and the chilly night, or whether he was already unconscious or possibly even dead when he fell into the water remains a mystery. Walter Arthur was around 41 years of age when he died, and his body was never recovered.[44]

Whaling became an employment path for at least six Van Diemen's Land Aboriginal men, including the 'part Tasmanian Aboriginal' George Morrison, who was in charge of the whaling station at Wairoa, on the east coast of New Zealand's North Island from 1844. Another 'Tasmanian half-caste' known only as 'Darkie Coon', was a member of a whaling crew at Wairoa and Mahia in New Zealand.[45] Others, such as William Lanne, Jack Allen and Adam, were forced into a seafaring life. As part of the cost-cutting measures affecting the Aboriginal Establishment in 1855 all three young men were apprenticed to whaling vessels.[46]

Notwithstanding the government's determination to reduce expenditure at Oyster Cove in 1855, the accommodation was in such a poor state that instructions were given in November to employ local men to carry out the necessary repairs. Dandridge and Kirwan were unable to find competent tradesmen, however, and it was not until April 1856 that the government finally accepted a tender for £275 from a Mr Rowlands to undertake the work.[47] But there was an alternative solution. From June 1854 right through to the end of 1855 former commandant of Wybalenna, Malcolm Laing Smith, offered to care for the remaining Aborigines at an annual cost of £30 each if the government relocated them back to Flinders Island. Laing Smith had continued his farming ventures on the island after his dismissal, and was fully cognisant of the deteriorating situation at Oyster Cove.

He insisted that the island climate was far more congenial than the perpetual dampness in which the Aborigines were forced to live, and initially the colonial secretary was receptive to his offer. The government nevertheless equivocated until the end of 1855, when John Dandridge was asked for his opinion. After advising against returning the Aboriginal people to Flinders Island the idea was quietly dropped and Laing Smith made no further offer. From the price he was asking there is no hint that Laing Smith intended to profit from the arrangement, as he was well aware that the majority of the Aborigines were rapidly ageing and of little use as cheap labour.[48] The government's final decision effectively condemned them to their fate.

The Aborigines may have fared better, as expenditure on Oyster Cove continued to be reduced. The meat ration, for example, was put out for tender every year, with the lowest price always accepted. The quality was of little concern. In June 1857 magistrate James Kirwan added his voice to Dandridge's protestations about the quality of the meat provided for the Aborigines. Although the contractor was advised that his product was below acceptable standards nothing was done to force him to comply with government regulations until the end of 1858, when the colonial treasurer happened to see the 'inferior' meat being loaded onto a vessel bound for Oyster Cove and personally took the matter up with the colonial secretary. It turned out that most of the meat ration was mutton from sheep which had died from natural causes — including old age.[49]

Nor was it just the meat; the quality of all the rations as well as the clothing supplied by the government were generally of exceptionally poor standard. Yet, despite their obvious physical wants, the lack of religious instruction became a major issue in 1859 when it was found that the Reverend Freeman had not visited Oyster Cove since January 1858. Archdeacon Davis was reportedly outraged at the absence of spiritual guidance, and immediately began negotiating with the colonial secretary to rectify the situation. It did not seem to matter that the Aborigines were living in sub-standard housing with little to eat and wear: they simply had to be taught the word of God. To that end, Francis Trappes was appointed catechist, largely on the basis that he lived locally. Trappes continued to provide religious instruction until 1862, his position becoming redundant when there were too few Aborigines left to instruct.[50]

In 1855 there was only one death at Oyster Cove, though owing to their already severely depleted numbers every one of them had a major impact on the population. Another died the following year, and in 1859 the Aboriginal Establishment was described by James Bonwick as 'a miserable collection of huts and outbuildings'. Rainwater poured through the roofs, many of the windows were broken and the interiors of the dwellings were virtually bereft of furnishings, much of it sold to pay for alcohol. The buildings were also swarming with fleas on account of the dogs.[51] Neither the complaints of Dandridge or rare visitors made any impression on the government, which insisted that all the blame lay squarely with the Aboriginal people themselves.[52]

Given their advancing ages it was not surprising that the mortality rate slowly began to accelerate. Two men, Tippo Saib and Augustus, as well as two women, Flora and Caroline, succumbed to illness and old age in 1860. The following year there were another two deaths at Oyster Cove, including that of Dray, who had accompanied Robinson on his very first 'Friendly Mission' to her south-west homeland in early 1830.[53] And Walter Arthur, of course, disappeared after the boating mishap in May 1861. Despite the mortality rate and the fact that the Aborigines were almost constantly in a state of poor health, no regular medical supervision was provided. Between 1858 and 1869, when the Aboriginal Establishment was officially finally closed down, Dr William Smith made periodic visits to Oyster Cove from his home at Kingston. Smith also attended Aboriginal patients in times of emergency, and he appears to have done the best he could.[54] But it was never enough. With only eight Aborigines left at Oyster Cove in 1861 Dandridge proposed relocating them to Hobart if suitable accommodation could be found. If all else failed he was willing to lodge the Aborigines in his own home, Dandridge estimating the cost at £560 per annum. As he was quick to point out, this arrangement would save the government £190 per year. Despite official enquiries being made, nothing eventuated. A number of private citizens made their own offers to care for the remaining Aborigines, including Henry Pybus of Kettering (Little Oyster Cove), who quoted the government £500 per annum. This seemingly generous offer did nothing more than ensure that the dithering continued along with the deaths.[55] In October 1863 only John Allen and five 'full-blood' Aboriginal women remained at Oyster Cove.[56]

Their numbers fell again in 1864 when both John Allen and Emma died. They were followed to the grave three years later by Patty, Wapperty and Bessy Clark. Patty and Wapperty were the last of the women who had been removed from the sealers in Bass Strait.[57] In 1865 Walter Arthur's widow, Mary Ann, remarried — this time to colonist Adam Booker — with the couple residing at the Aboriginal Establishment even though Mary Ann still held the occupation licence for the land granted to Walter. Mary Ann, a 'part-Aboriginal' woman, was destined to survive until August 1871, when she succumbed to an 'apoplectic fit'. Her occupation licence was then revoked and the government ordered Booker to quit the Aboriginal Establishment.[58] Of the 'full-blooded' Van Diemen's Land Aborigines, only Truganini and William Lanne remained alive in 1868, and when Lanne's luck ran out the following year his corpse was mutilated by ghouls working in the name of 'science'.

As noted previously, the Lanne or Lanna family captured by sealers near the Arthur River in north-west Van Diemen's Land in December

1842 are something of a mystery. They appear not to have been from the north-west, their origins possibly lying in the settled districts of the south-east. Lanne's mother's name was Labrunga, which bears no affinities to north-west nomenclature.[59] Question marks have also been raised over William Lanne's paternity: his father may have been an Aboriginal man from New South Wales.[60] Be that as it may, William Lanne was around seven years of age when his family arrived at Flinders Island, and his Aboriginal name was not recorded. Only William and two brothers, Barney and Albert, survived Wybalenna, and after repatriation to Oyster Cove in 1847 William spent a year in the Queen's Orphan School. Both his siblings were dead by 1851,[61] and although William was forced into a seafaring career in 1855 he found it much to his liking, possibly owing to the cosmopolitanism of shipmates who placed a greater emphasis on skill than skin colour.[62] The master mariners under whom he sailed also thought very highly of Lanne, who was generally known to one and all as 'King Billy'.[63] His base remained at Hobart, and whenever Lanne was in port he invariably made his way back to Oyster Cove, accepting full responsibility for the welfare of the remaining Aboriginal women. In 1864 he complained to Colonial Secretary Charles Meredith that the women were not receiving sufficient rations, his grievance resulting in a government investigation. It was subsequently found that when the supply vessel for the district failed to arrive from Hobart local settlers either purchased or 'borrowed' supplies from the Aboriginal Establishment to tide them over, frequently leaving the women on the verge of starvation. It is not clear whether any action was taken,[64] and it certainly did not result in the rations being increased or their quality improved. Like Lanne, Dandridge also tried to do the best he could, but he lacked any control over the Commissariat Store whose bungling had created major supply problems at Wybalenna.

In 1864 Lanne and the remaining four women were taken to Government House in Hobart, later having their photographs taken for 'posterity'. The high point of Lanne's life came four years later. In January 1868 he was dressed in a blue serge suit and together with Truganini the pair was presented to the visiting Duke of Edinburgh. This meeting of 'royals' (and Lanne certainly regarded himself as a local royal) was patently false. Neither 'King Billy' nor 'Queen Truganini', as she was now regularly dubbed, were Aboriginal leaders in the true sense, their elevation solely due to the decimation of their people. Two months after fraternising with the Duke, Lanne shipped out on the whaler *Runnymede*, returning to Hobart in February 1869 and taking up his usual lodgings at the Dog and Partridge Hotel, an old waterfront hostelry which still stands, albeit, no longer licensed and now serving a very different purpose. Lanne was seriously ill and taking regular medication purchased from Dr Thomas Smart's nearby dispensary, though his exact ailments are unclear. He appears to have contracted either cholera (possibly choleraic diarrhoea) or typhoid, the condition further aggravated by alcoholism. The publican became so concerned with Lanne's failing health that he sought the services of a physician, who attended Lanne and ordered him to hospital. It was while he was in the act of dressing that Lanne suddenly collapsed and died.[65]

The passing of the last 'full-blood' Aboriginal male was an event of no little consequence in Van Diemen's Land, and Lanne's death also exposed a deep schism existing within colonial society. On one hand he was well-known and highly-regarded by many colonists, particularly his seafaring companions and the master mariners under whom he served. On the other side of the divide stood prominent members of the medical fraternity, who viewed Lanne's death as a wonderful opportunity to advance their names by making a contribution to 'science'. No sooner had Lanne taken his last breath than the chairman of the Royal Society contacted Colonial Secretary Richard Dry requesting his remains.[66] Dry's brother had been a casualty of the Black War, but those days were now long gone. Instead of complying with the Royal Society's wish, the colonial secretary instructed Dr George Stokell, resident surgeon at Hobart General Hospital, to secure the body and ensure that it was not tampered with. Although Stokell obediently lodged the corpse in the hospital's locked morgue he had his own plans for Lanne's body. The good doctor was, after all, a prominent member of the Royal Society.[67]

But the Royal Society had strong competition. The hospital's visiting surgeon, Dr William Crowther, was determined to obtain Lanne's remains for the Royal College of Surgeons in London, a gift that would do much to raise his standing in the British scientific community. And it was Crowther who struck first. After obtaining a key to the morgue he lured Stockell and the gatekeeper away, allowing sufficient time for himself and one of his sons, Bingham Crowther, a medical student at the hospital, to remove Lanne's skull, replacing it with one from a non-Indigenous corpse lying in the adjoining dissection room. The substitute skull was inserted under Lanne's scalp and the skin drawn over it. Stokell returned to the hospital later that night to find the results of Crowther's grisly handiwork. Not to be outdone, however, Stokell received the Royal Society's blessing to remove Lanne's hands and feet, which were then lodged in the society's museum for safekeeping.[68]

Rumours of the mutilation soon spread and angry voices were raised, but they came too late. The following morning Lanne's coffin, draped in a union jack purchased by his former crewmates and further adorned with Aboriginal artefacts and a possum skin rug, was taken to St David's Church for the religious service. It was then conveyed to what should have been Lanne's final resting place.[69] But the battle for his remains was still far from over. Both Stokell and Crowther laid plans to disinter the body that same evening, a race narrowly won by the Royal Society, who removed the body back to the morgue for further dismemberment. A frustrated Crowther returned to the hospital the following morning and after being refused entry to the morgue battered down the door with either an axe or a hammer. All he found was 'masses of fat and blood'.[70] According to Lyndall Ryan, who does not provide any solid evidence, Stokell and other members of the Royal Society had removed Lanne's ears, nose, some of the skin and a section of an arm, with the remaining body parts temporarily buried in the garden of the hospital's house steward. It was later dug up, packed into a cask, and interred in the Campbell Street cemetery. Stokell is said to have used some of Lanne's skin to make a tobacco pouch. His hands and feet were later located in the Royal Society's rooms in Argyle Street, though it was to be a century before Lanne's skull was eventually tracked down in the School of Anatomy at the University of Edinburgh.[71] William Lanne had roamed widely in life; in death his travels were even more extensive.

This ghoulish affair and the anger it generated within the community resulted in an official inquiry. Crowther lost his position as the hospital's visiting surgeon and his son found that he was no longer enrolled as a medical student.[72] Stokell and the Royal Society were completely exonerated of any wrongdoing,[73] a curious result indeed and one which clearly reflected the society's powerful political influence. Not to be outdone, Crowther fought back through the press, indignantly insisting that it was Stokell and the Royal Society who were responsible for removing William Lanne's skull.[74] He had considerable support, which certainly rose to the fore during the Legislative Council elections held in March 1869 when Crowther successfully — and easily — won the seat of Hobart, holding it until the year of his death in 1885.[75] One of his opponents, Alfred Crisp, was backed by the Royal Society. The following year Crowther was awarded the gold medal of the Royal College of Surgeons for his contributions to their Hunterian Museum, one of only four recipients to attain that prestigious honour.[76] He later served as Premier of Tasmania from December 1878 to October 1879, the first medical practitioner to do so.[77] Much of his scientific reputation had, of course, been built on the bodies of the Van Diemen's Land Aborigines, and his eldest son, Edward, was not yet finished with harvesting their remains.

As Lynette Russell had rightly reminded us, however, the mutilation of William Lanne's body has overshadowed his remarkable achievements in life. He was not simply a helpless and passive victim of circumstance.[78] A young Aboriginal man whose origins are obscure, William Lanne survived Wybalenna and the Queen's Orphan School to become a highly-skilled and well-liked member of colonial society. Against almost incredible odds he forged an individual identity and became his own master, standing proudly as the protector of the remaining Van Diemen's Land Aboriginal women.

Lanne's death nevertheless left Truganini reputedly standing as the last of the 'full-blooded' Van Diemen's Land Aborigine, substantially raising her value as a commodity to the scientific community. She was well aware of her tenuous position and that her demise might result in similar mutilation.[79] Indeed, Truganini's entire life had been one of epic tragedy. Born around 1812 at Recherche Bay on the southern shores of the d'Entrecasteaux Channel, violence engulfed her from an early age. Truganini's mother was stabbed to death in a surprise attack by raiding seamen, and her two sisters had been forcibly abducted by the sealer John Baker and taken to Kangaroo Island.[80] Her father, Mangana, overcame his grief to marry a second time — only to suffer further at the hands of the colonists. In August 1829 he left Truganini on Bruny Island while he took his new wife and Truganini's brother Robert across the d'Entrecasteaux Channel. The timing could not have been worse. The brig *Cyprus* conveying convicts to Macquarie

Harbour had been forced to seek shelter at Recherche Bay, and it was there that 18 of the prisoners rose up and seized the vessel. The officers, crew and those convicts unwilling to join the mutiny were put ashore at an isolated location where the mutineers captured Truganini's stepmother, who was taken aboard the *Cyprus* which sailed out into the Pacific and eventually reached China. She was never heard from again. Robert appears to have been killed at Recherche Bay.[81]

In her late teens the diminutive Truganini, who stood only 1.3 metres high (4 feet 3 inches), blossomed into an attractive young woman possessed of keen intellect and a mischievous nature. She was also promiscuous, regularly visiting the convicts working at Birch's Bay across the channel from North Bruny Island. On one occasion she was followed to Birch's Bay by two young Aboriginal men, one of whom was her betrothed, Paraweena, who demanded her return. After an argument two of the convict sawyers, William Lowe and Patrick Newell, agreed to row the trio back to North Bruny Island. Midway across the channel they turned on the Aboriginal men and threw them overboard, and when Paraweena and his companion attempted to climb back into the boat one of the convicts seized a hatchet and severed their hands near the wrist. As the helpless Aboriginal men screamed and struggled in the water Lowe and Newell returned with Truganini to their camp.[82]

Yet, despite the horrors she had witnessed, Truganini continued to seek out the company of non-Indigenous men, often accompanied by her friends Dray and Pagerly. Whether it was to share in the spoils of the colonists, or simply a personal preference, we can no longer know.[83] Nor is it clear why she willingly joined George Augustus Robinson's 'Friendly Mission'. Vivienne Rae-Ellis has suggested that Truganini may have seen Robinson's scheme as the only means of saving the Aboriginal people from complete extermination,[84] but such a view overlooks the depth of enmity which existed between the Aboriginal groups of Van Diemen's Land. As pointed out earlier, their hostility towards one another was so strong that internecine conflict continued unabated even at the height of the Black War. It continues in muted form to the present day. Truganini is more likely to have been motivated by a spirit of adventure or self-preservation, perhaps a combination of both. At Wybalenna she was allegedly accused of having betrayed the Aboriginal people,[85] quite understandable given the rapidly mounting death toll. Traitor or not, it was Truganini's fate to watch the Aborigines continue to die one by one until she alone remained, and by the early 1870s Truganini was in failing health.

In July 1873 John Dandridge advised the colonial secretary that he had found a suitable home for Truganini in Macquarie Street, Hobart, where she could be comfortably lodged with him and his wife. The government finally — and somewhat belatedly — accepted medical advice that Oyster Cove was an unhealthy location and authorised Dandridge to make the necessary arrangements. He received £60 per annum to care for Truganini, and when Dandridge died in March 1874 his wife Matilda successfully petitioned the government for additional financial assistance, with the annual payment increased to £80.[86]

In September 1875 Truganini fell seriously ill from bronchitis and asthma, and the government agreed to employ a nurse to attend her needs.[87] This was the beginning of the end, and on 8 May 1876 a 'Rowra', or evil spirit, finally came calling for Truganini.[88] Terrified by what had happened to William Lanne, Truganini had begged the physician attending her in the final hours not to 'let them cut me', and expressed a wish to be buried 'behind the mountains'.[89] Instead, her body was interred in the grounds of the Cascades Gaol, close to the front door of the chapel and secure from grave-robbers behind the institution's formidable walls. The Royal Society was given a cast of Truganini's head,[90] but it was not enough, and members were prepared to bide their time.

Patience was finally rewarded in December 1878, when the society received government authorisation to exhume Truganini's remains. Under the terms of the agreement they were to be held in a secure location (which eventually devolved on the Tasmanian Museum) where access would only be granted to qualified scientific personnel. The agreement was a sham. In 1888 Truganini's bones were exhibited in a box at Melbourne's Centenary Exhibition, and the terms of custodianship were completely waived in 1904 when Truganini's skeleton was rearticulated and placed on public display in the Tasmanian Museum. It remained on display until 1947, when complaints from the general public finally forced museum authorities to place it in storage.[91] There the bones languished until an Aboriginal activist from mainland Australia, Harry Penrith (otherwise known as Burnum Burnum) led the campaign from 1970 to have Truganini's remains returned to the Tasmanian Aboriginal community for decent burial.[92] The culmination of these efforts resulted in the Tasmanian government passing legislation in January 1976 to have them returned to government control,[93] and after cremation the following April Truganini's ashes were passed to the Tasmanian Aboriginal community, who scattered them on the waters of d'Entrecasteaux Channel.[94] It had taken Truganini a century to return home.

There was to be no rest for those who had died at Oyster Cove. Adjoining land was owned by the Crowther family and in 1900 the site of the Aboriginal Establishment was acquired by Edward Crowther, William Crowther's eldest son.[95] Seven years later Edward Crowther and his own son began to systematically disinter Aboriginal skeletal remains from the unmarked graves.[96] Yet it was from this dismal setting that one success story emerged. After leaving the Aboriginal Establishment in October 1854 to marry the ex-convict sawyer

William Smith, Fanny Cochrane had prospered. Upon marriage she had received an annuity of £24 on account of her Aboriginality, and the couple largely focused their efforts on timber-splitting and fencing, though at one stage they also operated a boarding house. Eleven children were born from the union, and in 1889 the government increased Fanny's annuity to £50 and simultaneously granted her 300 acres (121 hectares) of land. None of this caused her to lose touch with her roots. Despite enjoying the trappings of colonial society, Fanny Cochrane Smith maintained a range of customary Aboriginal activities, knowledge of which was passed to her children.[97]

While she was always proud of her Aboriginal identity, others have questioned her paternity.[98] The father of Fanny's half-sister, Mary Ann, was definitely non-Indigenous, and weighing up all the available evidence Brian Plomley reasoned that Fanny was probably fathered by the sealer, John Smith.[99] Others have begged to disagree, citing Nicermenic, an Aboriginal man from Circular Head in the north-west, as the probable father.[100] There is a problem with this line of reasoning. Nicermenic was one of the first four Aborigines captured by George Augustus Robinson in 1830, all of whom were sent to Launceston. On the orders of Lieutenant Governor Arthur three were returned to the north-west, while Nicermenic was sent to Hobart for unspecified reasons. He was not among the early deportees at Wybalenna, and nor is there any evidence that he was attached to Robinson's 'Friendly Mission' as a guide. Nicermenic appears to have been released from captivity and whether assisted or not returned to the north-west. Robinson kept meticulous records of the names and dates of Aborigines arriving at Wybalenna, and Nicermenic is again absent. He may not have been recaptured until late 1834, by either George Robinson Jnr or an unofficial party, neither of whom recorded details. As Fanny Cochrane Smith was born at Wybalenna in December 1834 it is unlikely that Nicermenic could have been her father. The basis of this argument appears to have been the later 'marriage' of Nicermenic (renamed Eugene by Robinson) to Fanny Cochrane Smith's mother, Tanganuturra, from Cape Portland in north-east Van Diemen's Land.[101] Despite the controversy, the Tasmanian government accepted her claim of full Aboriginal descent. Fanny Cochrane Smith was also a pioneer recording artist. Between 1899 and 1903 she made Australia's very first sound recordings for Horace Watson of Sandy Bay, consisting of songs in customary Aboriginal language.[102] She was also well-versed in some of the dances of her people, and by the time of her death in February 1905 at Port Cygnet, south of Hobart, Fanny Cochrane Smith had become a highly respected member of Tasmania's wider community.[103] Elsewhere, on the Furneaux Islands of Bass Strait, were many other descendants of Tasmania's Indigenous people, their treatment by the Tasmanian government often at great variance from that extended to Fanny Cochrane Smith, a woman the islanders themselves regarded as being no more than 'a half caste like themselves'.[104]

12

THE BASS STRAIT ISLANDER COMMUNITY 1850–1910

When Wybalenna was closed down in October 1847 and the surviving Aborigines repatriated to Oyster Cove, they left behind the nucleus of what became a significant section of the modern Tasmanian Aboriginal community. In 1850 there were approximately 50 people, comprising 13 families, residing on eight of the Bass Strait Islands. Not all the women were Van Diemen's Land Aborigines: on the contrary, there were a number of Aboriginal women from mainland Australia, one from India, another from Tahiti and a New Zealand Maori as well as a woman of African origins.[1] When Gun Carriage Island was abandoned as a result of the Aboriginal Establishment being relocated to Flinders Island it was quickly reclaimed by the sealers, with Gun Carriage serving as the hub for the islander community over the next two decades. Around 1850 it was home to at least six sealers. John Smith claimed to be the first sealer to reside permanently on Gun Carriage Island, living at various times with two Van Diemen's Land Aboriginal women, notably

Pleenperrenner (otherwise known as Sarah or 'Mother Brown') by whom he sired a number of children.[2] Thomas Beedon (or Beeton) was also there with his Van Diemen's Land Aboriginal wife Woreterneemmerunnertatteyenne, usually abbreviated to Emerenna or Bet Smith, who had been abducted as a child from Cape Portland in north-eastern Van Diemen's Land by John Harrington. After Harrington's death she was claimed by Thomas Tucker, who then sold her to Beedon. The couple had two children who survived infancy, and Thomas Beedon remained on Gun Carriage Island until his death in January 1867.[3] Edward Mansell, who had previously lived on Preservation Island, was definitely a resident of Gun Carriage Island in the early 1850s, where he married his long-time consort, Julia Thomas (or 'Black Judy'), an Aboriginal woman from Van Diemen's Land.[4]

Thomas Tucker, a notorious killer of Aborigines, also lived on the island with his Indian wife Maria Bengally.[5] Another resident sealer was David Kelly, whose Van Diemen's Land Aboriginal wife Portripellaner (Maria) had been removed to Wybalenna by William Darling in late October 1832 before Kelly settled on Gun Carriage in November 1848. Then there was John Riddle, a former whaler who had previously lived with Maria Bengally.[6] At the western end of Franklin Sound lies Woody Island, which was the home of James Everett and Wottecowwidyer (or Wat), who had been given to Everitt by fellow sealer James Thompson after Everett murdered his first Aboriginal partner, Worethmaleyerpodeyer (allegedly for failing to clean mutton-birds to his satisfaction). After Wat died in the early 1850s, Everett married the New Zealand Maori, Elizabeth (Betsy) Mattai, at George Town in May 1856.[7] Also on Woody Island was Richard Maynard and his wife Elizabeth, an Aboriginal woman from the Australian mainland, whom Maynard married after the death of his Van Diemen's Land Aboriginal wife, Pollerwottelterrunner

(Margaret) sometime between 1840 and 1843. Maynard had two children by Margaret and four by Elizabeth.[8]

Maynard had previously lived on Clarke Island, to the south of Cape Barren Island, which by 1850 was home to Andrew Armstrong and his mainland Aboriginal wife, Jane Foster, and their three children. A fourth child was born in 1854.[9] Another mainland Aboriginal woman, Doogbyerumboroke (better known as Margery), the widow of sealing patriarch James Munro (died 1845), continued to dwell on Preservation Island for some time with her children, Robert and Polly. In 1862, however, the family were resident on Chappell Island, before relocating to Little Dog Island the following year.[10] Many other sealing families were equally transient. After the death of John Thomas on Clarke Island four of his children, the mother of whom was either Teekoolterme or Nimmeranna (both Aboriginal women from Van Diemen's Land), relocated to Tin Kettle Island. Two other sealers, Robert Rew and his Aboriginal wife, Frances Anderson, and William Proctor and his Aboriginal wife, Mary Ann Brown, may have also been living in the Furneaux Islands around this time.[11] At the western end of Bass Strait, David Howie lived with his New South Wales Aboriginal partner Mary Bogue on King Island. The couple produced one son, David Howie Bogue, but tragedy struck in 1851 when both Mary and David Jnr were drowned. Two years later Howie married Jane Wilson, a non-Aboriginal woman.[12]

In 1851 the Irishman, Samuel Bligh, married into the community, with his surname often appearing as a middle name among the modern islander people. Bligh did not stay long, abandoning his wife and children to search for gold in Victoria. He never returned. In the same decade three other European men married into the community, all of whom remained in the islands. William Brown initially married Sarah Maynard and, later, Marryann Smith and Frances Maynard. John Summers married Lydia Maynard, while George

Burgess married Julia Mansell. From that time onwards the islanders tended to marry amongst themselves.[13] Apart from largely futile attempts by the Wybalenna commandants to keep the sealers away from Flinders Island, the islander community was virtually ignored by government authorities until February 1848, when Colonial Secretary James Bicheno instructed Surveyor General Robert Power to survey the Furneaux Islands with the intention of regulating the inhabitants by extracting rents based on the estimated value of their landholdings.

Power was impressed by the islanders, describing them as peaceful and friendly people who lived in harmony with each other. The violence of earlier years had apparently mellowed with age, while the nautical skills of the men had been refined to the peak of perfection. Power commented on the superb quality of the islanders' longboats and their skill as small boatmen,[14] a reputation that would endure until the end of the nineteenth century. Given the maritime background of the sealers, and that boats were the only means of transport and communication around the islands which lie in one of the most dangerous stretches of water in the world, it is not surprising their skills were passed down through the generations.[15]

Power also noted that the economy of the Furneaux Islands was a unique blend of customary Aboriginal practices and European agricultural techniques. It revolved heavily around the exploitation of seasonal resources such as mutton-birds, wallabies and seals, with various families congregating together for often lengthy periods of time. But they also grew wheat and potatoes and raised pigs and goats. The latter were a particularly important source of meat, milk and butter. By the mid-1850s the goat herd on Gun Carriage Island alone numbered around 600, with another 200 foraging on Woody Island.[16] The islanders later ran a few sheep and cattle as well, but agriculture was always something of a struggle on the Furneaux Islands owing to the prevailing, and destructive, westerly winds.[17] Accepting their presence and the absence of a solid cash economy, Power issued the sealers on Clarke, Woody, Gun Carriage, Cape Barren and Tin Kettle Islands with tickets of occupation at a nominal rent of one shilling per annum. Thomas Beedon's application for the lease of Badger Island, on the other hand, was turned down because it was the only source of firewood for the lighthouse keepers stationed on nearby Goose Island.[18]

Looking ahead, Power advised the government that it should retain the right to resume any land that might be required for as yet unforeseen purposes, with the occupant to be given six months notice to quit.[19] All told, this was a reasonable compromise between the islanders who were already well-established and clearly wished to remain on the islands, and the government which would otherwise have been left with unimproved land or been forced to extract higher licence fees from occupants who had no means of paying. Flinders Island was the exception, with the former Wybalenna superintendent, Malcolm Laing Smith, acquiring a 10-year lease for £30 per year.[20]

That the islanders were bent on permanent occupation and a settled way of life was made abundantly clear in 1852, when they petitioned Lieutenant Governor William Denison to appoint a 'missionary-catechist' to educate their children. The islanders' use of the term 'missionary' was carefully framed to show that they identified with their Aboriginal, rather than European, roots. This was reinforced by their suggestion that the appointee's salary could be paid from the Land Fund used to administer the Aboriginal Establishment at Oyster Cove. Although well aware that at least some of the islanders were 'full-blood' Aborigines, Denison refused to accept all of them as such and denied their request.[21] In many ways this marked the beginning of a struggle to gain acceptance as either legitimate Aboriginal people or direct descendants of Van Diemen's Land's Indigenous inhabitants. The question of Aboriginal identity remains a current and at times controversial issue in Tasmania today.

Robert Power returned to the Furneaux Islands in 1854, this time with Francis Nixon, the first Anglican bishop of Van Diemen's Land (officially renamed Tasmania the following year). On Preservation Island they found the two Allen brothers, one of whom lived on Clarke Island with his wife and eight children. This was James Allen, the former medical officer of Wybalenna. James Allen, his wife Maria (*nee* Robinson), and their children had resided on Clarke Island for the previous eight years, but as neither of the Allen brothers had paid any rent at all, Power served them with eviction notices. As an indication of their straitened circumstances, the annual rent for Clarke Island amounted to just five shillings.[22]

Despite the eviction they were still there two years later when James Allen drowned, and the families continued to reside on these islands until 1860. They differed little from the general islander community, who tended to ignore eviction notices as the government seldom had the means to enforce them, and there was simply nowhere else to go except to another island — which was the invariable outcome. For the amount of revenue received it was not worth the expense of stationing either a Crown bailiff or a police constable in the Furneaux Islands, and visits by government officials were infrequent at best. Beginning with James Munro in 1831, the policy had been to appoint leading members of the community as special constables. Not surprisingly, they generally worked solely in the interests of their fellow islanders, and there is no record of any islanders being evicted by these quasi-officials. As it transpired, even James Allen's family continued to rent on one or another of the islands, making an unsuccessful attempt to purchase Preservation Island outright in 1870.[23]

On Gun Carriage Island in 1854 Edward Mansell seized the opportunity of Bishop Nixon's visit to marry Julia Thomas, with whom he had lived outside wedlock for 25 years. Julia Thomas's poor grasp of English elicited some mirth from Mansell, who was rebuked by Captain King of the *Beacon*.[24] There was no issue from this lengthy union, and although Edward Mansell produced a son, Thomas Sydney Mansell in 1837, there are question marks over his maternity. According to Archibald Meston (who confused father and son) the mother was 'a negress … from whom all the many Mansells to-day are descended'.[25] Later, of course, there was intermarriage with other islander families.

It was while on this cruise through the islands of eastern Bass Strait that Nixon discovered Lucy Beedon had taken on the task of educating the children of the islanders. Like many others, Bishop Nixon was impressed by the abilities of this remarkable woman. The daughter of Thomas Beedon and Emerenna, Lucy had been born on Gun Carriage Island in 1829. Two years later Thomas Beedon was evicted by George Augustus Robinson, who retained custody of both Emerenna and Lucy. They were returned to Beedon after his successful petition to Lieutenant Governor Arthur, and when the Aboriginal Establishment was relocated to Flinders Island the Beedon family moved back to Gun Carriage Island. In 1861 they shifted briefly to Preservation Island before finally settling permanently on Badger Island. Lucy was sent to school at either Launceston or George Town, where she learnt to read and write and embraced the Christian faith to which she held fast for the remainder of her life. From her father Lucy also acquired superb business skills which she used to benefit the entire islander community in their dealings with the merchants of Launceston. Prior to Lucy taking control of commercial transactions, the islanders were frequently cheated and on numerous occasions paid for their produce with alcohol. Not any more. Henceforth, all business was conducted strictly on a cash basis, and from all accounts Lucy Beedon drove a very hard bargain with the purchasers.[26]

Part of Lucy Beedon's success was undoubtedly due to her formidable size. By the time she had reached 25 years of age Lucy weighed 23 stone (146 kilograms), and she wielded considerable authority over the islanders. At this time the islanders rarely sailed singly to Launceston or other distant destinations; they gathered their boats together as a fleet, and it was Lucy Beedon who determined when the voyage would be made and the course it would take.[27] She never married, preferring the isolation of Badger Island which the government allowed Lucy to lease for life at £24 per annum as a reward for her services to the islander community. She later purchased 50 acres (20 hectares) freehold, as did her brother James. Lucy continued to teach the islander children until 1862, when she turned most of her restless energy towards controlling the islanders' financial interests. Known as the 'Queen of the Isles', she died at the age of 58 in July 1886.[28]

Like Power, Bishop Nixon also gained a very favourable impression of the islander community. 'I could see', he later wrote, 'that there was an air of quiet domestic union amongst them all that told well for their ordinary way of life'. According to Nixon, 'the men appeared sober, active and intelligent' while 'the women were unmistakably modest and retiring in their manner'.[29] For their part, the islanders sensed a powerful ally, and alerted Nixon to the illegal occupation of some of the islands by outsiders, who blocked access to important mutton-bird rookeries. As they expected, Nixon conveyed their concerns to the government, which responded in 1855 by allowing the islanders to acquire leasehold, a practice which continued until 1860.[30] By this means James Everett's son, George, as well as the Maynard family, secured leases on Cape Barren Island. But not everyone was satisfied with this arrangement. John Riddle, for instance, managed to acquire the lease of Gun Carriage Island for £15 per year, providing him with the legal right to evict other members of the islander community. Both Thomas Beedon and Edward Mansell protested to the government, which guaranteed to protect their occupation rights. Riddle was warned that his lease would be cancelled if he continued to harass the other island residents.[31]

But the government's hands were tied, and in 1861 both the Beedon and Mansell families shifted to Preservation Island to take advantage of the recently-passed *Waste Lands Amendment Act*. Under the provisions of this legislation the islanders could obtain a 14-year lease over the smaller islands and sections of the larger ones. Beedon subsequently took out a lease on Badger Island, and by 1865 the islander community more generally held 550 acres (222 hectares) of leasehold throughout the Furneaux Islands.[32] John Riddle later lost his lease to Gun Carriage Island and ended his days in Hobart Gaol while serving a prison sentence.[33]

In 1862 Archdeacon Thomas Reibey and the Reverend John Fereday, vicar of George Town, made their first visit to the Furneaux Islands, and while on Badger Island Lucy Beedon convinced them of the desperate need for a qualified teacher to educate the islander children. Although the islanders agreed to pay the teacher's salary the cost proved beyond their limited resources. While the government made available £250 to build a schoolhouse and employ a qualified teacher, it came with the proviso that it would have to be matched on a pound-for-pound basis by the islander community. They managed to raise only £80,[34] and to continue the education of the children Lucy Beedon hired two temporary teachers from Melbourne. In 1871, however, she opened a tent school on Badger Island, an action which finally prompted the government to appoint Henry Collis as teacher the following year.[35] The facilities available to him initially differed little from those offered by Lucy Beedon: 'A single-roomed tent of small dimensions constituted his dwelling place and the school-house in one. No black-board, nor maps, nor desks, nor indeed any proper school furniture graced its interior'. It was not long, though, before these primitive conditions were substantially improved.[36]

While Archdeacon Reibey was unable to provide much assistance in the secular matter of education, he did manage to raise sufficient funds to purchase a mission boat so that Anglican ministers could visit the islanders on a regular basis. In many ways it was a similar situation to Oyster Cove, where the appointment of a catechist to look after the spiritual needs of the remaining Aborigines was apparently deemed more important than adequate food and clothing. In this instance the Reverend Fereday proved to be more practical, undertaking to act as agent for the islander community in their dealings with the government.[37] While this was a positive outcome, a number of problems arose in 1866 when the islanders' misunderstanding over the terms of their leaseholds resulted in revocation by the government.

The confusion provided an opportunity for outsiders to purchase more land on the Furneaux Islands, including those with significant mutton-bird rookeries. Jules Virieux, for example, purchased 50 acres (20 hectares) on Chappell Island which contained the second largest rookery of all. Virieux's sheep collapsed and destroyed many of the burrows existing within the boundaries of his freehold. One influential outsider who had also purchased land on the islands of the Furneaux Group nevertheless became an important ally of the islander community. Benvenuto Smith drew Surveyor General James Erskine Calder's attention to the islanders' dependence on Chappell Island's mutton-bird rookery, insisting that the islanders would starve if deprived of this crucial resource. Smith further contended that Chappell Island should be reserved for the exclusive use of the islander community. Although Calder was not prepared to enter into the question of exclusive rights, he did order Virieux to remove his sheep from the island.

But what should have been an important gain for the islanders was soon negated when a bureaucratic muddle allowed another outsider to purchase 50 acres (20 hectares) of land on the island.[38]

In response to the difficulties faced by the islander community just to make a basic living, the Tasmanian government finally toyed with the idea of granting them exclusive rights in 1868. It came to nought. Surveyor Richard Hall was chosen to investigate the islanders' circumstances, concluding that while the islands contained good soil for agriculture the islanders were unwilling to cultivate it. Hall felt that it was their thriftlessness which kept them destitute, adding that the only activities in which they engaged were the harvesting of mutton-birds and sailing their small wooden vessels around the islands. In the face of this seeming lack of initiative, the subject of exclusive rights was quietly shelved.[39]

As it stood, the situation posed a grave threat to the continuing economic survival of the islanders, prompting members of the community to petition Governor Charles Du Cane for exclusive rights to Chappell and a number of other islands on which there were large mutton-bird rookeries. Du Cane met with a deputation of islanders on Goose Island in August 1871 and was swayed by their arguments,[40] his influence forcing the government to reconsider the question of exclusive rights. While it was agreed that something would have to be done to protect the livelihood of the islanders, the government was only prepared to go so far: exclusive rights were restricted solely to Chappell Island.[41]

By the early 1870s the growth of the Islander population had become a significant factor in their concentration on Cape Barren Island, even though it had never been a preferred location owing to its exposed position and poor soil. Although there were extensive areas for grazing livestock, the only place suitable for permanent settlement lay on the western extremity, especially around the

Corner, where sheltered coves provided relatively safe anchorages for the islanders' watercraft. The adjacent waters were also rich in marine resources.[42] One distinctive feature of the settlement pattern on Cape Barren Island was the tendency of each family to separate themselves from the next, the average distance between households being in the order of three kilometres. Yet, despite this spatial buffer the islanders regularly visited each other and pursued a host of communal activities. By the early 1870s George Everett's family had established themselves at Thunder and Lightning Bay, while John Smith's family was ensconced at Long Beach, with John Maynard's family to their immediate north. Thomas and James Mansell were residents at the Corner, Thomas Rew had settled at Rooks River, and William Brown's family was at Munro Bay.[43] The first government-appointed schoolteacher, Henry Collis, held classes in the summer months at Long Beach on Cape Barren Island, moving across to Badger Island for the winter.[44] By the mid-1870s, Long Beach had emerged as the focal point of the Cape Barren Island community, with around 42 residents. By the early 1880s the population had risen to 69.[45]

Right throughout this period the islanders continued to follow their regular seasonal cycle. The majority of families spent the summer months on Cape Barren, scattering among the islands containing the largest mutton-bird rookeries in March and April. By May, the majority settled on Badger Island for their winter quarters, and in July the women began combing the beaches to gather shells for stringing into the necklaces for which they were renowned. In November the families dispersed again to harvest the eggs of mutton-birds and other avian fauna, before returning to Cape Barren Island.[46] The mutton-bird industry had itself undergone something of a transformation by the early 1870s. Feathers used for stuffing commercially made mattresses and pillows were now put aside after being plucked from the carcases rather than being collected 'by the smothering process of old'. Fledglings were salted rather than smoked as previously, and their fat had become a valuable commodity in its own right.[47]

In February 1870 the Tasmanian government conducted the first census in which the Furneaux Islands were included as a separate district. This disclosed a total population of 242 — 138 men and 104 women. It was unclear how many of these people were of Aboriginal descent, though it is known that many descendants resided on the smaller islands. A year later two of the original sealers were still alive. Edward Mansell had by then settled on Passage Island, while Richard Maynard was living on Long Island.[48] The 1872 census estimated the total population of the Furneaux Islands at 227, 84 of whom (35 per cent) were deemed to be 'half-castes'.[49] Owing to the heavier concentration of islanders on Cape Barren, Canon Marcus Brownrigg made the first of his 13 annual visits to the island in 1872 to conduct marriages and baptise children, becoming an important link between the community and the outside world. Unlike the government, Brownrigg readily acknowledged Aboriginal identity, though by doing so he accorded them a lower social status. For that reason Brownrigg continued to advocate that the leasehold on Cape Barren Island should be converted to a 'reserve' where the islanders could be 'civilised'.[50] His was a paternalistic vision.

Charles Bromby, who succeeded Francis Nixon as Bishop of Tasmania, gained an even more negative view of the islanders when he visited the Furneaux Group in 1876. To Bromby, all fault lay with the Aboriginal origins of the people, leading them along a number of Godless paths, and he particularly focused on their alleged heavy drinking and lack of industrious habits. Like Brownrigg, the good bishop was convinced that the only way the islanders could be saved from themselves was through the abandonment of a transient lifestyle and the seasonal exploitation of natural resources. Salvation lay in grasping the plough and farming the land.[51] Yet even Bromby realised the importance of mutton-birding to the islanders' economy. He noted that 30 000 salted fledglings, 4000 gallons (18 184 litres) of fat and 1000 gallons (1546 litres) of oil had been harvested from Chappell Island alone during a single season. Bromby estimated that up to 40 000 birds were taken in the islands every year, and their eggs were no less significant, with as many as 300 000 gathered on Chappell Island in 1864.[52]

The problem was that both Bromby and Brownrigg were either unable, or unwilling, to recognise that agriculture could not be successfully carried out on Cape Barren Island — or many other islands for that matter. And right throughout the 1870s the islanders were engaged in a constant struggle to keep their leaseholds, though some deliberately refused to meet their annual payments on the grounds that the land was theirs by right of their Aboriginal ancestry.[53] The government recognised the Aboriginal origins of many, but did not recognise Aboriginality *per se*. As 'half-castes' they were not entitled to any land as a right, and by the mid-1870s very few members of the community held any leases. The major exceptions were James Maynard and Henry Beedon, who separately held the lease for the Northern Sisters between 1872 and 1878. James Everett also leased East Kangaroo Island in 1874, but the only other islanders who rented or owned freehold land apart from Cape Barren Island were Lucy Beedon and her brother James. They ran 1400 sheep on Badger Island, some of the animals owned by fellow islanders.[54]

At the same time more of the islands came under the control of outsiders. In 1873 nine islands were leased by outsiders; by 1883 leases on 28 islands were either owned or leased by outside interests.[55] One of them was Henry Robinson, youngest son of George Augustus Robinson, who purchased Green Island where he built his home. Robinson also held leases over Isabella, Woody and Tin Kettle Islands, all of which were used for grazing sheep.[56] Part of the reason for this steady takeover by outsiders during the 1870s was that more of the islanders were settling on Cape Barren Island, and as this was actively encouraged by the government they found it easier to acquire deeds in grant. In 1873 George Everett and Thomas Mansell separately held five acres (two hectares) on the island, while John Smith had 10 acres (four hectares). The following year John Maynard also acquired the deeds for five acres of land on Cape Barren. The cost amounted to £1 per acre. Several attempts were nevertheless made by members of the community to purchase freehold land on other islands in the Furneaux Group. It was largely unsuccessful. While they were occasionally able to raise the deposit they could seldom meet the ongoing annual payments, with the land invariably falling into the hands of outsiders.[57]

And it was outsiders who continued to block access to the crucial mutton-bird rookeries — with the exception of the all-important rookery on Chappell Island. In 1872 Canon Marcus Brownrigg penned a description of temporary living quarters on the island, structures which bore affinities with the customary abodes of their Aboriginal forebears, particularly those on the west coast of Tasmania. Brownrigg also stressed the communal aspect of mutton-birding:

> The island having been reserved by Government for the use of the half-caste population, is generally regarded as the principal seat of mutton-birding operations. The 'season,' or 'harvest,' as it is also called, is unquestionably the great event of the year. For about a month prior to the commencement of work, preparations are made which consist of repairing or erecting huts, and collecting firewood. These huts are odd looking structures; they seldom exceed four feet [1.2 metres] in height at the walls, and about six feet [1.8 metres] at the ridge. The sides and roof are made up of light sticks, and covered in with long coarse grass. An opening at

> the side forms a door, and a few stones built up at one end serves for the fireplace. Grass is then strewed upon the earthen floor, and the habitation is considered to be complete ... As the work of mutton-birding finds occupation even for the children, a general gathering of whole families, at Chappell Island, is an annual event. In almost each case, the usual place of abode is deserted; goods, chattels, poultry, dogs, and all moveable things are transferred, for the time, to the scene of labour, and generally, towards the close of February, work begins in earnest.[58]

This had indeed been a fortunate concession by the Tasmanian government as land throughout the Furneaux Group had been alienated so rapidly that by the end of the 1870s the rookeries on Chappell and Babel Islands were the only ones where access did not require permission from an outside landowner. In January 1877 the islander community also attempted to sway the government to set aside Great Dog Island for their exclusive use. In this instance the best they could manage was a recommendation from the Solicitor General that they should be allowed access to the rookery during stipulated months without hindrance. In practice, however, permission from the lessee, Robert Gardner, remained a necessary formality.[59]

Chappell Island, with its extensive rookeries, may have been the most heavily exploited island during the harvesting season, but it was also the most dangerous to work. Many of the Furneaux Islands are home to the deadly tiger snake (*Notechis scutatus*), which prey on the young chicks and shelter in the burrows. These reptiles have the ability to store large reserves of fat to survive winter hibernation and the lean months when the mutton-birds are absent. Most grow to a maximum length of around 1.5 metres; the Chappell Island variety, however, can reach an impressive 2.4 metres in length, though its venom potency is only one-third that of its smaller cousins. As they are not ophiophagus, they inhabit the island in exceptionally large numbers and in the 1960s the well-known herpetologist, Eric Worrell, named the Chappell Island variety as a separate subspecies, *Notechis scutatus serventyi*, after the pioneer mutton-bird researcher, Dr Dominic Serventy. This remains to be validated. Since exploitation of mutton-birds began on the island the snakes have posed a very serious threat to harvesters,[60] and even after the development of a tiger snake antivenene in 1930 the isolation of Chappell Island ensured that the danger remained acute. In early April 1931 Martin Hayward, a 'half-caste, of Cape Barren Island' was taken to Whitemark on Flinders Island after being bitten by a tiger snake while mutton-birding. He died 12 hours later, leaving 'a widow and six children'.[61] Almost exactly seven years later:

> Two more cases of snakebite have occurred during the mutton bird season on the Straits Islands. Claude E. Brown, a resident of the reservation at Cape Barren Island, was bitten by a tiger snake while mutton birding at Chappell Island … Brown was bitten through his trousers, which probably saved his life. He was taken to Whitemark [Flinders Island] by boat for medical aid, and is progressing favourably. The first man to be bitten at Chappell Island this season, Arthur Stanley King, died at Whitemark about 53 hours afterwards.[62]

Such were the risks, but it was also a question of economic survival. With the exception of Flinders Island, further sales of land in the Furneaux Group finally came to a halt in 1880, and with a growing population on Cape Barren Island the Tasmanian government set aside 6000 acres (2428 hectares) on the western end of the island in 1881 as a reserve for the exclusive use of the islander community. This seemingly generous provision simultaneously deprived the islanders of the right to acquire leasehold land which they could claim as their own. The right of occupation in the reserved area also left the islanders without any firm security of tenure: having been gazetted as a 'reserve' theoretically meant that it could be revoked at any time. And as it comprised large areas of scrub and lagoons the land was mostly unsuited for any agricultural purposes.[63]

The islanders were initially under the belief that the gazettal of the reserve automatically granted them freehold title, and accordingly began planning a small township complete with its own general store. It did not take long before the full realisation of the reserve's provisions created a sense of utter futility, with a number of disgruntled families relocating across to Flinders Island. Some of them later returned when they were assured by Canon Brownrigg that it was highly unlikely the reserve would be revoked. The majority of the sub-divisions were at the Corner, where possession of the various allotments was decided by ballot, and by 1884 a number of the recipients had erected cottages and fenced off small plots of land. Despite the persistence of some uncertainty a general store was opened at the Corner to compete with Thomas Barrett's establishment on nearby Long Island.[64] Opened at least as early as 1877, Barrett's was the first store in the Furneaux Islands, and it was also the major source of alcohol, including hard spirits, the cause of many social problems.[65] It was the islanders' consumption of alcohol which particularly concerned the men of the cloth who visited the islands, no less so than Canon Brownrigg. For his part, Brownrigg continued to ignore the deficiency of the soil and held fast to his belief that if the islanders abstained from liquor they would soon begin cultivating their blocks and slowly adopt a more settled lifestyle.[66] Most did abstain, but it brought them no closer to success.

In 1889 a new Anglican bishop, Henry Hutchinson Montgomery, arrived in Tasmania and he soon began to take an active interest in the 'half-caste' people of the Furneaux Islands, visiting every year between 1891 and 1901. Montgomery's reputation has been somewhat overshadowed by that of his son Bernard, the renowned British general (later field marshal) who defeated Erwin Rommel's Axis forces in North Africa during World War Two.[67] Bishop Montgomery noted the steadily increasing islander population and used his influence to have the government appoint a 'missionary-schoolteacher' to Cape Barren Island. The appointee's duties were extremely wide-ranging. Not only were they expected to provide secular education for children of all ages, they were also to serve as catechist, postmaster and general government representative. On top of all that they were to instruct children and adults alike in horticultural and agricultural techniques.[68] These combined duties demanded someone of exceptional competence, and it was regrettable that the man finally chosen to perform these multifarious tasks, Edward Stephens, was already battling a demon of his own in the form of alcoholism.

Stephens arrived at the Corner with his family in August 1890, by which time the local community had grown to 110 — 30 adults and 80 children — 54 of the latter being of school age. Most of the adults continued to earn a basic living exploiting seasonal resources and engaging in itinerant work when available. There was too little of it. The wooden cottages they had built at the Corner mostly consisted of two or four rooms and were often chronically overcrowded, with the average family numbering around 10 individuals. The islanders still ran pigs and goats, and in some instances sheep, with many also raising poultry for meat and eggs. Horses were owned by a fortunate few. Generally speaking, though, Cape Barren was a depressed community with little in the way of luxuries and survival was often dependent on sharing what was available.[69]

The arrival of the Stephens family was therefore one of great excitement, a sudden reminder for the islanders that they had not been completely forgotten by officialdom. At first they were happy with the new schoolteacher *cum* government representative, but as time went on and Stephens struggled to control his craving for alcohol while simultaneously seeking to control the lives of the islanders, cracks began to appear. It finally reached a point where the community was left with little choice except to resist the imposition of a repressive system by Stephens.[70] But the schoolteacher had a powerful ally in Bishop Montgomery, who returned to Cape Barren Island with school inspector Joseph Masters just six months after Stephens had taken up his position. At that stage the community was still content with the new schoolteacher; their real concerns were those directly affecting their daily lives. Owing to their mutual dependence they were particularly keen to gain communal rights over the land in the vicinity of the Corner as well as the major mutton-bird rookeries on other islands. They presented Montgomery with a list of their grievances, which he promised to personally place before the premier on his return to Hobart.[71] The islanders were unaware that what they felt was best for them was at complete odds with what Montgomery thought was best for the community.

Rather than communal land ownership, Montgomery recommended to the premier that individual families should be granted allotments in close proximity to the schoolhouse where they could be kept under surveillance by Edward Stephens. He further advised that if the islanders refused to cultivate the existing tracts of arable land it should be returned to the Crown, and rather than communal rights over the mutton-bird rookeries, Montgomery advocated that families be forced to compete against each other rather than being encouraged to work cooperatively. In other words, Montgomery did all in his power to destroy the communal system which the islanders preferred as he believed it to be a legacy of their Aboriginal ancestors and thus an impediment to future advancement.[72]

The islanders were completely unaware of Bishop Montgomery's broader aims, and when he paid a second visit to Cape Barren Island in 1892 he was warmly thanked for his influence on new regulations controlling the mutton-bird industry. From December 1891 the season for catching mutton-birds on Chappell, Babel, Forsyth, Store and Little Green Islands was restricted to the period from 20 March to 20 May, with any adult birds taken having to be 'consumed on the spot' — without stipulating exactly what 'on the spot meant'. The same rule applied to harvested eggs,[73] though not during the restricted harvest season when there were none to be gathered. Mutton-birds arrive back in Bass Strait from the northern hemisphere in September every year and with uncanny accuracy they lay their single egg on or about 28 November. That was when the eggs were harvested.[74]

While the islanders were well aware that some form of regulation needed to be introduced to ensure long-term sustainability of the industry, they specifically wanted it to be applied to outsiders involved in 'birding' rather than themselves. Montgomery soon realised that the islanders readily flouted the regulations whenever it suited them.[75] Interestingly, Babel Island was included in the new regulations. Although the island contained the largest mutton-bird rookery in Bass Strait and lies off the east coast of Flinders Island it was (and to some extent still is) extremely remote and particularly difficult to access. Two families attempted to harvest mutton-bird fledglings in 1891, quickly withdrawing when they found that, like Chappell Island, it was over-run with snakes.[76] Seven years later Bishop Montgomery suggested that legislation should be introduced to compel the islanders to harvest the birds on Babel Island.[77] Compulsion failed, and it was not until the early twentieth century that a concerted effort was made to exploit the Babel Island rookery as Chappell Island was by then no longer able to accommodate all the islander families involved in the annual harvest.[78]

In 1890, 21 families harvested 204 000 fledglings which, at ten shillings per hundred birds, netted £1020. The following year the harvest was poor owing to a waterspout which destroyed thousands of birds on Chappell and Green Islands, but 1892 — when the new regulations came into effect — proved to be 'exceptionally good'. They continued much the same way until 1896, which was described as 'anything but a payable season', but apart from similar fluctuations there were to be many good harvests in the years ahead.[79] To enforce the new mutton-bird regulations a police officer was stationed permanently at the Corner on Cape Barren Island. He soon showed himself to be just as erratic in his behaviour as Edward Stephens, and it was perhaps not surprising that the two were soon at loggerheads. Battling to keep away from the bottle, Stephens was incensed to find that the new constable was a heavy imbiber. And it went further. The policeman regularly used coarse language and refused to attend the Sunday services Stephens held in the schoolhouse. Stephens's avalanche of complaints finally pushed the constable to breaking point, with shots fired at the schoolhouse one Sunday morning while Stephens was conducting the service.[80] This clash of personalities was of brief duration. In early 1892 the law officer died suddenly and was not replaced, presenting at least some of the islanders with a wonderful opportunity to flout the new mutton-birding regulations.[81]

Within two years the islander community also had more than enough of Edward Stephens. In 1894 a number of families uprooted and moved across to Flinders Island, while most of those who remained refused to send their children to school. In the same year Stephens began making preparations for his retirement to a small farm at Badger Corner on Flinders Island, where he later established a small private school.[82] But the islanders still had three years to go before they could finally rid themselves of Edward Stephens. The battle of wills reached a new level in October 1895 when the mail ketch *GV Holyman* was wrecked with the loss of all hands on Bung's Reef off Cape Barren Island during a storm. Stephens accused some of the islanders of looting the vessel's cargo. The islanders counter-attacked by claiming that Stephens arrived at the school drunk and locked the children outside. Their concerted campaign finally pushed Stephens over the edge. Two islanders bringing their small wooden boat into the harbour had to scramble for cover when the school-teacher fired shots in their direction; they later reported that Stephens had threatened to shoot all the 'half-castes' on the island.[83]

After the islanders' allegations were laid before the authorities they instructed John Maclaine, an outsider grazier and justice of the peace on Clarke Island, to investigate. Maclaine upheld the charges made by the islander community and Stephens was called to Hobart to explain his actions. Although reprimanded for his drinking and forced to seek medical help, both the Director of Education (an unrelated Thomas Stephens) and Bishop Montgomery maintained their determination to assist the schoolteacher in his struggle against the community. Stephens was promptly sent back to Cape Barren Island to renew the contest, with the salvoes soon falling. Members of the community advised the Director of Education that if Stephens was not replaced all the children would be withdrawn from the school. Then, in September 1896, they complained that the schoolteacher had struck Thomas Mansell and threatened him with a pistol.[84] Stephens denied the allegations and argued that the parents should be prosecuted for not sending their children to school under the provisions of the *Education Act*. Montgomery threw his weight behind him, contending that everything Stephens said about the 'Half-Castes' was true.[85]

Stephens was finally removed from the contest in 1897 when he suffered a nervous breakdown. After tendering his resignation he shifted across to Flinders Island and retirement.[86] In a bizarre twist he later became a staunch defender of the rights of the Cape Barren Island 'half-castes',[87] and the poisoned chalice of teaching duties was passed to his son Charles, who soon lifted school attendance to 45 pupils.[88] The community initially had no complaints against Charles Stephens, and the defeat of his father had given them a measure of confidence in dealing with other government officials. In 1897 they formed the Islander Association, which petitioned the government on a range of issues affecting the community. Further regulation of the mutton-bird industry was high on the agenda, as was the question of land tenure. The Association also made a brave attempt to publish a local newspaper and institute a health benefits scheme, both ventures still-born in the face of widespread illiteracy and poverty.[89]

Bishop Montgomery and government officials were opposed to this overt display of independence, but they could do little to stop it. When Montgomery again visited Cape Barren Island with the Director of Education in 1898 and tried to intimidate the islanders he was largely ignored. Montgomery fared no better the following year despite being accompanied by the Minister for Justice. When the bishop called a public meeting to discuss the islanders' grievances only four members of the community bothered to turn up. In August 1899 Montgomery discussed with the Commissioner of Police the possibility of having a police magistrate visit the island on a regular basis. There was already some outstanding legal matters to be dealt with, and notwithstanding that most of them were of a trivial nature, Montgomery believed that if a police magistrate investigated more thoroughly he was bound to uncover far more serious offences. To strengthen control even further, the bishop urged the police chief to institute a commission of inquiry to examine conditions on the reserve as well as the mutton-bird industry.[90]

A Committee of Inquiry was duly authorised in 1900, by which time Charles Stephens had fallen foul of the islander community. In October 1899 he informed Montgomery that the new secular curriculum at the school would focus heavily on biblical history in the hope of frightening the islanders into submission. How this was to work was left unsaid, and there was little hope of success as Stephens was himself under close observation. Members of the community stationed themselves within sight of the school every morning, armed with a clock to check when Stephens entered the schoolhouse. His movements were monitored again in the afternoon. If the children were allowed to go home a few minutes early their parents would lodge a formal complaint against Stephens for neglecting his duties. If he kept the children back for a few minutes the parents complained to his superiors that he was overworking the children.[91] Like his father, Charles Stephens was no slouch when it came to psychological warfare, and he refused to give in.

In May 1900 the Committee of Inquiry recommended that an annual licensing fee should be introduced for those engaged in the harvesting of mutton-birds, and the first licences were issued three years later. In 1908 a total of 177 licences were issued for the season, and given that the total population of the Furneaux Islands at that time was approximately 500 islanders and outsiders,[92] it is clear that a large percentage of the people were engaged in the industry. The Committee of Inquiry also recommended that all land on Cape Barren Island which had been withdrawn from leasehold in 1881 to create the reserve should be thrown open for selection by the islanders who would have 14 years to pay off their holding. Any islander not wishing to cultivate the land should have the alternative of being able to lease a five acre (two hectare) homestead block for £1 per annum. All remaining land could then be leased to outsiders. Apart from the licensing fee for mutton-birding, none of the committee's other recommendations were introduced, which meant that the question of land tenure remained unanswered. The situation had therefore remained virtually unchanged since the Cape Barren Island reserve had been created in 1881. That there was cause for concern was highlighted in 1902, when Chappell Island was again leased to outside interests for grazing purposes during the off-season, with no thought given to the almost certain destruction of mutton-bird burrows by livestock.[93]

Bishop Montgomery returned to England in August 1901 following a final visit to Cape Barren Island. Montgomery's effort on behalf of the islander community has been called 'his greatest failure',[94] and the bishop was often held in contempt by the islanders. As a means of demonstrating his claim that the islanders were inveterate liars, Edward Stephens later related a false rumour circulating on Cape Barren Island that was held to be a 'fact':

> Bishop Montgomery, on one of his visits, found me sitting on the roof of the water closet, and I had only my night shirt on, and was singing the national anthem! He asked me what I was doing and I told him "I was showing my loyalty to the Queen". He said "Oh come down and come inside and we will make a night of it". And we did so. They said they knew I was a drunkard but the Bishop was a 'bloody' sight worse![95]

Although Montgomery's successor, John Mercer, visited Cape Barren Island on a number of occasions, his interest was primarily directed towards the education of the children,[96] and even in government circles the islanders virtually disappeared off the radar during the first few years of the twentieth century. There was nevertheless one government official who did gain considerable respect from the islanders. That was Gustavus Knight, who replaced Charles Stephens as schoolteacher in September 1906. Stephens had finally been forced to relinquish his post when serious illness struck his family, and the school was closed for a period of nine months until Knight took over. During the four-and-a-half years that Knight spent on Cape Barren Island the school attendance doubled,[97] though it must be admitted that he publicly — and quite undeservedly — denigrated the efforts of both his predecessors.[98] Knight was in turn replaced by Captain James Bladon in 1911, and apart from a year's break in 1923, Bladon remained in the position until 1928.[99]

In 1907 Cape Barren Island was incorporated into the newly created Flinders municipality, whose 250-odd ratepayers were incensed when the islanders made it known that they had no intention of paying any rates or taxes. There was a good reason for this obduracy. None of the islanders had been consulted about the incorporation, and nor were any of them elected as councillors so they could represent the interests of the community.[100] As far as they were concerned the reserve had been created specifically for themselves by the Tasmanian government and Flinders Island Council had no right to levy any charges. It was in the midst of all this turmoil that the Tasmanian Attorney General instructed Police Commissioner JEC Lord to investigate conditions on Cape Barren Island as well as the mutton-bird industry and to make recommendations.[101]

Lord quickly discovered that there were three widely divergent views regarding the reserve on Cape Barren Island. For their part, the islanders continued to insist that the land was theirs by right of their Aboriginal ancestry, and that they should have exclusive control over the major mutton-bird rookeries on other islands. Outsiders, on the other hand, believed that they were the ones being discriminated against. Unlike the 'half-castes' they had to purchase land, they had to use it, and they had to pay rates and taxes. The general feeling among them was that the islanders were being 'spoon-fed' by the government, which did nothing to encourage the islanders to improve their circumstances. The local municipal authority had its own thoughts on the Cape Barren Island reserve. They wanted it thrown open for selection, and although it was agreed that the islanders should have first preference it was recognised that few of them had sufficient economic resources to pay for any such land. As Flinders Island Council knew full well, if the reserve was thrown open for selection the bulk of it would inevitably fall into the hands of outsiders. Following in the footsteps of Bishop Montgomery, the aptly named Lord felt that the islanders should earn the right to any land by paying for short-term homestead and agricultural leases. If they could demonstrate their ability to use it — that is, cultivate the soil — then they could be rewarded with long-term leasehold.[102]

Despite his own ideals, Lord gave the islanders ample opportunity to express their wishes by holding open meetings with the community. He reported that they wanted alcohol banned from all the Furneaux Islands, not just Cape Barren,[103] and the police commissioner was soon aware that the islanders had formed a very exclusive sense of identity. They wanted members of the community who were descended from either mainland Australian Aborigines or New Zealand Maori banned from the reserve, and objected to four outsiders who had married islander women and had children by them. In his report, Lord came down on the side of the majority by agreeing that if white men married into the community they should be forced to take their wives away from the reserve. At the same time, though, he was fully cognisant of the inherent dangers of following an exclusivist policy. There were only around 190 islanders on Cape Barren Island, including those descended from mainland Aborigines and Maori. Diversity rather than exclusivity was clearly of the utmost importance, and Edward Stephens had previously raised the spectre of incestuous relationships on Cape Barren Island. As Lord insisted, the 'community was related and inter-related to such an extent as to be a very serious physiological problem and one which cannot be overlooked'.[104]

While he saw some future for the Furneaux Islands with their natural resources and tourism potential,[105] Lord found housing and the general conditions on the Cape Barren Island reserve to be extremely poor and a serious health risk to the inhabitants. He suggested that the 26 existing dwellings should be demolished and a major rebuilding program commenced, while also supporting a regime of close supervision. Again following Bishop Montgomery, the Police Commissioner believed that the islanders should be instructed in agricultural techniques as a means of making the community self-sufficient.[106] A number of previous reports on the islander community had invariably disappeared into government pigeon-holes, but not this time. The Tasmanian government accepted the bulk of Lord's recommendations and determined to implement them. It was to have profound consequences for the future, and indeed, Lord's report was to serve as a blueprint for government policies until as late as 1978.[107] The year 1908 was thus a major turning point for the Bass Strait islander community, though it was still to be another four years before Lord's recommendations came into effect.

Right throughout this period and into the near future another struggle was being fought by a lone islander woman in a largely forgotten episode of Tasmanian Aboriginal history. The epic battle waged by Louisa Briggs, however, was fought on the mainland of Australia rather than the islands of Bass Strait. Louisa Briggs was the daughter of sealer John Strugnell and Polly Munro, herself the product of a union between sealer James Munro and his mainland Australian Aboriginal wife Margery. Born in 1836 Louisa married John Briggs, the son of sealer George Briggs and his Van Diemen's Land Aboriginal partner, in 1853. The couple soon set out to make their fortune on the Victorian goldfields, instead finding itinerant pastoral work in the Beaufort and Violet Town districts. It was often hard to come by and with nine children to support John and Louisa settled on Coranderrk Aboriginal Reserve near Healesville in 1871. The following year the family was expelled after John Briggs attempted to find outside employment, but destitution forced their return in 1874. Louisa worked as a nurse and dormitory matron, becoming a salaried staff member two years later. Able to read but not write,[108] Louisa became an outspoken critic of Coranderrk's administration and gave evidence to a government inquiry in August 1876.[109] It came at a cost. When John Briggs died in 1878 the authorities again expelled Louisa and her family from the reserve and they found temporary sanctuary at the Ebenezer Aboriginal Station on Lake Hindmarsh, where Louisa's nursing skills led to her appointment as matron. She was just as vocal in her condemnation of the administration at Ebenezer, but in a surprising move Louisa was allowed to return to Coranderrk following another official inquiry in 1882.[110]

Four years later, though, the Victorian government passed legislation which declared that only 'full-blood' Aborigines and 'half-castes' over the age of 34 were entitled to aid, a stern measure which halved the populations on the reserves.[111] Despite being 50 years of age, Louisa Briggs was among the expelled, and with her family she crossed into southern New South Wales and finally settled at Cumeroogunga Aboriginal Reserve in 1889. Her appeals to be allowed to return to Coranderrk in 1889 and again in 1892 were rejected by the Victorian government on the grounds that she was a Tasmanian 'half-caste'. Then, in 1895, 'half-castes' were barred from Cumeroogunga Aboriginal Reserve and Louisa moved with her family to a makeshift camp at Barmah. At the age of 67 in 1903 she requested government rations, only to be denied yet again on the basis of her Tasmanian origins. After years of struggle Louisa was finally given permission to return to Cumeroogunga Aboriginal Reserve,[112] where she died in

September 1925. Louisa Briggs was buried with full religious rites, the service read by one of her relatives. Schoolchildren laid a large wreath of violets on the grave, and press reports wrongly credited her age at 107 years[113] Her life had nevertheless been a long and tortuous journey, and Louisa Briggs's compatriots on Cape Barren Island still had further battles of their own ahead after the Tasmanian government decided to accept the recommendations of JEC Lord.

13

THE BASS STRAIT ISLANDER COMMUNITY 1912–1970

JEC Lord's concerns that the inadequate housing and poor living conditions on Cape Barren Island posed a serious health risk were well-justified. The death of Julia Thomas in 1910 from consumption (pulmonary tuberculosis) was the eleventh in succession from this disease of poverty.[1] Having accepted Lord's recommendations, the Tasmanian government was determined to improve the situation, but delay was experienced through political debate and the slowly grinding wheels of bureaucracy. During the four years prior to the passing of the *Cape Barren Island Reserve Act* in December 1912, politicians argued over what was in the best interests of the islanders and of the government, which were often along quite divergent lines.[2] In January 1911 the State Governor, Premier, Minister for Lands and Minister for Health descended on Cape Barren Island to view the situation for themselves, and they were not particularly impressed with what they found. The reserve population was by then estimated at 160, the majority crammed into just

34 private dwellings, few of which were considered to be of adequate standard.[3]

A deputation of islanders suggested to the official visitors that the reserve land should be granted to the community as freehold: if that was not acceptable, their alternative was to sub-divide the reserve into 100 acre (40 hectare) blocks for married men with families and 25 acre (10 hectare) blocks for single men — the land to be leased by the recipients. Members of the deputation insisted that sub-divisions of this size would be sufficient for the islanders to achieve an independent living by grazing either sheep or cattle. To that end they also sought government assistance to improve the existing pasture and advice on the most suitable breeds of cattle.[4] They were only too well aware that agriculture stood little chance of success.

The legislation fell well short of their aspirations. Under the provisions of the Act all the reserve land reverted to Crown ownership, including those areas which had already been purchased as freehold by a small minority of islanders. The latter were to be compensated for their loss and the entire reserve was to be resurveyed into 50 acre (20 hectare) agricultural blocks and 3 acre (1.2 hectare) homestead allotments. All islanders over the age of 18, male and female, became eligible to obtain a short-term lease for either an agricultural block or a homestead allotment. They were then required to erect a dwelling within two years of occupancy and tender proof that they had lived on their land for at least six months every year. Housing loans up to £50 were made available through a special government fund. Agricultural blocks also had to be fenced, and if all requirements were met over a period of three years the recipient then qualified for a long-term lease of 99 years. Acknowledging community concerns, the legislation included a clause which stipulated that female leaseholders must surrender their lease if they married an outsider.[5]

Contrary to uncritical claims, the islanders were provided with security of tenure, though with good reason the government stopped short of freehold title. Leasehold was offered with the best of intentions as a means of ensuring the long-term integrity and security of the reserve for those it was specifically designed. As they were regularly in debt there was an obvious risk that the islanders would be tempted to sell freehold land, a course that would invariably lead to their dispossession. That concern was clearly spelled out during debate over the Bill:

> The main object of the Bill is, as we have said, to encourage the proper use of the land in the Reserve, by giving security of tenure, with the proviso that it shall not become freehold, and that it will not be possible for the holder to transfer his rights to outsiders. This is a necessary provision, because it is quite certain that if the fee simple were given, in a short time very little of the land would be in the possession of the half-castes, for whose use it was intended.[6]

The legislation also prohibited alcohol on the reserve, but the real reasoning behind all the provisions was to encourage the islanders to become self-sufficient and thereby release the government from providing any future assistance. Although it had originally been intended to appoint a reserve manager to ensure that the islanders met their obligations, it was eventually decided that adequate surveillance could be maintained by the schoolteacher and a resident police constable. Whichever way it is viewed, there can be no denying that the *Cape Barren Island Reserve Act* subjected the islanders to a loose form of institutionalisation, though there was a generous escape clause. Section 28 of the legislation allowed leaseholders to exchange their land on Cape Barren Island for up to 50 acres

(20 hectares) of Crown land available for selection anywhere on the Tasmanian mainland.[7] It appears there were no takers, and by 1914 the reserve had been resurveyed, freeholders compensated, licences to occupy either agricultural blocks or homestead allotments had been extended to 27 families, and a number of new houses built. Livestock had increased to 1000 head of sheep and 104 cattle, a network of roads constructed throughout the reserve, and horticultural gardens established.[8]

The outbreak of war in August 1914 saw at least 25 islander men enlist for overseas service and don khaki. Fifteen gave their place of residence as Cape Barren Island, eight joined up from Flinders Island and two from Launceston. Their sacrifice was great. Three islanders were killed in action, another during training. One islander died from wounds and two others succumbed to disease. Eleven were wounded, in some cases multiple times. Silas Mansell and Willard Brown were perhaps the most fortunate. Both were discovered to be under-age before they embarked for overseas and were discharged.[9] Combined with those for old-age and invalids, war pensions were to be an important source of income in the community over the years ahead.[10]

By the early 1920s very few islanders had qualified for 99-year leasehold or even managed to repay loans which had been taken out to build their private dwellings. Tuberculosis had increased its hold on the population, and the families of some of the deceased had burned down their homes in the hope of preventing further contagion. To put a roof over their heads they either constructed makeshift shelters or moved in with relatives, exacerbating the already overcrowded conditions. The agricultural blocks were mostly unfenced and farming was virtually non-existent. The government had failed to provide any advice on improving pastures or suitable breeds of cattle, so the possibility of reinvigorating the local economy through either beef or dairy production remained unrealised. As a consequence the community continued to rely heavily on the seasonal exploitation of mutton-birds.[11]

Although a few families often made sufficient money during those few short months to sustain themselves for quite some time, the situation was largely unchanged from what Police Commissioner Lord had found in 1908. When funds ran out the islanders obtained credit from storekeepers using future returns from the mutton-bird harvest as security. Although Lord denied it, there is abundant evidence to show that the islanders were regularly charged exorbitant prices for basic commodities such as flour, tea and sugar, as well as tobacco, while forced to accept payment well below the market price for their own produce. For that reason the islanders not infrequently attempted to avoid repaying loans to the merchants by either spending their returns quickly without the creditor's knowledge, or selling their produce to a rival storekeeper. For their part, the storekeepers — particularly those on Flinders Island — preferred not to enter into any agreement with the islanders, though they were also acutely aware that without credit many of the islanders faced the very real prospect of starvation.[12] The overall effect of this system was that the islanders owned very little themselves and were constantly in debt, sometimes for substantial amounts. With too much time on their hands drunkenness was rife.[13]

In a bid to break this vicious cycle the islanders petitioned the Minister for Lands, again requesting that reserve land be granted to them as freehold.[14] The Secretary for Lands, AE Counsel, advised his minister that little could be done for the older islanders (who were apparently beyond redemption) except to increase supervision. The only solution that Counsel could see was to encourage the younger people to leave the island — to assimilate into the broader Tasmanian community.[15]

A select parliamentary inquiry in October 1924 similarly failed to offer any real solutions. One of its recommendations was that pensions should be paid directly to recipients at Cape Barren Island rather than Whitemark on Flinders Island, where much of it passed across the hotel bar. The inquiry further recommended that the future issue of mutton-birding licences should be restricted solely to 'half-castes', and as a means of providing additional income a short open season on seals between December and February was proposed. Then there was the school curriculum, which members of the inquiry felt should be changed to allow the children to gain practical skills. This was as good as saying that the children were not up to an acceptable academic standard — no doubt owing to their Aboriginal origins. Another suggestion was that the adult islanders should elect a five-member committee to advise the Crown land bailiff (the resident police constable) on all matters affecting the community.[16] It was left unsaid whether the police officer had to accept any proffered advice.

The islanders regarded the parliamentary inquiry as yet another attempt to control their lives. On the other side of the ledger, Flinders Island Council viewed the inquiry as pampering to the wishes of the Cape Barren Island community. Caught between a rock and a hard place the Tasmanian government chose to do nothing. The biggest bugbear for the islanders was now the municipal authority, which continually pressured them to pay rates and local taxes. Although some islanders did make an effort to comply, their lack of a regular income ensured that they were constantly in arrears. The department of education was also of some concern. Despite school attendance reputedly being higher at Cape Barren Island than at most other schools in Tasmania, truancy inspectors made regular visits to harass parents.[17]

During the 1920s a number of islanders relocated to Flinders Island, where some settled on the south coast around Trousers Point, others along the east and north coasts, while eight families congregated at Pine Scrub on the northern end of Marshall Bay where they lived in relative isolation. Herbert Beedon was one of the first islanders at Pine Scrub, settling there in the 1890s following his marriage to Judith Thomas. Like their neighbours, the Beedon family relied heavily on the small trading vessels which called in two or three times a year to collect bales of wool and offload supplies for the residents. Beedon purchased a small farm where he grew vegetables and ran a few sheep and dairy cows. He supplemented his income by taking casual work with local white farmers, and he still maintained a shed on Chappell Island which his family used during the 'birding' season. Like many other islanders, Beedon snared wallabies and possums for food and sold their skins, and his family maintained the Aboriginal connection by gathering native plant foods, especially cranberries and the pith of grass trees. Every November the families harvested mutton-bird eggs on the small offshore islands. Cooking was done over an open fire, with camp ovens used for baking.[18]

Life was tough for the islanders on both Flinders and Cape Barren Islands. As cash was scarce they made their own clothes and footwear — moccasins from wallaby skin. These consisted of two pieces of wet skin wrapped around the feet with the fur on the inside and tied with string through the top. They dried to the shape of the feet.[19] Molly Mallett recalled the dresses made by her mother from hessian bags to wear around the house. They were all dyed green, apparently the only coloured dye stocked by the Cape Barren Island store.[20] Lighting was provided by candles, kerosene lamps or what were known as 'fat lights', mutton-bird fat in a used Nestlé powdered milk tin with a wick made from plaited flannel or wool. It was to be many years before electricity was supplied by diesel generators, and it was not until 1992 that a reliable electricity supply was finally available through wind generation.[21]

In 1929 the Tasmanian government once again focused attention on Cape Barren Island, when AW Burbury, a lawyer in the Attorney General's department, was instructed to investigate the circumstances of the islander community. Burbury had only recently completed a similar investigation on Pitcairn Island in the Pacific, where many of the descendants of the *Bounty* mutineers still lived.[22] Unlike Pitcairn Island, Burbury was surprised by the situation on Cape Barren Island. He estimated the population at somewhere around 250, all of whom were living in just 24 houses, 'more than half mere shacks of two rooms'.[23] Noting that the store on the island operated strictly on a cash-only basis and that there appeared to be no regular employment, Burbury was at a loss to explain how the islanders even survived.[24] They had been doing it for quite some time. Replacing the earlier establishment, the new store which opened on Cape Barren Island in 1910 had refused to extend credit from the very outset.[25]

Burbury also discovered that the islanders had 'an inferiority complex deeply ingrained', and considered they had 'been supplanted and exploited by white men'. The situation might have been considerably worse if the *Cape Barren Island Reserve Act* of 1912 had provided the islanders with freehold title. On the other hand, the Tasmanian government had clearly failed to provide the islanders with any tangible support. Given the prevailing conditions and governmental neglect, Burbury questioned why the reserve had even been created. As he acidly commented, the government had clearly recognised that the islanders were entitled to something, but it had effectively given them nothing.[26]

He noted that existing leaseholds were too small for anyone to make a living and recommended they be increased in size. Acknowledging that the islanders were not farmers, he suggested that a forestry plantation could be established with wage labour. Burbury also accepted the Aboriginality of the islanders by suggesting that a missionary society could assume some responsibility for the community, and given their crucial dependence on the mutton-bird harvest he advised that the government should undertake a thorough investigation of the industry. Looking to the future, Burbury agreed with AE Counsel that when the children had completed their schooling they should be encouraged to leave the island. The problems were clearly many, so many in fact that Burbury felt that the solutions were beyond the capacity of the Tasmanian government, and that Cape Barren Island should be 'taken over by the [Commonwealth] Home and Territories Department as is done at Norfolk Island'.[27] Burbury's report was released at the worst possible time, on the very eve of a global economic crisis. Yet, in an ironic twist, it was to be the impact of the 'Great Depression' which paved the way for improving the islanders' plight.

From the early 1920s the Australian economy had been in a generally depressed state, partly through the huge cost of involvement in World War One and heavy overseas borrowing, especially on the London money market. This was exacerbated by Australia's continuing dependence on primary production at the expense of secondary industry. Primary produce was at the mercy of fluctuating prices in the global marketplace, and following the Wall Street crash of 1929 that market constricted dramatically.[28] With the deepening economic crisis the Tasmanian government accepted Burbury's advice and turned to the Commonwealth for assistance in dealing with the situation on Cape Barren Island. With urgent problems of its own the Commonwealth government could initially do little, but it was at this very time that the Australian Board of Missions expressed an interest in the welfare of the Cape Barren Island community. The board chairman, Reverend JS Needham, visited Cape Barren Island in December 1930, though it quickly proved to be a disappointing sojourn. Needham refused to accept the islanders as Aborigines, commenting that the last true 'half-caste' had died two years earlier.[29] Needham was wrong. Captain Phillip Thomas, the last islander born to a 'full-blooded' Aboriginal woman and a white sealer had actually died fifteen years earlier at the age of 83 on 28 February 1915.[30]

Needham could barely hide his disgust when one of the islanders, to outward appearance a non-Aboriginal man, said with all seriousness that 'if a case were brought in a Federal Court the Tasmanian Government would be forced to pay the half-castes rent for the island of Tasmania'.[31] Needham was used to working with 'full-blood' Aborigines, particularly those in Queensland, and insisted that while a few of the islanders possessed a hint of Aboriginal features, they could — and should be — absorbed into the broader Tasmanian population. Counsel, Burbury and Needham were all in agreement that at least some of the problems besetting the Cape Barren Island community could be overcome by assimilation rather than segregation. Needham considered the matter to be especially urgent given the islanders' propensity to marry within the community, which he warned could have long-term genetic consequences.[32]

The Australian Board of Missions was therefore unwilling to offer any assistance, though the church did not entirely forsake Cape Barren Island. In 1934 the Salvationist, Miss Ada Hudson, established her non-denominational Bethel Peniel Mission in a small building at the Corner where she dedicated herself to offering practical assistance to the community.[33] By 1940 she had launched an annual appeal in Hobart and Launceston for funds to keep the mission operating, at the same time soliciting for second-hand clothing 'or other articles' for the islanders.[34] Hudson travelled as far afield as Melbourne and Adelaide to make her work known,[35] but it was not until 1949 that the Tasmanian government finally came to her aid by agreeing to erect a new mission building.[36] Her efforts were not always totally in accord with the islanders. Hudson emphasised their poverty and sought charitable assistance: the islanders wanted regular work, not charity. Nor did they appreciate donations of second-hand clothing, which they argued carried the possible risk of diseases prevalent on the Tasmanian mainland. But Hudson was dedicated and remained in the community until the early 1960s.[37]

Long before then, in late 1931, events had taken an unexpected turn for the islanders when the Scullin Federal government attempted to reinvigorate the Australian economy by extending grants to local authorities so they could employ those who were out of work on necessary public works projects. Flinders Island Council was one such recipient, and in this instance it came with the stipulation that at least some of the grant money had to be directed towards Cape Barren Island. The council initially refused to comply, directing funding into other areas, notably those on Flinders Island. When complaints were lodged, however, some of it finally began to channel into the Cape Barren Island community.[38] Many of the islander men now found work repairing roads and fences, constructing wells and water tanks and renovating and painting houses. Seeds were distributed free of charge to enable the islanders to grow their own vegetables. When combined with earnings from the mutton-bird harvest, the dole scheme proved to be a major windfall for the islanders.[39]

Another source of income was provided by the island's alluvial tin fields. Tin was first reported on Cape Barren Island in 1871, and alluvial mining began in 1882 at Rooks River, which flows into Deep Bay on the north coast of the island. Further deposits were found around the Modder River which enters Thunder and Lightning Bay on the south-west coast, though neither was conducive to large-scale operations. While impurities and the difficulty of extraction through an inadequate water supply have been the main barriers,[40] this did not prevent outside interests from attempting to cash in on potential profits at the expense of the islanders. In February 1899 a mining syndicate based at Zeehan on Tasmania's west coast expressed interest in the tin fields on Cape Barren Island, dispatching two experienced prospectors to carry out an investigation of the prospects. Encouraged by what they found, an attempt was made to form a company the following month.[41] Although that may not have been successful, tin-mining was reported to be 'going on nicely in a small way' by October 1906,[42] and two years later 'several half-castes' were working alongside six outsiders on the Rooks River field. All participants were said to be 'making very fair profits'.[43] Another attempt was made to form a mining company in Launceston in late 1912,[44] and eventually the Mount Munro Tin Mining Company was established. Operations were centred at the Modder River and by March 1934 the company was said to be obtaining 'a satisfactory output'.[45] In November 1936, 20 bags of ore were shipped to Launceston for processing,[46] and it was around this same time that another outsider syndicate was formed to bore for oil after gaining access to 9000 acres (3640 hectares) of land on Cape Barren Island.[47] The oil proved illusory. Tin was not, and in March 1937 a substantial rise in price triggered an expansion in mining activity.[48] Like any other industrial venture, however, it also had inherent dangers. In late January 1937:

> A fatal accident occurred at Rook's River tin mine … when J Sainty, a well-known tin miner, was killed by a sudden fall of earth. At the inquest a verdict of death by suffocation, in accordance with the doctor's examination, was returned. Deceased was interred in the Cape Barren Island Cemetery.[49]

For the majority of islanders not involved in tin-mining, the dole extended by the Commonwealth government gave their larders a much-needed boost. For a married man in the 1930s the dole consisted of a voucher valued at five shillings, by no means a princely sum, but sufficient to obtain a week's worth of flour, sugar, tea, butter, jam, sausages, camp pie (or tinned meat), potatoes, onions and even a quantity of tobacco. The Cape Barren Island store was only small and stocked a limited range of goods, with even fruit such as apples and oranges irregularly available. As an alternative, the islanders continued to gather seasonal native plants, including kangaroo apple, tater vines, pigface, wild cherry, wild currant and she-oak apples.[50]

Most of the islanders were able to supplement the dole still further by keeping poultry and, of course, growing their own vegetables. They also snared wallabies, caught echidnas and fish, mostly rockfish, flathead and flounder, the latter usually speared. This again brings up the subject of whether the Aborigines really abandoned scale-fish 3700 years ago, because their descendants certainly enjoyed a fish meal — and they deliberately burnt the bones to avoid the risk of cuts and infection. Perhaps their forebears did the same. Interestingly, though, Molly Mallett recalled that while the islanders often caught crayfish they seldom harvested abalone. Limpets were eaten on occasion, but abalone was only taken during the spring tides at a few scattered locations. No-one was apparently interested in diving for these succulent shellfish as in the past. The islanders also gathered mushrooms in autumn and when any livestock was slaughtered the meat was distributed among members of the community. Salted mutton birds were, of course, available all year round.[51]

By 1936 at least 100 islanders were benefitting from Commonwealth funding, though while it has been said that there was a general air of prosperity prevailing on Cape Barren Island, many of those who lived through the depression years remember it a little differently. Building materials, for example, were very costly and in short supply, forcing at least some of the islanders to gather driftwood from the beaches to use as construction material. Others scavenged whatever they could find around the island. Molly Mallett recalled that her family obtained drinking water from a natural spring 3 kilometres from their home. Her mother carried the washing there once a week, draping the clothes and linen over nearby bushes to dry. Washing was an all-day affair, with water for consumption brought home in old kerosene tins.[52]

The 1930s also ushered in further dispersal, more pronounced amongst those who had previously relocated to Flinders Island. It was at this time that all of Herbert Beedon's children left the Furneaux Islands to settle in Launceston. On Cape Barren Island families tended to move around and set up hessian tents and brush windbreaks wherever there was a supply of fresh water. When the water ran dry they moved on to another location. The basic staples for the majority of families were damper, potatoes and mutton-bird. They continued to gather other seasonal resources, and a substitute for the strong tea which the islanders (and their forebears) favoured was made locally and cheaply by boiling the leaves of tea-tree (*Leptospermum sp.*). When potatoes ran out the islanders managed on soda bread, a mixture of flour and water with a small amount of baking soda thrown in to make it rise. If milk was unaffordable, infants were fed with another flour and water substitute known as lily pea.[53]

Given the conditions which they were often forced to endure it is not surprising that the islanders were plagued by a host of medical problems. In the aftermath of the First World War the men who had gone away to fight brought back with them Spanish influenza, the most virulent form of influenza ever known. In the global pandemic of 1918–19 it claimed more lives than the previous four years of warfare. How many Cape Barren islanders died from the virus is not known; the ill were taken to hospitals in Launceston and Scottsdale. Another influenza epidemic struck the island in 1926, killing at least 12 people — eight in the month of June alone.[54] In 1934 the community also experienced an epidemic of poliomyelitis, with six people, mostly children, dying from the disease in August. Others were left permanently crippled, one of whom was Jimmy Maynard, who later gained local fame as a maker of guitars.[55] This epidemic prompted the State government to pay the medical practitioner on Flinders Island an annual fee to visit the islander community on a quarterly basis.[56]

Islanders, particularly the young, also died from tetanus, meningitis, measles, diphtheria and whooping cough, while tuberculosis became and remained the most serious health problem of all.[57] It was still claiming victims well into the 1990s.[58] The majority of these illnesses were once again a consequence of dire poverty, and until the permanent stationing of bush nurses on Cape Barren Island from 1939 even obtaining medical assistance was difficult. There were two methods, the most sophisticated of which was for the schoolteacher to contact the doctor at Whitemark on Flinders Island by Morse code and hope that weather conditions would allow medical assistance to arrive in time. The islanders' own method, equally dependent on weather conditions, was by smoke signal. One puff of smoke meant that someone was ill while two puffs indicated that a doctor was required. Three puffs signalled that it was too late for help.[59] Doctors on Flinders Island did their best. After Theodore Barrett was seriously injured when thrown from a horse in January 1936, Dr Heck Ewan made the trip across to Cape Barren Island in what was described as 'boisterous' conditions.[60] Like their Aboriginal forebears the islanders relied heavily on bush remedies which reputedly alleviated or even cured many maladies. Another legacy of the past was their heightened superstition. When lightning and thunder was about they made sure to cover all mirrors and wrap cutlery in tea towels. The islanders believed strongly in the spirit world and feared the twilight hours. If they were forced to travel at night through necessity the islanders whistled constantly to keep the evil spirits at bay.[61]

When death finally came calling, however, the burial practices of the Cape Barren islanders differed considerably from those of the Aboriginal past. Rather than customary cremation, deceased islanders were interred. The interior of the pine coffins were varnished with a dark oak stain and covered with calico, which was also used as a shroud to cover the body of the deceased almost to the chin. Buttonholes of wildflowers were placed on the shroud, and as the mourners filed past the body they lightly touched the forehead and removed one of the buttonholes of flowers to later press in the family bible. Wreaths and crosses made from wildflowers were also placed around the sides of the coffin. Mourners followed the hearse on foot as it slowly made its way from the church to the cemetery, and before the grave was filled the immediate family threw in either a wreath or a cross. All the family of the deceased wore black: the men black armbands and the women black frocks, and black would continue to be worn for six months after the funeral. During the mourning period all dances and other forms of entertainment were suspended. If the deceased was a child, the family wore deep purple, and it was a brave islander indeed who was prepared to venture past a cemetery at night. Fear of the dead was universal.[62]

Despite this divergence from the Aboriginal past, women continued the customary practice of gathering shells and stringing them into necklaces. The best shells are collected from kelp fronds and it was (and still is) a lengthy process. The shells are initially put aside in a tin for 12 months to allow the animal to rot away. They are then washed and dried before soaking in diluted spirits of salt to bring out their often exquisite colours. The shells were originally strung onto wallaby and kangaroo tail sinews; in the post-contact period strong cotton gained favour.[63] Shell necklaces are not everyday wearing apparel; just as in the past they are only worn on important occasions, particularly those of cultural significance.[64]And just as in customary

Aboriginal societies, it was the women and girls who continued to bear the brunt of work on Cape Barren Island during the twentieth century. It fell to the lot of the females to cut and split firewood as well as undertaking all domestic chores such as cooking, washing and cleaning. Women also dug out the white clay at Sandpit Beach known as 'pug' for whitewashing their dwellings as well as the 'birding' sheds on the outer islands. During the 1930s the men brought home dole vouchers for their work on council projects, but did very little else outside the mutton-bird season. Even on the mutton-birding islands it was women who did the bulk of the work in the sheds, and although there were exceptions to the rule, it was usually women who headed their respective households. As such it was they who made the primary decisions affecting their families. Mothers, rather than fathers, were the disciplinarians when it came to wayward children.[65]

For all that, quite a number of the men owned small fishing boats which they generally built themselves. Keels were made from Oyster Bay Pine (*Callitris rhomboidea*), locally known as Cape Barren Pine, with construction usually taking around 12 months to complete. The wood was left in the littoral zone and turned daily until the salt water and air had shrunk it to the required size. It then underwent a lengthy drying period before building even commenced. By the 1930s, though, the islanders' expertise as small boatmen was already well on the wane. The last keel was laid around 1940.[66]

From the mid-1920s the Tasmanian government decided there was no longer any need for a resident police constable on Cape Barren Island. As the nearest full-time police officers were stationed at Whitemark on Flinders Island, there still had to be some form of law enforcement to deal with any immediate problems within the community. The solution was not difficult to find. When Norman Hawkins took up the position of schoolteacher in 1928 he also found himself appointed as a special constable and paid a separate salary by the police department, a practice that was to be continued.[67] From the time of Edward Stephens it had been usual for schoolteachers to simultaneously perform bailiff duties for the department of lands as well as conducting Sunday services in lieu of an ordained minister. As the only residents on the island with an accomplished education and a fixed, secure and regular income, the schoolteachers regarded themselves as socially above the islanders and rarely mixed with members of the community. Hawkins deviated slightly owing to his penchant for films, regularly screening silent movies for the community, particularly the slapstick comedy of Charlie Chaplin. All teachers appointed to Cape Barren Island were married men whose wives were often qualified teachers themselves and taught the lower grades as well as domestic science to the older girls. Although some of their children were taught at the Cape Barren School, others were sent away to boarding schools on the Tasmanian mainland.[68]

A number of islander children were also sent away — but not to boarding schools. In 1931 Hawkins arranged for the forced removal of three girls named Downie who lived with their grandfather. In the schoolteacher's view the grandfather was incapable of caring for the girls and all three were sent to a government girl's home. The grandfather was illiterate, and while he did sign the consent form with a cross it remains questionable whether the children's carer was really aware of what he was signing.[69] Islander children continued to be sent to government institutions and white foster homes well into the 1960s — ostensibly for 'neglect'[70] — though it needs to be borne in mind that none of these children were removed on the basis of their Aboriginality which, of course, the government consistently refused to recognise.[71] What the case involving the Downie girls in 1931 does clearly demonstrate is the power that schoolteachers on Cape Barren Island were able to wield over at least some members of the community. Norman Hawkins, though, wanted a virtual dictatorship.

In 1933 the schoolteacher claimed that the islanders were pampered and wished to be treated as minors, and yet, at the same time, they demanded full citizenship and the franchise. In Hawkins's estimation they were 'mentally defective' and 'human parasites' who were holding themselves back. He dismissed any criticism of his actions and comments from members of the community by insisting that his opponents were 'wasters', particularly JC Everett, his most vocal critic. Hawkins believed that he alone could solve all the problems on Cape Barren Island if he was appointed as a full-time administrator. His idea was to put the islanders to work on a quasi-feudal basis and force them to pay rates and local taxes. Hawkins sought the authority to prosecute parents who failed to send their children to school and to enter the homes of islanders without their permission or a warrant. The schoolteacher wanted to control their movements and to banish offenders from the island, and to accomplish his aims he believed that a little back-up might be useful. To that end he requested a gun. Fortunately, the Tasmanian government declined Hawkins' generous offer of an insular dictatorship. But he continued as schoolteacher for another four years.[72]

Hawkins's successor in 1937, Gerald Smyth, was remembered by former pupils as a strict disciplinarian who caned both boys and girls for the most minor infringements of the rules. On one occasion he was offended by a boy's 'dirty' leg and set to work cleaning it with a scrubbing brush and sandsoap until the blood began to flow. It was only then that he realised it was actually the lad's dark skin.[73] As the only resident government representative, it also fell to the schoolteachers to administer the dole scheme in the 1930s. GE Maynard was refused sustenance by Smyth on the grounds that he had refused to work. While that may or may not have been the case, it could be relevant that Maynard was by then a leading agitator in the community, regularly forwarding letters and petitions to politicians calling for a better deal.[74] Unlike Hawkins and Smyth, later schoolteachers were often remembered with some affection.

Very little work was done on Cape Barren Island on Sundays, the community strictly observing God's rest day. All the islanders belonged to the Church of England, with children attending Sunday school in the morning and accompanying their parents to church later in the afternoon.[75] Social events featured regularly in islander life. Football was played by men and boys in the winter, and dances were held every Saturday night;[76] dance competitions became particularly popular after the public hall was opened in September 1936. Music was important, and in the 1930s it was the Brown brothers who usually provided the entertainment on a range of musical instruments, including guitars made by Jimmy Maynard. The Browns are said to have later made a recording of Cape Barren Island music,[77] and music in all its many genres has continued to be a powerful unifying force within the islander community.[78]

Major sporting events were held on Boxing Day, including wood-chopping, running, sack, three-legged and blindfold races, the highlight of which was the men's one-mile race. While horse racing was held at various times throughout the year the premier occasion was again on Boxing Day, a special feature being races between male and female riders. They might have been the depression years with most islander families struggling, but substantial bets were often wagered on the outcomes.[79] And just as at home, women played a pivotal role in organising sports — right down to making the jackets and caps for the jockeys and even erecting the barriers for horse races.[80]

Children were not surprisingly involved in all these activities, and yet despite strong Christian convictions, Easter was never celebrated on Cape Barren Island. The high point of the calendar for children was Christmas Eve, and when a fire appeared on Home Hill it signalled their retirement to bed. The fire, of course, was held to be the work of Santa Claus,[81] and the tradition of a fire on Home Hill continued until recent years.[82] Some of those children later remembered the politicians who made fleeting visits to their island home and threw boiled lollies in the dirt, hoping to watch the children scramble after them. It was a wasted exercise: parents refused to allow the children to touch them.[83] Pride was similarly reflected in the two football teams on Cape Barren Island in the 1930s and 1940s. One team comprised married men, the other singles, with the best players from both teams selected to play against Flinders Island. The inter-island competition was organised on a fortnightly basis, with each team taking turns to cross Franklin Sound and play the opposition.[84]

In 1935 the Australian State governments were requested to take a count of all Aborigines within their borders for the Commonwealth Bureau of Census and Statistics. Tasmania was uncertain how to proceed as the islanders were not recognised as 'Aboriginal'. The bureau was finally advised that there were no 'full-blooded Aborigines' in Tasmania, which explains why no Tasmanian representative attended the Commonwealth Conference on Assimilation two years later. That conference endorsed the assimilation of Aborigines into wider Australian society, a policy that was initially delayed owing to the outbreak of World War Two. The first official announcement made by the Tasmanian government regarding the status of the islander community came in 1940, when they were classified as 'octoroons' and therefore not Aboriginal people as it was understood at the time.[85]

The classification had much to do with the results of the Harvard–Adelaide Universities Anthropological Expedition of 1938–39, which itself was a product of growing concern in Australia. In the late nineteenth and early twentieth centuries there was a widespread Social Darwinian belief that 'full-blood' Aborigines were destined to slowly die out. As they were held to be racially pure but 'inferior' they were segregated on reserves to 'smooth the dying pillow' until their eventual demise. Their resilience fortunately ensured that extinction did not come to pass, but to the dismay of policy makers in the 1930s it was found that the part-Aboriginal population was actually on the increase.[86] Segregation had clearly been ineffectual, and there were two over-arching concerns. One was whether Aboriginal blood could be effectively 'bred out' through assimilation into the white community, and whether inter-marriage and assimilation would have any detrimental impact on the white population. It was not just about pigmentation: fears were also held that it might result in defective intellects and physical traits. The 1920s and 1930s were also the golden years of eugenics, when determined efforts were underway to 'improve' the white race, so the 'Aboriginal problem' was of considerable national concern.[87]

Among scientists probing for answers to this dilemma were the South Australian anthropologist Norman Tindale and his American colleague, Joseph Birdsell, a population geneticist. From May 1938 they made a wide ranging investigation of 'half-caste' populations across Australia and in January 1939 the pair made landfall on Cape Barren Island. Birdsell set to work collecting blood samples, taking anthropometric measurements and recording the physical characteristics of the islanders. Tindale used his anthropological expertise to document the islanders' genealogies and ethnology, the results of both researchers compared for accuracy. Tindale was provided with information concerning illegitimate and incestuous relationships which themselves were of some concern to a few members of the community, notably Ted Summers and GE Brown.[88]

The conclusion reached by the Harvard–Adelaide Universities Anthropological Expedition was that out-marriage into the white population would dilute the supposedly defective Aboriginal characteristics without any deleterious effects on white partners or the children of mixed unions. Tindale, in fact, was adamant that the islanders were already 'white people' with just 'a dark strain running through them'.[89] So, too, did a number of islanders, who wanted government assistance to leave the Furneaux Islands and make a new start on the Tasmanian mainland. Others, though, remembered the visit as particularly demeaning. Physical examinations by Birdsell and Tindale left them feeling as if they were nothing more than unusual zoological specimens.[90] Another off-shoot of the expedition was that Birdsell gathered additional evidence to support his 'tri-hybrid theory' of the Aboriginal colonisation of Australia, comparing the physical traits of the islanders with those of the rainforest Aborigines of north-east Queensland.[91] Importantly, the work of Tindale and Birdsell contributed to the Commonwealth policy of assimilation, and although it was held in abeyance owing to the outbreak of World War Two, that global conflict proved to be a major turning point for the islanders of Bass Strait.

As in 1914–18, at least 20 islander men once again enlisted for active service, and under the Manpower Regulations later introduced by the Curtin Federal government many others, both men and women, were drafted into industry. Some worked in Melbourne, but most were employed on the Tasmanian mainland at Hobart, Launceston, Burnie, and even at Roseberry and Queenstown on the west coast. Still others left Cape Barren Island to seek work in Launceston, a trend that was to continue over the next two decades, with many islanders settling in and around Invermay, at that time one of Launceston's poorest suburbs.[92] At the age of 14 Molly Mallett also left Cape Barren, first moving with her family to Lady Barron on Flinders Island where she worked in a fish canning factory. Twelve months later they left the Furneaux Islands for Launceston, where like many other islander girls Molly Mallett found work at Coats Paton's Woollen Mills. At the height of production the company employed up to 1000 people split into four shifts.[93]

By 1944 the population of Cape Barren Island had fallen from nearly 300 to 106, and as the Tasmanian government continued to deny the islanders their Aboriginality the decision was taken to revoke the reserve. In 1945 the government passed another *Cape Barren Island Reserve Act*, the provisions of which cancelled the reserve status as of 1951 — coincidentally the year that the Commonwealth government's assimilation policy came into effect. Members of the island community were thus given six years to make improvements to their existing holdings to the value of not less than £1 per acre. Having satisfied those requirements they became eligible to receive the land as a free grant.[94] The alternative was to relocate to the Tasmanian mainland where they were assured that economic opportunities awaited them.[95] Birdsell and Tindale's recommendations were clearly being brought to fruition. To all intent the islanders were now regarded as white people, something which had always been denied them in the past.

No sooner had the legislation been passed, however, than 19 families suddenly found that their leaseholds had been cancelled. And over the following years government expenditure on Cape Barren Island dwindled to a trickle as a means of placing additional pressure on the islanders to leave. The school remained open, but the small hospital operated by the bush nurses soon closed its doors. To the great disappointment of the government, few of the remaining people showed any inclination to depart their island home.[96] After press reports in 1947 that the islanders were living in squalor, the government launched yet another official inquiry into conditions on Cape Barren Island.

Members of the parliamentary select committee confirmed that the islanders — whose numbers had now risen to 130 — were indeed living in abject poverty, owing to the absence of regular employment and almost total dependence on the short mutton-bird season. There was nothing new in any of this. Not surprisingly, the committee could find no means of stimulating the local economy, and members dismissed claims that the islanders were a 'special people' whose Aboriginal ancestry should be recognised. On the contrary, the committee came to the conclusion that the islanders would have to leave Cape Barren Island for the Tasmanian mainland, where they could be absorbed into the general population. For the sake of the islanders themselves, the reserve would simply have to be closed down.[97]

By the time it ceased to exist in 1951, 35 leases had been taken out but only one family had qualified for a free land grant — and they appeared to be in no hurry to take it up. The legal disappearance of the reserve initially meant little, as the residents simply remained on their land: seven years later, in 1958, there were still 120 islanders living on the former reserve land. They continued to resist every move by the government to shift them, refusing to cooperate with welfare authorities and health department officials who occasionally came knocking on their doors.[98] For those who did relocate the reality of opportunity was not what they had been led to expect. Men usually only found low-paid jobs, particularly on the railways, while women generally worked as poorly paid factory hands. With little money, the islanders continued to rent in Launceston's cheaper suburbs such as Invermay and Mayfield, and there were more than a few occasions when even rental accommodation was difficult to come by when real estate agents discovered their island origins. Others faced eviction when relatives stayed too long or white neighbours complained about their activities. Discrimination extended to sluggish service in shops and hotels.[99]

Yet despite these problems more and more islanders were forced to resettle in mainland Tasmania by the mid-1960s as a consequence of government neglect, lack of employment and, perhaps more importantly, a run of poor mutton-bird seasons. Cape Barren Island was itself undergoing change. In 1960 a 16 000-hectare cattle run which included part of the former reserve was established in the Modder River district by an outsider. The islanders were offered good money for their leaseholds, and having no other prospects many sold out. For the 50 or so islanders who remained, fear was a constant companion. Many believed that if they vacated their land for even a brief period the government was likely to take it over.[100]

In 1968 Flinders Island Council made an attempt to have the remaining islanders removed by the Tasmanian government. Calling for the establishment of another parliamentary select committee to investigate the future potential of Cape Barren Island, the municipal authority argued that there was somewhere between 20 000 and 24 000 hectares of prime pastoral land and at least another 240 hectares suitable for agriculture. The State government nevertheless equivocated, maintaining that the islanders would leave voluntarily if attractive inducements were held out to them. For that reason Tasmania's Chief Secretary, Brian Miller, attended a Commonwealth and State conference on Aboriginal Affairs in July 1968. This was a major turnaround. The State government had previously denied the existence of any Aborigines and now it was seeking Commonwealth Aboriginal funding to resettle the islanders in either Hobart or Launceston. Nor were Miller's efforts entirely unsuccessful: he managed to extract $25 000 from the Commonwealth to assist with housing the islanders in Tasmania's two major cities.[101]

On Cape Barren Island, however, resistance to the government's overtures continued. Opinion on the islander question was polarised within the State. Many whites had little time for the islanders and many islanders felt the same towards whites, with both groups having supporters from the opposite side. By the middle of 1969 students from the University of Tasmania had also become increasingly vocal in their condemnation of the government's policy of pressuring the islanders to leave Cape Barren. By then the Liberals were in government, having brought an end to a quarter of a century of Labor domination in Tasmanian politics. At first the new government pursued the same course as its predecessor, but change was in the air. The Liberal government appointed a Launceston-based 'resettlement officer' to provide assistance to islanders who had made the move to the Tasmanian mainland in regard to housing and social security. The salary of this appointed official as well as the relocation of islander families came from Commonwealth funding, which was not entirely to the liking of the Commonwealth government.[102]

Following 12 months of squabbling between the two levels of government the title of 'resettlement officer' was altered to 'community advisor' and henceforth they were stationed permanently on Cape Barren Island.[103] This was an extraordinary development. In 1970 a Tasmanian government official in Launceston was expected to encourage the islanders to leave Cape Barren Island; one year later that same official was living on Cape Barren Island and encouraging the islanders to remain where they were. It was no accident that this dramatic policy shift coincided with a greater appreciation of Aboriginal (and Torres Strait Islander) issues within broader Australian society — as well as the emergence of Indigenous activism which, *inter alia*, promoted a separate identity. In 1964 the Commonwealth government initiated Abschol, Aboriginal scholarships designed to assist Indigenous Australians to achieve a higher education. Abschol also played a prominent role in the emerging activism, and in August 1971 it organised an Aboriginal conference in Launceston which attracted 200 islanders from all parts of Tasmania. On the second day of proceedings the participants agreed to push for full title to the former reserve land on Cape Barren Island. Taking it even further they demanded title to the entire island.[104] It was a sign of things to come, with the stakes now rising rapidly.

14

THE RESURGENCE OF TASMANIAN ABORIGINALITY

The early 1970s thus saw a convergence of two significant strands: the use of Commonwealth funds to redevelop Cape Barren Island, and a claim on that land by the modern Tasmanian Aboriginal community. Redevelopment essentially meant implementing local projects to employ the remaining islanders. Vegetation was cleared — particularly the noxious weed known as boxthorn — which had colonised large areas of Cape Barren. The islanders improved roads, installed concrete water tanks, constructed a retaining wall and tidied up the neglected war memorial and cemetery. A dam was built and facilities at the school upgraded and improved. By the end of 1973 the community advisor had also formed an island council, though this created division among the 90-odd islander residents, roughly one half of whom were children. Some of the adults regarded the continuing presence of a government official as yet another example of imposed external control, while others viewed it as proof that the government was genuinely concerned for their welfare and that positive outcomes would result.[1]

An initiative of Abschol, the Aboriginal Information Service (AIS) was established at Hobart in November 1972 to provide legal advice and general assistance to Tasmanian Aboriginal people in trouble with policing authorities. The first State Secretary (1972–75) was Rosalind Langford, an Aboriginal woman from New South Wales.[2] After the service began receiving both Commonwealth and State funding it was able to acquire its own office and employ larger numbers of Aboriginal people. A hostel was also opened, and in 1973 another State-wide conference on Tasmanian Aboriginal affairs attracted hundreds of participants, with discussions resulting in the opening of an AIS office in Launceston.[3]

Four years later — in 1977 — the service was renamed the Tasmanian Aboriginal Centre (TAC), with regional branches opened in Burnie and the Huon Valley. Amidst this resurgence of Aboriginality the term 'islander' faded from use, with the emphasis thereafter falling on maternal rather than paternal origins. Formal branch meetings identified key issues confronting the modern Aboriginal community, with discussions centring on finding practical solutions. The TAC also broadened its scope. While continuing to provide legal assistance, social welfare and family support services were added to its repertoire. Craft afternoons focusing on customary Aboriginal activities began to be held on a regular basis, while an unemployment scheme and adult education programs were introduced. A housing committee was formed to take responsibility for dwellings rented to Aboriginal people by the State Housing Department.[4]

The strength of Aboriginal resurgence was reflected in the increasing number of people openly identifying as Aboriginal. In the 1971 census 671 people claimed Aboriginality: at the next census in 1976 the figure rose to 2942.[5] Although white Australian attitudes were simultaneously undergoing a sympathetic shift, the Aboriginal community was confronted in 1978 by the release of Tom Haydon's film, *The Last Tasmanian*, which seemingly implied that the death of Truganini in May 1876 marked the end of the Aboriginal presence in Tasmania.[6] In many ways, then, Haydon's film was an important adjunct to the struggle for the recognition of Aboriginality in Tasmania. Its emphasis on 'extinction' became a *cause celebre*, with the Tasmanian Aboriginal community branding it a racist and denialist account of their very existence. That was not Haydon's intention, which was specifically aimed at highlighting the level of violence unleashed against the Aborigines by British colonists in the nineteenth century.[7] Nor can it be denied that in just seven decades the original societies and the people who comprised them had been effectively destroyed. Indeed, the acceptance of Aboriginality by their descendants is a relatively recent phenomenon. As popular writer Patsy Adam Smith found in the 1950s and 1960s, descendants invariably referred to themselves as 'islanders' or 'straitsmen', deliberately avoiding the label 'Aborigine'.[8] Two descendants who appeared in *The Last Tasmanian* similarly denied their Aboriginality, with the independent film producer accused of purposely selecting them to reinforce the idea that the Tasmanian Aborigines had indeed disappeared off the face of the earth.[9] On the contrary, Haydon chose both Annette Mansell (a cousin of leading Tasmanian Aboriginal activist Michael Mansell) and Melvyn Everett solely because of their standing within the community. Annette Mansell was then President of the Cape Barren Island community, and her comment in the film that 'there's a hell of a difference' between the original Aboriginal people and their descendants is quite pertinent. Recognising that a number of cultural activities had been passed down through the generations Everett's statement that 'it's only history what we've learnt' is exactly the source which is drawn on by modern Aboriginal Tasmanians to recreate what has been lost — albeit, not always critically or accurately.[10] For better or worse, *The Last Tasmanian* made an important contribution by disseminating information about the historic treatment of the Tasmanian Aborigines to a wider public and, at the same time, provided a springboard for the modern Aboriginal community to assert their survival.

By arguing that the Aborigines had not become extinct the TAC's tactic was to place land rights — specifically prior ownership and the control of Aboriginal heritage sites — at the forefront of its agenda. Under the guiding hands of Rosalind Langford and Michael Mansell those campaigns resulted in the TAC becoming one of the most significant Aboriginal organisations in Australia, encouraging active participation by all community members who were kept fully informed on developments through a newsletter, *Pungunna News*. Finances were carefully controlled, thus ensuring that the TAC avoided financial extinction following a penetrating audit by the Commonwealth government in 1987.[11]

The first foray into land rights came in 1974, when the TAC presented a submission to the Woodward Committee of Inquiry. The following year the organisation placed its weight behind the campaign for the return of Truganini's ashes to the Aboriginal community,[12] though it is conveniently forgotten that the genesis of this initiative lay with the mainland Aboriginal activist, Burnum Burnum.[13] Land rights nevertheless returned to the forefront in December 1977 when Michael Mansell managed to skirt a security cordon at Wrest Point Casino in an attempt to present Queen Elizabeth II with a petition demanding the recognition of prior Aboriginal land ownership during the royal visit to Hobart.[14] This incident, and the police harassment which followed, catapulted Tasmanian Aboriginal activism onto the national stage. The Nielsen government had already suffered embarrassment the previous month when the TAC emulated the Canberra example and erected a tent embassy in front of Hobart's parliament house where a list of land claims ranging from Cape Barren Island to archaeological and historically significant sites as well as all unalienated Crown land were presented.[15] The Tasmanian government responded by establishing an Aboriginal Affairs Study Group in 1978, charged with the task of investigating the TAC's demands as well as the mutton-bird industry on which many community members continued to depend. The Study Group, comprising government bureaucrats and representatives from the TAC, was further instructed to make recommendations for the social development of the modern Tasmanian Aboriginal community.[16]

Relations within the group quickly became strained when the chairman refused to acknowledge the continuity of Aboriginality, referring to the TAC representatives as 'hybrids'. The TAC withdrew from further discussions. It came as no real surprise, then, that when the Study Group completed its investigations it recommended that ancient Aboriginal sites, including the petroglyphs of north-west Tasmania, should be protected by government legislation, the *Aboriginal Relics Act* passed in 1975, rather than the Aboriginal community. To make their position even clearer, the group insisted that 'common and historical sites', such as those on the mutton-bird islands, should fall completely within the jurisdiction of the newly created Aboriginal Lands Trust.[17]

Draft legislation granting an extremely limited form of land rights finally emerged in 1981, but before anything concrete happened a major clash erupted between conservationists and the Hydro-Electric Commission over the proposed Gordon-below-Franklin dam in Tasmania's remote south-west. The TAC initially distanced itself from the Tasmanian Wilderness Society and other conservation groups owing to their concept of 'wilderness', which denied any prior Aboriginal occupation. That stance radically altered when the discovery of cave deposits bearing unmistakeable evidence of the Aboriginal presence extending back thousands of years drew the TAC into the campaign as an ally of the conservationists.[18] Construction of the dam would have effectively destroyed this rich Aboriginal heritage.

With the very real possibility of securing land rights in Tasmania's south-west the TAC gave its full support to archaeologists, only to alter its stance yet again when it was discovered that Aborigines had abandoned the region around 11 000 years ago and there had been no continuity down to historical times. The archaeologists suddenly became demons. Moreover, the TAC successfully gained possession of the artefacts which had been recovered during excavations. Their fate remains unknown, and if they were not destroyed their provenance is now seriously compromised. In 1994, for example, artefacts dating from around 17 000 years ago were excavated by archaeologists from the University of Western Australia in Tasmania's King River Valley which was to be inundated with the construction of a dam. The artefacts were returned to the Aboriginal community and subsequently thrown into the waters of the newly created lake 'to heal the site', an act of cultural vandalism bereft of any logical meaning. Importantly, this irresponsible action effectively denied future generations of Aboriginal people access to their heritage. As it transpired the Gordon-below-Franklin dam project did not go ahead when the newly elected Hawke government in Canberra fulfilled its promise to have the region listed as World Heritage.[19]

In 1984 the TAC occupied Oyster Cove south of Hobart and the site of the last Aboriginal Establishment, declaring that it belonged to the Aboriginal community and had been neglected while under the control of the National Parks and Wildlife Service. To increase the site's significance the TAC cremated Aboriginal skeletal remains which had been returned to the community from museums in Hobart and Launceston.[20] Oyster Cove had been the homeland of few, if any, of the Aboriginal people who had been cremated on the site and it was almost certainly enemy territory to many. Despite that, the TAC received strong support from the Commonwealth government in its bid for control of Oyster Cove. The State government, on the other hand, refused to budge. In 1986 the Commonwealth sought to break the deadlock by offering its State counterpart the old quarantine station on Bruny Island (which was under federal jurisdiction) in exchange for 30 hectares of land at Oyster Cove. At the same time the Commonwealth agreed to hand back its control of Swan Island off the north-east tip of Tasmania in exchange for a number of mutton-birding islands, all of which would then be returned to the Aboriginal community. Identifying these Commonwealth initiatives as little more than 'land rights by stealth' the Tasmanian government refused to negotiate.[21]

As the TAC had been effectively locked out of all these discussions the organisation embarked on a campaign for the recognition of Aboriginal sovereignty, and the establishment of a separate Aboriginal nation. It was an idea which found little support within the wider Australian community, and the TAC decided to take it offshore in April–May 1987 by seeking support from Libyan dictator Moamar al Gaddafi. Michael Mansell became the public face in this extraordinary episode, although he later claimed that he was thrust into the role only after the original TAC representative discovered their passport was invalid at the last minute. According to Mansell he was the twelfth member of the organisation who was contacted, and the first who possessed a valid passport. He agreed to go.[22] Libya gave recognition to Mansell's alternative Aboriginal passport the following year, and it was his provocative actions which resulted in the Commonwealth suspending further funding for the TAC and conducting a penetrating audit of the organisation's finances.[23]

Although no discrepancies were uncovered, Mansell's association with the Gaddafi regime aroused a considerable degree of paranoia within Australia. He played the publicity card to maximum effect. After arriving back in Australia Mansell announced his intention of returning to Libya in the near future to obtain financial assistance. In response the Commonwealth government threatened to withdraw its support for Aboriginal land claims in Tasmania, and Mansell inflamed the situation even further by stating that he would request Libya to impose economic sanctions against Australia by refusing to accept live sheep imports until Aboriginal sovereignty was recognised.[24]

Many viewed Mansell's actions as nothing short of 'treasonable', but they certainly achieved results for the Tasmanian Aboriginal community.[25] In 1988 Tasmania's Minister for Ethnic Affairs, Ray Groom, declared that his government recognised the Aboriginal community as a legitimate ethnic minority, and the following year he offered the TAC the opportunity to open an Aboriginal cultural centre at Oyster Cove. The Labor Opposition took these concessions even further by insisting that they were fully committed to returning several sites considered sacred to the Aboriginal community's control, and when they won government in 1990 Premier Michael Field pushed ahead with lands rights legislation.[26] Now in opposition, the Liberals were not prepared to let it go that far, and while debates continued Michael Mansell joined with mainland Aboriginal activists to form an Aboriginal Provisional Government (APG) in July 1991. They again sought official recognition of Aboriginal sovereignty, an idea that was still too ambitious for the time. When members of the TAC itself began to criticise their association with the APG Mansell began distancing himself from the national body to refocus on local issues.[27]

An Aboriginal Land Rights Bill was introduced in the Tasmanian Legislative Assembly in April 1991, with the intention of returning

21 areas of Crown land totalling 53 000 hectares to the Aboriginal community. Opposition spokesman John Barker reiterated the Liberal party's belief that Aboriginal land rights could only have a negative divisive impact on Tasmania, arguing that the Cape Barren Island community was also opposed to land rights on the basis that it would give the TAC too much power over them.[28] They were right, thus demonstrating the customary lack of consensus among Aboriginal Tasmanians who were never one united social entity. As it turned out the Bill passed through the Legislative Assembly with support from Green Independents only to come to grief in the Legislative Council.[29]

In February 1992 the Liberals under Ray Groom returned to power and pushed land rights off the agenda altogether, but there could be no denying that the strength of the Tasmanian Aboriginal community was continuing to grow. In the previous year's census 8948 people had identified as Aboriginal, and this steady growth was reflected within the TAC itself. In 1974 the organisation had been staffed by just six people; in 1991 staff numbers had increased to 25, and the following year a substantial building was purchased in Hobart to serve as TAC headquarters.[30]

Throughout this period the TAC continued to fight for the repatriation of Tasmanian Aboriginal skeletal remains. In 1990 the organisation played a key role in the return of William Lanne's severed head along with the remains of eight other Tasmanian Aborigines held in the collections of Scotland's Edinburgh University. They almost failed to make it back to Tasmania due to inept bungling. A squabble erupted between the TAC and the National Museum of Australia over who should rightly have custodianship over the remains. The Australian High Commission in London sided with the TAC and then its envoys lost the remains at Heathrow Airport. The setback was only brief, however, as they were eventually located in quarantine and flown back to Hobart.[31] This conflict was unusual at the time as it was widely accepted that there were no longer any moral, ethical or scientific grounds for retaining Aboriginal skeletal material from the recent past. But the National Museum of Australia was a new institution with not much of a collection of anything.

Division was equally apparent within the Tasmanian Aboriginal community. The concern of the Cape Barren Island residents with the growing power of the TAC in 1991 had long been foreshadowed by the Flinders Island Aboriginal Association (FIAA), formed in 1973. In the early 1970s non-Aboriginal residents of the island had largely ignored the presence among them of people who readily identified as Aboriginal. Given their neglect, the Association was specifically established to convey issues directly affecting the Aboriginal residents to the local municipal authority as well as the State and Commonwealth governments. The constitution also included a call for Aboriginal land rights, in this instance title to the historic Aboriginal Establishment site at Wybalenna.[32]

The Association increasingly distanced itself from the TAC, which it regarded as monopolistic and dismissive of purely local issues. In 1993, and on behalf of the FIAA, Ruby Roughley began proceedings in the High Court of Australia against both the Tasmanian and Commonwealth governments for the return of Wybalenna to the Flinders Island Aboriginal community. Although the case did not advance to a formal hearing it proved to be an effective means of moving forward with negotiations for the return of the site. Three years later an agreement was jointly signed by the FIAA and Flinders Island Council, whereby the latter gave its support to the aspirations of the local Aboriginal community, an accord that has since become known as the Treaty of Whitemark.[33]

This action by the FIAA also served as an inspiration for other Aboriginal groups throughout Tasmania to commence their own campaigns regarding local issues, a move that was given added stimulus by the 1995 Federal Court judgement that there was no real way of determining just who was an Aborigine in Tasmania. This ruling allowed a number of other self-identifying groups to break away from the control of the TAC to pursue their own agendas — a good example being the Lia Pootah's challenge for control over the Risdon Cove Historic Site. The power of the TAC was nevertheless amply demonstrated by its success in winning the struggle, albeit, leaving bitter recriminations in its wake.[34]

In 1995 the leasehold of a large section of Clarke Island in Bass Strait was purchased by the Aboriginal Land Council of Tasmania (an adjunct of the TAC), with an area set aside for troubled Aboriginal youths to undergo a program based on cultural experience as an alternative to formal sentencing.[35] The young of the past were also placed on the Tasmanian government's agenda in August 1997, when parliament unanimously supported a Statement of Apology expressing acknowledgement of, and regret for, the forced removal of Tasmanian Aboriginal children from their families.[36] That policy, of course, had not been racially based as Aboriginality had been consistently denied by successive governments at the time. The apology, however, was addressed in practical terms in late 2006, when Tasmania became the first Australian State to offer a compensation scheme for members of the 'Stolen Generation'.[37] The financial package amounting to $4 million was to some extent tempered by an amendment made to the *Aboriginal Lands Act* in June 2005 which substantially narrowed the definition of Aboriginality in Tasmania. Unlike their counterparts on the mainland of Australia, Tasmanian Aborigines must produce proof of their ancestry in addition to self-identification and recognition by the community.[38]

On 18 April 1999 the Bacon Labor government returned the title of Wybalenna to the FIAA,[39] and before standing down as premier in

2004 due to terminal illness, Jim Bacon set in motion plans for the return of Cape Barren, Clarke and Goose Islands to the Aboriginal community. This was warmly welcomed by the 70-odd residents of Cape Barren Island,[40] whose very presence stood as mute testimony of the strength of their determination to resist the assimilatory policies of past Tasmanian governments. Today, members of the Tasmanian Aboriginal community have achieved considerable success in many walks of life, though they still represent a small minority of the total population. That is why calls by Michael Mansell in June 2010 to have three seats in the Tasmanian parliament reserved for Aboriginal representatives have not been successful.[41] Such a demand also overlooks the divisiveness within modern Tasmanian Aboriginal society which has been well documented by Kathy Marks,[42] and despite Mansell's label of 'white fellas' the Lia Pootah and other marginal Aboriginal groups refuse to go away. In February 2007 the Lia Pootah were particularly vocal in their condemnation of the TAC's efforts to repatriate Aboriginal skeletal remains held by the British Museum of Natural History as a complete 'waste of money'.[43]

This criticism arose after the Commonwealth government had agreed to pay the legal costs for a TAC challenge in the British High Court, as well as any costs incurred if the case was lost.[44] It did not need to go so far. The Museum of Natural History finally agreed to hand over the remains of 17 Tasmanian Aboriginal people to the Commonwealth government which, in turn, passed them to the TAC.[45] Whether the TAC should rightly have had that control is another matter again. Few would argue that the repatriation of Aboriginal remains from overseas institutions is not the correct course to take, but an issue which remains unresolved is legitimate custodianship. This was highlighted in 2009 when two envoys of the TAC travelled to Britain and retrieved Aboriginal remains held by London's Royal College of Surgeons and the National Museum of Scotland. Little was known of the origins and collection of skeletal material held by the latter institution, and if they were Tasmanian they could well have come from anywhere on the island.[46] A similar scenario was played out five years later when TAC took possession of two crania from a museum in Chicago without knowing where they had originally been obtained.[47] Given that there were nine socio-political groups in Tasmania who were often in conflict with each other, there is a very real possibility that the envoys were actually descendants of customary enemies. Such a prospect would have been terrifying to the living, though this is an issue that is not unique to Tasmania. The problem is a global one, and it should be receiving more attention than it has thus far.

Owing to its comparatively small geographical size and the past treatment of the Indigenous population, the question of custodianship is nonetheless very acute in Tasmania. This was shown yet again in 2009 when the TAC led a campaign to block the auction of two plaster busts of Truganini and Woorrady in Melbourne. Thirty copies of these busts, which stand approximately 75 centimetres high, were made by Benjamin Law in the 1830s. The two busts were removed from auction but later sold privately.[48] TAC representatives argued that the busts should be 'returned' to the Tasmanian Aboriginal community (effectively the TAC) as they 'perpetuate the myth that [Truganini] and Woureddy [*sic*] were the last Tasmanian Aborigines'.[49] Woorrady died in July 1842,[50] and no-one has ever asserted that he was one of the 'last Tasmanian Aborigines'. Unlike Truganini (and William Lanne), Woorrady is not particularly well known and even one academic researcher was inadvertently led to believe that he was, in fact, a woman.[51] In this instance, though, the question of custodianship becomes somewhat blurred. While the subjects were Aboriginal the artistic creations were unmistakably British. As such it is a fine line indeed, and the demands of the TAC have continued to be ignored.

There is no question that the TAC and unaligned Aboriginal Tasmanians are rightly determined to protect their heritage, and their tenacity has been exhibited on numerous occasions. In at least one instance, however, the campaign was sadly misguided. One of the problems facing archaeologists throughout the world is that any potential new discovery of great antiquity can easily fall into the hands of an uncritical media before it has been accurately assessed. In a great many cases claims have been made and just as quickly dismissed by other archaeologists using different dating techniques or more rigorous methodology. To safeguard against this, new finds are now ideally published in peer-reviewed journals and time allowed for further discussion and examination prior to any public announcement. Those safeguards were ignored in late 2009 when the preliminary results of Don Ranson's excavations on the site of proposed road works just north of Hobart entered the public domain without the necessary precautions having been taken. The resultant media frenzy proclaimed the discovery of Aboriginal artefacts dating from beyond 40 000 years,[52] claims which were understandably seized on by the TAC and other Aboriginal people as well as their supporters. If correct, this would have provided confirmation of Aboriginal occupation extending from the deep past down to historical times in the south-east, and as the site was earmarked for destruction it quickly became a target for protests — all of which, it needs to be added, were peaceful in their intent.

Less easy to understand, however, was the longevity of the protest campaign when the preliminary results of the excavation were found to be seriously flawed. Sediments rather than artefacts had been dated, and bioturbation had resulted in even post-colonial refuse filtering down to the earliest levels.[53] This was acknowledged by an Aboriginal heritage officer who was among the first to be arrested at the site for trespass. Aaron Everett insisted that post-colonial artefacts such as glass provided clear evidence of the area having 'been used for thousands of years'.[54] How European-manufactured glass can be used as evidence of Aboriginal occupation over millennia was left unexplained, but uncritical acceptance was a hallmark of the campaign, which by mid-December 2009 had already resulted in more than 40 arrests.[55] Interestingly, senior archaeologist Rob Paton 'stood in solidarity with the Aboriginal community', commenting in February 2010 that occupation at this location extended from '10 000 years up to the present'.[56] While 30 000 years had thus been eliminated from the original estimate, there was still no evidence to suggest that occupation extended even to 10 000 years.

Yet, faced with the level of protest the Tasmanian government had revised its plans by the middle of 2010 to include a 70-metre bridge to span the site and minimise damage.[57] The press continued to add fuel to the fire by maintaining that the site dated from at least 40 000 years ago,[58] thereby encouraging the TAC and non-Aboriginal supporters to call for Commonwealth intervention and to mount expensive legal action in the Supreme Court to halt further construction.[59] Although the action failed, the protest continued.[60] In November 2011, and with all other avenues blocked, a number of Aboriginal protesters who had been arrested defended their actions by claiming 'a spiritual connection to the site'. To his credit, magistrate Glenn Hay did not dismiss the defence out-of-hand, instead calling for a written submission to explain 'the extent to which their spiritual connection with the land has been affected by this construction'.[61] Veteran activist Jim Everett hailed the magistrate's request as a 'victory' for the protesters, but the claim was never going to be substantiated. The battle was clearly lost, and a smoking ceremony was subsequently held to heal the site — itself an alien concept in Aboriginal Tasmania.[62] Farce, however, characterised both sides of the debate. In December 2011 Aaron Everett and the TAC received Human Rights Awards from Governor-General Quentin Bryce for their protest actions. A bemused Everett commented: 'It's a bit strange getting an award after what they've done … it did not stop the government from destroying [the site]'.[63] Indeed it did not.

The destruction of any Aboriginal heritage is, of course, a matter of deep regret, and nor can it be denied that Tasmanian governments have at times been complicit in the erasure of Aboriginal heritage from the landscape. In the wake of the Jordan River Levee protest the Giddings Labor government proposed the introduction of new heritage legislation.[64] After examining the draft provisions the TAC discovered that the proposed legislation allowed very little direct input from the Aboriginal community, and was considerably weaker than the existing *Historic Cultural Heritage Act* designed to protect non-Aboriginal heritage.[65] Hopefully, a balance will ultimately be reached, but there have been significant gains on other fronts. In May 2013 a rare act of unity saw the Tasmanian Aboriginal community gain possession of the 6750-hectare property known as Gowan Brae in the Central Highlands — the largest area of land ever returned on the mainland of Tasmania. Previously owned by the eccentric Texan millionaire lawyer, Martin Polin, the land had become available following his death in 2007. Securing it depended on cooperation between a number of Aboriginal groups, a conservation organisation and the Commonwealth government. The latter advanced $2.2 million to the Tasmanian Land Conservancy (TLC) from its National Reserve System, an amount which fell $1.1 million short of the total funding required:

> [The TLC] contacted the Tasmanian Aboriginal Centre … which in turn called the Aboriginal Land Council of Tasmania … and brokered a deal to return the entire property to the Aboriginal community should it secure the remaining funds. The Indigenous

> Land Corporation (ILC) came to the party [with the result that] the TLC will have an ongoing role in supporting the TAC with land management of the property.[66]

Divisiveness rather than cooperation is more the norm in Aboriginal Tasmania, highlighted later that same year when the Commonwealth government decided to issue mining permits in the Tarkine River region of the north-west. The Aboriginal Land Council of Tasmania immediately expressed its concerns that Aboriginal heritage assessment had not been fully taken into account. That claim was denied by the Circular Head Aboriginal Corporation, with chair Graeme Heald insisting that 'some of our people went out with … environmental officers [and] we couldn't see any issues'. The corporation was keen to see mining take place, with a very real prospect of jobs in a region which suffers from a chronically high level of unemployment.[67] Difference and divisiveness have been present in Aboriginal Tasmania since the earliest migrations from 40 000 years ago, and in this instance it was a case of the past converging with the present. Only time will tell if the two can ever be fully reconciled.

CONCLUSION

The Aboriginal people of Van Diemen's Land/Tasmania have indeed been engaged in a journey of epic proportions, an odyssey which continues to wind its way towards the future. Culture, however, is not frozen in time, and despite misguided attempts to recapture a lost past the Aboriginal people of today's Tasmania are not the same as those who lived 35 000, 10 000 or even 200 years ago. A few threads have nevertheless survived that immense span of time, one of which is the regionalism and difference which characterised the Aboriginal people of ancient times just as it impacts today on the Aboriginal community. They were not, are not still, a single united entity.

At the very outset of this work the discussion centred on early European perceptions of those people, who were often not even recognised as being Aboriginal. Observers and theorists alike believed that the Indigenous inhabitants of Van Diemen's land were 'negritos', and New Caledonia often featured as their imaginary original homeland. We know now, of course, that the origins of the Aboriginal people lay on the mainland of Australia, and that over millennia a number of distinct groups colonised what was then the Tasmanian Peninsula. By at least 35 000 years ago at least one of those groups had penetrated as far as the river valleys of the south-west, and at that time they were the most southerly people in the world, living and hunting within sight of glaciers and ranging across the sub-alpine tundra. This was a remarkable human achievement, though there are limitations to what humans can physically endure. Even the south-west was abandoned some 11 000 years ago owing to changing environmental factors. One thousand years later the flooding of the Bassian Plain severed the remaining link with mainland Australia, with the Aboriginal people isolated until just a few centuries ago — an isolation of considerable magnitude.

How many Aborigines inhabited the island of Van Diemen's Land at first contact can only be conjectured, the general consensus being in the order of 4500–5000. If this figure is correct it means that Van Diemen's Land was as densely populated as the richest coastal regions of the south-east of mainland Australia. Isolation certainly had its impact on the Aboriginal people, both culturally and physically. Over time their toolkit was reduced in size to the very basics necessary to ensure survival, an island-wide anomaly amidst cultural diversity. Woolly hair, often reddish-brown pigmentation and generally stocky bodies were another consequence of both isolation and adaptation to cooler moister conditions. Societies consisted of bands tied to clearly defined tracts of territory, with those sharing a common culture and language grouped into one of possibly nine larger socio-political entities. Just as on mainland Australia there was a gendered division of labour, though in Van Diemen's Land it is apparent that the contribution of women was even more significant. It was women who gathered vegetable foods and birds eggs, climbed for possums, hunted seals and dived for abalone and crayfish. It was also women who mined the highly prized ochre.

Men, on the other hand, generally hunted the larger game with spears approximately 3 metres in length, missiles which could be hurled with remarkable accuracy over exceptional distances without the aid of a spear-thrower. Rather than boomerangs, the Tasmanians possessed hand-held waddies which could also be thrown with a rotary motion to down game, including birds on the wing. Both weapons were utilised during internecine conflict with deadly effect, just as they were during the 'Black War' against British colonists. While Van Diemen's Land contained more than sufficient natural resources, it was certainly no utopia. The Aborigines of these southern climes probably depended less on vegetable foods than their counterparts on mainland Australia, but the coastal marine life was particularly rich. At least 31 species of scale-fish featured regularly in the ancient diet, but then, around 3700 years ago, fish bones suddenly disappear from coastal middens. Whether fish were entirely abandoned as a food source right around the island as is often suggested remains questionable: depending on the region, the consumption of scale-fish may well have persisted. There can be no denying, though, that there was a systemic change in the coastal economy around 3700 years ago, with greater emphasis placed on the exploitation of the sub-littoral zone as opposed to inter-tidal areas. It is equally clear that bone tools fell out of favour at roughly the same time, indicative of a correlation between the two. But exactly what that connection was has remained elusive.

Despite a number of mysteries we do have a reasonable body of knowledge regarding Aboriginal material culture in Van Diemen's Land. The same cannot be said about religion and spirituality, and even the recent publication of the Cotton Papers has shed little light on the subject owing to its highly questionable authenticity. The meaning of Tasmanian Aboriginal art is no less obscure, particularly the petroglyphs which occur in a number of widely separated regions. There is no evidence of the Dreaming in Tasmania, which is no surprise as it was a relatively recent development on mainland Australia — certainly well within the last 10 000 years — and therefore after the Aboriginal people of Van Diemen's Land had been isolated by the flooding of the Bassian Plain. Only one creation myth has been documented, which suggests that there were probably more, but it is known that celestial bodies, notably Earth's own lunar satellite, played significant roles in religious life.

When European mariners first began to touch on the shores of Van Diemen's Land from the mid-seventeenth century the overall health profile of the Aboriginal people appears to have been quite good, and rather than retrogressing their cultural universe was still in the process of expanding. The invention of the bundled canoe within the last 3000–4000 years allowed the Aborigines of the south and north-west to recolonise and exploit a number of offshore islands which had previously been beyond reach. This is more than adequate proof that the Tasmanians were not 'doomed to a slow strangulation of the mind' as once suggested, though no level of intellect could prevent the detrimental impact of Europeans.

The Dutch were the first to arrive, a fleeting visit by Abel Tasman in 1642, who departed the shores of the island that would later bear his name with a strong suspicion that it was inhabited by giant beings and tigers. The Frenchman, Marion Dufresne, realised otherwise when he stepped ashore in 1772 to make the first known contact with the Van Diemen's Land Aborigines. Imbued with the idealised imagery of the 'noble savage', du Fresne's beliefs were rudely shattered through a grave misunderstanding which led to the death of an Aboriginal man, the first known Aboriginal blood shed by outsiders. Unfortunately, it was not to be the last. The British, particularly James Cook and William Bligh, managed to establish cordial relationships, as did Marion du Fresne's compatriot, Bruny d'Entrecasteaux, in 1793. Of all these early mariners it was the French who were the first to gain real insights into the Aboriginal societies of Van Diemen's Land, notably through the efforts of the proto-anthropologist Francois Péron, who accompanied the Baudin expedition of 1801–03.

It was the French presence in these southern waters which finally convinced their British rivals to colonise the island in 1803. A small settlement was initially established by Lieutenant John Bowen on the east bank of the Derwent River at Risdon Cove in August 1803, an outpost soon superseded by a second settlement on the present site of Hobart. The following year Colonel William Paterson formed the first British settlement in the north, on the Tamar River, and within a week there was a violent confrontation with the Indigenous people. In the south a survey party led by James Meehan was frightened off by the Aborigines in February 1804, and a fatal clash occurred at Risdon Cove the following May. Often labelled a 'massacre', this incident has been grossly exaggerated. To do so portrays the Aborigines as simplistic passive victims — which they were certainly not. Unfortunately, this emphasis on often non-existent 'massacres' has persisted in scholarship to the present day. There were very few large-scale clashes on the Van Diemen's Land frontier, where the Aboriginal people quickly proved adept at countering their British opponents until the weight of numbers finally told against them.

The first two decades of British colonisation were marked by both confrontation and collaboration. Bushrangers, convict pastoral workers and frontiersmen are certainly known to have killed Aborigines, although they not infrequently paid the ultimate price for their aggression. Conversely, the Aboriginal people often assisted British settlers as they established their landholdings. The situation differed considerably in the north, particularly the north-east, where the first effects of the British impact were felt. The discovery of immense colonies of seals on the Bass Strait islands in 1798 resulted in an influx of adventurers, seamen and runaway convicts seeking their fortunes. Their depredations quickly led to the virtual extinction of their quarry, yet for a multitude of reasons a small number of these men chose to make the islands their home. Trading seal and wallaby skins, vegetables and meat with passing vessels, they also required women. For that reason they regularly raided the coast of northern Van Diemen's Land and the southern Australian mainland to procure Aboriginal 'wives', with their activities playing a key role in the demographic collapse of Aboriginal societies within their sphere of operations. Although it has been stated that the Aboriginal people were themselves active agents in this sexual trade, such claims are based on the flimsiest evidence. Similarly, attempts by new revisionists to portray Aboriginal women as equal partners in these relationships flies in the face of all the available evidence. With the occasional exception, the women were taken by force and treated brutally by their sealer captors.

Violence in all its manifestations escalated from 1824 throughout eastern Van Diemen's Land, when the spread of British settlement between Hobart and Launceston severed the migratory routes of the Aboriginal people and concomitantly deprived them of essential resources. The activities of Musquito, Black Dick, Jack and Dick and their subsequent executions were side issues rather than the catalyst for what became known as the 'Black War', which was actually a series of frontier conflicts erupting whenever the British impact became intolerable. It was also characterised by continuing internecine conflict which seriously weakened the overall Aboriginal response. Despite that, the Aboriginal warriors fought so well that they seriously worried their opponents. At times they seized the initiative, and it was the British who were forced to take defensive measures. To placate his subjects and to avoid the possibility of the Aborigines being totally annihilated, Lieutenant Governor George

Arthur implemented a range of confused policies in his search for an effective means of ending hostilities. One of them was the farcical 'Black Line' of late 1830, a human cordon aimed at trapping the Big River and Oyster Bay peoples on the Tasman Peninsula where they could be captured. The whole exercise from start to finish was an exorbitantly expensive fiasco, and it is unlikely that the 'Black Line' had any bearing on the final outcome of frontier conflict in the east.

On the contrary, the conclusion of hostilities largely resulted from attrition. The 'Black War' was characterised by small-scale continuing clashes, particularly campfire ambushes, which steadily decimated the Aboriginal people of eastern Van Diemen's Land. Constantly on the run, they suffered enormous privations, with starvation and exposure contributing to the overall death toll. The Aboriginal people were literally fought to a standstill, and it was at this point that George Arthur's acceptance of 'conciliation' finally proved its worth. The idea of negotiating with the Aboriginal people had its genesis years earlier, but in the hands of George Augustus Robinson, a builder who believed that he was destined to save the Aborigines, the idea became a reality. Vain and arrogant, Robinson had both the determination and stamina to travel throughout Van Diemen's Land contacting different Aboriginal groups and convincing them to lay down their arms. There can be no doubt that his terms were fraudulent, with the Aborigines expecting that their grievances would be addressed. They never were. Instead, they were shunted off to exile on the islands of Bass Strait, a supposedly temporary measure from which most did not return.

Some of those exiles came from the north-west, fortunate to survive a war of total extirpation. From the beginning of 1827 extensive tracts of land in this region were taken up by the Van Diemen's Land Company, a London-based joint stock company under the management of Edward Curr. For the first two years, however, there was only minimal contact with the Indigenous people, a situation which altered markedly after Curr's assigned convicts began taking liberties with Aboriginal women. This triggered a chain of events which culminated in the 'Cape Grim Massacre' and the implementation by Curr of an unofficial policy of genocide. The north-west was a separate and brutal theatre of conflict, and yet the local Aboriginal people were able to maintain resistance until at least February 1842, years after hostilities in the east had been concluded.

Dolly Dalrymple's family remained intact, and while there is a distinct possibility that a few other Aboriginal people, including members of the Big River nation, were able to avoid the wholesale round-up of the survivors of frontier conflict, to all intent the landscape of Van Diemen's Land was devoid of its Indigenous inhabitants by the mid-1840s. Hunter, Swan and Guncarriage (Vansittart) Islands were all tried as places of incarceration before the Aboriginal Establishment was finally located on Flinders Island, first at The Lagoons and then Wybalenna. William Darling was clearly the most humane supervisor, who attempted to ensure some degree of comfort for his charges, albeit, not always successfully. Henry Nickolls followed Darling's lead, but with the appointment of George Augustus Robinson as commandant in November 1835 the situation rapidly deteriorated. Even with the exit of Robinson to Port Phillip in February 1839 conditions did not improve, with death continuing to stalk the exiles until the 46 survivors were finally repatriated back to the mainland of Van Diemen's Land in October 1847. Unfortunately, the new setting for the Aboriginal Establishment was an abandoned penal settlement at Oyster Cove, south of Hobart, a place even less conducive to long-term survival.

Among the repatriates were a handful of Aborigines from the group of 15 who had accompanied Robinson to Port Phillip.

Increasingly neglected, Pevay, Timme, Truganini, Fanny and Matilda decided to take fate into their own hands and unleashed a campaign of violence against the colonists. This short-lived episode claimed two European lives and ended with the execution of Pevay and Timme, the first public execution at Melbourne. The neglect experienced at Port Phillip was comparable to the treatment of the repatriated Aborigines at Oyster Cove, as one by one they fell ill and died until, in 1876, Truganini was the last to be buried. Even in death, both William Lanne and Truganini received barbaric treatment at the hands of the 'scientific' fraternity. Fanny Cochrane Smith, on the other hand, was fortunate to escape the confines of Oyster Cove by marrying an English ex-convict sawyer and prospering. Although doubts about her paternity persist, during her own lifetime the Tasmanian government recognised her claim to be a 'full blooded' Aborigine and, like Dolly Dalrymple in the north, she was highly respected by wider society. The same cannot be said for the families which descended from unions between European sealers and Aboriginal women and remained on the islands of Bass Strait.

Blending Aboriginal and European practices, the Bass Strait islanders were a largely impoverished social group who relied heavily on the annual harvest of mutton-birds for their very survival. Government assistance was minimal and usually proffered only as a means of social control. In 1881 the government finally reserved a large section of land on the western end of Cape Barren Island for their exclusive use — but it came with strings attached. Further legislation in 1912 focusing on the reserve proved no more fruitful. Despite a plethora of government inquiries over succeeding decades the economic and social circumstances of the islanders altered little until the 1950s, when the revocation of the Cape Barren Island reserve ushered in government attempts to assimilate members of the community into Tasmania's dominant society. Notwithstanding attempts at resistance, poverty and the lack of opportunity ultimately prevailed, and more and more islanders relocated to the Tasmanian mainland.

Some of them nevertheless held fast to their Aboriginal origins, and with the resurgence of Aboriginal identity throughout Australia from the 1960s the islanders began to reassert their own distinctiveness. They were initially aided by Aboriginal activists from mainland Australia, notably Burnum Burnum and Rosalind Langford. Gradually, however, members of the modern Tasmanian Aboriginal community took matters into their own hands. Michael Mansell, in particular, loomed large in the reassertion of Aboriginality and the development of Aboriginal organisations in Tasmania. While they have since gone from strength to strength they still exhibit the deep schisms which have existed within the Aboriginal community since time immemorial. Notwithstanding that customary divisiveness, there can be no denying that taken as a whole the Aboriginal people of Van Diemen's Land/Tasmania are among the great survivors of human history.

NOTES

INTRODUCTION

1 N. Porch and J. Allen, 'Tasmania: archaeological and palaeo-ecological perspectives', *Antiquity*, Vol.69, No.265 (October 1995), p.714.
2 S. Macintyre and A. Clark, *The History Wars* (Melbourne: Melbourne University Press, 2004), pp.8–9.
3 Macintyre and Clark, *The History Wars*, p.13.
4 R. Callick, 'Publisher pilloried for attacking historian', *Australian* (Sydney), 7 December 2010, p.4.
5 W. Smith, 'By Order of Lenin', "Weekend", in *Courier-Mail* (Brisbane), 24 August 1996, pp.1–2.
6 K. Windschuttle, *The Fabrication of Aboriginal History Volume One: Van Diemen's Land 1803–1847* (Sydney: Macleay Press, 2003), pp.6–7.
7 S. Macintyre, 'The History Wars', *Sydney Papers*, Vol.15, Nos.3–4 (Winter–Spring 2003), p.77.
8 K. Windschuttle, 'The myths of Aboriginal history', *Sunday Mail* (Brisbane), 5 January 2003, p.54.
9 L. Ryan, 'The Extinction of the Tasmanian Aborigines: Myth and Reality', *Tasmanian Historical Research Association Papers and Proceedings* [hereafter *THRA*], Vol.19, No.2 (June 1972), p.63.
10 Windschuttle, *The Fabrication of Aboriginal History Volume One*, p.371.
11 Windschuttle, *The Fabrication of Aboriginal History Volume One*, pp.377, 383 and 386.
12 J. Hirst, 'In the Middle of the History Wars', *Sydney Papers*, Vol.18, Nos.3–4 (Winter–Spring 2006), p.51.
13 P. Cobern, 'Who really killed Tasmania's aborigines?', *Bulletin* (Sydney), 23 February 1982, p.32.
14 Cobern, 'Who really killed Tasmania's aborigines?', p.32.
15 Cobern, 'Who really killed Tasmania's aborigines?', p.34.
16 Cobern, 'Who really killed Tasmania's aborigines?', p.32.
17 Cobern, 'Who really killed Tasmania's aborigines?', p.34.

18 S. Bowdler, 'Tasmania's Aborigines', *Bulletin* (Sydney), 16 March 1982, p.6.

19 R. Travers, *The Tasmanians: The Story of a Doomed Race* (Melbourne: Cassell, 1968), p.233.

20 J. Cooper (comp.), *The Cotton Papers: Land of the Sleeping Gods* (Hobart: Wellington Bridge Press, 2013), pp.3 and 10.

21 N. Brodie, 'History's mysteries: The Cotton papers 2', *40° South*, No.72 (Autumn 2014), p.26.

22 J. Mundy, 'Book lifts shroud', *Koori Mail* (Lismore), 4 December 2013, p.21.

1 ORIGINS ... IN FACT AND FICTION

1 T. Flannery, The Future Eaters: An ecological history of the Australasian lands and people (Sydney: Reed New Holland, 1999), p.264.

2 J. Wunderly, 'The origin of the Tasmanian race', Man, Vol.38 (December 1938), pp.199–200.

3 A. Lubbock, Owen Stanley R.N. 1811–1850: Captain of the 'Rattlesnake' (Melbourne: Heinemann, 1968), pp.190–1 and 203–4.

4 R. Blench, 'The Languages of the Tasmanians and Their Relation to the Peopling of Australia: Sensible and Wild Theories', Australian Archaeology [hereafter AA], No.67 (December 2008), p.14.

5 A. Meston, 'The Problem of the Tasmanian Aborigine', Papers and Proceedings of the Royal Society of Tasmania for the year 1936 (1937), p.88.

6 F. Allen, 'The Original Range of the Papuan and Negritto Races', Journal of the Anthropological Institute of Great Britain and Ireland, Vol.8 (1879), p.49.

7 Allen, 'The Original Range of the Papuan and Negritto Races', pp.40–1.

8 Blench, 'The Languages of the Tasmanians and Their Relation to the Peopling of Australia', p.14.

9 Wunderly, 'The Origin of the Tasmanian Race', p.199.

10 J. Bonwick, 'On the Origin of the Tasmanians Geologically Considered', Journal of the Ethnological Society of London, Vol.2, No.2 (1870), p.129.

11 J. Mathew, Eaglehawk and Crow: A study of the Australian Aborigines including an inquiry into their origin and a survey of Australian languages (London: David Nutt, 1899), p.5.

12 Meston, 'The Problem of the Tasmanian Aborigine', pp.91–2.

13 J. Taylor, 'The Tasmanian Languages', Launceston Historical Society Papers and Proceedings, Vol.11 (1999), p.45.

14 J. Mulvaney and J. Kamminga, Prehistory of Australia (Sydney: Allen & Unwin, 1999), p.154.

15 J. Flood, The Original Australians: Story of the Aboriginal People (Sydney: Allen & Unwin, 2006), p.185.

16 K. Windschuttle and T. Gillin, 'The Extinction of the Australian Pygmies', Quadrant, Vol.46, No.6 (June 2002), pp.7 and 11–12.

17 R.M.W. Dixon, The Dyirbal Language of North Queensland (Cambridge: Cambridge University Press, 1972), pp.22–3.

18 J. Taylor, 'The Aboriginal Discovery and Colonisation of Tasmania', THRA, Vol.50, No.4 (December 2003), p.220.

19 Taylor, 'The Aboriginal Discovery and Colonisation of Tasmania', p.217; J. Taylor, 'The Palawa (Tasmanian Aboriginal) Languages' (unpublished MA thesis, University of Tasmania, 2004), p.47.

20 C. Turney et.al., 'Late-surviving megafauna in Tasmania, Australia, implicate human involvement in their extinction', Proceedings of the National Academy of Sciences of the United States of America, Vol.105, No.34 (26 August 2008), pp.12152–3.

21 G. Calder, Levée, Line and Martial Law: A History of the Dispossession of the

Mairremmener People of Van Diemen's Land 1803–1832 (Launceston, Tas: Fullers Bookshop, 2010), p.15.

22 R. Cosgrove, 'Late Pleistocene behavioural variation and time trends: the case from Tasmania', Archaeology in Oceania, Vol.30, No.3 (October 1995), p.83.

23 F. Morello et.al., 'Hunter-gatherers, biogeographic barriers and the development of human settlement in Tierra del Fuego', Antiquity, Vol.86, No.331 (March 2012), p.74.

24 Calder, Levée, Line and Martial Law, p.15.

25 Calder, Levée, Line and Martial Law, p.15.

26 Calder, Levée, Line and Martial Law, p.15.

27 L. Ryan, The Aboriginal Tasmanians (Sydney: Allen & Unwin, 1996), pp.14–15.

28 Taylor, 'The Palawa (Tasmanian Aboriginal) Languages', pp.7–8.

29 Z. Edwards, 'Bypass site set for human history claim', Examiner (Launceston), 11 March 2010, p.7; D. Brown, 'Bypass finds date to 40,000 years', Mercury (Hobart), 27 April 2010, p.3.

30 D. Arndt, 'Aborigines mount spiritual defence', Examiner (Launceston), 11 November 2011, p.8.

31 CHMA, 'Interim Report on the Jordan River Levee Excavations' (Sandy Bay, Tasmania, April 2010), pp.1–2; J. Olley, 'Peer Review of the TASI10757 Jordan River, Brighton, Tasmania: Luminescence Chronology' (Cupper, May 2010), pp.3–5; J. Allen Archaeological Consultancies, 'Peer Review of the Draft Final Archaeological Report on the Test Excavations of the Jordan River Levee Site Southern Tasmania' (Broulee, NSW, 22 October 2010), pp.15ff.

32 Personal communication from Dr Nicholas Brodie, Hobart, 19 September 2010.

33 Taylor, 'The Palawa (Tasmanian Aboriginal) Languages', pp.41–2.

34 L. Gaffney and J. Stockton, 'Results of the Jordan River Midden Excavation', AA, No.10 (June 1980), p.73.

35 J. Flood, Archaeology of the Dreamtime: The story of prehistoric Australia and its people (Marleston, SA: JB Publishing, 2004), pp.195–7.

36 R. Jones, 'Tasmanian Archaeology: Establishing the Sequences', Annual Review of Anthropology, Vol.24 (October 1995), p.428.

37 Flood, Archaeology of the Dreamtime, pp.197–9.

38 H. Lourandos, Continent of Hunter-Gatherers: New perspectives in Australian prehistory (Cambridge: Cambridge University Press, 1997), pp.245–6.

39 Flood, Archaeology of the Dreamtime, pp.118 and 120.

40 J. Garvey, 'The Wallaby Hunters of Ice Age Tasmania', Australasian Science, Vol.28, No.5 (June 2007), pp.30 and 32; I. McFarlane, Beyond Awakening —The Aboriginal Tribes of North West Tasmania: A History (Launceston, Tas: Fullers Bookshop, Riawunna Aboriginal Studies Centre and Community, Place and Heritage Research Unit, University of Tasmania, 2008), pp.3–4.

41 Flood, Archaeology of the Dreamtime, p.124.

42 J.H. Calaby, 'Red-necked Wallaby: Macropus rufogriseus', in R. Strahan (ed.), The Australian Museum Complete Book of Australian Mammals (Sydney: Angus & Robertson, 1983), p.239.

43 R. Fudali and R. Ford, 'Darwin Glass and Darwin Crater: A Progress Report', Meteoritics, Vol.14 (September 1979), pp.284–7; R. Jones, 'Ice-Age Hunters of the Tasmanian Wilderness', Australian Geographic, No.8 (October–December 1987), p.39.

44 J. Flood, The Riches of Ancient Australia: a journey into prehistory (Brisbane: University of Queensland Press, 1990), p.327.

45 I. McNiven, 'Technological organization and settlement in southwest Tasmania after the last glacial maximum', Antiquity, Vol.68, No.258 (March 1994), p.75.

46 Jones, 'Tasmanian Archaeology', p.430.

47 Cosgrove, 'Late Pleistocene behavioural variation and the trends: the case from Tasmania', pp.92 and 97.

48 Jones, 'Tasmanian Archaeology', p.430.
49 Flood, Archaeology of the Dreamtime, p.124.
50 Jones, 'Ice-Age Hunters of the Tasmanian Wilderness', p.44.
51 Jones, 'Tasmanian Archaeology', p.432.
52 J. Garvey, 'Preliminary zooarchaeological interpretations from Kutikina Cave, south-west Tasmania', Australian Aboriginal Studies, No.1 (2006), p.58.
53 J. Flood, Rock Art of the Dreamtime: Images of Ancient Australia (Sydney: Angus & Robertson, 1997), p.224.
54 Lourandos, Continent of Hunter-Gatherers, pp.245–7.
55 Flood, Archaeology of the Dreamtime, p.125.
56 K. Kiernan, R. Jones and D. Ranson, 'New evidence from Fraser Cave for glacial age man in south-west Tasmania', Nature, Vol.301 (6 January 1983), p.31; Lourandos, Continent of Hunter-Gatherers, p.248.
57 Garvey, 'Preliminary zooarchaeological interpretations of Kutikina Cave, south-west Tasmania', p.60.
58 R. Cosgrove, 'Forty-Two Degrees South: The Archaeology of Late Pleistocene Tasmania', Journal of World Prehistory, Vol.13, No.4 (December 1999), p.393.
59 J. Garvey, 'Economic anatomy of the Bennett's wallaby (Macropus rufogriseus): Implications for understanding human hunting strategies in late Pleistocene Tasmania', Quaternary International, Vol.211, Nos.1–2 (1 January 2010), pp.151–2.
60 R. Cosgrove and A. Pike-Tay, 'The Middle Palaeolithic and Late Pleistocene Tasmania Hunting Behaviour: a Reconsideration of the Attributes of Modern Human Behaviour', International Journal of Osteoarchaeology, Vol.14, No.3 (August 2004), p.323.
61 J. Garvey, 'Surviving an Ice Age: The Zooarchaeological Record from Southwestern Tasmania', Palaios, Vol.22, No.6 (November 2007), p.584.
62 Cosgrove and Pike-Tay, 'The Middle Palaeolithic and Late Pleistocene Tasmania Hunting Behaviour', p.323.
63 A. Pike-Tay, R. Cosgrove and J. Garvey, 'Systematic land use by late Pleistocene Tasmanian Aborigines', Journal of Archaeological Science, Vol.35, No.9 (September 2008), pp.2541–2.
64 S. Harris, D. Ranson and S. Brown, 'Maxwell River Archaeological Survey 1986', AA, No.27 (1988), pp.94–5.
65 Flood, Rock Art of the Dreamtime, pp.225–6.
66 I. Thomas, 'Models and prima-donnas in southwest Tasmania', AA, No.41 (December 1995), pp.22–3.
67 Cosgrove, Late Pleistocene behavioural variation and trends', pp.83 and 85.
68 Cosgrove, Late Pleistocene behavioural variation and trends', pp.92–3.
69 Cosgrove, Late Pleistocene behavioural variation and trends', p.94.
70 Lourandos, Continent of Hunter-Gatherers, pp.263–4.
71 Cosgrove, 'Forty-Two Degrees South', p.365.
72 S. Webb, The Willandra Lakes Hominids (Canberra: Department of Prehistory, Research School of Pacific Studies, Australian National University, 1989), pp.67–70; T. Stone and M. Cupper, 'Last Glacial Maximum ages for robust humans at Kow Swamp, southern Australia', Journal of Human Evolution, Vol.45, No.2 (August 2003), p.99.
73 R. Sim, 'Prehistoric human occupation in the King and Furneaux Island regions, Bass Strait', in M. Sullivan, S. Brockwell and A. Webb (eds), Archaeology in the North: Proceedings of the 1993 Australian Archaeological Association Conference (Darwin: North Australian Research Unit of Australian National University, 1994), p.359.
74 Brockwell and Webb (eds), Archaeology in the North: Proceedings of the 1993 Australian Archaeological Association Conference, pp.361–2.
75 Brockwell and Webb (eds), Archaeology in the North: Proceedings of the 1993 Australian Archaeological Association Conference, p.369.
76 Flannery, The Future Eaters, p.264.

77 B. Plomley, The Tasmanian Aborigines (Launceston, Tas: Plomley Foundation, 1993), p.55; Flood, Archaeology of the Dreamtime, p.207.
78 Flood, Archaeology of the Dreamtime, pp.204–5.
79 N.J.B. Plomley, Friendly Mission: The Tasmanian Journal and Papers of George Augustus Robinson 1829–1834 (Launceston, Tas: Queen Victoria Museum and Art Gallery and Quintus Publishing, 2008), pp.23–4.
80 Plomley, Friendly Mission: The Tasmanian Journal and Papers of George Augustus Robinson 1829–1834, p.18.
81 H. Ling Roth, The Aborigines of Tasmania (Halifax: F. King & Sons, 1899), p.163.
82 R. Jones, 'The Demography of Hunters and Farmers in Tasmania', in D.J. Mulvaney and J. Golson (eds), Aboriginal Man and Environment in Australia (Canberra: Australian National University Press, 1971), p.274.
83 Jones, 'The Demography of Hunters and Farmers in Tasmania', p.281.
84 Jones, 'The Demography of Hunters and Farmers in Tasmania', p.281.
85 Ryan, The Aboriginal Tasmanians, pp.14–15.
86 Jones, 'The Demography of Hunters and Farmers in Tasmania', p.281.

2 LIFE-WAYS AND MATERIAL CULTURE OF PRE-CONTACT VAN DIEMEN'S LAND

1 Ling Roth, *The Aborigines of Tasmania*, pp.9 and 11; J. Wunderly, 'The West Coast Tribe of Tasmanian Aborigines', *Man*, Vol.38 (August 1938), p.121.
2 Plomley, *The Tasmanian Aborigines*, p.1.
3 N.J.B., Plomley, *The Baudin Expedition and the Tasmanian Aborigines 1802* (Hobart: Blubber Head Press, 1983), p.168.
4 Plomley, *The Tasmanian Aborigines*, p.30; Flood, *Archaeology of the Dreamtime*, p.202.
5 J.B. Walker, *Early Tasmania* (Hobart: M.C. Reed, Govt. Printer, 1989), p.249; L. Johnston, 'Artistry in jewels of Tassie's foreshore', *Examiner* (Launceston), 10 January 2009, p.33.
6 Ling Roth, *The Aborigines of Tasmania*, pp.128–9.
7 Plomley, *The Tasmanian Aborigines*, p.29.
8 Plomley, *The Tasmanian Aborigines*, p.2.
9 J. Isaacs, *Australia's Living Heritage: Arts of the Dreaming* (Sydney: Lansdowne Press, 1997), p.55.
10 Isaacs, *Australia's Living Heritage: Arts of the Dreaming*, pp.2 and 7.
11 Plomley, *Friendly Mission*, p.613.
12 McFarlane, *Beyond Awakening*, p.30.
13 Flood, *Archaeology of the Dreamtime*, p.199.
14 R. Jones, 'The Tasmanian paradox', in R.V.S. Wright (ed.), *Stone tools as Cultural Markers: Change, evolution and complexity* (Canberra: Australian Institute of Aboriginal Studies, 1977), p.203.
15 R. Jones, 'Tasmanian Tribes', appendix in N. Tindale, *Aboriginal Tribes of Australia: Their Terrain, Environmental Controls, Distribution, Limits, and Proper Names* (Canberra: Australian National University Press, 1974), p.323.
16 Jones, 'The Demography of Hunters and Farmers in Tasmania', p.277.
17 Plomley, *The Baudin Expedition and the Tasmanian Aborigines 1802*, p.169.
18 N.J.B. Plomley, *Jorgen Jorgenson and the Aborigines of Van Diemen's Land* (Hobart: Blubber Head Press, 1991), p.11.
19 Ryan, *The Aboriginal Tasmanians*, pp.13–14.
20 Plomley, *Jorgen Jorgenson and the Aborigines of Van Diemen's Land*, p.56.
21 Jones, 'The Demography of Hunters and Farmers in Tasmania', p.280.
22 McFarlane, *Beyond Awakening*, p.35.
23 Plomley, *Jorgen Jorgenson and the Aborigines of Van Diemen's Land*, p.55.
24 McFarlane, *Beyond Awakening*, p.36.

25 McFarlane, *Beyond Awakening*, pp.36-37.
26 Plomley, *Friendly Mission*, p.314.
27 Plomley, *Friendly Mission*, p.805.
28 McFarlane, *Beyond Awakening*, p.8.
29 Plomley, *Friendly Mission*, pp.888–9.
30 McFarlane, *Beyond Awakening*, p.11.
31 Plomley, *The Tasmanian Aborigines*, p.34.
32 Plomley, *The Tasmanian Aborigines*, p.47.
33 Plomley, *Friendly Mission*, p.460.
34 Plomley, *Jorgen Jorgenson and the Aborigines of Van Diemen's Land*, p.114.
35 McFarlane, *Beyond Awakening*, p.17.
36 Travers, *The Tasmanians*, p.19.
37 Plomley, *Friendly Mission*, p.659.
38 Plomley, *Friendly Mission*, p.788.
39 Plomley, *Friendly Mission*, p.759.
40 I. Skira, 'Tasmanian Aborigines and Muttonbirding: A Historical Examination' (unpublished PhD thesis, University of Tasmania, 1993), p.35.
41 B. Hiatt, 'The Food Quest and the Economy of the Tasmanian Aborigines [Part 1]', *Oceania*, Vol.38, No.2 (December 1967), pp.110–11.
42 Plomley, *The Tasmanian Aborigines*, p.37.
43 J. Boyce, 'Canine revolution: the social and environmental impact of the introduction of the dog to Tasmania', *Environmental History*, Vol.11, No.1 (January 2006), p.117.
44 Walker, *Early Tasmania*, p.257.
45 Plomley, *The Tasmanian Aborigines*, p.37.
46 Plomley, *Friendly Mission*, p.658.
47 Flood, *Archaeology of the Dreamtime*, p.203.
48 Hiatt, 'The Food Quest and the Economy of Tasmanian Aborigines [Part 1]', p.110.
49 Plomley, *Friendly Mission*, p.665.
50 V. Matson-Green and T. Harper, 'Palawa Women: Carrying the Burdens and Finding the Solutions', *Labour History*, No.69 (November 1995), p.66.
51 Ling Roth, *The Aborigines of Tasmania*, pp.87–8; F. Noetling, 'The Food of the Tasmanian Aborigines', *Papers and Proceedings of the Royal Society of Tasmania for the year 1910*, pp.288–9.
52 Boyce, 'Canine revolution', p.117.
53 H.S. Dove, 'The Tasmanian Emu', *Emu*, Vol.25, No.4 (April 1926), p.290.
54 Skira, 'Tasmanian Aborigines and Muttonbirding', p.9.
55 Skira, 'Tasmanian Aborigines and Muttonbirding', p.34.
56 M.S.R. Sharland, 'Mutton-Birds of Bass Strait: A little-known island industry', *Walkabout* (1 December 1935), p.33; I. Stuart, 'To kill a mutton bird: the archaeology of birding in the Outer Furneaux Islands', *Historic Environment*, Vol.14, No.1 (1998), p.19.
57 B. d'Entrecasteaux, *Voyage to Australia & the Pacific 1791–1793* (ed.), E. Duyker and M. Duyker (Melbourne: Melbourne University Press, 2001), p.144.
58 Flood, *Archaeology of the Dreamtime*, p.201.
59 McFarlane, *Beyond Awakening*, pp.13 and 16.
60 R. Jones, 'Why did the Tasmanians stop eating fish?', in R. Gould (ed.), *Explorations in Ethnoarchaeology* (Albuquerque, NM: University of New Mexico, 1978), p.46.
61 Jones, 'Why did the Tasmanians stop eating fish?', p.34.
62 D. Horton, 'Tasmanian Adaptation', *Mankind*, Vol.12, No.1 (1979), p.30; S. Bowdler, 'Fish and Culture: a Tasmanian Polemic', *Mankind*, Vol.12, No.4 (December 1980), p.339.
63 P. Hiscock, *Archaeology of Ancient Australia* (London: Routledge, 2008), p.133.
64 R. Taylor, 'The polemics of eating fish in Tasmania: the historical evidence revisited', *Aboriginal History*, Vol.31 (2007), p.10.
65 Flood, *Archaeology of the Dreamtime*, p.206.
66 Flannery, *The Future Eaters*, pp.268–9.
67 E. Bassett, 'Reconsidering Evidence of Tasmanian Fishing', *Environmental Archaeology*, Vol.9, No.2 (October 2004), p.139.

68 J. Bonwick, *The Lost Tasmanian Race* (London: Sampson Low, Marston, Searle, and Rivington, 1884), pp.4–5.
69 D.J. Mulvaney, *Encounters in Place: Outsiders and Aboriginal Australians 1606–1985* (Brisbane: University of Queensland Press, 1989), p.37.
70 Taylor, 'The polemics of eating fish in Tasmania', p.11.
71 Plomley, *The Baudin Expedition and the Tasmanian Aborigines 1802*, p.205.
72 E. Duyker (ed.), *The Discovery of Tasmania: Journal Extracts from the Expeditions of Abel Janszoon Tasman and Marc-Joseph Marion Dufresne 1642 & 1772* (trans.), E. Duyker, H. Duyker and M. Duyker (Hobart: St. David's Park Publishing, 1992), pp.33–4.
73 E. Duyker, *Citizen Labillardière: A Naturalist's Life in Revolution and Exploration (1755–1834)* (Melbourne: Miegunyah Press, 2003), p.154.
74 Plomley, *The Baudin Expedition and the Tasmanian Aborigines 1802*, pp.205–6.
75 McFarlane, *Beyond Awakening*, p.13.
76 Plomley, *Friendly Mission*, p.59.
77 Extract from the Minutes of the Executive Council in Lieutenant-Governor George Arthur to Sir George Murray, 4 April 1831, Colonial Secretary's Office [CSO] 1/280/28, Tasmanian Archive and Heritage Office, Hobart [hereafter TAHO].
78 Plomley, *Friendly Mission*, p.687.
79 Plomley, *Friendly Mission*, p.757.
80 Ling Roth, *The Aborigines of Tasmania*, p.101.
81 CSO 1/493/10853/2, pp.84–6, TAHO.
82 J. West, *The History of Tasmania: With copious information respecting the Colonies of New South Wales Victoria South Australia &c., &c., &c.* (ed.) A.G.L. Shaw (Sydney: Angus & Robertson, 1981), p.328.
83 Taylor, 'The polemics of eating fish in Tasmania', p.15.
84 Jones, 'The Tasmanian paradox', p.196.
85 Jones, 'The Tasmanian paradox', p.22.
86 J. Stockton, 'Stone Wall Fish-Traps in Tasmania', *AA*, No.14 (June 1982), p.112.
87 McFarlane, *Beyond Awakening*, p.13.
88 McFarlane, *Beyond Awakening*, pp.15–16.
89 McFarlane, *Beyond Awakening*, pp.15–16.
90 Hiatt, 'The Food Quest and the Economy of the Tasmanian Aborigines [Part 1]', p.115.
91 Plomley, *The Tasmanian Aborigines*, pp.38–9.
92 Plomley, *Friendly Mission*, pp.566–7.
93 Calder, *Levée, Line and Martial Law*, p.43.
94 S. Cane, J. Stockton and A. Vallance, 'A Note on the Diet of the Tasmanian Aborigines', *AA*, No.9 (1979), p.79.
95 Plomley, *The Tasmanian Aborigines*, p.39.
96 P.A.C. Richards, 'Iodine nutrition in two Tasmanian cultures', *Medical Journal of Australia*, Vol.163, Nos.11–12 (4–18 December 1995), pp.628–9.
97 Plomley, *The Tasmanian Aborigines*, p.56.
98 Duyker (ed.), *The Discovery of Tasmania*, p.35.
99 Duyker (ed.), *The Discovery of Tasmania*, pp.57–8.
100 D. Woodward, 'Diet in Tasmania over a Thousand Generations: A Preliminary History', *Tasmanian Historical Studies*, Vol.3, No.1 (1990–1991), p.144.
101 B. Gammage, 'Plain Facts: Tasmania under Aboriginal Management', *Landscape Research*, Vol.33, No.2 (2008), p.247.
102 R. Jones, 'Fire-Stick Farming', *Australian Natural History*, Vol.16, No.7 (15 September 1969), p.226.
103 B. Gammage, *The Biggest Estate on Earth: How Aborigines made Australia* (Sydney: Allen & Unwin, 2011), p.174.
104 Gammage, *The Biggest Estate on Earth: How Aborigines made Australia*, pp.82–3.
105 S. Breen, 'Tasmanian Aborigines—Making Fire', *THRA*, Vol.39, No.1 (March 1992), pp.40 and 42.
106 Plomley, *The Tasmanian Aborigines*, pp.40–1.
107 Plomley, *Friendly Mission*, p.599.

108 Plomley, *Friendly Mission*, p.143.
109 B. Gott, 'Fire-Making in Tasmania: Absence of Evidence is Not Evidence of Absence', *Current Anthropology*, Vol.43, No.4 (August–October 2002), p.653.
110 G. Volger, 'Making Fire by Percussion in Tasmania', *Oceania*, Vol.44, No.1 (September 1973), p.60.
111 J. Mulvaney, 'French strangers on Tasmanian shores', in P. Veth, P. Sutton and M. Neale (eds), *Strangers on the Shore: Early coastal contacts in Australia* (Canberra: National Museum of Australia Press, 2008), p.121.
112 McFarlane, *Beyond Awakening*, p.24.
113 R. Taylor, 'The polemics of making fire in Tasmania: the historical evidence revisited', *Aboriginal History*, Vol.32 (2008), pp.5–7.
114 I. McFarlane, 'Adolphus Schayer: Van Diemen's Land and the Berlin Papers', *THRA*, Vol.57, No.2 (August 2010), p.112.
115 J. Harris, 'Robinson, George Augustus', in B. Dickey (ed.), *The Australian Dictionary of Evangelical Biography* (Sydney: Evangelical History Association, 1994), p.324.
116 H. Melville, *The history of Van Diemen's Land from the year 1824 to 1835, inclusive during the administration of Lieutenant-Governor George Arthur* (ed.) G. Mackaness (Sydney: Horwitz-Grahame, 1965), p.59.
117 J. Clark, 'Devils and Horses: Religious and Creative Life in Tasmanian Aboriginal Society', in M. Roe (ed.), *The Flow of Culture: Tasmanian studies* (Canberra: Australian Academy of the Humanities, 1987), p.59; Plomley, *Friendly Mission*, p.406.
118 Plomley, *The Tasmanian Aborigine*, p.62.
119 C. Lord, 'A Note on the Burial Customs of the Tasmanian Aborigines', *Papers and Proceedings of the Royal Society of Tasmania for the year 1923* (1924), p.45.
120 F. Noetling, 'A Native Burial Ground on Charlton Estate, Near Ross', *Papers and Proceedings of the Royal Society of Tasmania for the year 1908* (1909), pp.37–9.
121 Ling Roth, *The Aborigines of Tasmania*, p.57; E.A. Worms, 'Tasmanian Mythological Terms', *Anthropos*, BD.55, H.1–2 (1960), p.12.
122 Ling Roth, *The Aborigines of Tasmania*, p.54.
123 Plomley, *The Tasmanian Aborigines*, p.62.
124 R. Jones, 'Tasmanian Aborigines and Dogs', *Mankind*, Vol.7, No.4 (December 1970), p.259.
125 McFarlane, 'Adolphus Schayer', p.113.
126 Plomley, *Friendly Mission*, p.334.
127 Plomley, *Friendly Mission*, p.406; M. Johnson, 'Indigenous People of the Cataract', in P.A.C. Richards and M. Johnson (eds), *Health, Wealth and Tribulation: Launceston's Cataract Gorge* (Launceston, Tas: Myola House of Publishing, 2007), p.60.
128 Plomley, *Friendly Mission*, p.406.
129 N.J.B. Plomley, 'French Manuscripts referring to the Tasmanian Aborigines', *Records of the Queen Victoria Museum*, No.23 (June 1966), p.3; S. Anderson, 'French anthropology in Australia, a prelude: the encounters between Aboriginal Tasmanians and the expedition of Bruny d'Entrecasteau, 1793', *Aboriginal History*, Vol.24 (2000), p.221.
130 Plomley, *Friendly Mission*, pp.143 and 260.
131 Plomley, *The Tasmanian Aborigines*, pp.62–5; Flood, *The Riches of Ancient Australia*, pp.341–3. See also: A.L. Meston, 'Aboriginal Rock-Carvings on the North-West Coast of Tasmania', *Papers and Proceedings of the Royal Society of Tasmania for the year 1931* (1932), pp.12–19; L.E. Luckman, 'The Aboriginal Rock Carvings at Mt. Cameron West, Tasmania, Photographs and Notes on the Excavations', *Papers and Proceedings of the Royal Society of Tasmania for the year 1950* (1951), pp.25–7.
132 Plomley, *Friendly Mission*, p.950.
133 O. Reid, 'Further Discoveries of

Aboriginal Rock Engravings in Tasmania', *Papers and Proceedings of the Royal Society of Tasmania*, Vol.96 (1962), pp.87–9; Plomley, *The Tasmanian Aborigines*, p.65.

134 Plomley, *The Tasmanian Aborigines*, p.66.

135 R. Jones, 'Excavations on a Stone Arrangement in Tasmania', *Man*, Vol.65 (May–June 1965), pp.78–9; Flood, *The Riches of Ancient Australia*, pp.331–3.

136 Plomley, *The Tasmanian Aborigines*, pp.32–4.

137 Plomley, *Jorgen Jorgenson and the Aborigines of Van Diemen's Land*, p.58.

138 Plomley, *The Tasmanian Aborigines*, p.35.

139 Flood, *Archaeology of the Dreamtime*, pp.228–30 and 248.

140 S. Bowdler, 'Hunters and Farmers in the Hunter Islands: Aboriginal and European Land-use of north-west Tasmanian islands in the historical period', *Records of the Queen Victoria Museum*, No.70 (1980), p.13.

141 J. Flood, *Archaeology of the Dreamtime: The story of prehistoric Australia and its people* (Sydney: Collins, 1989), p.186.

142 R.L. Vanderwal, 'Pre-History and the Archaeology of Louisa Bay', in H. Gee and J. Fenton (eds), *The South West Book: A Tasmanian Wilderness* (Melbourne: Australian Conservation Foundation, 1979), p.19.

143 R.L. Vanderwal, 'Adaptive Technology in Southwest Tasmania', *AA*, No.8 (September 1978), p.122.

144 Plomley, *Friendly Mission*, p.682; Calder, *Levée, Line and Martial Law*, p.71.

145 R. Jones, 'Tasmania: aquatic machines and off-shore islands', in G. de G. Sieveking, I.H. Longworth and K.E. Wilson (eds), *Problems in Economic and Social Archaeology* (London: Duckworth, 1976), p.240.

146 Jones, 'Tasmania: aquatic machines and off-shore islands', p.244.

147 Flood, *Archaeology of the Dreamtime* (2004), p.207.

148 Vanderwal, 'Pre-History and the Archaeology of Louisa Bay', p.19.

3 FIRST ENCOUNTERS AND BRITISH COLONISATION

1 J.B. Walker, *Abel Janszoon Tasman: His Life and Voyages* (Hobart: William Grahame Jnr, Govt. Printer, 1896), pp.29 and 31–2.

2 C.M.H. Clark, *A History of Australia Vol.1: From the Earliest Times to the Age of Macquarie* (Melbourne: Melbourne University Press, 1968), pp.31–2.

3 Duyker (ed.), *The Discovery of Tasmania*, pp.13–15.

4 M. Cannon, *The Exploration of Australia* (Sydney: Reader's Digest Services, 1987), p.29.

5 Cannon, *The Exploration of Australia*, p.29.

6 E. Duyker, 'Marion Dufresne, Marc-Joseph (1724–1772)', *Australian Dictionary of Biography* [hereafter *ADB*], Supplementary Volume 1580–1980, p.259.

7 J. Dunmore, *Storms and Dreams — Louis Bougainville: Soldier, Explorer, Statesman* (Sydney: ABC Books, 2005), pp.220 and 273.

8 Ryan, *The Aboriginal Tasmanians*, p.50.

9 Duyker (ed.), *The Discovery of Tasmania*, pp.46–7.

10 Mulvaney, 'French strangers on Tasmanian shores', p.115.

11 Duyker, 'Marion Dufresne, Marc-Joseph (1724–1772)', p.259.

12 Ryan, *The Aboriginal Tasmanians*, p.50.

13 R. Rienits and T. Rienits, *The Voyages of Captain Cook* (London: Hamlyn, 1968), pp.82, 85 and 87.

14 E.C. Nelson, 'The Natural History Obsevations and Collections Made During Furneaux's Visit to Tasmania

(Van Diemen's Land) in 1773, With Special Reference to Botany', *Papers and Proceedings of the Royal Society of Tasmania*, Vol.115 (1981), pp.77–8.
15 A.W. Reed (ed.), *Captain Cook in Australia: Extracts from the journals of Captain James Cook giving a full account in his own words of his adventures and discoveries in Australia* (Wellington: A.H. and A.W. Reed, 1969), pp.163–4.
16 Mulvaney, *Encounters in Place*, p.33.
17 Mulvaney, *Encounters in Place*, pp.33–4.
18 Mulvaney, *Encounters in Place*, p.36.
19 Mulvaney, *Encounters in Place*, p.36.
20 W. Bligh, *A Voyage to the South Seas, undertaken by command of His Majesty, for the purpose of conveying bread-fruit to the West Indies in His Majesty's ship Bounty* (Adelaide: Libraries Board of South Australia, 1969), pp.50–1.
21 G. Mackaness, *Captain William Bligh's Discoveries and Observations in Van Diemen's Land* (Sydney: D.S. Ford, 1943), pp.20–1.
22 I. Lee, 'A Forgotten Navigator: Captain (Afterwards Sir) John Hayes, and His Voyage of 1793', *Geographical Journal*, Vol.38, No.6 (December 1911), pp.580 and 584.
23 L. Marchant, 'La Perouse, Jean-Francois de Galaup, Comte de (1741–1788)', *ADB*, Vol.2, p.85.
24 L. Marchant, 'Bruny d'Entrecasteaux, Joseph-Antoine Raymond (1739-1793)', *ADB*, Vol.1, pp.171–2.
25 d'Entrecasteaux, *Voyage to Australia & the Pacific 1791-1793*, pp.34 and 55.
26 Mulvaney, 'French strangers on Tasmanian shores', p.116.
27 d'Entrecasteaux, *Voyage to Australia & the Pacific 1791–1793*, p.147.
28 d'Entrecasteaux, *Voyage to Australia & the Pacific 1791–1793*, pp.147–8.
29 Duyker, *Citizen Labillardière:* pp.150 and 152.
30 Anderson, 'French anthropology in Australia, a prelude', p.218.
31 Duyker, *Citizen Labillardière*, p.151.
32 Anderson, 'French anthropology in Australia, a prelude', p.218.
33 Anderson, 'French anthropology in Australia, a prelude', p.221.
34 Boyce, *Van Diemen's Land*, pp.20–1.
35 McFarlane, *Beyond Awakening*, p.45.
36 McFarlane, *Beyond Awakening*, p.45.
37 McFarlane, *Beyond Awakening*, p.45; L. Marchant and J. Reynolds, 'Baudin, Nicolas Thomas (1754–1803) and Freycinet, Louis-Claude Desaules de (1779–1842)', *ADB*, Vol.1, pp.71–2.
38 McFarlane, *Beyond Awakening*, p.46.
39 P. Valder, 'Plant Explorers: Who Discovered Our Plants?', *Australian Garden History*, Vol.9, No.4 (January–February 1998), p.6.
40 F. Horner, *The French Reconnaissance: Baudin in Australia 1801–1803* (Melbourne: Melbourne University Press, 1987), p.81.
41 L. Marchant and J. Reynolds, 'Péron, Francois (1775–1810)', *ADB*, Vol.2, p.323; G. Hewes, 'On Francois Pèron: The First Official Expedition Anthropologist', *Current Anthropology*, Vol.9, No.4 (October 1968), p.287.
42 S. Anderson, 'French anthropology in Australia, the first fieldwork report: Francois Pèron's "Maria Island — anthropological observations"', *Aboriginal History*, Vol.25 (2001), p.233; S. Konishi, 'Francois Pèron and the Tasmanians: an unrequited romance', in I. Macfarlane and M. Hannah (eds), *Transgressions: Critical Australian Indigenous histories* (Canberra: ANU E-Press, 2007), p.5.
43 Konishi, 'Francois Pèron and the Tasmanians', p.10.
44 Konishi, 'Francois Pèron and the Tasmanians', p.11.
45 P. O'Brien, 'Divine Browns and the Mighty Whiteman: exotic primitivism and the Baudin voyage to Tasmania in 1802', *Journal of Australian Studies*, Vol.23, No.63 (1999), p.14.
46 Konishi, 'Francois Pèron and the Tasmanians', pp.12–13.
47 Anderson, 'French anthropology in Australia, the first fieldwork report', p.236.

48 Anderson, 'French anthropology in Australia, p.238.
49 Hewes, 'On Francois Pèron', p.288; Horner, *The French Reconnaissance*, p.2.
50 Marchant and Reynolds, 'Baudin, Thomas Nicholas (1754–1803) and Freycinet, Louis-Claude Desaules de (1779–1842)', p.72.
51 A.J. Brown, *Ill-Starred Captains: Flinders and Baudin* (Fremantle, WA: Fremantle Arts Centre Press, 2004), pp.234–6.
52 Brown, *Ill-Starred Captains: Flinders and Baudin*, pp.239–41.
53 Brown, *Ill-Starred Captains: Flinders and Baudin*, p.252.
54 Horner, *The French Reconnaissance*, pp.251 and 263.
55 A. Jose, 'Nicolas Baudin', *Journal of the Royal Australian Historical Society*, Vol.20, Pt.6 (1934), pp.262–3; N. Shakespeare, *In Tasmania* (Sydney: Vintage 2004), pp.45–6.
56 Horner, *The French Reconnaissance*, pp.271–2.
57 Clark, *A History of Australia Vol.1*, p.190.
58 D. Phillips, 'Early Settlement on the Tamar', *Launceston Historical Society Papers and Proceedings*, Vol.16 (2004), p.32.
59 Walker, *Early Tasmania*, pp.25–6.
60 M. Johnson, 'People, Place and Identity in the Tamar Valley Precinct', in F. Gale (ed.), *Pulp Friction in Tasmania: A review of the environmental assessment of Gunns' proposed mill* (Launceston, Tas: Pencil Pine Press, 2011), p.4.
61 *Historical Records of New South Wales* [hereafter *HRNSW*], Vol.5, p.782.
62 C. Macknight, *Low Head to Launceston: the earliest reports of Port Dalrymple and the Tamar* (Launceston, Tas: Historical Survey of Northern Tasmania, 1998), p.47.
63 T. Valance, D. Moore and E. Groves, *Nature's Investigator: The Diary of Robert Brown in Australia, 1801–1805* (Canberra: Australian Biological Resources Study, 2001), p.470.
64 Valance, Moore and Groves, *Nature's Investigator: The Diary of Robert Brown in Australia, 1801–1805*, p.470.
65 R. Giblin, 'Robert Brown at Port Dalrymple', *Papers and Proceedings of the Royal Society of Tasmania for the year 1929* (1930), p.31.
66 Johnson, 'People, Place and Identity in the Tamar Valley Precinct', p.5.
67 Johnson, 'People, Place and Identity in the Tamar Valley Precinct'; *Historical Records of Australia* [hereafter *HRA*], Ser.3, Vol.1, p.605.
68 Lieutenant-Governor Paterson to Governor King, Camp at Outer Cove, Port Dalrymple, 26 November 1804, *HRNSW*, Vol.5, p.484.
69 'Exploration of Port Dalrymple and the Tamar', Journal of Lieutenant-Governor Paterson, 28 November 1804, p.499.
70 Ryan, *The Aboriginal Tasmanians*, p.77.
71 J. Connor, *The Australian Frontier Wars 1788–1838* (Sydney: University of New South Wales Press, 2005), p.38.
72 A. Frost, 'New South Wales as *Terra Nullius*: The British Denial of Aboriginal Rights', *Historical Studies*, Vol.19, No.77 (October 1981), p.514.
73 E. Scott, 'Taking Possession of Australia — The Doctrine of "Terra Nullius" (No-Man's Land)', *Journal of the Royal Australian Historical Society*, Vol.26, Pt.1 (1940), p.13.
74 H. Reynolds, *Aboriginal Sovereignty: Reflections on race, state and nation* (Sydney: Allen & Unwin, 1996), pp.98–9.
75 Earl Bathurst to Governor Darling, 14 July 1825, *HRA*, Ser.1, Vol.12, p.21; H. Reynolds, *Fate of a free people: a radical re-examination of the Tasmanian wars* (Melbourne: Penguin, 1995), p.92.
76 *Hobart Town Gazette and Van Diemen's Land Advertiser* [hereafter *HTG*] (Hobart), 16 September 1826, p.4; Ryan, *The Aboriginal Tasmanians*, p.90.

77 *Colonial Times* [hereafter *CT*] (Hobart), 15 September 1826, p.3.

78 West, *The History of Tasmania*, p.272.

79 McFarlane, *Beyond Awakening*, p.xiv.

4 RISDON COVE AND THE LONG MARCH TO WAR

1 Walker, *Early Tasmania*, p.49.

2 J. Ritchie (intro.), *A charge of mutiny: The Court Martial of Lieutenant Colonel George Johnston for deposing Governor William Bligh in the Rebellion of 26 January 1808* (Canberra: National Library of Australia, 1988), p.9.

3 P. Tardiff, *John Bowen's Hobart: The beginning of European settlement in Tasmania* (Hobart: Tasmanian Historical Research Association, 2003), p.142.

4 *Sydney Gazette and New South Wales Advertiser* (Sydney), 18 March 1804, p.4; K.V. Smith, *Mari Nawa: Aboriginal Odysseys* (Sydney: Rosenberg Publishing, 2010), p.52.

5 J. Owen, *Risdon Cove 3 May 1804* (Sydney: Macleay Press, 2010), pp.3–4.

6 West, *The History of Tasmania*, p.262.

7 Walker, *Early Tasmania*, pp.48–9.

8 P. Tardiff, 'Risdon Cove', in R. Manne (ed.), *Whitewash: On Keith Windschuttle's Fabrication of Aboriginal History* (Melbourne: Black Inc. Agenda, 2003), p.221.

9 Lieutenant-Governor Collins to Governor King, 15 May 1804, *HRA*, Ser.3, Vol.1, pp.237–8.

10 M. Nicholls (ed.), *The Diary of the Reverend Robert Knopwood 1808–1838* (Hobart: Tasmanian Historical Research Association, 1977), p.51.

11 Walker, *Early Tasmania*, p.51.

12 Lieutenant Moore to Lieutenant-Governor Collins, 7 May 1804, *HRA*, Ser.3, Vol.1, pp.242–3.

13 Lieutenant Moore to Lieutenant-Governor Collins, p.243.

14 W.F. Refshauge, 'An analytical approach to the events at Risdon Cove on 3 May 1804', *Journal of the Royal Australian Historical Society*, Vol.93, No.1 (June 2007), p.47.

15 Moore to Collins, 7 May 1804, pp.242–3

16 Collins to King, 15 May 1804, p.238.

17 *Sydney Gazette and New South Wales Advertiser* (Sydney), 2 September 1804, p.2.

18 Nicholls (ed.), *The Diary of the Reverend Robert Knopwood 1808–1838*, p.51.

19 Windschuttle, *The Fabrication of Aboriginal History Vol.*, p.18.

20 Tardiff, *John Bowen's Hobart*, p.147.

21 *Sydney Gazette and New South Wales Advertiser* (Sydney), 2 September 1804, p.2.

22 Nicholls (ed.), *The Diary of the Reverend Robert Knopwood 1808–1838*, p.51.

23 F. Voss, 'Surgeon became a shady operator', "Examiner Extra: Soldiers, Settlers and Bushrangers", in *Examiner* (Launceston), 9 November 2004, P.A34.

24 A. Bartlett, 'Fall from grace — Jacob Mountgarrett: Launceston's first doctor', "Examiner Extra: 2004 Bicentenary of Tasmania", in *Examiner* (Launceston), 16 February 2004, p.A12.

25 Voss, 'Surgeon became a shady operator', p.A34.

26 Voss, 'Surgeon became a shady operator', p.A34.

27 Anon, 'Mills, Peter (1786-1816)', *ADB*, Vol.2, pp.231–2.

28 I. Mead, 'Mountgarrett, Jacob (1773?-1828)', *ADB*, Vol.2, p.264.

29 D. Wyllie, *Dolly Dalrymple* (Childers, Qld: Diana Wyllie, 2004), pp.11 and 79–80.

30 Refshauge, 'An analytical approach to the events at Risdon Cove on 3 May 1804', p.43.

31 Anon, *Copies of all Correspondence between Lieutenant-Governor Arthur and His Majesty's Secretary of State for the Colonies, on the Subject of the Military Operations lately carried on against the Aboriginal Inhabitants of Van Diemen's Land* (Hobart: Tasmanian Historical Research Association, 1971), p.37.

32 Anon, *Copies of all Correspondence between Lieutenant-Governor Arthur and His Majesty's Secretary of State for the Colonies, on the Subject of the Military Operations lately carried on against the Aboriginal Inhabitants of Van Diemen's Land*, p.53.

33 M. Asten, 'The Risdon Cove Site: Birth of a State or Site of a Massacre; Bone of Contention or Future Site of Reconciliation?, *Tasmanian Historical Studies*, Vol.18 (2013), pp.112–13 and 115.

34 A. McGrath, 'Tasmania: 1', in A. McGrath (ed.), *Contested Ground: Australian Aborigines under the British Crown* (Sydney: Allen & Unwin, 1995), p.314.

35 Anon, *Copies of all Correspondence between Lieutenant-Governor Arthur and His Majesty's Secretary of State for the Colonies*, p.53.

36 Walker, *Early Tasmania*, p.55.

37 Anon, *Copies of all Correspondence between Lieutenant-Governor Arthur and His Majesty's Secretary of State for the Colonies*, p.53.

38 Anon, *Copies of all Correspondence between Lieutenant-Governor Arthur and His Majesty's Secretary of State for the Colonies*, p.51.

39 Anon, *Copies of all Correspondence between Lieutenant-Governor Arthur and His Majesty's Secretary of State for the Colonies*, p.37.

40 M. Binks, 'Violence at Risdon Cove', *Mercury* (Hobart), 12 September 1988, p.1; L. Ryan, 'Risdon Cove and the Massacre of 3 May 1804: Their Place in Tasmanian History', *Tasmanian Historical Studies*, Vol.9 (2004), p.119.

41 G. Lehman, 'Our Story of Risdon Cove', *Puganna News*, No.34 (May 1992), p.2. Copy held at Riawunna Centre for Aboriginal Studies, Launceston campus, University of Tasmania.

42 Ryan, *The Aboriginal Tasmanians*, pp.17 and 19.

43 Refshauge, 'An analytical approach to the events at Risdon Cove on 3 May 1804', p.45.

44 Ryan, *The Aboriginal Tasmanians*, pp.17 and 19.

45 Refshauge, 'An analytical approach to the events at Risdon Cove on 3 May 1804', p.45.

46 Refshauge, 'An analytical approach to the events at Risdon Cove on 3 May 1804', p.48.

47 R. Broome, 'The struggle for Australia: Aboriginal–European warfare, 1770–1930', in M. McKernan and M. Browne (eds), *Australia: Two Centuries of War and Peace* (Canberra: Australian War Memorial and Allen & Unwin, 1988), pp.97–8.

48 Refshauge, 'An analytical approach to the events at Risdon Cove on 3 May 1804', p.48.

49 Broome, 'The struggle for Australia', pp.97–8.

50 Refshauge, 'An analytical approach to the events at Risdon Cove on 3 May 1804', p.48.

51 Refshauge, 'An analytical approach to the events at Risdon Cove on 3 May 1804', p.50.

52 Ryan, 'Risdon Cove and the Massacre of 3 May 1804', p.118.

53 Windschuttle, *The Fabrication of Aboriginal History Vol.1*, p.19.

54 J. Maynard, 'The Shark, Remora and Aboriginal History', *International Journal of Critical Indigenous Studies*, Vol.1, No.1 (2008), p.48.

55 J. Talbott, 'The Rise and Fall of the Carronade', *History Today*, Vol.39, No.8 (August 1989), pp.25–6.

56 Talbott, 'The Rise and Fall of the Carronade', p.30.

57 Refshauge, 'An analytical approach to the events at Risdon Cove on 3 May 1804', p.47.
58 Refshauge, 'An analytical approach to the events at Risdon Cove on 3 May 1804', pp.47–8.
59 Talbott, 'The Rise and Fall of the Carronade', p.27.
60 Windschuttle, *The Fabrication of Aboriginal History*, p.24.
61 Tardiff, 'Risdon Cove', p.222.
62 J. Cove, *What The Bones Say: Tasmanian Aborigines, Science and Domination* (Ottawa: Carleton University Press, 1995), p.46.
63 J. Boyce, 'Fantasy Island', in Manne (ed.), *Whitewash*, p.41.
64 I. Williams, *Rum: A Social and Sociable History of the Real Spirit of 1776* (New York: Nation Books, 2005), p.226.
65 Ryan, 'Risdon Cove and the Massacre of 3 May 1804', p.122.
66 J. Bonwick, *The Last of the Tasmanians, or The Black War of Van Diemen's Land* (London: Sampson Low, Son, & Marston, 1870), p.35.
67 See for example: C. Turnbull, *Black War: The Extermination of the Tasmanian Aborigines* (Melbourne: F.W. Cheshire, 1948), p.34.
68 Bonwick, *The Last of the Tasmanians*, p.35.
69 Windschuttle, *The Fabrication of Aboriginal History*, p.25.
70 A. Alexander, *Governors' Ladies: The Wives and Mistresses of Van Diemen's Land Governors* (Hobart: Tasmanian Historical Research Association, 1987), pp.6 and 14.
71 S. Ison, 'A Rum Lot', *Australian Military History*, No.3 (October–November 1994), p.44.
72 F. Smith, *Caribbean Rum: A Social and Economic History* (Gainesville, FL: University Press of Florida, 2005), pp.136–7.
73 Refshauge, 'An analytical approach to the events at Risdon Cove on 3 May 1804', pp.48–9.
74 Bonwick, *The Last of the Tasmanians*, p.35.
75 See for example: B. Elder, *Blood on the Wattle: Massacres and Maltreatment of Australian Aborigines since 1788* (Sydney: National Book Distributors, 1992), p.28.
76 Ryan, 'Risdon Cove and the Massacre of 3 May 1804', p.112.
77 Ryan, 'Risdon Cove and the Massacre of 3 May 1804', p.117.
78 A. McGowan, 'Archaeological Investigations at Risdon Cove Historic Site 1978–1980', National Parks and Wildlife Service Tasmania, Occasional Paper No.10 (April 1985), pp.25–35 and 79–80.
79 Binks, 'Violence at Risdon Cove', p.1.
80 Ryan, 'Risdon Cove and the Massacre of 3 May 1804', p.119.
81 Ryan, 'Risdon Cove and the Massacre of 3 May 1804', p.119.
82 Calder, *Levée, Line and Martial Law*, p.242.
83 Jones, 'Tasmanian Aborigines and Dogs', pp.259–60; Boyce, 'Canine revolution', pp.111–12.
84 Boyce, *Van Diemen's Land*, pp.59–60.
85 W. Joy and T. Prior, *The Bushrangers* (Adelaide: Rigby, 1971), p.21; M. Johnson, *Trials and Tribulations: A Social History of Europeans in Australia 1788–1960* (Launceston, Tas: Myola House of Publishing, 2007), p.34.
86 Johnson, *Trials and Tribulations*, p.34.
87 C. White, *History of Australian Bushranging: Vol.1* (Melbourne: Currey O'Neil, 1980), p.30.
88 G. Boxall, *Australian Bushrangers: An Illustrated History* (Adelaide: Rigby, 1976), p.18.
89 M. Fels, 'Culture Contact in the County of Buckinghamshire, Van Diemen's Land 1803-11', *THRA*, Vol.29, No.2 (June 1982), p.60.
90 C. Smith, *Tales of Old Tasmania: The First Fifty Years* (Adelaide: Rigby, 1978), pp.81–82.
91 L. Mickleborough, 'Colonel William Sorell Lieutenant-Governor of Van Diemen's Land 1817–1824: An Examination of his Convict System and Establishment of Free Settlement'

(unpublished MA thesis, University of Tasmania, 2002), p.192.
92 L. Robson, *A History of Tasmania Vol.1: Van Diemen's Land from the Earliest Times to 1855* (Melbourne: Oxford University Press, 1983), p.48.
93 Reynolds, *Fate of a Free People*, p.90.
94 McGrath, 'Tasmania:1', p.315.
95 S. Robinson, '"Something like slavery?" The exploitation of Aboriginal child labour in Queensland, 1842–1945' (unpublished PhD thesis, University of Queensland, 2002), p.281.
96 B. Madley, 'From Terror to Genocide: Britain's Tasmanian Penal Colony and Australia's History Wars', *Journal of British Studies*, Vol.47, No.1 (January 2008), p.87.
97 See for example: R. Lemkin, 'Tasmania' (ed.) A. Curthoys, *Patterns of Prejudice*, Vol.39, No.2 (2005), pp.185–86.
98 *Sydney Gazette and New South Wales Advertiser* (Sydney), 18 July 1818, p.3.
99 M. Moneypenny, '"Going out and coming in": Cooperation and Collaboration between Aborigines and Europeans in early Tasmania', *Tasmanian Historical Studies*, Vol.5, No.1 (1995–1996), p.69.
100 N. Parry, '"Hanging no good for blackfellow": Looking into the life of Musquito', in Macfarlane and Hannah (eds), *Transgressions*, pp.154–5.
101 Parry, '"Hanging no good for blackfellow"', p.156.
102 Smith, *Mari Nawi*, pp.73–4.
103 Parry, '"Hanging no good for blackfellow"', p.157.
104 K. Harman, 'Aboriginal Convicts: Race, Law and Transportation in Colonial New South Wales' (unpublished PhD thesis, University of Tasmania, 2008), p.51.
105 *HTG*, 3 December 1824, p.3.
106 R. Cox, 'Black Tom Birch: Fact and Fiction', *THRA*, Vol.60, No.1 (April 2013), pp.8–9.
107 Plomley, *Friendly Mission*, p.347.
108 *HTG*, 3 December 1824, p.3.
109 Cox, 'Black Tom Birch', p.9.
110 Parry, '"Hanging no good for blackfellow"', pp.160–1.
111 Parry, '"Hanging no good for blackfellow"', p.161.
112 Parry, '"Hanging no good for blackfellow"', p.161.
113 *HTG*, 3 December 1824, p.3.
114 R. Travers, *Rogue's March: A Chronicle of Colonial Crime in Australia* (Melbourne: Hutchinson, 1973), p.73.
115 *HTG*, 25 February 1825, p.2.
116 *CT*, 6 January 1826, p.4.
117 *CT*, 5 May 1826, p.3.
118 *CT*, 22 September 1826, p.3.
119 *CT*, 17 November 1826, p.3; *HTG*, 18 November 1826, p.2.
120 *HTG*, 25 November 1826, p.2.
121 *CT*, 29 December 1826, p.3.
122 Bonwick, *The Last of the Tasmanians*, pp.103–4.
123 Ryan, *The Aboriginal Tasmanians*, p.83.
124 S. Morgan, *Land Settlement in Early Tasmania: Creating an Antipodean England* (Cambridge: Cambridge University Press, 1992), p.19.

5 THE SEALING FRATERNITY AND THE 'BLACK WAR'

1 C. Bateson, *Dire Strait: A History of Bass Strait* (Sydney: A.H. & A.W. Reed, 1973), pp.29 and 31.
2 B. Plomley and K.A. Henley, 'The Sealers of Bass Strait and the Cape Barren Island Community', *THRA*, Vol.37, No.1 (March 1990), p.38.
3 Plomley and Henley, 'The Sealers of Bass Strait and the Cape Barren Island Community', p.39.
4 M. Roe, 'Charles Bishop, Pioneer of Pacific Commerce', *THRA*, Vol.10 (1962–1963), p.12.
5 M. Veitch, *The Forgotten Islands: A*

personal adventure through the islands of Bass Strait (Melbourne: Viking, 2011), pp.78–9 and 221–2.

6 Plomley, *Friendly Mission*, p.1049.

7 D.R. Hainsworth, 'Iron Men in Wooden Ships: The Sydney Sealers 1800–1820', *Labour History*, No.13 (November 1967), p.19.

8 G. Bolton, *Spoils and Spoilers: A history of Australians shaping their environment* (Sydney: Allen & Unwin, 1992), p.50.

9 J. King, 'Elephant Seal Oil from King Island, Bass Strait, 1802–1819: with estimates of numbers killed and size of the original population', *Papers and Proceedings of the Royal Society of Tasmania*, Vol.133, Pt.1 (31 October 1999), p.51.

10 B. Little, 'The Sealing and Whaling Industry in Australia before 1850', *Australian Economic History Review*, Vol.9, No.2 (September 1969), pp.112–13.

11 *Sydney Gazette and New South Wales Advertiser* (Sydney), 24 July 1813, p.2; Johnson, *Trials and Tribulations*, p.17.

12 I. Stuart, 'Sea rats, bandits and roistering buccaneers: What were the Bass Strait sealers really like?', *Journal of the Royal Australian Historical Society*, Vol.83, Pt.1 (June 1997), p.49.

13 Hainsworth, 'Iron Men in Wooden Ships', p.22.

14 Little, 'The Sealing and Whaling Industry in Australia before 1850', pp.111–12.

15 Johnson, *Trials and Tribulations*, p.17.

16 Johnson, *Trials and Tribulations*, p.17.

17 Plomley and Henley, 'The Sealers of Bass Strait and the Cape Barren Island Community', p.54.

18 Ryan, *The Aboriginal Tasmanians*, p.67.

19 See: P. Cameron, *Grease and Ochre: The blending of two cultures at the colonial sea frontier* (Launceston, Tas: Fullers Bookshop, 2011).

20 William Stewart to Colonial Secretary Campbell, 28 September 1815, HRA, Ser. 3, Vol.2, p.576; S. Murray-Smith, 'Beyond the Pale: The Islander Community of Bass Strait in the Nineteenth Century', *THRA*, Vol.20, No.4 (December 1973), p.172.

21 'Miscellaneous Papers of George Augustus Robinson 1829–1833' A7059, State Library of New South Wales, Sydney, pp.34–7.

22 K. James, 'Wife or Slave: Australian Sealing Slavery, Australia's own slavery system using Indigenous women workers on Kangaroo Island and Bass Strait islands 1802–1835', in A. Chittleborough et.al., *Alas for the Pelicans! Flinders, Baudin & Beyond: Essays and Poems* (Kent Town, SA: Wakefield Press, 2002), p.178.

23 McFarlane, *Beyond Awakening*, p.56.

24 J.S. Cumpston, *Kangaroo Island 1800–1836* (Canberra: Roebuck Society, 1986), pp.89–90.

25 McFarlane, *Beyond Awakening*, pp.56–7.

26 R. Taylor, *Unearthed: The Aboriginal Tasmanians of Kangaroo Island* (Kent Town, SA: Wakefield Press, 2008), pp.212–13.

27 McFarlane, *Beyond Awakening*, pp.58–9.

28 N. Clements, 'Frontier Conflict in Van Diemen's Land' (unpublished PhD thesis, University of Tasmania, 2013), p.76.

29 K.M. Bowden, *Captain James Kelly of Hobart Town* (Melbourne: Melbourne University Press, 1964), pp.57–8.

30 George Robinson to Lieutenant-Colonel Arthur, 20 November 1830, CSO 1/317, pp.231–2, TAHO.

31 Plomley and Henley, 'The Sealers of Bass Strait and the Cape Barren Island Community', pp.54–5.

32 V. Matson-Green, 'Tarenorerer (c.1800–1831)', ADB, Supplementary Volume 1580–1880, p.376; S. De Vries, *Strength of Spirit: Pioneering Women of Achievement from First Fleet to Federation* (Sydney: Millennium Books, 1995), pp.111–12.

33 F. Voss, 'Aboriginal woman a "resistance leader"', 'Examiner Extra: 200 Great Tasmanians', in *Examiner* (Launceston), 22 November 2005, p.A29; McFarlane, *Beyond Awakening*, p.119.

34 Matson-Green, 'Tarenorerer (c.1800–1831)', p.376.
35 Plomley, *Friendly Mission*, p.872.
36 McFarlane, *Beyond Awakening*, p.119.
37 N.J.B. Plomley, 'The Tasmanian Tribes & Cicatrices as Tribal Indicators among the Tasmanian Aborigines', Queen Victoria Museum and Art Gallery, Launceston, Occasional Paper No.5 (1992), p.32; Plomley, *Friendly Mission*, p.658.
38 Clements, 'Frontier Conflict in Van Diemen's Land', pp.156–7.
39 S. Breen, The PALL-I-TORRE: The Black native people of Meander', in Anon, *Meander Valley Memories: A History of Meander and Surrounding Areas* (Meander, Tas: Meander Centenary Writers, 1991), p.2.
40 Jones, 'Tasmanian Tribes', pp.343–4.
41 L. Ryan, 'Massacre in the Black War in Tasmania 1823–34: a case study of the Meander River Region, June 1827', *Journal of Genocide Research*, Vol.10, No.4 (2008), pp.488–9.
42 Ryan, 'Massacre in the Black War in Tasmania 1823–34', p.489.
43 Plomley, *Friendly Mission*, p.231.
44 L. Ryan, 'Who Is the Fabricator?', in Manne (ed.), *Whitewash*, p.241.
45 Windschuttle, *The Fabrication of Aboriginal History: Vol.1*, pp.271–2.
46 W.F. Refshauge, 'The Swivel Gun Massacre', *THRA*, Vol.57, No.1 (April 2010), pp.41 and 44.
47 Ryan, 'Massacre in the Black War in Tasmania 1823–34', p.490.
48 I. McFarlane, 'Dalrymple, Dolly (c.1808–1864)', *ADB*, Supplementary Volume 1580–1880, p.94.
49 Ryan, 'Massacre in the Black War in Tasmania 1823–34', p.490.
50 Breen, 'The PALL-I-TORRE', p.3.
51 Ryan, 'Massacre in the Black War in Tasmania 1823–34', p.492.
52 Ryan, *Tasmanian Aborigines*, p.94.
53 Depositions of John Skinner and Thomas Williams, 30 June 1827, CSO 1/1/316, pp.23–28 and 34–36, TAHO.
54 CT, 6 July 1827, p.4.
55 Ryan, 'Massacre in the Black War in Tasmania 1823–34', p.493.
56 Ryan, 'Massacre in the Black War in Tasmania 1823–34', p.488.
57 Ryan, 'Massacre in the Black War in Tasmania 1823–34', p.493.
58 Reynolds, *Fate of a Free People*, p.94.
59 J.C.H. Gill, 'Notes on the Tasmanian "Black War" 1827–1830', *Journal of the Royal Historical Society of Queensland*, Vol.8, No.3 (1967–1968), p.508.
60 R. Cox, *Steps to the Scaffold: The untold story of Tasmania's black bushrangers* (Pawleena, Tas: Cornhill Publishing, 2004), pp.72–3.
61 CSO 1/316/7578, p.832, TAHO.
62 Cox, *Steps to the Scaffold*, pp.82–4.
63 Cox, *Steps to the Scaffold*, pp.85–6.
64 *Australian* (Sydney), 16 May 1827, p.4.
65 Cox, *Steps to the Scaffold*, pp.86–8 and 95.
66 N.J.B. Plomley, 'The Aboriginal-Settler Clash in Van Diemen's Land 1803–1831', Queen Victoria Museum and Art Gallery, Launceston, Occasional Paper No.16 (1992), p.58.
67 Calder, *Lèvee, Line and Martial Law*, p.161.
68 Calder, *Lèvee, Line and Martial Law*, p.166.
69 *HTG*, 29 April 1825, p.3.
70 W.H. Hudspeth, 'Experiences of a Settler in the Early Days of Van Diemen's Land', *Papers and Proceedings of the Royal Society of Tasmania for the Year 1935* (1936), pp.150–1.
71 Calder, *Lèvee, Line and Martial Law*, p.166.
72 Calder, *Lèvee, Line and Martial Law*, pp.166 and 168.
73 L. Ryan, *Tasmanian Aborigines: A history since 1803* (Sydney: Allen & Unwin, 2012), pp.80 and 82.
74 J.F. McMahon, 'The British Army: Its Role in Counter-Insurgency in the Black War in Van Diemen's Land', *Tasmanian Historical Studies*, Vol.5, No.1 (1995–1996), p.58.
75 Plomley, *Jorgen Jorgenson and the Aborigines of Van Diemen's Land*, p.81.

76 Ryan, *The Aboriginal Tasmanians*, p.92.
77 Ryan, *Tasmanian Aborigines*, p.83.
78 N. Clements, '"Wriggle, and Shuffle, and Twist": Attitudes Towards Aborigines in the Vandemonian Press 1825–1831' (unpublished Honours thesis, University of Tasmania, 2007), p.32.
79 Ryan, *The Aboriginal Tasmanians*, p.95.
80 Connor, *The Australian Frontier Wars 1788–1838*, p.89.
81 Connor, *The Australian Frontier Wars 1788–1838*, pp.84–5.
82 Ryan, *The Aboriginal Tasmanians*, p.95.
83 *Hobart Town Courier* (Hobart), 12 April 1828, p.3.
84 Clements, 'Frontier Conflict in Van Diemen's Land', p.136.
85 Windschuttle, *The Fabrication of Aboriginal History*: Vol.1, p.149.
86 P. Edmonds, '"Failing in every endeavour to conciliate": Governor Arthur's Proclamation Boards to the Aborigines, Australian conciliation narratives and their transnational connections', *Journal of Australian Studies*, Vol.35, No.2 (June 2011), pp.201–2.
87 Anon, *Copies of all Correspondence between Lieutenant-Governor George Arthur and His Majesty's Secretary of State for the Colonies*, p.7.
88 Ryan, *The Aboriginal Tasmanians*, p.97.
89 Anon, *Copies of all Correspondence between Lieutenant-Governor George Arthur and His Majesty's Secretary of State for the Colonies*, pp.11–12.
90 R. Davis, *The Tasmanian Gallows: A Study of Capital Punishment* (Hobart: Cat & Fiddle Press, 1974), pp.6–7.
91 J. Connor, 'British Frontier Warfare Logistics and the "Black Line", Van Diemen's Land (Tasmania), 1830', *War in History*, Vol.9, No.2 (April 2002), p.148.
92 Plomley, *Jorgen Jorgenson and the Aborigines of Van Diemen's Land*, pp.81–3; Clements, 'Frontier Conflict in Van Diemen's Land', pp.133–4.
93 S. Bakewell, *The English Dane: A Life of Jorgen Jorgenson* (London: Chatto & Windus, 2005), pp.217–20.
94 Ryan, *The Aboriginal Tasmanians*, pp.101 and 155.
95 Clements, 'Frontier Conflict in Van Diemen's Land', pp.136–7.
96 K. Harman, 'Send in the Sydney Natives! Deploying Mainlanders Against Tasmanian Aborigines', *Tasmanian Historical Studies*, Vol.14 (2009), pp.7 and 9.
97 *Hobart Town Courier* (Hobart), 26 September 1829, p.2.
98 Harman, 'Send in the Sydney Natives!', pp.16–17.
99 Harman, 'Send in the Sydney Natives!', pp.20–1.
100 R. Stirling, John Batman: Aspirations of a Currency Lad', *Australian Heritage* (Spring 2007), p.41.
101 Harman, 'Send in the Sydney Natives!', p.12.
102 Ryan, *The Aboriginal Tasmanians*, p.102.
103 Ryan, *The Aboriginal Tasmanians*, p.102.
104 Ryan, *The Aboriginal Tasmanians*, p.103.
105 Ryan, *The Aboriginal Tasmanians*, p.103.
106 Plomley, 'The Aboriginal-Settler Clash in Van Diemen's Land 1803-1831', pp.81–3.
107 Plomley, 'The Aboriginal-Settler Clash in Van Diemen's Land 1803-1831', p.83.
108 Plomley, *Friendly Mission*, p.236; G.A. Robinson to Lieutenant-Governor Arthur, 20 November 1830, CSO 1/317, p.223, TAHO.
109 Boyce, 'Fantasy Island', pp.31–2; Stirling, 'John Batman', p.41.
110 L. Ryan, 'The Black Line in Van Diemen's Land: success or failure?', Journal of Australian Studies, Vol.37, No.1 (2013), p.5.
111 Plomley, 'The Aboriginal-Settler Clash in Van Diemen's Land 1803–1831', p.84.
112 Plomley, 'The Aboriginal-Settler Clash in Van Diemen's Land 1803–1831', pp.84–5.
113 Ryan, *The Aboriginal Tasmanians*, p.104.
114 Ryan, *The Aboriginal Tasmanians*, p.104.
115 Ryan, *The Aboriginal Tasmanians*, p.106.

116 Ryan, *The Aboriginal Tasmanians*, pp.107–8.
117 Reynolds, *Fate of a Free People*, pp.114–15.
118 Windschuttle, *The Fabrication of Aboriginal History*: Vol.1, pp.171–2.

6 THE 'BLACK LINE' AND 'FRIENDLY MISSION'

1 Calder, *Levée, Line and Martial Law*, pp.181–2.
2 N. Clements, '"Army of sufferers": the experience of Tasmania's Black Line', *Journal of Australian Studies*, Vol.37, No.1 (2013), pp.21–2.
3 Connor, *The Australian Frontier Wars 1788–1838*, p.94.
4 Melville, *The History of Van Diemen's Land*, p.92.
5 Connor, *The Australian Frontier Wars 1788–1838*, p.97.
6 Connor, *The Australian Frontier Wars 1788–1838*, pp.95 and 98.
7 Connor, 'British Frontier Warfare Logistics and the "Black Line"', p.152.
8 Bonwick, *The Last of the Tasmanians*, p.152.
9 Clements, 'Frontier Conflict in Van Diemen's Land', pp.196–7.
10 Connor, *The Australian Frontier Wars 1788–1838*, p.95.
11 E. Cave, '"Journal during the expedition against the blacks": Robert Lawrence's experience on the Black Line', *Journal of Australian Studies*, Vol.37, No.1 (2013), p.38.
12 Connor, *The Australian Frontier Wars 1788–1938*, p.95.
13 Cave, '"Journal during the expedition against the blacks"', pp.36 and 39–40.
14 Cave, '"Journal during the expedition against the blacks"', pp.40–1; Clements, '"Army of sufferers"', p.27.
15 Clements, '"Army of sufferers"', p.25.
16 Connor, 'British Frontier Warfare Logistics and the "Black Line"', p.155.
17 N. Clements, *The Black War: Fear, Sex and Resistance in Tasmania* (St Lucia, Qld: University of Queensland Press, 2014, p.127.
18 M. Roe, 'Eumarrah (c.1798–1832)', *ADB*, Supplementary Volume 1580–1880, p.117.
19 Plomley, 'The Aboriginal-Settler Clash in Van Diemen's Land 1803–1831', p.94.
20 *HTG*, 23 October 1830, p.2.
21 Plomley, 'The Aboriginal–Settler Clash in Van Diemen's Land 1803–1831', p.95.
22 Ryan, *The Aboriginal Tasmanians*, p.157.
23 Roe, 'Eumarrah (c.1798–1832)', p.117.
24 Plomley, 'The Aboriginal-Settler Clash in Van Diemen's Land 1803–1831', p.95.
25 Clements, 'Frontier Conflict in Van Diemen's Land', pp.196–7.
26 Clements, *The Black War*, pp.134–5.
27 J. McMahon, 'The Black Line: Military Operations in Van Diemen's Land, October to November 1830', *THRA*, Vol.55, No.3 (December 2008), p.179.
28 Lieutenant-Governor Arthur to Major Douglas, 25 October 1830, CSO 1/324, pp.18-19, TAHO.
29 Connor, *The Australian Frontier Wars 1788–1838*, p.98.
30 Bonwick, *The Last of the Tasmanians*, pp.151–2.
31 Connor, 'British Frontier Warfare Logistics and the "Black Line"', p.156.
32 Cave, '"Journal during the expedition against the blacks"', p.43.
33 McMahon, 'The Black Line', p.181.
34 Calder, *Levée, Line and Martial Law*, p.189.
35 Connor, 'British Frontier Warfare Logistics and the Black Line', p.157.
36 Clements, '"Army of sufferers"', p.19.
37 Connor, *The Australian Frontier Wars 1788–1838*, p.100.
38 Ryan, 'The Black Line in Van Diemen's Land: success or failure?', pp.3–4.
39 Clements, 'Frontier Conflict in Van Diemen's Land', pp.225–6.
40 Plomley, 'The Aboriginal-Settler Clash in Van Diemen's Land 1803-1831',

pp.96–8.
41 Plomley, 'The Aboriginal-Settler Clash in Van Diemen's Land 1803-1831', p.98.
42 Wyllie, *Dolly Dalrymple*, pp.28–31.
43 McFarlane, 'Dalrymple, Dolly (c.1808–1864)', p.94.
44 H.R. Thomas, 'Thomas, Jocelyn Henry Connor (1780–1862) and Bartholomew Boyle (1785?–1831)', *ADB*, Vol.2, pp.516–17.
45 CT, 28 September 1831, p.2; Plomley, 'The Aboriginal-Settler Clash in Van Diemen's Land 1803–1831', p.100.
46 *Examiner* (Launceston), 2 November 1831, p.341; Hobart Town Courier (Hobart), 10 December 1831, p.2.
47 Calder, *Levée, Line and Martial Law*, p.198.
48 'Copy of a letter by James Erskine Calder upon the existence of natives in unexplored parts of Tasmania in 1847', University of Tasmania Library, Special and Rare Materials Collection, Hobart.
49 N.J.B. Plomley, 'Robinson, George Augustus (1788-1866)', ADB, Vol.2, pp.385–6.
50 Plomley, 'Robinson, George Augustus (1788–1866)', p.386; A. Johnston, 'George Augustus Robinson, the "Great Conciliator": colonial celebrity and its postcolonial aftermath', *Journal of Postcolonial Studies*, Vol.12, No.2 (2009), p.157.
51 Ryan, *The Aboriginal Tasmanians*, pp.126 and 129.
52 Ryan, *The Aboriginal Tasmanians*, p.129.
53 V. Rae-Ellis, *Black Robinson: Protector of Aborigines* (Melbourne: Melbourne University Press, 1988), p.33.
54 Rae-Ellis, *Black Robinson: Protector of Aborigines*, pp.38–9.
55 Ryan, *Tasmanian Aborigines*, p.160.
56 Plomley, *Friendly Mission*, p.164.
57 Plomley, *Friendly Mission*, pp.168–9.
58 Ryan, *The Aboriginal Tasmanians*, p.134.
59 Ryan, *The Aboriginal Tasmanians*, p.134.
60 Roe, 'Eumarrah (c.1798–1832)', p.117; Plomley, *Friendly Mission*, p.191.
61 Ryan, *The Aboriginal Tasmanians*, p.137; Plomley, *Friendly Mission*, p.195.
62 I. McFarlane, 'Cape Grim', in Manne (ed.), *Whitewash*, pp.282–3.
63 McFarlane, *Beyond Awakening*, p.142.
64 Plomley, *Friendly Mission*, pp.225 and 243.
65 Plomley, *Friendly Mission*, p.144; Ryan, *The Tasmanian Aborigines*, p.170.
66 Rae-Ellis, *Black Robinson*, pp.57–9.
67 Plomley, *Friendly Mission*, pp.259 and 277–8.
68 Ryan, *The Aboriginal Tasmanians*, p.145.
69 Ibid, p.146; Plomley, *Friendly Mission*, pp.295 and 470.
70 Rae-Ellis, *Black Robinson*, pp.65–6.
71 Plomley, *Friendly Mission*, pp.296–301.
72 Plomley, *Friendly Mission*, p.490.
73 Plomley, *Friendly Mission*, pp.305–6.
74 Anon, 'McKay, Alexander (1802?–1882)', *ADB*, Vol.2, p.170; Rae-Ellis, *Black Robinson*, pp.64–5; T. McKay, *Alexander McKay: This Prince of Bush Travellers* (Kingston, Tas: Thelma McKay, 1994), p.50.
75 Plomley, *Friendly Mission*, p.324.
76 Plomley, *Friendly Mission*, 328.
77 Ryan, *The Aboriginal Tasmanians*, p.150.
78 Ryan, *The Aboriginal Tasmanians*, pp.150–1.
79 Plomley, *Friendly Mission*, p.381.
80 Ryan, *Tasmanian Aborigines*, p.182.
81 Anon, *Copies of all Correspondence between Lieutenant-Governor Arthur and His Majesty's Secretary of State for the Colonies*, p.82; Reynolds, *Fate of a Free People*, p.153.
82 Plomley, *Friendly Mission*, pp.489–91.
83 Ryan, *The Aboriginal Tasmanians*, p.157.
84 Ryan, *The Aboriginal Tasmanians*, pp.154–5.
85 Ryan, *The Aboriginal Tasmanians*, p.157.
86 Ryan, *The Aboriginal Tasmanians*, p.157.
87 Ryan, *The Aboriginal Tasmanians*, p.158.
88 *Hobart Town Courier* (Hobart), 14 January 1832, p.2; J.E. Calder, *Some Account of the Wars, Extirpation, Habits, etc. of the Native Tribes, of Tasmania* (Hobart: Fullers Bookshop, 1972), p.62.

89 Ryan, *The Tasmanian Aborigines*, pp.200 and 202.
90 Plomley, *Friendly Mission*, p.640.
91 McFarlane, *Beyond Awakening*, p.156.
92 Plomley, *Friendly Mission*, pp.653 and 657.
93 Plomley, *Friendly Mission*, pp.653 and 655.
94 Ryan, *The Aboriginal Tasmanians*, p.163.
95 McFarlane, *Beyond Awakening*, pp.157–8.
96 Plomley, *Friendly Mission*, pp.684–6.
97 Plomley, *Friendly Mission*, p.686.
98 Plomley, *Friendly Mission*, pp.686–7.
99 McFarlane, *Beyond Awakening*, p.159.
100 McFarlane, *Beyond Awakening*, pp.160–1.
101 McFarlane, *Beyond Awakening*, pp.161–2.
102 McFarlane, *Beyond Awakening*, p.162.
103 McFarlane, *Beyond Awakening*, p.163; Plomley, *Friendly Mission*, p.909.
104 Cox, 'Black Tom Birch', p.12.
105 Plomley, *Friendly Mission*, p.960.
106 McFarlane, *Beyond Awakening*, p.169.
107 Reynolds, *Fate of a Free People*, pp.122 and 154.
108 H. Reynolds, 'George Augustus Robinson in Van Diemen's Land: Race, Status and Religion', in A. Johnston and M. Rolls (eds), *Reading Robinson: Companion Essays to Friendly Mission* (Hobart: Quintus Publishing, 2008), p.162. For Robinson's questionable linguistic skills see: T. Crowley, 'Tasmanian Aboriginal Language: Old and New Identities', in M. Walsh and C. Yallop (eds), *Language and Culture in Aboriginal Australia* (Canberra: Aboriginal Studies Press, 1993), pp.59–60.
109 Reynolds, 'George Augustus Robinson in Van Diemen's Land: Race, Status and Religion', pp.165–6; Reynolds, *Fate of a Free People*, pp.154–5.
110 Reynolds, 'George Augustus Robinson in Van Diemen's Land', p.167.

7 THE NORTH-WEST FRONTIER

1 McFarlane, *Beyond Awakening*, pp.7 and 220–1.
2 T. Flannery (ed.), *Terra Australis: Matthew Flinders' Great Adventures in the Circumnavigation of Australia* (Melbourne: Text Publishing, 2000), p.23.
3 Plomley (ed.), *The Baudin Expedition and the Tasmanian Aborigines 1802*, p.102.
4 *Sydney Gazette and New South Wales Advertiser* (Sydney), 15 May 1803, p.1.
5 J. Kelly, 'First Discovery of Port Davey and Macquarie Harbour', *Papers and Proceedings of the Royal Society of Tasmania for the year 1920*, pp.166–8.
6 Plomley and Henley, 'The Sealers of Bass Strait and the Cape Barren Island Community', p.74.
7 I. McFarlane, 'Aboriginal Society in North West Tasmania: Dispossession and Genocide' (unpublished PhD thesis, University of Tasmania, 2002), pp.57–8.
8 Anon, 'Boat Expeditions Round Tasmania, 1815–16 and 1824: Reports' (Hobart: Tasmanian Legislative Council, 1881), pp.17 and 19–20.
9 Plomley, *Friendly* Mission, p.238; McFarlane, 'Aboriginal Society in North West Tasmania', p.59.
10 McFarlane, 'Aboriginal Society in North West Tasmania', pp.59–60.
11 A.L. Meston, *The Van Diemen's Land Company 1825–1842* ed. F. Ellis (Launceston, Tas: Museum Committee, Launceston City Council, 1958), pp.11–12.
12 *Ibid.*, pp.15-16; McFarlane, *Beyond Awakening*, p.66.
13 McFarlane, *Beyond Awakening*, pp.71–72.
14 Anon, 'Curr, Edward (1798–1850)',

ADB, Vol.1, p.270.

15 Anon, 'Curr, Edward (1798–1850)', pp.269–70.

16 Anon, 'Curr, Edward (1798–1850)', p.270.

17 Anon, 'Curr, Edward (1798-1850)', p.270; Meston, *The Van Diemen's Land Company 1825–1842*, pp.17–18.

18 Meston, *The Van Diemen's Land Company 1825–1841*, pp.20–21.

19 J. Bischoff, *Sketch of the History of Van Diemen's Land, illustrated by a map of the island, and an account of the Van Diemen's Land Company* (London: John Richardson, Royal Exchange, 1832), pp.157–8.

20 Meston, *The Van Diemen's Land Company 1825-1842*, pp.20–1.

21 Bischoff, *Sketch of the History of Van Diemen's Land*, pp.117–21; R. Onfray, 'Cultural artefacts or "neglected old parks": the colonisation of rainforests in north-western Tasmania', in B. Stubbs (ed.), *Australia's Ever-Changing Forests VI: Proceedings of the Eighth National Conference on Australian Forest History* (Canberra: Australian Forest History Society and Tankard Books, 2012), p.13.

22 B. Rollins, 'Henry Hellyer, Esquire, 1790–1832 Van Diemen's Land Company Surveyor: In His Footsteps', *Australian Surveyor*, Vol.34, No.2 (June 1988), pp.111 and 114.

23 S. Eldershaw, 'Hellyer, Henry (1790–1832)', *ADB*, Vol.1, pp.528–9.

24 McFarlane, *Beyond Awakening*, p.80.

25 McFarlane, *Beyond Awakening*, pp.123–4.

26 Jones, 'Aboriginal Tribes', p.333.

27 McFarlane, 'Aboriginal Society in North West Tasmania', pp.42–3.

28 G. Lennox, 'The Van Diemen's Land Company and the Tasmanian Aborigines: A Reappraisal', *THRA*, Vol.37, No.1 (March 1990), pp.167–8.

29 McFarlane, 'Aboriginal Society in North West Tasmania', p.86.

30 Lennox, 'The Van Diemen's Land Company and the Tasmanian Aborigines', p.167.

31 Plomley, *Friendly Mission*, p.215.

32 McFarlane, *Beyond Awakening*, p.90.

33 Edward Curr to Directors, 14 January 1828, Despatch No.2, Van Diemen's Land Company Records 5/1, TAHO.

34 R. Hare, *The Voyage of the Caroline from England to Van Diemen's Land and Batavia in 1827–28* (ed.) I. Lee (London: Longmans, Green, 1927), p.41.

35 J.H. Wedge, 'Official Report of Journies made by J.H. Wedge, Esq., Assistant Surveyor, in the North-west portion of Van Diemen's Land in the early part of the Year 1828', (Hobart: Govt. Printer, 1828), p.1.

36 Justice Crawford, W.F. Ellis and G.M. Stancombe (eds), *The Diaries of John Helder Wedge 1824–1835*, (Hobart: Royal Society of Tasmania, 1962), p.48.

37 Crawford, Ellis and Stancombe (eds), *The Diaries of John Helder Wedge 1824–1835*, p.48.

38 McFarlane, 'Aboriginal Society in North West Tasmania', pp.90–100.

39 G.H. Stancombe, 'Wedge, John Helder (1793-1872)', *ADB*, Vol.2, p.576.

40 CSO 1/326/7578, pp.109–11, TAHO.

41 McFarlane, 'Aboriginal Society in North West Tasmania', p.123.

42 McFarlane, *Beyond Awakening*, p.110.

43 Colonial Office, 280/25, pp.434–5, TAHO.

44 Edward Curr to Directors, 11 December 1829, Despatch No.103,Van Diemen's Land Company Records 5/2, pp.227–8, TAHO.

45 McFarlane, *Beyond Awakening*, pp.111 and 113.

46 Henry Hellyer to Edward Curr, 25 September 1828, Van Diemen's Land Company Records 23/2, p.304, TAHO.

47 McFarlane, *Beyond Awakening*, pp.111–12.

48 McFarlane, *Beyond Awakening*, pp.112–13.

49 P. Turnbull, 'British Anthropological Thought in Colonial Practice: the appropriation of Indigenous Australian bodies, 1860–1880', in B. Douglas and C. Ballard (eds), *Foreign Bodies: Oceania and the Science of Race 1750–1940*

(Canberra: Australian National University, 2008), p.221.
50 McFarlane, *Beyond Awakening*, pp.112–13.
51 McFarlane, *Beyond Awakening*, p.114.
52 Lennox, 'The Van Diemen's Land Company and the Tasmanian Aborigines', pp.189–90.
53 McFarlane, *Beyond Awakening*, p.114.
54 I. McFarlane, 'NJB Plomley's Contribution to North-West Tasmanian Regional History', in Johnston and Rolls (eds), *Reading Robinson*, p.131.
55 Plomley, *Friendly Mission*, pp.206–7.
56 Windschuttle, *The Fabrication of Aboriginal History: Vol.1*, p.263.
57 Plomley, *Friendly Mission*, pp.229–30.
58 Plomley, *Friendly Mission*, p.225.
59 Plomley, *Friendly Mission*, p.217.
60 Windschuttle, *The Fabrication of Aboriginal History: Vol.1*, p.264.
61 Plomley, *Friendly Mission*, p.217.
62 McFarlane, 'NJB Plomley's Contribution to North-West Tasmanian Regional History', p.136.
63 Plomley, *Friendly Mission*, pp.131–2.
64 Windschuttle, *The Fabrication of Aboriginal History: Vol.1*, p.262.
65 Plomley, *Friendly Mission*, p.216.
66 McFarlane, *Beyond Awakening*, p.257.
67 Windschuttle, *The Fabrication of Aboriginal History: Vol.1*, p.251.
68 Windschuttle, *The Fabrication of Aboriginal History: Vol.1*, pp.251–3.
69 C. Pybus, *Community of Thieves* (Melbourne: Minerva, 1992), p.90.
70 McFarlane, 'Cape Grim', pp.278–9.
71 McFarlane, 'NJB Plomley's Contribution to North-West Tasmanian Regional History', p.134.
72 Windschuttle, *The Fabrication of Aboriginal History: Vol.1*, p.268.
73 McFarlane, 'Cape Grim', p.291.
74 Plomley, *Friendly Mission*, p.229.
75 J.L. Bruce, 'A Gentleman from Silesia: Adolphus Schayer and the Van Diemen's Land Company 1830–1843' (unpublished research paper, Tasmanian State Institute of Technology, 1990), p.72.
76 Lennox, 'The Van Diemen's Land Company and the Tasmanian Aborigines', pp.199–200.
77 McFarlane, *Beyond Awakening*, p.123.
78 Directors to Edward Curr, 6 April 1829, Despatch No.93, Van Diemen's Company Records, 1/4 , TAHO.
79 McKay, *Alexander McKay*, p.74.
80 Plomley, *Friendly Mission*, p.961.
81 *CT*, 26 November 1839, p.5.
82 McFarlane, *Beyond Awakening*, pp.169–70.
83 McFarlane, *Beyond Awakening*, p.173.
84 McFarlane, *Beyond Awakening*, p.170.
85 Lennox, 'The Van Diemen's Land Company and the Tasmanian Aborigines', p.199.
86 Edward Curr to Colonial Secretary, 21 September 1841, Van Diemen's Land Company Records, 23/9, pp.323–4 , TAHO.
87 McFarlane, 'Aboriginal Society in North West Tasmania', p.199.
88 McFarlane, 'Aboriginal Society in North West Tasmania', pp.207–8.
89 Lennox, 'The Van Diemen's Land Company and the Tasmanian Aborigines', p.200; McFarlane, *Beyond Awakening*, pp.171–2 and 177.
90 H. Reynolds, *The Other Side of the Frontier: Aboriginal resistance to the European invasion of Australia* (Melbourne: Penguin, 1995), pp.55–6.
91 McFarlane, *Beyond Awakening*, p.172.
92 McFarlane, *Beyond Awakening*, pp.179–80.
93 T. Murray, 'The childhood of William Lanne: contact archaeology and Aboriginality in Tasmania', *Antiquity*, Vol.67, No.256 (September 1993), p.514.
94 *Courier* (Hobart), 23 December 1842, p.2.
95 Plomley, *Friendly Mission*, p.961.
96 S. Petrow, 'The Last Man: The mutilation of William Lanne in 1869 and its aftermath', *Aboriginal History*, Vol.21 (1997), p.90.
97 James Gibson to Directors, 10 December 1842, Despatch No.23, Van Diemen's Land Company Records 5/7, p.111, TAHO.
98 'Copy of a letter by James Erskine

Calder upon the existence of natives in unexplored parts of Tasmania in 1847'.
99 McFarlane, *Beyond Awakening*, pp.216–17.
100 Clements, *The Black War*, p.208.
101 Windschuttle, *The Fabrication of Aboriginal History: Vol.1*, p.397.
102 Clements, *The Black War*, p.208.
103 Clements, *The Black War*, pp.77–9.
104 Windschuttle, *The Fabrication of Aboriginal History: Vol.1*, pp.372–5.
105 H. Maxwell-Stewart, 'Competition and Conflict on the Forgotten Frontier: Western Van Diemen's Land 1822–33', *History Australia*, Vol.6, No.3 (December 2009), pp.66.9–66.10 and 66.12.
106 Plomley, *Friendly Mission*, p.922.
107 Maxwell-Stewart, 'Competition and Conflict on the Forgotten Frontier', p.66.15.
108 N.J.B. Plomley, *Weep in Silence: A History of the Flinders Island Aboriginal Settlement* (Hobart: Blubber Head Press, 1987), pp.803, 813, 817, 819, 826–8. The exiled Peternidic people were Larratong, Laywoodeen, Noburic, Parderbonedim, Parpattee, Pennebope, Pennemoonooper, Teddeheburer, Tidderap, Toeernac and Tymenedic.

8 CAPTIVITY AND EXILE

1 McFarlane, *Beyond Awakening*, p.164.
2 V. Rae-Ellis, *Trucanini: Queen or Traitor?* (Hobart: O.B.M. Publishing Company, 1976), p.57.
3 Anon, *Copies of all Correspondence between Lieutenant-Governor Arthur and His Majesty's Secretary of State for the Colonies*, p.81; George Arthur to Sir George Murray, 4 April 1831, *HRA*, Ser.3, Vol.10, p.465.
4 *Tasmanian and Austral-Pacific Review* (Hobart), 21 April 1837, p.129.
5 Robson, *A History of Tasmania Vol.1*, p.151.
6 Robson, *A History of Tasmania Vol.1*, p.83.
7 McFarlane, *Beyond Awakening*, p.165.
8 Plomley, *Friendly Mission*, pp.106–7.
9 Rae-Ellis, *Black Robinson*, pp.37–8.
10 Plomley, *Friendly Mission*, p.965.
11 Rae-Ellis, *Black Robinson*, p.37.
12 *Tasmanian and Austral-Pacific Review* (Hobart), 21 April 1837, p.129.
13 Plomley, *Friendly Mission*, p.481.
14 Turnbull, *Black War*, pp.97–8.
15 McFarlane, *Beyond Awakening*, pp.165–6.
16 Plomley, *Friendly Mission*, p.243.
17 McFarlane, *Beyond Awakening*, p.166.
18 McFarlane, *Beyond Awakening*, pp.166–7.
19 *Tasmanian and Austral-Pacific Review* (Hobart), 21 April 1837, p.129.
20 *Tasmanian and Austral-Pacific Review*, p.129.
21 Plomley, *Weep in Silence*, p.638.
22 Rae-Ellis, *Black Robinson*, pp.80 and 84.
23 *Tasmanian and Austral-Pacific Review* (Hobart), 21 April 1837, p.129.
24 Calder, *Some Account of the Wars, Extirpation, Habits etc. of the Native Tribes, of Tasmania*, p.23.
25 Reynolds, *Fate of a Free People*, pp.152–3.
26 McFarlane, *Beyond Awakening*, pp.151–2.
27 Reynolds, *Fate of a Free People*, p.154.
28 *CT*, 1 December 1826, p.2.
29 *CT*, 16 March 1827, p.3.
30 Plomley, *Weep in Silence*, p.13.
31 Plomley, *Friendly Mission*, p.91.
32 McFarlane, *Beyond Awakening*, pp.150–1.
33 Plomley, *Friendly Mission*, pp.95–6.
34 Captain George Jackson to the Aborigines Committee, 18 June 1831, CSO 1/323/7578, Vol.8, pp.14–15, TAHO
35 Plomley, *Weep in Silence*, pp.14–15.
36 Plomley, *Friendly Mission*, p.301.
37 Plomley, *Weep in Silence*, pp.26–7.
38 Plomley, *Weep in Silence*, pp.27–9.

39 Anon, 'McKay, Alexander (1802?–1882)', p.170.
40 Plomley, *Weep in Silence*, pp.30 and 228.
41 Plomley, *Weep in Silence*, p.15.
42 Anon, *Copies of all Correspondence between Lieutenant-Governor Arthur and His Majesty's Secretary of State for the Colonies*, p.81.
43 Ryan, *The Aboriginal Tasmanians*, p.152.
44 Plomley, *Weep in Silence*, p.15; Plomley, *Friendly Mission*, p.481.
45 Plomley, *Weep in Silence*, pp.32 and 964.
46 Plomley, *Friendly Mission*, pp.356–7.
47 Plomley, *Friendly Mission*, p.493.
48 Plomley, *Friendly Mission*, pp.358–60 and 491.
49 Plomley, *Friendly Mission*, p.361.
50 Plomley, *Weep in Silence*, pp.33–4.
51 Plomley, *Weep in Silence*, p.34; Plomley, *Friendly Mission*, p.367.
52 Ryan, *The Aboriginal Tasmanians*, p.153.
53 Plomley, *Weep in Silence*, p.34.
54 *Advertiser* (Launceston), 9 May 1831, p.150.
55 Plomley, *Friendly Mission*, pp.380 and 489.
56 Plomley, *Weep in Silence*, p.35.
57 Plomley, *Friendly Mission*, pp.717–18.
58 Plomley, *Weep in Silence*, pp.47–8.
59 Plomley, *Weep in Silence*, pp.35-36.
60 Plomley, *Weep in Silence*, p.54.
61 Plomley, *Weep in Silence*, p.37; Plomley, *Friendly Mission*, p.718.
62 Plomley, *Friendly Mission*, p.36.
63 Ryan, *The Aboriginal Tasmanians*, pp.161–2.
64 Plomley, *Weep in Silence*, pp.39–40.
65 Plomley, *Weep in Silence*, pp.40–1.
66 Plomley, *Friendly Mission*, pp.624–5.
67 Plomley, *Weep in Silence*, p.57.
68 Plomley, *Friendly Mission*, pp.625–6.
69 Plomley, *Weep in Silence*, pp.224 and 226.
70 Rae-Ellis, *Trucanini*, p.6.
71 Crowley, 'Tasmanian Aboriginal Language', p.64.
72 Plomley, *Weep in Silence*, p.58.
73 Plomley, *Weep in Silence*, p.58; J. Backhouse, *A Narrative of a Visit to the Australian Colonies* (London: Hamilton, Adams, and Co., 1843), pp.83 and 87.
74 Plomley, *Weep in Silence*, p.59.
75 Plomley, *Weep in Silence*, pp.60–61.
76 Plomley, *Weep in Silence*, pp.59–60; Backhouse, *A Narrative of a Visit to the Australian Colonies*, pp.82–3.
77 Walker, *Early Tasmania*, p.243.
78 Walker, *Early Tasmania*, p.243.
79 Walker, *Early Tasmania*, p.246.
80 Walker, *Early Tasmania*, pp.244–5; Plomley, *Weep in Silence*, p.61.
81 Plomley, *Weep in Silence*, p.60.
82 Plomley, *Weep in Silence*, p.61.
83 Plomley, *Weep in Silence*, p.61.
84 Plomley, *Weep in Silence*, p.62.
85 Plomley, *Weep in Silence*, pp.48–9 and 62–3.
86 Plomley, *Weep in Silence*, pp.62–3.
87 G. Shaw, 'Wybalenna', in A. Alexander (ed.), *The Companion to Tasmanian History* (Hobart: Centre for Tasmanian Historical Studies, University of Tasmania, 2005), p.390.
88 Plomley, *Weep in Silence*, pp.44–5.
89 Plomley, *Weep in Silence*, pp.44–5.
90 Plomley, *Weep in Silence*, p.46.
91 Walker, *Early Tasmania*, p.245.
92 Plomley, *Weep in Silence*, pp.46 and 228.
93 Plomley, *Weep in Silence*, pp.60–1.
94 Plomley, *Weep in Silence*, pp.396–7 and 645–6.
95 Plomley, *Weep in Silence*, p.47.
96 Plomley, *Weep in Silence*, p.47.

9 WYBALENNA

1 Plomley, *Weep in Silence*, p.65.
2 M. Johnson, 'Honour Denied: A Study of Soldier Settlement in Queensland, 1916–1929' (unpublished PhD thesis, University of Queensland, 2002), pp.176–7.
3 Plomley, *Weep in Silence*, p.65.
4 Plomley, *Weep in Silence*, pp.65–6.

5 Plomley, *Weep in Silence*, p.75.
6 J. Kociumbas, *Possessions 1770–1860*, Vol.2 in G. Bolton (ed.), *The Oxford History of Australia* (Melbourne: Oxford University Press, 1992), pp.284–5.
7 Plomley, *Weep in Silence*, p.66.
8 Plomley, *Weep in Silence*, pp.66–7.
9 Plomley, *Weep in Silence*, p.73.
10 Plomley, *Weep in Silence*, p.74.
11 Plomley, *Weep in Silence*, p.96; M. Rose (ed.), *For the record: 160 years of Aboriginal print journalism* (Sydney: Allen & Unwin, 1996), p.15.
12 Plomley, *Weep in Silence*, p.73.
13 Plomley, *Weep in Silence*, p.67.
14 Plomley, *Weep in Silence*, pp.67–8.
15 Plomley, *Weep in Silence*, p.69 and 71.
16 Plomley, *Weep in Silence*, p.69.
17 Plomley, *Weep in Silence*, p.70.
18 Plomley, *Weep in Silence*, pp.69 and 71.
19 Backhouse, *A Narrative of a Visit to the Australian Colonies*, p.165.
20 A. Johnston, 'The "little empire of Wybalenna": Becoming Colonial in Australia', *Journal of Australian Studies*, Vol.28, No.81 (2004), pp.26–7.
21 Plomley, *Weep in Silence*, p.71.
22 Plomley, *Weep in Silence*, pp.71–2.
23 Plomley, *Weep in Silence*, p.75.
24 Plomley, *Weep in Silence*, p.79.
25 Plomley, *Weep in Silence*, pp.78–9.
26 Plomley, *Weep in Silence*, p.79.
27 Ryan, *The Aboriginal Tasmanians*, p.180.
28 Plomley, *Weep in Silence*, pp.79–80.
29 Plomley, *Weep in Silence*, pp.80–1.
30 Plomley, *Weep in Silence*, p.82.
31 Plomley, *Weep in Silence*, pp.86–7.
32 Plomley, *Weep in Silence*, pp.83–4.
33 Plomley, *Weep in Silence*, pp.84–5.
34 Plomley, *Weep in Silence*, p.84–5.
35 Plomley, *Weep in Silence*, p.88.
36 Rae-Ellis, *Trucanini*, pp.76–7.
37 Rae-Ellis, *Black Robinson*, p.112.
38 Plomley, *Weep in Silence*, p.96.
39 Ryan, *Tasmanian Aborigines*, pp.236–7.
40 Rae-Ellis, *Black Robinson*, pp.113–14.
41 Plomley, *Weep in Silence*, p.92.
42 Plomley, *Weep in Silence*, p.92.
43 Plomley, *Weep in Silence*, pp.91 and 97.
44 Plomley, *Weep in Silence*, p.97; Rae-Ellis, *Black Robinson*, p.126.
45 Rose (ed.), *For the record*, p.2.
46 Rae-Ellis, *Black Robinson*, pp.126–7.
47 Plomley, *Weep in Silence*, p.93.
48 Rae-Ellis, *Black Robinson*, p.116.
49 R. Blackburn, *The Making of New World Slavery* (London: Verso, 1999), p.325.
50 I. Berlin, *Many Thousands Gone: The First Two Centuries of Slavery in North America* (Cambridge: Belknap Press, 1998), p.96.
51 Plomley, *Weep in Silence*, pp.336–7 and 878–80.
52 Rae-Ellis, *Black Robinson*, p.123; Plomley, *Weep in Silence*, pp.97–8.
53 Plomley, *Weep in Silence*, pp.97–8.
54 Rae-Ellis, *Black Robinson*, p.123.
55 Rae-Ellis, *Black Robinson*, p.126.
56 Rae-Ellis, *Black Robinson*, p.125.
57 Plomley, *Weep in Silence*, p.93.
58 Rae-Ellis, *Black Robinson*, pp.125–6.
59 Rae-Ellis, *Black Robinson*, p.114; Plomley, *Weep in Silence*, p.103.
60 J. Birmingham, 'Wybalenna: The Archaeology of Cultural Accommodation in Nineteenth Century Tasmania' (Sydney: Australian Society for Historical Archaeology Incorporated, 1992), p.164.
61 *CT*, 20 November 1838, p.5.
62 Plomley, *Weep in Silence*, pp.98 and 104.
63 Plomley, *Weep in Silence*, p.403.
64 J. Birmingham and A. Wilson, 'Archaeologies of Cultural Interaction: Wybalenna Settlement and Killalpaninna Mission', *International Journal of Historical Archaeology*, Vol.14, No.1 (2010), p.19.
65 Plomley, *Weep in Silence*, pp.402–3 and 670–1.
66 Plomley, *Weep in Silence*, p.94.
67 P. van Toorn, *Writing Never Arrives Naked: Aboriginal cultures of writing in Australia* (Canberra: Aboriginal Studies Press, 2006), p.104.
68 Plomley, *Weep in Silence*, p.97.
69 S. Newitt, 'The Aboriginal Children who went to the Orphan Schools,

New Town 1828–1861' (unpublished Honours thesis, University of Tasmania, 2011), p.16.
70 Plomley, *Weep in Silence*, p.96.
71 Plomley, *Weep in Silence*, p.315.
72 Plomley, *Weep in Silence*, pp.312–13.
73 Rae-Ellis, *Black Robinson*, pp.129–131.
74 Plomley, *Weep in Silence*, p.530.
75 Plomley, *Weep in Silence*, p.539.
76 Plomley, *Weep in Silence*, p.784.
77 Plomley, *Weep in Silence*, p.575.
78 Rae-Ellis, *Black Robinson*, p.132.
79 Rae-Ellis, *Trucanini*, pp.32–3.
80 Plomley, *Weep in Silence*, p.100.
81 Rae-Ellis, *Black Robinson*, p.115.
82 Plomley, *Weep in Silence*, pp.634–5; Ryan, *The Aboriginal Tasmanians*, p.186.
83 Rae-Ellis, *Black Robinson*, p.118.
84 Rae-Ellis, *Black Robinson*, p.111.
85 Ryan, *Tasmanian Aborigines*, p.239.
86 Plomley, *Weep in Silence*, pp.99 and 110.
87 Plomley, *Weep in Silence*, p.109.
88 Ryan, *The Aboriginal Tasmanians*, p.195.
89 Plomley, *Weep in Silence*, pp.109 and 111.
90 Ryan, *The Aboriginal Tasmanians*, pp.195–6.
91 Plomley, *Weep in Silence*, pp.134 and 156.
92 Plomley, *Weep in Silence*, p.132.
93 M. Walter and L. Daniels, 'Personalising the History Wars: Woretemoeteryenner's Story', *International Journal of Critical Indigenous Studies*, Vol.1, No.1 (2008), p.38.
94 Wyllie, *Dolly Dalrymple*, pp.43–4 and 47.
95 Walter and Daniels, 'Personalising the History Wars', p.41.
96 McFarlane, 'Dalrymple, Dolly (c.1808–1864)', p.94.
97 Walter and Daniels, 'Personalising the History Wars', pp.41–2.
98 Ryan, *The Aboriginal Tasmanians*, p.196.
99 Plomley, *Weep in Silence*, p.142.
100 Plomley, *Weep in Silence*, pp.139–40 and 143.
101 Ryan, *The Aboriginal Tasmanians*, p.200.
102 Plomley, *Weep in Silence*, p.148.
103 Plomley, *Weep in Silence*, pp.148–9.
104 Reynolds, *Fate of a Free People*, pp.156–7.
105 van Toorn, *Writing Never Arrives Naked*, p.121.
106 Plomley, *Weep in Silence*, pp.153–5.
107 Ryan, *The Aboriginal Tasmanians*, p.202.
108 Ryan, *The Aboriginal Tasmanians.*
109 *Examiner* (Launceston), 14 June 1848, p.5; Pybus, *Community of Thieves*, p.161.
110 L.A. Meredith, *My Home in Tasmania, during a residence of nine years* (London: John Murray, 1852), pp.189–90.
111 Plomley, *Weep in Silence*, p.172.

10 THE PORT PHILLIP INTERLUDE (1839–1842)

1 J. Roberts, *Jack of Cape Grim: A Victorian Adventure* (Melbourne: Greenhouse Publications, 1986), p.40; D.J. Mulvaney, 'Thomas, William (1793-1867)', *ADB*, Vol.2, p.518.
2 A.S. Kenyon, 'The Aboriginal Protectorate of Port Phillip: Report of an Expedition to the Aboriginal Tribes of the Western Interior by the Chief Protector, George Augustus Robinson', *Victorian Historical Magazine*, Vol.12, No.3 (March 1928), p.136.
3 Anon, 'Robinson, George Augustus (1788-1866)', p.387.
4 Roberts, *Jack of Cape Grim*, p.37.
5 Roberts, *Jack of Cape Grim*, pp.39–40.
6 D. Reilly, 'Charles Joseph La Trobe: An Appreciation', *La Trobe Journal*, No.71 (Autumn 2003), p.11.
7 Roberts, *Jack of Cape Grim*, p.40.

8 I. Clark, 'George Augustus Robinson and Charles Joseph La Trobe: personal insights into a problematical relationship', *La Trobe Journal*, No.85 (May 2010), p.16.
9 Roberts, *Jack of Cape Grim*, p.41.
10 McFarlane, *Beyond Awakening*, p.197; S. Dammery, 'Walter George Arthur: A Health Profile of a 19th-Century Van Diemen's Land Aboriginal Man', *Health and History*, Vol.4, No.2 (2002), p.86.
11 Rae-Ellis, *Black Robinson*, p.212.
12 J. Toscano, 'The Tunnerminnerwait and Maulboyheenner Saga' (Melbourne: Anarchist Media Institute, 2008), p.15.
13 Roberts, *Jack of Cape Grim*, pp.46–7.
14 Roberts, *Jack of Cape Grim*, p.49.
15 Roberts, *Jack of Cape Grim*, pp.49–50.
16 Roberts, *Jack of Cape Grim*, pp.51 and 54.
17 Roberts, *Jack of Cape Grim*, p.53.
18 Roberts, *Jack of Cape Grim*, pp.56–7.
19 I. McFarlane, 'Pevay: A Casualty of War', *THRA*, Vol.48, No.4 (December 2001), p.297.
20 McFarlane, *Beyond Awakening*, p.199.
21 H. Felton, *Living with the land Book Four: From Optimism to Despair* (Hobart: Department of Education and The Arts, 1990), p.34.
22 McFarlane, 'Pevay', p.299.
23 McFarlane, *Beyond Awakening*, p.274.
24 Plomley and Henley, 'The Sealers of Bass Strait and the Cape Barren Island Community', p.115.
25 Toscano, 'The Tunnerminnerwait and Maulboyheenner Saga', p.15.
26 Roberts, *Jack of Cape Grim*, p.60.
27 Roberts, *Jack of Cape Grim*, p.66.
28 McFarlane, 'Pevay', p.300; Toscano, 'The Tunnerminnerwait and Maulboyheenner Saga', p.16.
29 McFarlane, 'Pevay', p.300.
30 Roberts, *Jack of Cape Grim*, pp.61–2.
31 Rae-Ellis, *Black Robinson*, p.214.
32 McFarlane, 'Pevay', pp.300–1.
33 Roberts, *Jack of Cape Grim*, pp.73–4.
34 Roberts, *Jack of Cape Grim*, pp.75–7; S. Davies, 'Aborigines, murder and the criminal law in early Port Phillip 1841–1851', *Historical Studies*, Vol.22, No.88 (April 1987), p.315.
35 McFarlane, 'Pevay', p.301.
36 *Geelong Advertiser* (Geelong), 27 December 1841, p.2.
37 *Bathurst Free Press and Mining Journal* (Bathurst), 20 June 1890, p.4; Roberts, *Jack of Cape Grim*, p.78.
38 McFarlane, 'Pevay', p.302.
39 J. Barry, 'Willis, John Walpole (1793–1877)', *ADB*, Vol.2, pp.603–4.
40 Roberts, *Jack of Cape Grim*, p.84.
41 *Port Phillip Patriot* (Melbourne), 20 September 1841, p.1; *Geelong Advertiser* (Geelong), 20 September 1841, pp.2–3.
42 'Decisions of the Superior Courts of New South Wales, 1788–1899: R. v. Bonjon' (Sydney: Macquarie Law School, n.d.), n.p.
43 B. Bridges, 'The Extension of English Law to the Aborigines for Offences Committed Inter Se, 1829–1842', *Journal of the Royal Australian Historical Society*, Vol.59, Pt.4 (December 1973), p.267.
44 *Geelong Advertiser* (Geelong), 6 December 1841, p.3.
45 Roberts, *Jack of Cape Grim*, p.82.
46 *Sydney Herald* (Sydney), 8 February 1836, p.3; *Sydney Gazette and New South Wales Advertiser* (Sydney), 5 May 1836, p.2.
47 Roberts, *Jack of Cape Grim*, p.82.
48 *Port Phillip Gazette* (Melbourne), 22 December 1841, pp.2–3; *Geelong Advertiser* (Geelong), 27 December 1841, p.2; *Sydney Herald* (Sydney), 3 January 1842, p.2.
49 McFarlane, *Beyond Awakening*, p.205.
50 McFarlane, *Beyond Awakening*, p.205.
51 McFarlane, 'Pevay', p.303.
52 McFarlane, *Beyond Awakening*, p.206.
53 Davies, 'Aborigines, murder and the criminal law in early Port Phillip, 1841–1851', p.317.
54 *Geelong Advertiser* (Geelong), 27 December 1841, pp.2–3.
55 Roberts, *Jack of Cape Grim*, p.88.
56 Rae-Ellis, *Black Robinson*, p.215.
57 Roberts, *Jack of Cape Grim*, p.90.

58 McFarlane, 'Pevay', pp.304–5.
59 Pybus, *Community of Thieves*, p.152.
60 Roberts, *Jack of Cape Grim*, p.92.
61 'James Dredge Diary' MS5244, Box 16/4, 20 January 1842, pp.218–22, La Trobe Australian Manuscripts Collection, State Library of Victoria.
62 Roberts, *Jack of Cape Grim*, p.89.
63 Plomley, *Weep in Silence*, p.787.
64 McFarlane, *Beyond Awakening*, p.212.

11 THE TRAGEDY OF OYSTER COVE

1 Mulvaney, *Encounters in Place*, pp.57–8; P. Dowling, 'Mercury Poisoning at Oyster Cove? Suspected cases of unintentional poisoning of Tasmanian Aboriginal Internees', *Tasmanian Historical Studies*, Vol.11 (2006), p.60.
2 Ryan, *Tasmanian Aborigines*, p.257.
3 Plomley, *Weep in Silence*, p.172.
4 Plomley, *Weep in Silence*, p.176.
5 Plomley, *Weep in Silence*, pp.176–7.
6 Plomley, *Weep in Silence*, p.173.
7 Plomley, *Weep in Silence*, p.175.
8 Ryan, *The Aboriginal Tasmanians*, pp.205, 207 and 209.
9 Plomley, *Weep in Silence*, pp.176–7.
10 'Aboriginal Establishment — Oyster Cove: Reports made by Visiting Magistrate, Surgeon and Chaplain when making calls to the establishment' (entry for 7 January 1867), CSO 89, TAHO.
11 C. Pybus, 'Oyster Cove 1988', *Meanjin*, Vol.47, No.4 (Summer 1988), p.579.
12 Rae-Ellis, *Trucanini*, p.120; Plomley, *Weep in Silence*, p.173.
13 Plomley, *Weep in Silence*, pp.174–5.
14 Plomley, *Weep in Silence*, p.178.
15 L. Russell, *Roving Mariners: Australian Aboriginal Whalers and Sealers in the Southern Oceans, 1790–1870* (New York: State University of New York Press, 2012), p.3.
16 Dowling, 'Mercury Poisoning at Oyster Cove?', p.60.
17 Plomley, 'Robinson, George Augustus (1788-1866)', p.387.
18 Ryan, *The Aboriginal Tasmanians*, p.209.
19 Rae-Ellis, *Trucanini*, pp.125-126; S. Maloney, 'Truganini & George Augustus Robinson', *The Monthly*, No.66 (May 2012), p.66.
20 Plomley, *Weep in Silence*, p.178.
21 Dowling, 'Mercury Poisoning at Oyster Cove?', pp.62 and 68.
22 Dowling, 'Mercury Poisoning at Oyster Cove?', p.63.
23 Bonwick, *The Last of the Tasmanians*, pp.279–80 and 282–3.
24 Plomley, *Weep in Silence*, p.178.
25 J. Clark, 'Smith, Fanny Cochrane (1834-1905)', *ADB*, Vol.11, p.642.
26 Plomley, *Weep in Silence*, p.178.
27 *Examiner* (Launceston), 3 May 1855, p.2.
28 Plomley, *Weep in Silence*, p.181.
29 H. Felton, 'Mathinna', in Alexander (ed.), *The Companion to Tasmanian History*, p.229.
30 *Examiner* (Launceston), 19 August 1884, p.3.
31 Felton, 'Mathinna', p.229.
32 N. Cree, *Oyster Cove: Last home of the Tasmanian Aboriginal* (Melbourne: Nicholas Cree, 1979), p.52; Plomley, *Weep in Silence*, pp.181 and 865.
33 Cree, *Oyster Cove: Last home of the Tasmanian Aboriginal*, p.182.
34 Rae-Ellis, *Trucanini*, p.126.
35 Plomley, *Weep in Silence*, p.183.
36 Pybus, 'Oyster Cove 1988', p.578.
37 Morgan, *Land Settlement in Early Tasmania*, pp.159–60.
38 Morgan, *Land Settlement in Early Tasmania*, pp.159–60.
39 Plomley, *Weep in Silence*, p.183.
40 Dammery, 'Walter George Arthur', p.87.
41 Plomley, *Weep in Silence*, p.183.
42 Plomley, *Weep in Silence*, p.183; Dammery, 'Walter George Arthur', p.88.
43 W. Crowther, 'The Final Phase of the Extinct Tasmanian Race 1847-1876', *Records of the Queen Victoria Museum*,

No.49 (1974), p.13.
44 H. Reynolds, 'Arthur, Walter George (c.1820–1861)', *ADB*, Supplementary Volume 1580–1980, p.11; Dammery, 'Walter George Arthur', p.88.
45 N. Prickett, 'Trans-Tasman stories: Australian Aborigines in New Zealand sealing and shore whaling', in G. Clark, F. Leach and S. O'Connor (eds), 'Islands of Inquiry: Colonisation, Seafaring and the Archaeology of Maritime Landscapes', *Terra Australis*, Vol.29 (June 2008), pp.357–8 and 363; Russell, *Roving Mariners*, pp.49 and 68.
46 Ryan, *The Aboriginal Tasmanians*, p.210.
47 Plomley, *Weep in Silence*, p.182.
48 Plomley, *Weep in Silence*, p.184.
49 Plomley, *Weep in Silence*, pp.184–5.
50 Plomley, *Weep in Silence*, p.186.
51 Bonwick, *The Last of the Tasmanians*, pp.274–5.
52 Ryan, *The Aboriginal Tasmanians*, p.212.
53 Ryan, *The Aboriginal Tasmanians.*
54 Dowling, 'Mercury Poisoning at Oyster Cove?', pp.59 and 61.
55 Cree, *Oyster Cove*, p.54; Pybus, *Community of Thieves*, p.166.
56 Plomley, *Weep in Silence*, pp.187–8.
57 Ryan, *The Aboriginal Tasmanians*, p.214.
58 Plomley, *Weep in Silence*, p.189.
59 McFarlane, 'Aboriginal Society in North West Tasmania', p.267.
60 Rae-Ellis, *Trucanini*, pp.122–3.
61 McFarlane, 'Aboriginal Society in North West Tasmania', p.267.
62 L. Russell, '"A New Holland Half-Caste": Sealer and Whaler Tommy Chaseland', *History Australia*, Vol.5, No.1 (April 2008), pp.8.5–8.6.
63 Russell, *Roving Mariners*, pp.77 and 83–5.
64 'Complaint of King "Billy"', 5 December 1864, CSD 4/77/231, TAHO.
65 Petrow, 'The Last Man', pp.94–5; Russell, *Roving Mariners*, p.82.
66 *Cornwall Chronicle* (Launceston), 31 March 1869, p.3.
67 Russell, *Roving Mariners*, p.82.
68 *Cornwall Chronicle* (Launceston), 27 March 1869, p.2; Petrow, 'The Last Man', p.96.
69 Russell, *Roving Mariners*, pp.83–4.
70 *Cornwall Chronicle* (Launceston), 13 March 1869, p.3.
71 Ryan, *Tasmanian Aborigines*, p.267.
72 *Mercury* (Hobart), 9 March 1869, pp.2–3.
73 *Examiner* (Launceston), 16 March 1869, p.3.
74 *Cornwall Chronicle* (Launceston), 13 March 1869, p.3.
75 W.E.L.H. Crowther, 'Crowther, William Lodewyk (1817–1885)', *ADB*, Vol.3, p.502.
76 Petrow, 'The Last Man', pp.106–7.
77 Crowther, 'Crowther, William Lodewyk (1817-1885)', pp.502–3.
78 Russell, *Roving Mariners*, p.88.
79 L. Ryan and N. Smith, 'Trugernanner (Truganini) (1812?-1876)', *ADB*, Vol.6, p.305.
80 V. Rae-Ellis, 'Trucanini', *THRA*, Vol.23, No.2 (June 1976), pp.26-27.
81 De Vries, *Strength of Spirit*, pp.115-116; D.C.S. Sissons, 'The Voyage of the *Cyprus* Mutineers: Did They Enter Japanese Waters?', *Journal of Pacific History*, Vol.43, No.2 (September 2008), p.253.
82 Rae-Ellis, 'Trucanini', pp.28–9.
83 Rae-Ellis, 'Trucanini', p.29.
84 Rae-Ellis, 'Trucanini', p.31.
85 Rae-Ellis, 'Trucanini', p.31.
86 Plomley, *Weep in Silence*, p.190.
87 Plomley, *Weep in Silence*, p.190.
88 Rae-Ellis, 'Trucanini', p.38.
89 Turnbull, *Black War*, p.236.
90 'Summary', in *Mercury* (Hobart), 13 May 1876, p.3.
91 Ryan and Smith, 'Trugernanner (Truganini) (1812?-1876)', p.305; De Vries, *Strength of Spirit*, p.128.
92 M. Norst, *Burnum Burnum: A Warrior for Peace* (Sydney: Kangaroo Press, 1999), p.76; M. Rolls and M. Johnson, *Historical Dictionary of Australian Aborigines* (Lanham, MY: Scarecrow

Press, 2011), p.44.
93 Rae-Ellis, 'Trucanini', p.39.
94 I. West, *Pride Against Prejudice: Reminiscences of a Tasmanian Aborigine* (Canberra: Australian Institute of Aboriginal Studies, 1984), pp.87–8.
95 Cree, *Oyster Cove*, p.63.
96 Pybus, 'Oyster Cove 1988', p.581.
97 Clark, 'Smith, Fanny Cochrane (1834-1905)', p.642.
98 H. Ling Roth, '*Is* Mrs. F.C. Smith a "last living Aboriginal *of* Tasmania"?', *Journal of the Anthropological Institute of Great Britain and Ireland*, Vol.27 (1898), p.454; Rae Ellis, *Trucanini*, pp.113–14.
99 Plomley and Henley, 'The Sealers of Bass Strait and the Cape Barren Island Community', p.99.
100 McFarlane, *Beyond Awakening*, p.216.
101 Plomley, *Weep in Silence*, p.869.
102 M. Longman, 'Songs of the Tasmanian Aborigines as Recorded by Mrs. Fanny Cochrane Smith', *Papers and Proceedings of the Royal Society of Tasmania*, Vol.94 (1960), pp.79 and 85. B. Watson, 'The Man and the Woman and the Edison Phonograph: Race, History and Technology through Song', *Australasian Journal of Ecocriticism and Cultural Ecology*, Vol.1 (2011-2012), p.4; *Courier-Mail* (Brisbane), 15 March 1983, p.9.
103 Clark, 'Smith, Fanny Cochrane (1834-1905)', p.642.
104 J.G.S., 'Cape Barren Island, Bass Straits', *Mercury* (Hobart), 14 August 1890, p.2.

12 THE BASS STRAIT ISLANDER COMMUNITY 1850–1910

1 Meston, 'The Halfcastes of the Furneaux Group', pp.48–9.
2 B. Mollison and C. Everitt, 'The Tasmanian Aborigines and Their Descendants (Chronology, Genealogies and Social Data): Part 2 (Hobart: University of Tasmania, December 1978), n.p.; Plomley and Henley, 'The Sealers of Bass Strait and the Cape Barren Island Community', p.99.
3 Mollison and Everitt, 'The Tasmanian Aborigines and Their Descendants: Part 2', n.p.; Plomley and Henley, 'The Sealers of Bass Strait and the Cape Barren Island Community', p.104.
4 Mollison and Everitt, 'The Tasmanian Aborigines and Their Decendants: Part 2', n.p.; Plomley, *Friendly Mission*, p.1055.
5 Mollison and Everitt, 'The Tasmanian Aborigines and Their Descendants: Part 2', n.p.
6 Plomley and Henley, 'The Sealers of Bass Strait and the Cape Barren Island Community', pp.85 and 96.
7 Plomley and Henley, 'The Sealers of Bass Strait and the Cape Barren Island Community', p.80; Mollison and Everitt, 'The Tasmanian Aborigines and Their Descendants: Part 2, n.p.; Plomley, *Friendly Mission*, p.1053.
8 Plomley and Henley, 'The Sealers of Bass Strait and the Cape Barren Island Community', p.90; Mollison and Everitt, 'The Tasmanian Aborigines and Their Descendants: Part 2', n.p.
9 Mollison and Everitt, 'The Tasmanian Aborigines and Their Descendants: Part 2', n.p.
10 T. Reibey, 'Half-Caste Islanders in Bass's Straits: A Report of the Venerable Archdeacon Reibey', *Journal of the Tasmanian Legislative Council*, Vol.9 (1863), p.4.
11 Mollison and Everitt, 'The Tasmanian Aborigines and Their Descendants: Part 2', n.p.
12 H. Trethewie, 'David Howie — Bass Strait Constable', *THRA*, Vol.39, No.1 (March 1992), pp.46–7; P. Buckby, *David Howie: Devil or Saint?* (Smithton, Tas: Jamala Press, 2003), pp.138 and 146.

13 A.L. Meston, 'The Halfcastes of the Furneaux Group', *Records of the Queen Victoria Museum*, Vol.11, No.1 (July 1947), p.51; P. Adam-Smith, *Moonbird People* (Adelaide: Rigby, 1965), p.68; P. Sutton, 'Cape Barren English', *Working Papers of the Linguistic Society of Australia*, Vol.13 (1975), pp.63–4.
14 L. Ryan, 'The struggle for recognition: Part-Aborigines in Bass Strait in the nineteenth century', *Aboriginal History*, Vol.1, Pt.1 (1977), p.37.
15 I. Skira, 'Always Afternoon: Aborigines on Cape Barren Island, in the Nineteenth Century', *THRA*, Vol.44, No.2 (June 1997), pp.124–6.
16 Murray-Smith, '*Beyond the Pale*', pp.177–8.
17 Ryan, 'The struggle for recognition', p.37.
18 I. Skira, '"I hope you will be my friend": Tasmanian Aborigines in the Furneaux Group in the nineteenth-century—population and land tenure', *Aboriginal History*, Vol.21 (1997), p.33.
19 Ryan, 'The struggle for recognition', p.37.
20 Skira, '"I hope you will be my friend"', p.33.
21 Ryan, 'The struggle for recognition', pp.37–8.
22 F. Nixon, *The Cruise of the Beacon: A Narrative of a Visit to The Islands of Bass's Straits* (London: Bell & Daldry, 1857), p.50; Skira, '"I hope you will be my friend"', p.34.
23 Skira, '"I hope you will be my friend"', pp.34–5.
24 Nixon, *The Cruise of the Beacon*, pp.41–2.
25 Meston, 'The Halfcastes of the Furneaux Group', p.49.
26 *Tasmanian* (Hobart), 2 October 1886, 'Supplement', n.p.; S. Breen, 'Beeton, Lucy (1829-1886)', *ADB*, Supplementary Volume 1580–1980, p.24.
27 Adam-Smith, *Moonbird People*, pp.90–1.
28 *Tasmanian* (Hobart), 2 October 1886, 'Supplement', n.p.; Breen, 'Beeton, Lucy (1829-1886)', p.24.
29 Nixon, *The Cruise of the Beacon*, pp.46–7.
30 Ryan, 'The struggle for recognition', p.38.
31 Skira, '"I hope you will be my friend"', p.38.
32 Ryan, 'The struggle for recognition', p.38.
33 Murray-Smith, '*Beyond the Pale*', p.183.
34 Reibey, 'Half-Caste Islanders in Bass's Straits', p.3; M. Howard, 'Archdeacon Thomas Reibey's 1862 Missionary Voyage to the Islands of Bass Strait', *THRA*, Vol.38, No.1 (March 1991), p.86.
35 Breen, 'Beeton, Lucy (1829–1886)', p.24.
36 [M.] Rev. Canon Brownrigg, *The Cruise of the Freak: A Narrative of a Visit to the Islands of Bass and Banks Straits with some account of the islands* (Launceston, Tas: J.S.V. Turner, 1872), p.5.
37 J. Guenther, 'The Failure of Christian Response to Tasmanian Aboriginals: 1803–1901 A Valid Assessment', *THRA*, Vol.44, No.3 (September 1997), p.214.
38 Skira, '"I hope you will be my friend"', p.39.
39 Skira, '"I hope you will be my friend"', p.39.
40 Skira, '"I hope you will be my friend"', p.40.
41 Brownrigg, *The Cruise of the Freak*, p.61.
42 Skira, '"I hope you will be my friend"', p.40.
43 Murray-Smith, '*Beyond the Pale*', p.183.
44 Ryan, 'The struggle for recognition', p.41.
45 Murray-Smith, '*Beyond the Pale*', p.183.
46 Ryan, 'The struggle for recognition', p.41.
47 Murray-Smith, '*Beyond the Pale*', p.185.
48 Skira, '"I hope you will be my friend"',

pp.39–40.
49 Brownrigg, *The Cruise of the Freak*, p.iv.
50 Ryan, *The Aboriginal Tasmanians*, p.229.
51 Ryan, 'The struggle for recognition', pp.41–2.
52 Murray-Smith, '*Beyond the Pale*', p.185.
53 Ryan, *The Aboriginal Tasmanians*, p.229.
54 Skira, '"I hope you will be my friend"', p.41.
55 Skira, 'Always Afternoon', p.122.
56 *Examiner* (Launceston), 23 May 1883, p.3.
57 Skira, '"I hope you will be my friend"', p.41.
58 Brownrigg, *The Cruise of the Freak*, pp.61–2.
59 Skira, 'Tasmanian Aborigines and Muttonbirding', pp.159–60.
60 E. Worrell, *Reptiles of Australia* (Sydney: Angus & Robertson, 1970), p.131; H. Cogger, *Reptiles & Amphibians of Australia* (Sydney: Reed New Holland, 2000), p.659.
61 *Mercury* (Hobart), 7 April 1931, p.5.
62 *Examiner* (Launceston), 7 April 1938, p.3.
63 Skira, '"I hope you will be my friend"', pp.41–2.
64 Ryan, *The Aboriginal Tasmanians*, pp.229–30.
65 Skira, 'Always Afternoon', p.127.
66 Ryan, *The Aboriginal Tasmanians*, p.230.
67 G. Stephens, 'H.H. Montgomery—The Mutton Bird Bishop', *University of Tasmania Occasional Paper*, No.39 (1985), p.10; P. Hart, 'Montgomery, Henry Hutchinson (1847–1932)', in Alexander (ed.), *The Companion to Tasmanian History*, p.241.
68 Ryan, 'The struggle for recognition', p.43.
69 Ryan, 'The struggle for recognition', p.43.
70 Ryan, 'The struggle for recognition', p.43.
71 Ryan, *The Aboriginal Tasmanians*, p.231.
72 Ryan, *The Aboriginal Tasmanians*, p.231.
73 Skira, 'Tasmanian Aborigines and Muttonbirding', p.168.
74 P. Adam-Smith, *There was a Ship* (Melbourne: Thomas Nelson, 1983), p.55.
75 Skira, 'Tasmanian Aborigines and Muttonbirding', p.169.
76 Skira, 'Tasmanian Aborigines and Muttonbirding', p.165.
77 *Examiner* (Launceston), 26 September 1898, p.3.
78 Skira, 'Tasmanian Aborigines and Muttonbirding', p.165.
79 Skira, 'Tasmanian Aborigines and Muttonbirding', pp.165–6; *Mercury* (Hobart), 4 June 1892, p.3.
80 Ryan, 'The struggle for recognition', p.44.
81 *Mercury* (Hobart), 14 May 1892, p.2.
82 Skira, 'Tasmanian Aborigines and Muttonbirding', p.112.
83 A.T. Morgan, 'Aboriginal Education in the Furneaux Islands (1798–1986): a study of Aboriginal racial policy, curriculum and teacher/community relations, with specific reference to Cape Barren Island' (unpublished MA thesis, University of Tasmania, 1986), pp.123–4.
84 Morgan, 'Aboriginal Education in the Furneaux Islands (1798–1986)', pp.125–6.
85 Morgan, 'Aboriginal Education in the Furneaux Islands (1798–1986)', pp.125–6.
86 Morgan, 'Aboriginal Education in the Furneaux Islands (1798–1986)', pp.125–6., p.127; N. Parry, '"Such a Longing": Black and white children in welfare in New South Wales and Tasmania, 1880-1940' (unpublished PhD thesis, University of New South Wales, 2007), p.108.
87 *Mercury* (Hobart), 30 August 1902, p.6; *Examiner* (Launceston), 14 November 1907, p.7.
88 *Examiner* (Launceston), 26 September 1898, p.3.

89 Ryan, 'The struggle for recognition', p.48.
90 *Ibid.*
91 Morgan, 'Aboriginal Education in the Furneaux Islands (1798-1986)', p.129.
92 Skira, 'Tasmanian Aborigines and Muttonbirding', p.173.
93 Ryan, *Tasmanian Aborigines*, p.291.
94 Stephens, 'H.H. Montgomery — The Mutton Bird Bishop', p.10.
95 E.W. Stephens, 'The Furneaux Island: Their Early Settlement and some Characteristics of their Inhabitants' (Launceston, Tas: Royal Society of Tasmania, 1899), p.9.
96 *Examiner* (Launceston), 7 October 1905, p.5.
97 Morgan. 'Aboriginal Education in the Furneaux Island (1798–1986)', p.132.
98 *Mercury* (Hobart), 1 February 1909, p.6; *Mercury* (Hobart), 15 April 1909, p.8.
99 Morgan, 'Aboriginal Education in the Furneaux Islands (1798–1986)', p.139.
100 Parry, '"Such a Longing"', p.109.
101 Ryan, *The Aboriginal Tasmanians*, p.239.
102 Ryan, *The Aboriginal Tasmanians*, pp.239-240.
103 J.E.C. Lord, 'Furneaux Islands: Report upon the State of the Islands, the Condition and Mode of Living of the Half-Castes, the Existing Methods of Regulating the Reserves, and Suggesting Lines for Future Administration', *Journals and Printed Papers of the Parliament of Tasmania*, Vol.59, No.57 (1908), p.8.
104 Lord, 'Furneaux Islands: Report upon the State of the Islands, p.8.
105 Lord, 'Furneaux Islands: Report upon the State of the Islands, pp.11–12.
106 Lord, 'Furneaux Islands: Report upon the State of the Islands, pp.9–10.
107 Ryan, *The Aboriginal Tasmanians*, p.239.
108 L. Barwick, 'Briggs, Louisa (1836-1925)', *ADB*, Supplementary Volume 1580–1980, p.45.
109 *Argus* (Melbourne), 29 August 1876, p.5.
110 Barwick, 'Briggs, Louisa (1836–1925)', p.45.
111 D. Barwick, 'Coranderrk and Cumeroogunga: Pioneers and Policy', in T.S. Epstein and D.H. Penny (eds), *Opportunity and Response: Case Studies in Economic Development* (London: C. Hurst & Company, 1972), p.36.
112 Barwick, 'Briggs, Louisa (1836-1925)', pp.45–6.
113 *Brisbane Courier* (Brisbane), 15 September 1925, p.6.

13 THE BASS STRAIT ISLANDER COMMUNITY 1912–1970

1 *Mercury* (Hobart), 25 February 1910, p.7.
2 K. Harman, 'Protecting Tasmanian Aborigines: American and Queensland Influences on the Cape Barren Island Reserve Act, 1912', *Journal of Imperial and Commonwealth History*, Vol.41, No.5 (2013), pp.753–4 and 758.
3 Ryan, *The Aboriginal Tasmanians*, p.240.
4 Ryan, *The Aboriginal Tasmanians*, p.240.
5 *An Act to provide for the Subdivision of the Cape Barren Island Reserve, and for other purposes* (1912), pp.116–22. Hereafter the *Cape Barren Island Reserve Act* (copy held by Riawunna, Centre for Aboriginal Studies, University of Tasmania, Launceston campus); I. Skira, 'Aboriginals in Tasmania: Living on Cape Barren Island in the Twentieth Century', *THRA*, Vol.44, No.3 (September 1997), p.188.
6 *Mercury* (Hobart), 13 September 1912, p.4.
7 *Cape Barren Island Reserve Act*, p.123.
8 Ryan, *The Aboriginal Tasmanians*, pp.242–3.
9 *Kurbingui Star* (Zillmere), 20 October 2006, pp.8, 10–11 and 14.
10 *Mercury* (Hobart), 18 November 1929, p.7; *Mercury* (Hobart), 24 November

1932, p.5; Parry, '"Such a Longing"', p.217.

11 A.E. Counsel, 'Report on the Management of the Half Castes at Cape Barren Island', 4 December 1922, LSD 643/30/1646/22, TAHO.

12 Counsel, 'Report on the Management of the Half Castes at Cape Barren Island'; Lord, 'Furneaux Islands', p.10.

13 Ryan, *The Aboriginal Tasmanians*, p.243.

14 'Petition from Residents of Cape Barren Island Reserve to the Minister for Lands', 8 December 1922, LSD 643/30/1646/22, TAHO.

15 ' Memorandum to Minister for Lands', 4 December 1922, LSD 1/576, File 643/30, TAHO.

16 A. Marshall (Chairman), 'Furneaux Islands Half-Castes: Report of Select Committee' (Hobart: Government Printer, 19 December 1924), pp.2–3.

17 Ryan, *The Aboriginal Tasmanians*, pp.244–5.

18 Felton (ed.), *Living with the land Book Seven: Family and Community*, pp.16–18 and 24.

19 Felton (ed.), *Living with the land Book Seven*, pp.19–20.

20 M. Mallett, *On Being Aboriginal Book 4: When Cape Barren Island was an Aboriginal Reserve* (Hobart: Education Department of Tasmania, 1984), p.8.

21 M. Mallett, *My Past—Their Future: Stories from Cape Barren Island* (Hobart: Blubber Head Press in association with Riawunna, Centre for Aboriginal Education, University of Tasmania, 2001), p.27.

22 Ryan, *Tasmanian Aborigines*, p.298.

23 *Mercury* (Hobart), 18 November 1929, p.7.

24 A.W. Burbury, 'Report on the Condition of the Half Castes at Cape Barren Island Reservation' (Hobart: Government Printer, 16 September 1929), pp.3–4.

25 *Examiner* (Launceston), 18 June 1910, p.8.

26 Burbury, 'Report on the Condition of the Half Castes at Cape Barren Island Reservation', pp.5–7.

27 *Mercury* (Hobart), 18 November 1929, p.8.

28 Johnson, *Trials and Tribulations*, p.111.

29 J.S. Needham, Chairman, Australian Board of Missions, Sydney, to Attorney General, Hobart, 24 December 1930, LSD 1/576, File 643/70, TAHO.

30 Skira, 'Aboriginals in Tasmania', p.187.

31 Morgan, 'Aboriginal Education in the Furneaux Islands (1798-1986)', p.71.

32 J.S. Needham, Chairman, Australian Board of Missions, Sydney, to Attorney General, Hobart, 24 December 1930, LSD 1/576, File 643/70, TAHO.

33 Parry, '"Such a Longing"', p.231.

34 *Mercury* (Hobart), 17 May 1940, p.10; *Mercury* (Hobart), 12 September 1940, p.5.

35 *Advocate* (Burnie), 2 July 1940, p.8; *Advertiser* (Adelaide), 25 April 1947, p.8.

36 *Examiner* (Launceston), 30 March 1949, p.6.

37 Morgan, 'Aboriginal Education in the Furneaux Islands (1798-1986)', pp.72–3.

38 Ryan, *The Aboriginal Tasmanians*, p.246.

39 Felton (ed.), *Family and Community*, p.28.

40 R.A. Perrin, 'Land Use on Cape Barren Island, Tasmania', *Papers and Proceedings of the Royal Society of Tasmania*, Vol.122, No.2 (1988), pp.76 and 79.

41 *Examiner* (Launceston), 23 February 1899, p.3; *Examiner* (Launceston), 1 April 1899, p.7.

42 *Examiner* (Launceston), 8 October 1906, p.7.

43 *Examiner* (Launceston), 13 August 1908, p.6.

44 *Examiner* (Launceston), 21 November 1912, p.2.

45 *Mercury* (Hobart), 29 March 1934, p.8.

46 *Mercury* (Hobart), 24 November 1936, p.7.

47 *Advocate* (Burnie), 3 September 1936, p.7.

48 *Examiner* (Launceston), 9 March 1937, p.5.

49 *Examiner* (Launceston), 2 February 1937, p.5.

50 Mallett, *My Past—Their Future*, pp.16–18.
51 Mallett, *My Past—Their Future*, pp.16–17.
52 Mallett, *My Past—Their Future*, pp.1 and 3.
53 Felton (ed.), *Family and Community*, p.22.
54 Felton (ed.), *Family and Community*, pp.23–4.
55 Mallett, *My Past—Their Future*, p.22.
56 *Mercury* (Hobart), 31 August 1934, p.7.
57 Felton (ed.), *Family and Community*, p.24.
58 Mallett, *My Past—Their Future*, p.23.
59 Felton (ed.), *Family and Community*, p.27.
60 *Mercury* (Hobart), 15 January 1936, p.5.
61 Felton (ed.), *Family and Community*, p.35.
62 Mallett, *My Past—Their Future*, pp.20 and 22.
63 Mallett, *My Past—Their Future*, p.34; Felton (ed.), *Family and Community*, p.34.
64 R. Norman, 'Jewellery and Cultural Identity: A Tasmanian Perspective' (unpublished MA thesis, Monash University, 1995), pp.3–4.
65 Mallett, *My Past — Their Future*, pp.5–6, 8 and 14.
66 Mallett, *My Past — Their Future*, p.19.
67 Morgan, 'Aboriginal Education in the Furneaux Islands (1798–1986)', p.154.
68 Mallett, *My Past — Their Future*, pp.11–12.
69 Parry, '"Such a Longing"', p.229.
70 M. Denholm , 'Torn from mother, brother', *Australian* (Sydney), 15 December 2004, p.6.
71 C. Evans and N. Parry, 'Vessels of Progressivism? Tasmanian State Girls and Eugenics, 1900–1940', *Australian Historical Studies*, Vol.32, No.117 (October 2001), p.323.
72 Evans and Parry, 'Vessels of Progressivism?, pp.230–31.
73 Mallett, *My Past — Their Future*, p.12.
74 Morgan, 'Aboriginal Education in the Furneaux Islands (1798–1986)', p.156.
75 Mallett, *My Past — Their Future*, p.13.
76 Felton (ed.), *Family and Community*, pp.29 and 31.
77 Mallett, *My Past — Their Future*, p.14.
78 R. Ryan, '"Synchronicity Happened": Dance and Music as a Social Force in the Furneaux Group, 1954–2004', in H. Johnson (ed.), *Refereed Papers from the 2nd International Small Island Cultures Conference*, Museum Theatre, Norfolk Island Museum, 9–13 February 2006.
79 Mallett, *When Cape Barren Island was an Aboriginal Reserve*, p.12.
80 Mallett, *My Past — Their Future*, pp.15–16.
81 Mallett, *When Cape Barren Island was an Aboriginal Reserve*, pp.11–12.
82 Personal communication from Aunty Phyllis Pitchford, 21 October 2011.
83 Mallett, *My Past — Their Future*, p.41.
84 Felton (ed.), *Family and Community*, p.31.
85 Parry, '"Such a Longing"', pp.231–2.
86 H. Reynolds, *The Indelible Stain? The question of genocide in Australia's history* (Melbourne: Viking, 2001), pp.148–9.
87 J. D'Arcy, '"The Same but Different": Aborigines, Eugenics, and the Harvard-Adelaide Universities' Anthropological Expedition to Cape Barren Island Reserve, January 1939', *Tasmanian Historical Studies*, Vol.12 (2007), pp.61–3.
88 D'Arcy, '"The Same but Different"', pp.73, 78, 81 and 87.
89 D'Arcy, '"The Same but Different", p.88.
90 Mallett, *My Past — Their Future*, p.45.
91 D'Arcy, '"The Same but Different"', pp.80–1.
92 Felton (ed.), *Family and Community*, pp.33–4.
93 Mallett, *My Past — Their Future*, p.60.
94 Skira, 'Aboriginals in Tasmania', p.195.
95 Felton (ed.), *Family and Community*, p.34.
96 Felton (ed.), *Family and Community*, pp.33–4.
97 Ryan, *The Aboriginal Tasmanians*, p.247.
98 Ryan, *The Aboriginal Tasmanians*, p.248.

99 Felton (ed.), *Family and Community*, pp.34 and 39.
100 Ryan, *The Aboriginal Tasmanians*, p.249.
101 Ryan, *The Aboriginal Tasmanians*, pp.250–1.
102 Ryan, *The Aboriginal Tasmanians*, pp.250–1.
103 Morgan, 'Aboriginal Education in the Furneaux Islands (1798–1986)', p.79.
104 Ryan, *The Aboriginal Tasmanians*, pp.251 and 253.

14 THE RESURGENCE OF ABORIGINALITY

1 Ryan, *The Aboriginal Tasmanians*, p.253.
2 S. Bowdler, 'Rosalind Langford (1946–2012)', AA, No.75 (December 2012), p.137.
3 Felton (ed.), *Family and Community*, p.46.
4 Felton (ed.), *Family and Community*, pp.47–9.
5 K. Marks, 'Channelling Mannalargenna: Surviving, belonging, challenging, enduring', *Griffith Review*, No.39 (Autumn 2013), p.182.
6 M. Mansell, 'Black Tasmanians Now', *Arena*, No.51 (1978), pp.5–6.
7 Anon, *The Last Tasmanian: Study Guide* (s.1: s.n., n.d.), p.7.
8 Windschuttle, *The Fabrication of Aboriginal History*: Vol.1, pp.432–3.
9 Mansell, 'Black Tasmanians Now', p.7.
10 Anon, *The Last Tasmanian*, pp.4–5.
11 Ryan, *The Aboriginal Tasmanians*, p.264.
12 Ryan, *The Aboriginal Tasmanians*, p.264.
13 Norst, *Burnum Burnum*, p.76.
14 G. Vowles, 'No Surrender', "Saturday Magazine", in *Mercury* (Hobart), 18 September 2010, p.5.
15 R. Jones, 'Tom Haydon 1938–1991: Film Interpreter of Australian Archaeology', *AA*, No.35 (1992), p.58.
16 Ryan, *The Aboriginal Tasmanians*, p.266.
17 Ryan, *The Aboriginal Tasmanians*, pp.266–7.
18 Ryan, *The Aboriginal Tasmanians*, pp.267–8.
19 G. Maslem, 'Battle of the bones', Bulletin (Sydney), 3 October 1995, pp.52–3.
20 Ryan, *The Aboriginal Tasmanians*, pp.271 and 273.
21 Ryan, *The Aboriginal Tasmanians*, pp.276–7.
22 Vowles, 'No Surrender', p.6.
23 B. Primsall, 'Gaddafi loses touch with people: Mansell', *Examiner* (Launceston), 8 March 2011, p.8.
24 Ryan, *The Aboriginal Tasmanians*, pp.280–1.
25 Primsall, 'Gaddafi loses touch with people', p.8.
26 Ryan, *The Aboriginal Tasmanians*, p.282.
27 Ryan, *The Aboriginal Tasmanians*, pp.284–5.
28 Ryan, *The Aboriginal Tasmanians*, p.285.
29 Jones, 'Tom Haydon 1938-1991', p.58.
30 Ryan, *The Aboriginal Tasmanians*, p.288.
31 *Courier-Mail* (Brisbane), 19 January 1991, p.19.
32 M. Roughley-Shaw, 'Wybalenna and the Treaty of Whitemark', *Indigenous Law Bulletin*, Vol.4, No.22 (July 1999), pp.10–11.
33 Roughley-Shaw, 'Wybalenna and the Treaty of Whitemark', pp.10–11.
34 Ryan, 'Risdon Cove and the Massacre of 3 May 1804', pp.119–20.
35 Anon, *Lungtalanana Clarke Island* (Hobart: Tasmanian Aboriginal Centre, 2004), p.8.
36 Ryan, *Tasmanian Aborigines*, p.341.
37 M. Denholm, 'First payout for stolen generation children', *Australian* (Sydney), 18 October 2006, pp.1–2; M. Denholm, 'Stolen generation bill set to pass parliament', *Australian* (Sydney), 22 November 2006, p.5.
38 M. Denholm, 'We're black and proud, say "whites"', *Weekend Australian* (Sydney), 25–26 June 2005, p.11.
39 B. Montgomery, 'Black ghosts finally put to rest', *Australian* (Sydney), 1 March

1999, p.5; Roughley-Shaw, 'Wybalenna and the Treaty of Whitemark', p.10.

40 M. Denholm, 'Stall on Bacon plan to return native island land', *Australian* (Sydney), 17 November 2004, p.4.

41 L. Johnston, 'Mansell calls for Aboriginal MP quota', *Examiner* (Launceston), 24 June 2010, p.8.

42 Marks, Channelling Mannalargenna', pp.182-189.

43 M. Denholm and P. Wilson, 'Museum bones legal fight a "waste" of $1m', *Weekend Australian* (Sydney), 24–5 February 2007, pp.1 and 4.

44 Denholm and Wilson, 'Museum bones legal fight a "waste" of $1m', p.1.

45 D. Shanahan, 'Scottish museum to return set of six Aboriginal skulls', *Australian* (Sydney), 9 April 2008, p.3.

46 J. Mundy, 'Remains back in safe hands', *Koori Mail* (Lismore) [hereafter *KM*], 23 September 2009, p.9.

47 Courier-Mail (Brisbane), 21 June 2014, p.30.

48 D. Coyne, 'Call to return busts', *KM*, 9 September 2009, p.32.

49 *KM*, 23 September 2009, p.19.

50 Plomley, *Weep in Silence*, p.136.

51 Russell, *Roving Mariners*, p.100.

52 Edwards, 'Bypass site set for human history claim', p.7; Brown, 'Bypass finds date from 40,000 years', p.3.

53 Olley, 'Peer review of the TAS110757 Jordan River, Brighton, Tasmania', pp.3-5; Allen, 'Peer Review of the *Draft Final Archaeological Report on the Test Excavations of the Jordan River Levee Site Southern Tasmania*', pp.15ff.

54 J. Mundy, 'Tassie bypass protest arrests', *KM*, 2 December 2009, p.12.

55 J. Mundy, 'Protest arrests', *KM*, 16 December 2009, p.8.

56 J. Mundy, 'Tas work restarts', *KM*, 10 February 2010, p.13.

57 J. Mundy, 'Bypass battle goes on', *KM*, 16 June 2010, p.7.

58 J. Mundy, 'Bypass campaign', *KM*, 11 August 2010, p.12.

59 Mundy, 'Bypass battle goes on', *KM*, 16 June 2010, p.7; J. Mundy, 'Tas battle in court', *KM*, 25 August 2010, p.8; J. Mundy, 'Hopeful of Federal intervention', *KM*, 6 October 2010, p.9.

60 J. Mundy, 'Brighton campaign vow as court challenge fails', *KM*, 9 March 2011, p.6.

61 Arndt, 'Aborigines mount spiritual defence', p.8.

62 J. Mundy, 'Activist hails magistrate's decision a victory', *KM*, 16 November 2011, p.7.

63 J. Mundy, 'Recipient puzzled by award', *KM*, 14 December 2011, p.3.

64 J. Mundy, 'Anger and hope after Tas talks', *KM*, 30 November 2011, p.14.

65 J. Mundy, '1 July deadline for Tas heritage', *KM*, 19 June 2013, p.18; J. Mundy, 'Last-ditch Tas plea to "kill" heritage bill', *KM*, 20 November 2013, p.6.

66 J. Mundy, 'Land in safe hands', *KM*, 22 May 2013, p.35.

67 R. Maxwell, 'Tas split on mining', *KM*, 14 August 2013, p.14.

BIBLIOGRAPHY

TASMANIAN ARCHIVE AND HERITAGE OFFICE

CO 280/25.
CSD 4/77/231.
CSO 89.
CSO 1/280/28.
CSO 1/1/316.
CSO 1/317.
CSO 1/323/7578.
CSO 1/324.
CSO 1/326/7578.
CSO 1/493/10853/2.
LSD 1/576, File 643/30.
LSD 1/576, File 643/70.
Van Diemen's Land Company Records, 1/4.
Van Diemen's Land Company Records, 5/1.
Van Diemen's Land Company Records, 5/2.
Van Diemen's Land Company Records 5/7.
Van Diemen's Land Company Records, 23/2.
Van Diemen's Land Company Records 23/9.

TASMANIAN GOVERNMENT

An Act to provide for the Subdivision of the Cape Barren Island Reserve, and for other purposes (1912).

Burbury, A.W., 'Report on the Condition of the Half Castes at Cape Barren Island Reservation' (Hobart: Government Printer, 16 September 1929).

Lord, J.E.C., 'Furneaux Islands: Report upon the State of the Islands, the Condition and Mode of Living of the Half-Castes, the Existing Methods of Regulating the Reserves, and Suggesting Lines for Future Administration', *Journals and Printed Papers of the Parliament of Tasmania*, Vol.59, No.57 (1908).

Marshall, A. (Chairman), 'Furneaux Islands Half-Castes: Report of the Select Committee' (Hobart: Government Printer, 19 December 1924).

Reibey, T., 'Half-Caste Islanders in Bass's Straits: A Report of the Venerable Archdeacon Reibey', *Journal of the*

Tasmanian Legislative Council, Vol.9 (1863).
Wedge, J.H., 'Official Report of Journies made by J.H. Wedge, Esq., Assistant Surveyor, in the North-west portion of Van Diemen's Land in the early part of the year 1828' (Hobart: Govt. Printer, 1828).

UNIVERSITY OF TASMANIA, HOBART

'Copy of a letter by James Erskine Calder upon the existence of natives in unexplored parts of Tasmania in 1847', University of Tasmania Library, Special and Rare Materials Collection, Hobart.

STATE LIBRARY OF NEW SOUTH WALES, SYDNEY

'Miscellaneous Papers of George Augustus Robinson 1829–1833', A7059.

MACQUARIE LAW SCHOOL

'Decisions of the Superior Courts of New South Wales, 1788–1899: *R. v. Bonjon*'.

STATE LIBRARY OF VICTORIA

'James Dredge Diary' MS5244, Box 16/4, La Trobe Manuscripts Collection.

NEWSPAPERS

Advertiser (Adelaide).
Advertiser (Launceston).
Advocate (Burnie).
Australian (Sydney).
Bathurst Free Press and Mining Journal (Bathurst).
Brisbane Courier (Brisbane).
Colonial Times (Hobart).
Cornwall Chronicle (Launceston).
Courier (Hobart).
Courier-Mail (Brisbane).
Examiner (Launceston).
Geelong Advertiser (Geelong).
Hobart Town Courier (Hobart).
Hobart Town Gazette and Van Diemen's Land Advertiser (Hobart).
Koori Mail (Lismore).
Kurbingui Star (Zillmere).
Mercury (Hobart).
Port Phillip Gazette (Melbourne).
Port Phillip Patriot (Melbourne).
Sydney Gazette and New South Wales Advertiser (Sydney).
Sydney Herald (Sydney).
Tasmanian (Hobart).
Tasmanian and Austral-Pacific Review (Hobart).

BOOKS

Adam-Smith, P., *Moonbird People* (Adelaide: Rigby, 1965).

——, *There was a Ship* (Melbourne: Thomas Nelson, 1983).

Alexander, A., *Governors' Ladies: The Wives and Mistresses of Van Diemen's Land Governors* (Hobart: Tasmanian Historical Research Association, 1987).

Anon, *Copies of all Correspondence between Lieutenant-Governor Arthur and His Majesty's Secretary of State for the Colonies, on the Subject of the Military Operations lately carried on against the Aboriginal Inhabitants of Van Diemen's Land* (Hobart: Tasmanian Historical Research Association, 1971).

Backhouse, J., *A Narrative of a Visit to the Australian Colonies* (London: Hamilton, Adams, and Co, 1843).

Bakewell, A., *The English Dane: A Life of Jorgen Jorgenson* (London: Chatto & Windus, 2005).

Bateson, C., *Dire Strait: A History of Bass Strait* (Sydney: A.H. & A.W. Reed, 1973).

Berlin, I., *Many Thousands Gone: The First Two Centuries of Slavery in North America* (Cambridge: Belknap Press, 1998).

Bischoff, J., *Sketch of the History of Van Diemen's Land, illustrated by a map of the island, and an account of the Van Diemen's Land Company* (London: John Richardson, Royal Exchange, 1832).

Blackburn, R., *The Making of New World Slavery* (London: Verso, 1999).

Bligh, W., *A Voyage in the South Seas, undertaken by command of His Majesty, for the purpose of conveying bread-fruit to the West Indies in His Majesty's ship Bounty* (Adelaide: Libraries Board of South Australia, 1969).

Bolton, G., *Spoils and Spoilers: A history of Australians shaping their environment* (Sydney: Allen & Unwin, 1992).

Bonwick, J., *The Last of the Tasmanians, or The Black War of Van Diemen's Land* (London: Sampson Low, Son, & Marston, 1870).

——, *The Lost Tasmanian Race* (London: Sampson Low, Marston, Searle, and Rivington, 1884).

Bowden, K.M., *Captain James Kelly of Hobart Town* (Melbourne: Melbourne University Press, 1964).

Boxall, G., *Australian Bushrangers: An Illustrated History* (Adelaide: Rigby, 1976).

Brown, A.J., *Ill-Starred Captains: Flinders and Baudin* (Fremantle, WA: Fremantle Arts Centre Press, 2004).

Brownrigg, [M], Rev. Canon, *The Cruise of the Freak: A Narrative of a Visit to the Islands of Bass and Banks Straits with some account of the islands* (Launceston, Tas: J.S.V. Turner, 1872).

Buckby, P., *David Howie: Devil or Saint?* (Smithton, Tas: Jamala Press, 2003).

Calder, G., *Levée, Line and Martial Law: A History of the Dispossession of the Mairremmener People of Van Diemen's Land 1803–1832* (Launceston, Tas: Fullers Bookshop, 2010).

Calder, J., *Some Account of the Wars, Extirpation, Habits, etc. of the Native Tribes, of Tasmania* (Hobart: Fullers Bookshop, 1972).

Cameron, P., *Grease and Ochre: The Blending of Two Cultures at the Colonial Sea Frontier* (Launceston, Tas: Fullers Bookshop, 2011).

Cannon, M., *The Exploration of Australia* (Sydney: Reader's Digest Services, 1987).

Clark, C.M.H., *A History of Australia Vol.1: From the Earliest Times to the Age of Macquarie* (Melbourne: Melbourne University Press, 1968).

Clements, N., *The Black War: Fear, Sex and Resistance in Tasmania* (St Lucia, Qld: University of Queensland Press, 2014).

Cogger, H., *Reptiles & Amphibians of Australia* (Sydney: Reed New Holland, 2000).

Connor, J., *The Australian Frontier Wars 1788–1838* (Sydney: University of New South Wales Press, 2005).

Cooper, J. (comp.), *The Cotton Papers: Land*

of the Sleeping Gods (Hobart: Wellington Bridge Press, 2013).
Cove, J., *What The Bones Say: Tasmanian Aborigines, Science and Domination* (Ottawa: Carleton University Press, 1995).
Cox, R., *Steps to the Scaffold: The untold story of Tasmania's black bushrangers* (Pawleena, Tas: Cornhill Publishing, 2004).
Crawford, Justice, W.F. Ellis and G.M. Stancombe (eds), *The Diaries of John Helder Wedge 1824–1835* (Hobart: Royal Society of Tasmania, 1962).
Cree, N., *Oyster Cove: Last home of the Tasmanian Aboriginal* (Melbourne: Nicholas Cree, 1979).
Cumpston, J.S., *Kangaroo Island 1800–1836* (Canberra: Roebuck Society, 1986).
Davis, R., *The Tasmanian Gallows: A Study of Capital Punishment* (Hobart: Cat & Fiddle Press, 1974).
d'Entrecasteaux, B., *Voyage to Australia & the Pacific 1791–1793* (ed.), E. Duyker and M. Duyker (Melbourne: Melbourne University Press, 2001).
De Vries, S., *Strength of Spirit: Pioneering Women of Achievement from First Fleet to Federation* (Sydney: Millennium Books, 1995).
Dixon, R.M.W., *The Dyirbal Language of North Queensland* (Cambridge: Cambridge University Press, 1972).
Dunmore, J., *Storms and Dreams — Louis Bougainville: Soldier, Explorer, Statesman* (Sydney: ABC Books, 2005).
Duyker, E. (ed.), *The Discovery of Tasmania: Journal extracts from the expeditions of Abel Janszoon Tasman and Marc-Joseph Dufresne 1642 and 1772* (Hobart: St. David's Park Publishing, 1992).
——, *Citizen Labillardière: A Naturalists Life in Revolution and Exploration (1755–1834)* (Melbourne: Miegunyah Press, 2003).
Elder, B., *Blood on the Wattle: Massacres and Maltreatment of Australian Aborigines since 1788* (Sydney: National Book Distributors, 1992).
Felton, H., *Living with the land Book Four: From Optimism to Despair* (Hobart: Department of Education and The Arts, 1990).
——, *Living with the land Book Seven: Family and Community* (Hobart: Department of Education and The Arts, 1991).
Flannery, T., *The Future Eaters: An ecological history of the Australasian lands and people* (Sydney: Reed New Holland, 1999).
—— (ed.), *Terra Australis: Matthew Flinders' Great Adventures in the Circumnavigation of Australia* (Melbourne: Text Publishing, 2000).
Flood, J., *Archaeology of the Dreamtime: The story of prehistoric Australia and its people* (Sydney: Collins, 1989).
——, *The Riches of Ancient Australia: a journey into prehistory* (Brisbane: University of Queensland, 1990).
——, *Rock Art of the Dreamtime: Images of Ancient Australia* (Sydney: Angus & Robertson, 1997).
——, *Archaeology of the Dreamtime: The story of prehistoric Australia and its people* (Marleston, SA: JB Publishing, 2004).
——, *The Original Australians: Story of the Australian People* (Sydney: Allen & Unwin, 2006).
Gammage, B., *The Biggest Estate on Earth: How Aborigines Made Australia* (Sydney: Allen & Unwin, 2011).
Hare, R., *The Voyage of the Caroline from England to Van Diemen's Land and Batavia in 1827–28* ed. I. Lee (London: Longmans, Green, 1927).
Hiscock, P., *Archaeology of Ancient Australia* (London: Routledge, 2008).
Historical Records of Australia, Ser.1, Vol.12.
Historical Records of Australia, Ser.3, Vol.1.
Historical Records of Australia, Ser.3, Vol.2.
Historical Records of Australia, Ser.3, Vol.10.
Historical Records of New South Wales, Vol.5.
Horner, F., *The French Reconnaissance: Baudin in Australia 1801–1803* (Melbourne: Melbourne University Press, 1987).
Isaacs, J., *Australia's Living Heritage: Arts of the Dreaming* (Sydney: Lansdowne Press, 1997).

Johnson, M., *Trials and Tribulations: A Social History of Europeans in Australia 1788–1960* (Launceston, Tas: Myola House of Publishing, 2007).

Joy, W. and T. Prior, *The Bushrangers* (Adelaide: Rigby, 1971).

Kociumbas, J., *Possessions 1770–1860*, Vol.2 in G. Bolton (ed.), *The Oxford History of Australia* (Melbourne: Oxford University Press, 1992).

Lourandos, H., *Continent of Hunter-Gatherers: New perspectives in Australian prehistory* (Cambridge: Cambridge University Press, 1997).

Lubbock, A., *Owen Stanley R.N. 1811–1850: Captain of the 'Rattlesnake'* (Melbourne: Heinemann, 1968).

McFarlane, I., *Beyond Awakening — The Aboriginal Tribes of North West Tasmania: A History* (Launceston, Tas: Fullers Bookshop, Riawunna Aboriginal Studies Centre and Community, Place and Heritage Research Unit, University of Tasmania, 2008).

Macintyre, S. and A. Clark, *The History Wars* (Melbourne: Melbourne University Press, 2004).

Mackaness, G., *Captain William Bligh's Discoveries and Observations in Van Diemen's Land* (Sydney: D.S. Ford, 1943).

McKay, T., *Alexander McKay: The Prince of Travellers* (Kingston, Tas: Thelma McKay, 1994).

Macknight, C., *Low Head to Launceston: the earliest reports of Port Dalrymple and the Tamar* (Launceston, Tas: Historical Survey of Northern Tasmania, 1998).

Mallett, M., *On Being Aboriginal Book 4: When Cape Barren Island was an Aboriginal Reserve* (Hobart: Education Department of Tasmania, 1984).

——, *My Past — Their Future: Stories from Cape Barren Island* (Hobart: Blubber Head Press in association with Riawunna, Centre for Aboriginal Education, University of Tasmania, 2001).

Mathew, J., *Eaglehawk and Crow: A study of the Australian Aborigines including an inquiry into their origin and a survey of Australian languages* (London: David Nutt, 1899).

Melville, H., *The history of Van Diemen's Land from the year 1824 to 1835, inclusive During the Administration of Lieutenant-Governor George Arthur* (ed.), G. Mackaness (Sydney: Horowitz-Grahame, 1965).

Meredith, L.A., *My Home in Tasmania, during a residence of nine years* (London: John Murray, 1852).

Meston, A., *The Van Diemen's Land Company 1825–1842* (ed.) F. Ellis (Launceston, Tas: Museum Committee, Launceston City Council, 1958).

Morgan, S., *Land Settlement in Early Tasmania: Creating an Antipodean England* (Cambridge: Cambridge University Press, 1992).

Mulvaney, D.J., *Encounters in Place: Outsiders and Aboriginal Australians 1606–1985* (Brisbane: University of Queensland Press, 1989).

Mulvaney, J. and J. Kamminga, *Prehistory of Australia* (Sydney: Allen & Unwin, 1999).

Nicholls, M. (ed.), *The Diary of the Reverend Robert Knopwood 1808–1838* (Hobart: Tasmanian Historical Research Association, 1977).

Nixon, F., *The Cruise of the Beacon: A Narrative of a Visit to The Islands of Bass's Straits* (London: Bell & Daldry, 1857).

Norst, M., *Burnum Burnum: A Warrior for Peace* (Sydney: Kangaroo Press, 1999).

Owen, L., *Risdon Cove 3 May 1804* (Sydney: Macleay Press, 2010).

Plomley, N.J.B., *The Baudin Expedition and the Tasmanian Aborigines 1802* (Hobart: Blubber Head Press, 1983).

——, *Jorgen Jorgenson and the Aborigines of Van Diemen's Land* (Hobart: Blubber Head Press, 1991).

——, *Weep in Silence: A History of the Flinders Island Aboriginal Settlement* (Hobart: Blubber Head Press, 1987).

——, *The Tasmanian Aborigines* (Launceston, Tas: Plomley Foundation, 1993).

——, *Friendly Mission: The Tasmanian*

Journal and Papers of George Augustus Robinson 1829–1834 (Launceston, Tas: Queen Victoria Museum and Art Gallery and Quintus Publishing, 2008).

Pybus, C., *Community of Thieves* (Melbourne, Vic: Minerva, 1992).

Rae-Ellis, V., *Trucanini: Queen or Traitor?* (Hobart: O.B.M. Publishing Company, 1976).

——, *Black Robinson: Protector of Aborigines* (Melbourne: Melbourne University Press, 1988).

Reed, A.W. (ed.), *Captain Cook in Australia: Extracts from the journals of Captain James Cook giving a full account in his own words of his adventures and discoveries in Australia* (Wellington: A.H. and A.W. Reed, 1969).

Reynolds, H., *The Other Side of the Frontier: Aboriginal resistance to the European invasion of Australia* (Melbourne: Penguin, 1995).

——, *Fate of a Free People: A Radical Re-Examination of the Tasmanian Wars* (Melbourne: Penguin, 1995).

——, *Aboriginal Sovereignty: Reflections on race, state and nation* (Sydney: Allen & Unwin, 1996).

——, *The Indelible Stain? The question of genocide in Australia's history* (Melbourne: Viking, 2001).

Rienits, R. and T. Rienits, *The Voyages of Captain Cook* (London: Hamlyn, 1968).

Ritchie, J. (intro.), *A Charge of Mutiny: The Court Martial of Lieutenant Colonel George Johnston for deposing Governor William Bligh in the Rebellion of 26 January 1808* (Canberra: National Library of Australia, 1988).

Roberts, J., *Jack of Cape Grim: A Victorian Adventure* (Melbourne: Greenhouse Publications, 1986).

Robson, L., *A History of Tasmania Vol.1: Van Diemen's Land from the Earliest Times to 1855* (Melbourne: Oxford University Press, 1983).

Rolls, M. and M. Johnson, *Historical Dictionary of Australian Aborigines* (Lanham, MY: Scarecrow Press, 2011).

Rose, M. (ed.), *For the record: 160 years of Aboriginal print journalism* (Sydney: Allen & Unwin, 1996).

Roth, H. Ling, *The Aborigines of Tasmania* (Halifax: F. King & Sons, 1899).

Russell, L., *Roving Mariners: Australian Aboriginal Whalers and Sealers in the Southern Oceans, 1790–1870* (New York: State University of New York Press, 2012).

Ryan, L., *The Aboriginal Tasmanians* (Sydney: Allen & Unwin, 1996).

——, *Tasmanian Aborigines: A history since 1803* (Sydney: Allen & Unwin, 2012).

Shakespeare, N., *In Tasmania* (Sydney: Vintage, 2004).

Smith, C., *Tales of Old Tasmania: The First Fifty Years* (Adelaide: Rigby, 1978).

Smith, F., *Caribbean Rum: A Social and Economic History* (Gainesville, FL: University Press of Florida, 2005).

Smith, K.V., *Mari Nawi: Aboriginal Odysseys* (Sydney: Rosenberg Publishing, 2010).

Tardiff, P., *John Bowen's Hobart: The beginning of European settlement in Tasmania* (Hobart: Tasmanian Historical Research Association, 2003).

Taylor, R., *Unearthed: The Aboriginal Tasmanians of Kangaroo Island* (Kent Town, SA: Wakefield Press, 2008).

Travers, R., *The Tasmanians: The Story of a Doomed Race* (Melbourne: Cassell, 1968).

——, *Rogue's March: A Chronicle of Colonial Crime in Australia* (Melbourne: Hutchinson, 1973).

Turnbull, C., *Black War: The Extermination of the Tasmanian Aborigines* (Melbourne: F.W. Cheshire, 1948).

Valance, T., D. Moore and E. Groves, *Nature's Investigator: The Diary of Robert Brown in Australia, 1801–1805* (Canberra: Australian Biological Resources Study, 2001).

Van Toorn, P., *Writing Never Arrives Naked: Early Aboriginal cultures of writing in Australia* (Canberra:

Aboriginal Studies Press, 2006).
Veitch, M., *The Forgotten Islands: a personal adventure through the islands of Bass Strait* (Melbourne: Viking, 2011).
Walker, J.B., *Abel Janszoon Tasman: His Life and Voyages* (Hobart: William Grahame Jnr., Govt. Printer, 1896).
——, *Early Tasmania* (Hobart: M.C. Reed, Govt. Printer, 1989).
West, I., *Pride Against Prejudice: Reminiscences of a Tasmanian Aborigine* (Canberra: Australian Institute of Aboriginal Studies, 1984).
West, J., *The History of Tasmania: with copious information respecting the Colonies of New South Wales Victoria South Australia &c., &c.* (ed.), A.G.L. Shaw (Sydney: Angus & Robertson, 1981).
White, C., *History of Australian Bushranging: Vol.1* (Melbourne: Currey O'Neil, 1980).
Williams, I., *Rum: A Social and Sociable History of the Real Spirit of 1776* (New York: Nation Books, 2005).
Windschuttle, K., *The Fabrication of Aboriginal History Vol.1: Van Diemen's Land 1803–1847* (Sydney: Macleay Press, 2002).
Worrell, E., *Reptiles of Australia* (Sydney: Angus & Robertson, 1970).
Wyllie, D., *Dolly Dalrymple* (Childers, Qld: Diana Wyllie, 2004).

MONOGRAPHS

Allen, J. Archaeological Consultancies, 'Peer Review of the *Draft Final Archaeological Report on the Test Excavations of the Jordan River Levee Site Southern Tasmania*' (Broulee, NSW, 22 October 2010).
Anon, 'Boat Expeditions Round Tasmania, 1815–16 and 1824: Reports' (Hobart: Legislative Council, 1881).
Anon, *The Last Tasmanian: Study Guide* (s.1: s.n., n.d.).
Anon, *Lungtalanana Clarke Island* (Hobart: Tasmanian Aboriginal Centre, 2004).
Birmingham, J., 'Wybalenna: The Archaeology of Cultural Accommodation in Nineteenth Century Tasmania' (Sydney: Australian Society for Historical Archaeology Incorporated, 1992).
Bruce, J.L., 'A Gentleman from Silesia: Adolphus Schayer and the Van Diemen's Land Company 1830–1843' (unpublished research paper, Tasmanian State Institute of Technology, 1990).
CHMA, 'Interim Report on the Jordan River Levee Excavations' (Hobart, April 2010).
Crowther, W., 'The Final Phase of the Extinct Tasmanian Race 1847–1876', *Records of the Queen Victoria Museum*, No.49 (1974).
McGowan, A., 'Archaeological Investigations at Risdon Cove Historic Site 1978–1980', National Parks and Wildlife Service Tasmania, Occasional Paper No.10 (April 1985).
Mollison, B. and C. Everitt, 'The Tasmanian Aborigines and Their Descendants (Chronology, Genealogies and Social Data): Part 2' (Hobart: University of Tasmania, December 1978).
Olley, J., 'Peer Review of the TAS110757 Jordan River, Brighton, Tasmania: Luminescence Chronology' (Cupper, May 2010).
Plomley, N.J.B., 'The Tasmanian Tribes & Cicatrices as Tribal Indicators among the Tasmanian Aborigines', Queen Victoria Museum and Art Gallery, Launceston, Occasional Paper No.5 (1992).
——, 'The Aboriginal–Settler Clash in Van Diemen's Land 1803–1831', Queen Victoria Museum and Art Gallery, Launceston, Occasional Paper No.16 (1992).
Stephens, E.W., 'The Furneaux Islands: Their Early Settlement and some Characteristics of the Inhabitants'

(Launceston, Tas: Royal Society of Tasmania, 1899).
Stephens, G., 'H.H. Montgomery—The Mutton Bird Bishop', *University of Tasmania Occasional Paper*, No.39 (1985).
Toscano, J., 'The Tunnerminnerwait and Maulboyheener Saga' (Melbourne: Anarchist Media Institute, 2008).
Webb, S., *The Willandra Lakes Hominids* (Canberra: Department of Prehistory, Research School of Pacific Studies, Australian National University, 1989).

CHAPTERS

Barwick, D., 'Coranderrk and Cumeroogunga: Pioneers and Policy', in T.S. Epstein and D.H. Penny (eds), *Opportunity and Response: Case Studies in Economic Development* (London: C. Hurst & Company, 1972), pp.11–68.
Boyce, J., 'Fantasy Island', in R. Manne (ed.), *Whitewash: On Keith Windschuttle's Fabrication of Aboriginal History* (Melbourne: Black Inc. Agenda, 2003), pp.17–78.
Breen, S., 'The PALL-I-TORRE: The Black native people of Meander', in Anon, *Meander Valley Memories: A History of Meander and Surrounding Areas* (Meander, Tas: Meander Centenary Writers, 1991), pp.1–7.
Broome, R., 'The struggle for Australia: Aboriginal–European warfare, 1770–1930', in M. McKernan and M. Browne (eds), *Australia: Two Centuries of War and Peace* (Canberra: Australian War Memorial and Allen & Unwin, 1988), pp.92–120.
Calaby, J.H., 'Red-necked Wallaby: *Macropus rufogriseus*', in R. Strahan (ed.), *The Australian Museum Complete Book of Australian Mammals* (Sydney: Angus & Robertson, 1983), pp.239–41.
Clark, J., 'Devils and Horses: Religious and Creative Life in Tasmanian Aboriginal Society', in M. Roe (ed.), *The Flow of Culture: Tasmanian Studies* (Canberra: Australian Academy of the Humanities, 1987), pp.50–72.
Crowley, T., 'Tasmanian Aboriginal Language: Old and New Identities', in M. Walsh and C. Yallop (eds), *Language and Culture in Aboriginal Australia* (Canberra: Aboriginal Studies Press, 1993), pp.51–71.
James, K., 'Wife or Slave: Australian Sealing Slavery, Australia's own slavery system using Indigenous women workers on Kangaroo Island and Bass Strait islands 1802–1835', in A. Chittleborough *et.al.*, *Alas for the Pelicans! Flinders, Baudin & Beyond: Essays and Poems* (Kent Town, SA: Wakefield Press, 2002), pp.175–83.
Johnson, M., 'Indigenous People of the Cataract', in P.A.C. Richards and M. Johnson (eds), *Health, Wealth and Tribulation: Launceston's Cataract Gorge* (Launceston, Tas: Myola House of Publishing, 2007), pp.57–67.
——, 'People, Place and Identity in the Tamar Valley Precinct', in F. Gale (ed.), *Pulp Friction in Tasmania: a review of the environmental assessment of Gunns' proposed mill* (Launceston, Tas: Pencil Pine Press, 2011), pp.1–17.
Jones, R., 'The Demography of Hunters and Farmers in Tasmania', in D.J. Mulvaney and J. Golson (eds), *Aboriginal Man and Environment in Australia* (Canberra: Australian National University Press, 1971), pp.271–87.
——, 'Tasmanian Tribes', Appendix in N. Tindale, *Aboriginal Tribes of Australia: Their Terrain, Environmental Controls, Distribution, Limits, and Proper Names* (Canberra: Australian National University Press, 1974), pp.317–54.
——, 'Tasmania: aquatic machines and off-shore islands', in G. de G. Sieveking, I.H. Longworth and K.E. Wilson (eds), *Problems in Economic and Social Archaeology* (London: Duckworth, 1976), pp.235–63.

——, 'The Tasmanian paradox', in R.V.S. Wright (ed.), *Stone tools as cultural markers: change, evolution and complexity* (Canberra: Australian Institute of Aboriginal Studies, 1977), pp.189–204.

——, 'Why did the Tasmanians stop eating fish?', in R. Gould (ed.), *Explorations in Ethnoarchaeology* (Albuquerque, NM: University of New Mexico, 1978), pp.11–48.

Konishi, S., 'Francois Pèron and the Tasmanians: an unrequited romance', in I. Macfarlane and M. Hannah (eds), *Transgressions: critical Australian indigenous histories* (Canberra: ANU E Press, 2007), pp.1–18.

McFarlane, I., 'Cape Grim', in R. Manne (ed.), *Whitewash: On Keith Windschuttle's Fabrication of Aboriginal History* (Melbourne: Black Inc. Agenda, 2003), pp.277–98.

——, 'NJB Plomley's Contribution to North-West Tasmanian Regional History', in A. Johnston and M. Rolls (eds), *Reading Robinson: Companion Essays to Friendly Mission* (Hobart: Quintus Publishing, 2008), pp.127–41.

McGrath, A., 'Tasmania: 1', in A. McGrath (ed.), *Contested Ground: Australian Aborigines under the British Crown* (Sydney: Allen & Unwin, 1995), pp.306–37.

Mulvaney, J., 'French strangers on Tasmanian shores', in P. Veth, P. Sutton and M. Neale (eds), *Strangers on the Shore: Early coastal contacts in Australia* (Canberra: National Museum of Australia Press, 2008), pp.113–23.

Onfray, R., 'Cultural artefacts or "neglected old parks": the colonisation of rainforests in north-western Tasmania', in B. Stubbs (ed.), *Australia's Ever-Changing Forests VI: Proceedings of the Eighth National Conference on Australian Forest History* (Canberra: Australian Forest History Society and Tankard Books, 2012), pp.1–24.

Parry, N., '"Hanging no good for blackfellow": Looking into the life of Musquito', in I. Macfarlane and M. Hannah (eds), *Transgressions: critical Australian Indigenous histories* (Canberra: ANU E Press, 2007), pp.153–76.

Prickett, N., 'Trans-Tasman stories: Australian Aborigines in New Zealand sealing and shore whaling', in G. Clark, F. Leach and S. O'Connor (eds), 'Islands of Inquiry: Colonisation, Seafaring and the Archaeology of Maritime Landscapes', *Terra Australis*, Vol.29 (June 2008), pp.351–66.

Reynolds, H., 'George Augustus Robinson in Van Diemen's Land: Race, Status and Religion', in A. Johnston and M. Rolls (eds), *Reading Robinson: Companion Essays to Friendly Mission* (Hobart: Quintus Publishing, 2008), pp.161–69.

Ryan, L., 'Who Is the Fabricator?', in R. Manne (ed.), *Whitewash: On Keith Windschuttle's Fabrication of Aboriginal History* (Melbourne: Black Inc. Agenda, 2003), pp.230–57.

Ryan, R., '"Synchronicity Happened": Dance and Music as a Social Force in the Furneaux Group, 1954–2004', in H. Johnson (ed.), *Refereed Papers from the* 2nd *International Small Island Cultures Conference*, Museum Theatre, Norfolk Island Museum, 9–13 February 2006, pp.129–41.

Sim, R., 'Prehistoric human occupation in the King and Furneaux Island regions, Bass Strait', in M. Sullivan, S. Brockwell and A. Webb (eds), *Archaeology in the North: Proceedings of the 1993 Australian Archaeological Association Conference* (Darwin: North Australian Research Unit of Australian National University, 1994), pp.358–74.

Tardiff, P., 'Risdon Cove', in R. Manne (ed.), *Whitewash: On Keith Windschuttle's Fabrication of Aboriginal History* (Melbourne: Black Inc. Agenda, 2003), pp.218–24.

Turnbull, P., 'British Anthropological Thought in Colonial Practice: the appropriation of Indigenous Australian bodies, 1860–1880', in B. Douglas and C. Ballard (eds), *Foreign Bodies: Oceania and the Science of Race 1750–1940* (Canberra: Australian National University, 2008), pp.205–28.

Vanderwal, R.L., 'Pre-History and the Archaeology of Louisa Bay', in H. Gee and J. Fenton (eds), *The South West Book: A Tasmanian Wilderness* (Melbourne: Australian Conservation Foundation, 1979), pp.17–21.

ARTICLES

Allen, F., 'The Original Range of the Papuan and Negritto Races', *Journal of the Anthropological Institute of Great Britain and Ireland*, Vol.8 (1879), pp.38–50.

Anderson, S., 'French anthropology in Australia, a prelude: the encounters between Aboriginal Tasmanians and the expedition of Bruny d'Entrecasteaux, 1793', *Aboriginal History*, Vol.24 (2000), pp.212–23.

——, 'French anthropology in Australia, the first fieldwork report: Francois Pèron's "Maria Island — anthropological observations"', *Aboriginal History*, Vol.25 (2001), pp.228–42.

Anon, 'Curr, Edward (1798–1850)', *Australian Dictionary of Biography*, Vol.1, pp.269–72.

Anon, 'McKay, Alexander (1802?–1882)', *Australian Dictionary of Biography*, Vol.2, p.170.

Anon., 'Mills, Peter (1786–1816)', *Australian Dictionary of Biography*, Vol.2, pp.231–32.

Arndt, D., 'Aborigines mount spiritual defence', *Examiner* (Launceston), 11 November 2011, p.8.

Asten, M., 'The Risdon Cove Site: Birth of a State or Site of a Massacre; Bone of Contention or Future Site of Reconciliation?', *Tasmanian Historical Studies*, Vol.18 (2013), pp.103–21.

Barnard, J., 'Notes on the Last Living Aboriginal of Tasmania', *Papers and Proceedings of the Royal Society of Tasmania for the Year 1889* (1890), pp.60–4.

Barry, J., 'Willis, John Walpole (1793-1877)', *Australian Dictionary of Biography*, Vol.2, pp.602–04.

Bartlett, A., 'Fall from grace — Jacob Mountgarrett: Launceston's first doctor', "Examiner Extra: 2004 Bicentenary of Tasmania", in *Examiner* (Launceston), 16 February 2004, p.A12.

Barwick, L, 'Briggs, Louisa (1836–1925)', *Australian Dictionary of Biography*, Supplementary Volume 1580-1980, pp.45–6.

Bassett, E., 'Reconsidering Evidence of Tasmanian Fishing', *Environmental Archaeology*, Vol.9, No.2 (October 2004), pp.135–42.

Binks, M., 'Violence at Risdon Cove', *Mercury* (Hobart), 12 September 1988, p.1.

Birmingham, J. and A. Wilson, 'Archaeologies of Cultural Interaction: Wybalenna Settlement and Killalpaninna Mission', *International Journal of Historical Archaeology*, Vol.14, No.1 (2010), pp.15–38.

Blench, R., 'The Languages of the Tasmanians and Their Relation to the Peopling of Australia: Sensible and Wild Theories', *Australian Archaeology*, No.67 (December 2008), pp.13–18.

Bonwick, J., 'On the Origin of the Tasmanians Geologically Considered', *Journal of the Ethnological Society of London*, Vol.2, No.2 (1870), pp.121–31.

Bowdler, S., 'Hunters and Farmers in the Hunter Islands: Aboriginal and European Land-use of north-west Tasmanian islands in the historical period', *Records of the Queen Victoria Museum*, No.70 (1980), pp.1–17.

——, 'Fish and Culture: a Tasmanian Polemic', *Mankind*, Vol.12, No.4 (December 1980), pp.334–40.

——, 'Tasmania's Aborigines', *Bulletin* (Sydney), 16 March 1982, pp.6–7.

——, 'Rosalind Langford (1946–2012)',

Australian Archaeology, No.75 (December 2012), pp.137–8.

Boyce, J., 'Canine revolution: the social and environmental impact of the introduction of the dog to Tasmania', *Environmental History*, Vol.11, No.1 (January 2006), pp.102–29.

Breen, S., 'Beeton, Lucy (1829–1886)', *Australian Dictionary of Biography*, Supplementary Volume 1580-1980, pp.24–25.

——, 'Tasmanian Aborigines—Making Fire', *Tasmanian Historical Research Association Papers and Proceedings*, Vol.39, No.1 (March 1992), pp.40–2.

Bridges, B., 'The Extension of English Law to the Aborigines for Offences Committed Inter Se, 1829-1842', *Journal of the Royal Australian Historical Society*, Vol.59, Pt.4 (December 1973), pp.264–9.

Brodie, N., 'History's mysteries: The Cotton Papers 2', *40° South*, No.72 (Autumn 2014), pp.20–6.

Brown, D., 'Bypass finds date to 40,000 years', *Mercury* (Hobart), 27 April 2010, p.3.

Callick, R., 'Publisher pillories for attacking historian', *Australian* (Sydney), 7 December 2010, p.4.

Cane, S., J. Stockton and A. Vallance, 'A Note on the Diet of the Tasmanian Aborigines', *Australian Archaeology*, No.9 (1979), pp.77–81.

Cave, E., '"Journal during the expedition against the blacks": Robert Lawrence's experience on the Black Line', *Journal of Australian Studies*, Vol.37, No.1 (2013), pp.34–47.

Clark, I., 'George Augustus Robinson and Charles Joseph La Trobe: personal insights into a problematical relationship', *La Trobe Journal*, No.85 (May 2010), pp.13–20.

Clark, J., 'Smith, Fanny Cochrane (1834–1905)', *Australian Dictionary of Biography*, Vol.11, p.642.

Clements, N., '"Army of sufferers": the experience of Tasmania's Black Line', *Journal of Australian Studies*, Vol.37, No.1 (2013), pp.19–33.

Cobern, P., 'Who really killed Tasmania's aborigines?', *Bulletin* (Sydney), 23 February 1982, pp.32 and 34.

Connor, J., 'British Frontier Warfare Logistics and the "Black Line", Van Diemen's Land (Tasmania), 1830', *War in History*, Vol.9, No.2 (April 2002), pp.143–58.

Cosgrove, R., 'Late Pleistocene behavioural variation and time trends: the case from Tasmania', *Archaeology in Oceania*, Vol.30, No.3 (October 1995), pp.83–104.

——, 'Forty-Two Degrees South: The Archaeology of Late Pleistocene Tasmania', *Journal of World Prehistory*, Vol.13, No.4 (December 1999), pp.357–402.

—— and A. Pike-Tay, 'The Middle Palaeolithic and Late Pleistocene Tasmania Hunting Behaviour: a Reconsideration of the Attributes of Modern Human Behaviour', *International Journal of Osteoarchaeology*, Vol.14, No.3 (August 2004), pp.321–32.

Cox, R., 'Black Tom Birch: Fact and Fiction', *Tasmanian Historical Research Association Papers and Proceedings*, Vol.60, No.1 (April 2013), pp.6–13.

Coyne, D., 'Call to return bust', *Koori Mail* (Lismore), 9 September 2009, p.32.

Crowther, W.E.L.H., 'Crowther, William Lodewyk (1817–1885)', *Australian Dictionary of Biography*, Vol.3, pp.501–3.

Dammery, S., 'Walter George Arthur: A Health Profile of a 19th Century Van Diemen's Land Aboriginal Man', *Health and History*, Vol.4, No.2 (2002), pp.80–92.

D'Arcy, J., '"The Same but Different": Aborigines, Eugenics, and the Harvard-Adelaide Universities' Anthropological Expedition to Cape Barren Island Reserve, January 1939', *Tasmanian Historical Studies*, Vol.12 (2007), pp.59–90.

Davies, S., 'Aborigines, murder and the criminal law in early Port Phillip, 1841–1851', *Historical Studies*, Vol.22, No.88 (April 1987), pp.313–35.

Denholm, M., 'Stall on Bacon plan to return

native island land', *Australian* (Sydney), 17 November 2004, p.4.
——, 'Torn from mother, brother', *Australian* (Sydney), 15 December 2004, p.6.
——, 'We're black and proud, say "whites"', *Weekend Australian* (Sydney), 25–6 June 2005, p.11.
——, 'First payout for stolen generation children', *Australian* (Sydney), 18 October 2006, pp.1–2.
——, 'Stolen generation bill set to pass parliament', *Australian* (Sydney), 22 November 2006, p.5.
—— and P. Wilson, 'Museum bones legal fight a "waste" of $1m', *Weekend Australian* (Sydney), 24–5 February 2007, pp.1 and 4.
Dove, H.S., 'The Tasmanian Emu', *Emu*, Vol.25, No.4 (April 1926), pp.290–1.
Dowling, P., 'Mercury Poisoning at Oyster Cove? Suspected cases of unintentional poisoning of Tasmanian Aboriginal internees', *Tasmanian Historical Studies*, Vol.11 (2006), pp.59–68.
Duyker, E., 'Marion Dufresne, Marc-Joseph (1724–1772)', *Australian Dictionary of Biography*, Supplementary Volume 1580–1980, pp.258–9.
Edmonds, P., '"Failing in every endeavour to conciliate": Governor Arthur's Proclamation Boards to the Aborigines, Australian conciliation narratives and their transnational connections', *Journal of Australian Studies*, Vol.35, No.2 (June 2011), pp.201–18.
Edwards, Z., 'Bypass site set for human history claim', *Examiner* (Launceston), 11 March 2010, p.7.
Eldershaw, S., 'Hellyer, Henry (1790–1832)', *Australian Dictionary of Biography*, Vol.1, pp.528–9.
Evans, C. and N. Parry, 'Vessels of Progressivism? Tasmanian State Girls and Eugenics, 1900–1940', *Australian Historical Studies*, Vol.32, No.117 (October 2001), pp.322–33.
Fels, M., 'Culture Contact in the County of Buckinghamshire, Van Diemen's Land 1803–11', *Tasmanian Historical Research Association Papers and Proceedings*, Vol.29, No.2 (June 1982), pp.47–79.
Felton, H., 'Mathinna', in A. Alexander (ed.), *The Companion to Tasmanian History* (Hobart: Centre for Tasmanian Historical Studies, University of Tasmania, 2005), p.229.
Frost, A., 'New South Wales as *Terra Nullius*: The British Denial of Aboriginal Rights', *Historical Studies*, Vol.19, No.77 (October 1981), pp.513–23.
Fudali, E. and R. Ford, 'Darwin Glass and Darwin Crater: A Progress Report', *Meteoritics*, Vol.14 (September 1979), pp.283–96.
Gaffney, L. and J. Stockton, 'Results of the Jordan River Midden Excavation', *Australian Archaeology*, No.10 (June 1980), pp.68–78.
Gammage, B., 'Plain Facts: Tasmania under Aboriginal Management', *Landscape Research*, Vol.33, No.2 (2008), pp.241–54.
Garvey, J., 'Preliminary zooarchaeological interpretations from Kutikina Cave, south-west Tasmania', *Australian Aboriginal Studies*, No.1 (2006), pp.57–62.
——, 'The Wallaby Hunters of Ice Age Tasmania', *Australasian Science*, Vol.28, No.5 (June 2007), pp.30 and 32–3.
——, 'Surviving an Ice Age: The Zooarchaeological Record from Southwestern Tasmania', *Palaios*, Vol.22, No.6 (November 2007), pp.583–5.
——, 'Economic anatomy of the Bennett's wallaby (*Macropus rufogriseus*): Implications for understanding human hunting strategies in late Pleistocene Tasmania', *Quaternary International*, Vol.211, Nos.1–2 (1 January 2010), pp.144–56.
Giblin, R., 'Robert Brown at Port Dalrymple', *Papers and Proceedings of the Royal Society of Tasmania for the year 1929* (1930), pp.25–32.
Gill, J.C.H., 'Notes on the Tasmanian "Black War" 1827–1830', *Journal of the Royal Historical Society of Queensland*, Vol.8, No.3 (1967–68), pp.495–524.
Gott, B., 'Fire-Making in Tasmania: Absence of Evidence is Not Evidence of Absence',

Current Anthropology, Vol.43, No.4 (August–October 2002), pp.650–6.
Guenther, J., 'The Failure of the Christian Response to Tasmanian Aboriginals: 1803–1901 A Valid Assessment', *Tasmanian Historical Research Association Papers and Proceedings*, Vol.44, No.3 (September 1997), pp.202–17.
Hainsworth, D.R., 'Iron Men in Wooden Ships: The Sydney Sealers 1800-1820', *Labour History*, No.13 (November 1967), pp.19–25.
Harman, K., 'Send in the Sydney Natives! Deploying Mainlanders Against Tasmanian Aborigines', *Tasmanian Historical Studies*, Vol.14 (2009), pp.5–24.
——, 'Protecting Tasmanian Aborigines: American and Queensland Influences on the Cape Barren Island Reserve Act, 1912', *Journal of Imperial and Commonwealth History*, Vol.41, No.5 (2013), pp.744–64.
Harris, J., 'Robinson, George Augustus', in B. Dickey (ed.), *The Australian Dictionary of Evangelical Biography* (Sydney: Evangelical History Association, 1994), p.324.
Harris, S., D. Ranson and S. Brown, 'Maxwell River Archaeological Survey 1986', *Australian Archaeology*, No.27 (1988), pp.89–97.
Hart, P., 'Montgomery, Henry Hutchinson (1847–1932)', in A. Alexander (ed.), *The Companion to Tasmanian History* (Hobart: Centre for Tasmanian Historical Studies, University of Queensland, 2005), p.241.
Hewes, G., 'On Francois Pèron: The First Official Expedition Anthropologist', *Current Anthropology*, Vol.9, No.4 (October 1968), pp.287–8.
Hiatt, B., 'The Food Quest and the Economy of the Tasmanian Aborigines [Part 1]', *Oceania*, Vol.38, No.2 (December 1967), pp.99–133.
Hirst, J., 'In the Middle of the History Wars', *Sydney Papers*, Vol.18, Nos.3–4 (Winter–Spring 2006), pp.51–8.
Horton, D., 'Tasmanian Adaptation', *Mankind*, Vol.12, No.1 (1979), pp.28–34.
Howard, M., 'Archdeacon Thomas Reibey's 1862 Missionary Voyage to the Islands of Bass Strait', *Tasmanian Historical Research Association Papers and Proceedings*, Vol.38, No.1 (March 1991), pp.78–87.
Hudspeth, W.H., 'Experiences of a Settler in the Early Days of Van Diemen's Land', *Papers and Proceedings of the Royal Society of Tasmania for the Year 1935* (1936), pp.139–54.
Ison, S., 'A Rum Lot', *Australian Military History*, No.3 (October-November 1994), pp.42–4.
'J.G.S.', 'Cape Barren Island, Bass Straits', *Mercury* (Hobart), 14 August 1890, p.2.
Johnston, A., 'The "little empire of Wybalenna": Becoming Colonial in Australia', *Journal of Australian Studies*, Vol.28, No.81 (2004), pp.17–31.
——, 'George Augustus Robinson, the "Great Conciliator": colonial celebrity and its postcolonial aftermath', *Journal of Postcolonial Studies*, Vol.12, No.2 (2009), pp.153–72.
Johnston, L., 'Artistry in jewels of Tassie's foreshore', *Examiner* (Launceston), 10 January 2009, p.33.
——, 'Mansell calls for Aboriginal MP quota', *Examiner* (Launceston), 24 June 2010, p.8.
Jones, R., 'Excavations on a Stone Arrangement in Tasmania', *Man*, Vol.65 (May–June 1965), pp.78–9.
——, 'Fire-Stick Farming', *Australian Natural History*, Vol.16, No.7 (15 September 1969), pp.224–8.
——, 'Tasmanian Aborigines and Dogs', *Mankind*, Vol.7, No.4 (December 1970), pp.256–71.
——, 'Ice-Age Hunters of the Tasmanian Wilderness', *Australian Geographic*, No.8 (October-December 1987), pp.26–45.
——, 'Tom Haydon 1938–1991: Film Interpreter of Australian Archaeology', *Australian Archaeology*, No.35 (1992), pp.51–64.
——, 'Tasmanian Archaeology: Establishing

the Sequences', *Annual Review of Archaeology*, Vol.24 (October 1995), pp.423–46.
Jose, A., 'Nicolas Baudin', *Journal of the Royal Australian Historical Society*, Vol.20, Pt.6 (1934), pp.337–96.
Kelly, J., 'First Discovery of Port Davey and Macquarie Harbour', *Papers and Proceedings of the Royal Society of Tasmania for the year 1920*, pp.160–81.
Kenyon, A.S., 'The Aboriginal Protectorate of Port Phillip: Report of an Expedition to the Aboriginal Tribes of the Western Interior by the Chief Protector, George Augustus Robinson', *Victorian Historical Magazine*, Vol.12, No.3 (March 1928), pp.134–71.
Kiernan, K., R. Jones and D. Ranson, 'New evidence from Fraser Cave for glacial age man in south-west Tasmania', *Nature*, Vol.301 (6 January 1983), pp.28–32.
King, J., 'Elephant Seal Oil from King Island, Bass Strait, 1802–1819: with estimates of numbers killed and size of the original population', *Papers and Proceedings of the Royal Society of Tasmania*, Vol.133, Pt.1 (31 October 1999), pp.51–6.
Lee, I., 'A Forgotten Navigator: Captain (Afterwards Sir) John Hayes, and His Voyage of 1793', *Geographical Journal*, Vol.38, No.6 (December 1911), pp.580–90.
Lehman, G., 'Our Story of Risdon Cove', *Puganna News*, No.34 (May 1992), pp.1–3.
Lemkin, R., 'Tasmania', (ed.) A. Curthoys, *Patterns of Prejudice*, Vol.39, No.2 (2005), pp.170–96.
Lennox, G., 'The Van Diemen's Land Company and the Tasmanian Aborigines: A Reappraisal', *Tasmanian Historical Research Association Papers and Proceedings*, Vol.37, No.1 (March 1990), pp.165–208.
Little, B., 'The Sealing and Whaling Industry in Australia before 1850', *Australian Economic History Review*, Vol.9, No.2 (September 1969), pp.109–27.
Longman, M., 'Songs of the Tasmanian Aborigines as recorded by Mrs. Fanny Cochrane Smith', *Papers and Proceedings of the Royal Society of Tasmania*, Vol.94 (1960), pp.79–86.
Lord, C., 'A Note on the Burial Customs of the Tasmanian Aborigines', *Papers and Proceedings of the Royal Society of Tasmania for the year 1923* (1924), pp.45–6.
Luckman, L.E., 'The Aboriginal Rock Carvings at Mt. Cameron West, Tasmania, Photographs and Notes on the Excavations', *Papers and Proceedings of the Royal Society of Tasmania for the year 1950* (1951), pp.25–7.
McFarlane, I., 'Dalrymple, Dolly (c.1808–1864)', *Australian Dictionary of Biography*, Supplementary Volume 1580-1980, p.94.
——, 'Pevay: A Casualty of War', *Tasmanian Historical Research Association Papers and Proceedings*, Vol.48, No.4 (December 2001), pp.280–305.
——, 'Adolphus Schayer: Van Diemen's Land and the Berlin Papers', *Tasmanian Historical research Association Papers and Proceedings*, Vol.57, No.2 (August 2010), pp.105–18.
Macintyre, S., 'The History Wars', *Sydney Papers*, Vol.15, Nos.3–4 (Winter–Spring 2003), pp.77–83.
McMahon, J.F., 'The British Army: Its Role in Counter-Insurgency in the Black War in Van Diemen's Land', *Tasmanian Historical Studies*, Vol.5, No.1 (1995–6), pp.56–63.
——, 'The Black Line: Military Operations in Van Diemen's Land, October to November 1830', *Tasmanian Historical Research Association Papers and Proceedings*, Vol.55, No.3 (December 2008), pp.175–82.
McNiven, I., 'Technological organization and settlement in southwest Tasmania after the last glacial maximum', *Antiquity*, Vol.68, No.258 (March 1994), pp.75–82.
Madley, B., 'From Terror to Genocide: Britain's Tasmanian Penal Colony and Australia's History Wars', *Journal of British Studies*, Vol.47, No.1 (January 2008), pp.77–106.
Maloney, S., 'Truganini & George Augustus Robinson', *The Monthly*, No.66 (May

2012), p.66.
Mansell, M., 'Black Tasmanians Now', *Arena*, No.51 (1978), pp.5–8.
Marchant, L. and J. Reynolds, 'Baudin, Nicolas Thomas (1754–1803) and Freycinet, Louis-Claude Desaules de (1779–1842)', *Australian Dictionary of Biography*, Vol.1, pp.71–73.
——, 'Bruny D'Entrecasteaux, Joseph Antoine Raymond (1739–1793)', *Australian Dictionary of Biography*, Vol.1, pp.171–2.
——, 'La Perouse, Jean-Francois de Galaup, Comte de (1741–1788)', *Australian Dictionary of Biography*, Vol.2, pp.85–6.
—— and J. Reynolds, 'Peron, Francois (1775–1810)', *Australian Dictionary of Biography*, Vol.2, pp.323–24.
Marks, K., 'Channelling Mannalargenna: Surviving, belonging, challenging, enduring', *Griffith Review*, No.39 (Autumn 2013), pp.174–92.
Maslem, G., 'Battle of the bones', *Bulletin* (Sydney), 3 October 1995, pp.52–4.
Matson-Green, V., 'Tarenorerer (c.1800–1831)', *Australian Dictionary of Biography*, Supplementary Volume 1580–1880, p.376.
—— and R. Harper, 'Palawa Women: Carrying the Burdens and Finding the Solutions', *Labour History*, No.69 (November 1995), pp.65–74.
Maxwell, R., 'Tas split on mining', *Koori Mail* (Lismore), 14 August 2013, p.14.
Maxwell-Stewart, H., 'Competition and Conflict on the Forgotten Frontier: Western Van Diemen's Land 1822–33', *History Australia*, Vol.6, No.3 (December 2009), pp.66.1–20.
Maynard, J., 'The Shark, Remora and Aboriginal History', *International Journal of Critical Indigenous Studies*, Vol.1, No.1 (2008), pp.45–51.
Mead, I., 'Mountgarrett, Jacob (1773?–1828)', *Australian Dictionary of Biography*, Vol.2, p.264.
Meston, A.L., 'Aboriginal Rock-Carvings on the North-West Coast of Tasmania', *Papers and Proceedings of the Royal Society of Tasmania for the year 1931* (1932), pp.12–19.
——, 'The Problem of the Tasmanian Aborigine', *Papers and Proceedings of the Royal Society of Tasmania for the year 1936* (1937), pp.85–92.
——, 'The Halfcastes of the Furneaux Group', *Records of the Queen Victoria Museum*, Vol.11, No.1 (July 1947), pp.47–52.
Moneypenny, M., '"Going out and coming in": Cooperation and Collaboration between Aborigines and Europeans in early Tasmania', *Tasmanian Historical Studies*, Vol.5, No.1 (1995-96), pp.64–75.
Montgomery, B., 'Black ghosts finally put to rest', *Australian* (Sydney), 1 March 1999, p.5.
Morello, F. *et.al.*, 'Hunter-gatherers, biogeographic barriers and the development of human settlement in Tierra del Fuego', *Antiquity*, Vol.86, No.331 (March 2012), pp.71–87.
Mulvaney, D.J., 'Thomas, William (1793–1867)', *Australian Dictionary of Biography*, Vol.2, pp.518–19.
Mundy, J., 'Remains back in safe hands', *Koori Mail* (Lismore), 23 September 2009, p.9.
——, 'Tassie bypass protest arrests', *Koori Mail* (Lismore), 2 December 2009, p.12.
——, 'Protest arrests', *Koori Mail* (Lismore), 16 December 2009, p.8.
——, 'Tas work restarts', *Koori Mail* (Lismore), 10 February 2010, p.13.
——, 'Bypass battle goes on', *Koori Mail* (Lismore), 16 June 2010, p.7.
——, 'Bypass campaign', *Koori Mail* (Lismore), 11 August 2010, p.12.
——, 'Tas battle in court', *Koori Mail* (Lismore), 25 August 2010, p.8.
——, 'Hopeful of Federal intervention', *Koori Mail* (Lismore), 6 October 2010, p.9.
——, 'Brighton campaign vow as court challenge fails', *Koori Mail* (Lismore), 9 March 2011, p.6.
——, 'Activist hails magistrate's decision a victory', *Koori Mail* (Lismore), 16 November 2011, p.7.
——, 'Anger and hope after Tas talks', *Koori*

Mail (Lismore), 30 November 2011, p.14.
——, 'Recipient puzzled by award', *Koori Mail* (Lismore), 14 December 2011, p.3.
——, 'Land in safe hands', *Koori Mail* (Lismore), 22 May 2013, p.35.
——, '1 July deadline for Tas heritage', *Koori Mail* (Lismore), 19 June 2013, p.18.
——, 'Last-ditch Tas plea to "kill" heritage bill', *Koori Mail* (Lismore), 20 November 2013, p.6.
——, 'Book lifts shroud', *Koori Mail* (Lismore), 4 December 2013, p.21.
Murray, T., 'The childhood of William Lanne: contact archaeology and Aboriginality in Tasmania', *Antiquity*, Vol.67, No.256 (September 1993), pp.504–19.
Murray-Smith, S., '*Beyond the Pale*: The Islander Community of Bass Strait in the Nineteenth Century', *Tasmanian Historical research Association Papers and Proceedings*, Vol.20, No.4 (December 1973), pp.167–200.
Nelson, E.C., 'The Natural History Observations and Collections Made During Furneaux's Visit to Tasmania (Van Diemen's Land) in 1773, With Special Reference to Botany', *Papers and Proceedings of the Royal Society of Tasmania*, Vol.115 (1981), pp.77–84.
Noetling, F., 'A Native Burial Ground on Charlton Estate, Near Ross', *Papers and Proceedings of the Royal Society of Tasmania for the year 1908* (1909), pp.36–43.
——, 'The Food of the Tasmanian Aborigines', *Papers and Proceedings of the Royal Society of Tasmania for the year 1910*, pp.279–305.
O'Brien, P., 'Divine Browns and Mighty Whiteman: Exotic Primitivism and the Baudin Voyage to Tasmania in 1802', *Journal of Australian Studies*, Vol.23, No.63 (1999), pp.13–21.
Perrin, R.A., 'Land Use on Cape Barren Island, Tasmania', *Papers and Proceedings of the Royal Society of Tasmania*, Vol.122, No.2 (1988), pp.73–83.
Petrow, S., 'The Last Man: The mutilation of William Lanne in 1869 and its aftermath', *Aboriginal History*, Vol.21 (1997), pp.90–112.
Phillips, D., 'Early Settlement on the Tamar', *Launceston Historical Society Papers and Proceedings*, Vol.16 (2004), pp.32–6.
Pike-Tay, A., R. Cosgrove and J. Garvey, 'Systematic land use by late Pleistocene Tasmanian Aborigines', *Journal of Archaeological Science*, Vol.35, No.9 (September 2008), pp.2532–44.
Plomley, N.J.B., 'Robinson, George Augustus (1788–1866)', *Australian Dictionary of Biography*, Vol.2, pp.385–7.
——, 'French Manuscripts referring to the Tasmanian Aborigines', *Records of the Queen Victoria Museum*, No.23 (June 1966), pp.1–4.
—— and K.A. Henley, 'The Sealers of Bass Strait and the Cape Barren Island Community', *Tasmanian Historical Research Association Papers and Proceedings*, Vol.37, No.1 (March 1990), pp.37–127.
Porch, N. and J. Allen, 'Tasmania: archaeological and palaeo-ecological perspectives', *Antiquity*, Vol.69, No.265 (October 1995), pp.714–32.
Primsall, B., 'Gaddafi loses touch with people: Mansell', *Examiner* (Launceston), 8 March 2011, p.8.
Pybus, C., 'Oyster Cove 1988', *Meanjin*, Vol.47, No.4 (Summer 1988), pp.573–84.
Rae-Ellis, V., 'Trucanini', *Tasmanian Historical Research Association Papers and Proceedings*, Vol.23, No.2 (June 1976), pp.26–43.
Refshauge, W.F., 'An analytical approach to the events at Risdon Cove on 3 May 1804', *Journal of the Royal Australian Historical Society*, Vol.93, No.1 (June 2007), pp.39–54.
——, 'The Swivel Gun Massacre', *Tasmanian Historical Research Association Papers and Proceedings*, Vol.57, No.1 (April 2010), pp.40–4.
Reid, O., 'Further Discoveries of Aboriginal

Rock Engravings in Tasmania', *Papers and Proceedings of the Royal Society of Tasmania*, Vol.96 (1962), pp.87–9.

Reilly, D., 'Charles Joseph La Trobe: An Appreciation', *La Trobe Journal*, No.71 (Autumn 2003), pp.5–15.

Reynolds, H., 'Arthur, Walter George (c.1820–1861)', *Australian Dictionary of Biography*, Supplementary Volume 1580-1980, pp.10–11.

Richards, P.A.C., 'Iodine nutrition in two Tasmanian cultures', *Medical Journal of Australia*, Vol.163, Nos.11–12 (4–18 December 1995), pp.628–30.

Roe, M., 'Charles Bishop, Pioneer of Pacific Commerce', *Tasmanian Historical Research Association Papers and Proceedings*, Vol.10 (1962-63), pp.6–15.

——, 'Eumarrah (c.1898–1832)', *Australian Dictionary of Biography*, Supplementary Volume 1580–1980, pp.117–18.

Rollins, B., 'Henry Hellyer, Esquire, 1790–1832 Van Diemen's Land Company Surveyor: In His Footsteps', *Australian Surveyor*, Vol.34, No.2 (June 1988), pp.110–41.

Roth H. Ling, '*Is* Mrs. F.C. Smith a "last living Aboriginal *of* Tasmania"?', *Journal of the Anthropological Institute of Great Britain and Ireland*, Vol.27 (1898), pp.451–4.

Roughley-Shaw, M., 'Wybalenna and the Treaty of Whitemark', *Indigenous Law Bulletin*, Vol.4, No.22 (July 1999), pp.10–11.

Russell, L., '"A New Holland Half-Caste": Sealer and Whaler Tommy Chaseland', *History Australia*, Vol.5, No.1 (April 2008), pp.8.1–15.

Ryan, L. and N. Smith, 'Trugernanner (Truganini) (1812?-1876)', *Australian Dictionary of Biography*, Vol.6, p.305.

Ryan, L., 'The Extinction of the Tasmanian Aborigines: Myth and Reality', *Tasmanian Historical Research Association Papers and Proceedings*, Vol.19, No.2 (June 1972), pp.61–77.

——, 'The struggle for recognition: Part-Aborigines in Bass Strait in the nineteenth century', *Aboriginal History*, Vol.1, Pt.1 (1977), pp.27–51.

——, 'Risdon Cove and the Massacre of 3 May 1804: Their Place in Tasmanian History', *Tasmanian Historical Studies*, Vol.9 (2004), pp.107–23.

——, 'Massacre in the Black War in Tasmania 1823–34: a case study of the Meander River Region, June 1827', *Journal of Genocide Research*, Vol.10, No.4 (2008), pp.479–99.

——, 'The Black Line in Van Diemen's Land: success or failure?', *Journal of Australian Studies*, Vol.37, No.1 (2013), pp.3–18.

Scott, E., 'Taking Possession of Australia — The Doctrine of "Terra Nullius" (No-Man's Land)', *Journal of the Royal Australian Historical Society*, Vol.26, Pt.1 (1940), pp.1–19.

Shanahan, D., 'Scottish museum to return set of six Aboriginal skulls', *Australian* (Sydney), 9 April 2008, p.3.

Sharland, M.S.R., 'Mutton-Birds of Bass Strait: A little-known island industry', *Walkabout* (1 December 1935), pp.32–5.

Shaw, G., 'Wybalenna', in A. Alexander (ed.), *The Companion to Tasmanian History* (Hobart: Centre for Tasmanian Historical Studies, University of Tasmania, 2005), p.390.

Sissons, D.C.S., 'The Voyage of the *Cyprus* Mutineers: Did They Enter Japanese Waters?', *Journal of Pacific History*, Vol.43, No.2 (September 2008), pp.253–65.

Skira, I., 'Always Afternoon: Aborigines on Cape Barren Island, in the Nineteenth Century', *Tasmanian Historical Research Association Papers and Proceedings*, Vol.44, No.2 (June 1997), pp.120–31.

——, 'Aboriginals in Tasmania: Living on Cape Barren Island in the Twentieth Century', *Tasmanian Historical Research Association Papers and Proceedings*, Vol.44, No.3 (September 1997), pp.187–201.

——, '"I hope you will be my friend": Tasmanian Aborigines in the Furneaux Group in the nineteenth-century—population and land tenure', *Aboriginal History*, Vol.21 (1997), pp.30–45.

Smith, W., 'By Order of Lenin', "Weekend", in *Courier-Mail* (Brisbane), 24 August 1996, pp.1–2 and 4.
Stancome, G.H., 'Wedge, John Helder (1793–1872)', *Australian Dictionary of Biography*, Vol.2, pp.575–6.
Stirling, R., 'John Batman: Aspirations of a Currency Lad', *Australian Heritage* (Spring 2007), pp.38–43.
Stockton, J., 'Stone Wall Fish-Traps in Tasmania', *Australian Archaeology*, No.14 (June 1982), pp.107–14.
Stone, T. and M. Crupper, 'Last Glacial Maximum ages for robust humans at Kow Swamp, southern Australia', *Journal of Human Evolution*, Vol.45, No.2 (August 2003), pp.99–111.
Stuart, I., 'Sea rats, bandits and roistering buccaneers: What were the Bass Strait sealers really like?', *Journal of the Royal Australian Historical Society*, Vol.83, Pt.1 (June 1997), pp.47–58.
——, 'To kill a mutton bird: the archaeology of birding in the Outer Furneaux Islands', *Historic Environment*, Vol.14, No.1 (1998), pp.19–28.
Sutton, P., 'Cape Barren English', *Working Papers of the Linguistic Society of Australia*, Vol.13 (1975), pp.61–97.
Talbott, J., 'The Rise and Fall of the Carronade', *History Today*, Vol.39, No.8 (August 1989), pp.24–30.
Taylor, J., 'The Tasmanian Languages', *Launceston Historical Society Papers and Proceedings*, Vol.11 (1999), pp.44–54.
——, 'The Aboriginal Discovery and Colonisation of Tasmania', *Tasmanian Historical Research Association Papers and Proceedings*, Vol.50, No.4 (December 2003), pp.216–24.
Taylor, R., 'The polemics of eating fish in Tasmania: the historical evidence revisited', *Aboriginal History*, Vol.31 (2007), pp.1–26.
——, 'The polemics of making fire in Tasmania: the historical evidence revisited', *Aboriginal History*, Vol.32 (2008), pp.1–26.
Thomas, H.R., 'Thomas, Jocelyn Henry Connor (1780–1862) and Bartholomew Boyle (1785?–1831)', *Australian Dictionary of Biography*, Vol.2, pp.516–18.
Thomas, I., 'Models and prima-donnas in southwest Tasmania', *Australian Archaeology*, No.41 (December 1995), pp.21–9.
Trethewie, H., 'David Howie — Bass Strait Constable', *Tasmanian Historical Research Association Papers and Proceedings*, Vol.39, No.1 (March 1992), pp.44–7.
Turney, C. *et.al.*, 'Late-surviving megafauna in Tasmania, Australia, implicate human involvement in their extinction', *Proceedings of the National Academy of Sciences of the United States of America*, Vol.105, No.34 (26 August 2008), pp.12150–3.
Valder, P., 'Plant Explorers: Who Discovered Our Plants?', *Australian Garden History*, Vol.9, No.4 (January–February 1998), pp.4–6.
Vanderwal, R.L., 'Adaptive Technology in Southwest Tasmania', *Australian Archaeology*, No.8 (1978), pp.107–27.
Volger, G., 'Making Fire by Percussion in Tasmania', *Oceania*, Vol.44, No.1 (September 1973), pp.58–63.
Voss, F., 'Surgeon became a shady operator', "Examiner Extra: Soldiers, Settlers and Bushrangers", in *Examiner* (Launceston), 9 November 2004, p.A34.
——, 'Aboriginal woman a "resistance leader"', 'Examiner Extra: 200 Great Tasmanians', in *Examiner* (Launceston), 22 November 2005, p.A29.
Vowles, G., 'No Surrender', "Saturday Magazine", in *Mercury* (Hobart), 18 September 2010, pp.4–7.
Walters, M. and L. Daniels, 'Personalising the History Wars: Woretemoeteryenner's Story', *International Journal of Critical Indigenous Studies*, Vol.1, No.1 (2008), pp.35–44.
Watson, B., 'The Man and the Woman and the Edison Phonograph: Race, History and Technology through Song', *Australasian Journal of Ecocriticism and Cultural Ecology*, Vol.1 (2011–2012), pp.1–8.

Windschuttle, K. and T. Gillin, 'The Extinction of the Australian Pygmies', *Quadrant*, Vol.46, No.6 (June 2002), pp.7–18.

Windschuttle, K., 'The myths of Aboriginal history', *Sunday Mail* (Brisbane), 5 January 2003, pp.54 and 75.

Woodward, D., 'Diet in Tasmania over a Thousand Generations: A Preliminary History', *Tasmanian Historical Studies*, Vol.3, No.1 (1990–1991), pp.139–49.

Worms, E.A., 'Tasmanian Mythological Terms', *Anthropos*, BD.55, H.1–2 (1960), pp.1–16.

Wunderly, J., 'The West Coast Tribe of Tasmanian Aborigines', *Man*, Vol.38 (August 1938), pp.121–4.

——, 'The Origin of the Tasmanian Race', *Man*, Vol.38 (December 1938), pp.198–203.

THESES

Clements, N., '"Wriggle, and Shuffle, and Twist": Attitudes Towards Aborigines in the Vandemonian Press 1825–1831' (unpublished Honours thesis, University of Tasmania, 2007).

——, 'Frontier Conflict in Van Diemen's Land' (unpublished PhD thesis, University of Tasmania, 2013).

Harman, K., 'Aboriginal Convicts: Race, Law and Transportation in Colonial New South Wales' (unpublished PhD thesis, University of Tasmania, 2008).

Johnson, M., 'Honour Denied: A Study of Soldier Settlement in Queensland, 1916–1929' (unpublished PhD thesis, University of Queensland, 2002).

McFarlane, I., 'Aboriginal Society in North West Tasmania: Dispossession and Genocide' (unpublished PhD thesis, University of Tasmania, 2002).

Mickleborough, L., 'Colonel William Sorell Lieutenant-Governor of Van Diemen's Land 1817–1824: An Examination of his Convict System and Establishment of Free Settlement' (unpublished MA thesis, University of Tasmania, 2002).

Morgan, A.T., 'Aboriginal Education in the Furneaux Islands (1798–1986): a study of Aboriginal racial policy, curriculum and teacher/community relations, with specific reference to Cape Barren Island' (unpublished MA thesis, University of Tasmania, 1986).

Newitt, S., 'The Aboriginal Children who went to the Orphan Schools, New Town 1828–1861' (unpublished Honours thesis, University of Tasmania, 2011).

Norman, R., 'Jewellery and Cultural Identity: A Tasmanian Perspective' (unpublished MA thesis, Monash University, 1995).

Parry, N., '"Such a Longing": Black and white children in welfare in New South Wales and Tasmania, 1880–1940' (unpublished PhD thesis, University of New South Wales, 2007).

Robinson, S., '"Something like slavery?" The exploitation of Aboriginal child labour in Queensland, 1842–1945' (unpublished PhD thesis, University of Queensland, 2002).

Skira, I., 'Tasmanian Aborigines and Muttonbirding: A Historical Examination' (unpublished PhD thesis, University of Tasmania, 1993).

Taylor, J., 'The Palawa (Tasmanian Aboriginal) Languages' (unpublished MA thesis, University of Tasmania, 2004).

PERSONAL COMMUNICATION

Brodie, N., Hobart, 19 September 2010.

Pitchford, P., Launceston, 21 October 2011.

ACKNOWLEDGMENTS

The idea for this book grew out of our time teaching Aboriginal Studies at the University of Tasmania, when it was apparent there was no over-arching accurate and critical history of Aboriginal Van Diemen's Land, particularly one which placed an emphasis on regional differences. By compiling material from a multitude of sources we were able to provide our students with sufficient study material, and it is those students on the Launceston and Cradle Coast campuses of the University of Tasmania, many of whom became and remain close friends, that we wish to thank. Special thanks must also go to our colleagues, Mitchell Rolls, Carol Pybus, Kristyn Harman, Nicholas Brodie and Nicholas Clements, who have all been very supportive of this work. We would also like to acknowledge the Plomley Foundation for their valuable support in acquiring and translating the works of Adolphus Schayer. Support and encouragement have similarly been the hallmark of our respective wives, Marianne and Yuk-Han, which both of us have always valued and appreciated. The doyen of Aboriginal history in Australia, Professor Henry Reynolds, was kind enough to write the foreword for this book, and we thank him both as a mutual friend and fellow academic. Finally, a debt of gratitude is owed to our publisher, Phillipa McGuinness, for having faith and confidence in this work in the already crowded field of Tasmanian Aboriginal Studies.

INDEX

A UNSW Press book

Published by

NewSouth Publishing
University of New South Wales Press Ltd
University of New South Wales
Sydney NSW 2052
AUSTRALIA
newsouthpublishing.com

First published 2015
10 9 8 7 6 5 4 3 2 1

National Library of Australia Cataloguing-in-Publication
Author: Johnson, Murray (Murray David), 1956– author.
Title: Van Diemen's Land: an Aboriginal history/Murray Johnson, Ian McFarlane.
ISBN: 9781742234212 (paperback)
9781742241890 (ePub/Kindle)
9781742247151 (ePDF)
Subjects: Aboriginal Australians – Tasmania – History.
Aboriginal Tasmanians – History.
Ethnology – Australia.
Tasmania – History.
Other Authors/Contributors: McFarlane, Ian 1945– author.
Dewey Number: 994.6

Design Di Quick
Cover design Xou Creative
Printer Griffin Press

This project has been assisted by the Australian Academy of the Humanities.

UNSW
AUSTRALIA